The
TIME-LIFE
International
Cookbook

The
TIME-LIFE
International
Cookbook

The Editors of TIME-LIFE Books

Holt, Rinehart and Winston
New York

Published simultaneously in Canada by Holt, Rinehart and Winston of Canada, Limited.

Library of Congress Cataloging in Publication Data
Main entry under title:
Time–Life international cookbook
  Includes index.
  1. Cookery, International. I. Time–Life Books.
II. Title: International cookbook.
TX725.AlT55   641.5   76–29918
ISBN 0–03–018496–7

First Edition

Produced by Media Projects Incorporated. Designer, Mary Gale Moyes. The fabric design reproduced on the cover is "Bonny Dundee," designed by Laura Ashley for Raintree Designs Inc., 6 N.E. 39th Street, Miami, Florida 33137.

Printed in the United States of America
10 9 8 7 6 5 4 3 2 1

The TIME-LIFE International Cookbook is a collection of tested recipes by leading authorities in the world of cooking which were originally published in a series entitled the TIME-LIFE Illustrated Library of Cooking. This volume contains recipes by the experts listed below:

The late Michael Field, consulting editor for the Foods of the World series, was one of America's top-ranking cooking experts and a contributor to leading magazines.

James A. Beard, a leading authority on America cuisine, is also an accomplished teacher and writer of the culinary arts.

Dione Lucas attended the famous Ecole du Cordon Bleu in Paris and received its diploma, Europe's highest award for fine cooking.

Ann Roe Robbins is the author of *How to Cook Well* and co-author of *The Dione Lucas Meat and Poultry Cook Book.*

Ruth Wakefield, who owned and managed the famous Toll House Restaurant at Whitman, Massachusetts, is the author of *Toll House Cook Book.*

Allison Williams is the author of *The Embassy Cookbook,* her collection of authentic recipes from various embassies in Washington.

Table of Contents

Appetizers

Hot Anchovy Canapés

Anchoyade

To serve 4 to 5

2 two-ounce cans flat anchovy fillets
2 medium garlic cloves, finely chopped
1 teaspoon tomato paste
1 to 1½ tablespoons olive oil
2 teaspoons lemon juice or red-wine
  vinegar

Freshly ground black pepper
8 to 10 slices fresh French bread
  (½- to ¾-inch slices)
1 teaspoon finely chopped fresh
  parsley

Drain the anchovies of all their oil and place them in a large mortar or heavy bowl with the garlic and the tomato paste. Mash with a pestle, wooden masher or wooden spoon until the mixture is a very smooth purée. Dribble the oil in, a few drops at a time, stirring constantly, until the mixture becomes thick and smooth like mayonnaise. Stir in the lemon juice and a few grindings of pepper.

Preheat the oven to 500°. Under the broiler, brown the bread lightly on one side. While the bread is warm, spread the untoasted, soft side with the anchovy mixture, pressing it into the bread with the back of a fork or spoon. Arrange the bread on a baking sheet and bake in the oven for 10 minutes. Sprinkle with parsley and serve at once.

NOTE: For less saltiness, after draining the anchovies soak them for 10 minutes in cold water and then pat them thoroughly dry with paper towels.

A colorful spread of Italian appetizers combines olives, fish, cold cuts and vegetables. The recipe for marinated mushrooms appears on page 19.

Anchovy, Tuna and Olive Dip

Tapanade

To make approximately 2 cups

3 two-ounce cans flat anchovy fillets, drained

A 7-ounce can tuna fish, drained

A 7-ounce can black pitted olives, if possible the imported Mediterranean type

¼ cup capers, thoroughly drained

4 medium cloves garlic, coarsely chopped

⅓ cup lemon juice

¼ to ½ cup olive oil

1 teaspoon freshly ground black pepper

If you have an electric blender, use it to make the *tapanade*—it is the quickest and easiest way to prepare this piquant vegetable dip from the South of France. Place in the jar of the blender the anchovies, the tuna fish, olives, capers, garlic and lemon juice. Blend at medium speed for about 2 minutes, stopping the blender after every 30 seconds to scrape down the sides of the jar with a rubber spatula. Continue to blend until the mixture becomes a smooth purée. With a rubber spatula, scrape it into a small mixing bowl. Using a wire whisk or wooden spoon, beat into it the olive oil, a tablespoon at a time, until ¼ cup of the oil has been absorbed. The *tapanade* should hold its shape lightly in a spoon. If it doesn't, beat in the remaining oil by tablespoons until it reaches the proper consistency. Stir in the black pepper and taste for seasoning, adding more pepper if you prefer the *tapanade* more highly seasoned.

To make the *tapanade* by hand, chop the anchovy fillets, tuna fish, olives, capers and garlic as finely as possible, and combine them by beating them together vigorously with a spoon for 2 or 3 minutes in a medium-sized bowl. Beat in the lemon juice and then the olive oil, following the directions above for the seasoning.

VEGETABLES

1 sweet red pepper and 1 green pepper, cut into strips 2 to 3 inches long and ½ inch wide

2 to 3 medium carrots, scraped and cut into strips 2 to 3 inches long

and ½ inch wide

2 to 3 stalks celery, cut into strips 2 to 3 inches long and ½ inch wide

8 to 12 whole red radishes

8 to 12 scallions, well trimmed

Although the vegetable strips may be served with the dip without any further preparation, they will be crisper if they are first soaked in ice water for about an hour and then thoroughly dried. Vegetables other than the ones listed may also be used: small raw mushrooms, raw broccoli or cauliflower flowerettes, strips of raw turnips, or endive spears.

Avocado-and-Tomato Dip
Guacamole

To make about 2 cups

2 large ripe avocados
1 tablespoon finely chopped
   onion
1 tablespoon rinsed and finely
   chopped canned *serrano* chili
1 medium tomato, peeled, seeded and
   coarsely chopped
1 tablespoon finely chopped fresh
   coriander
½ teaspoon salt
⅛ teaspoon freshly ground black
   pepper

Cut the avocados in half. With the tip of a small knife, loosen the seeds and lift them out. Remove any brown tissuelike fibers clinging to the flesh. Strip off the skin with your fingers starting at the narrow or stem end (the dark-skinned variety does not peel as easily; use a knife to pull the skin away, if necessary). Chop the avocados coarsely; then, in a large mixing bowl, mash with a fork to a smooth purée. Add the chopped onion, chili, tomato, coriander, salt and a few grindings of black pepper, and mix them together gently but thoroughly. Taste for seasoning. To prevent the *guacamole* from darkening as it stands, cover it with plastic wrap or aluminum foil and refrigerate until ready to use. Stir before serving, and serve as a dip, either at room temperature or chilled.

Caviar and Eggs

To serve 6

6 hard-cooked eggs
6 tablespoons caviar (red or black)
1 tablespoon chopped chives or
   green onion
1 tablespoon chopped parsley
1 tablespoon mayonnaise or sour
   cream
1 teaspoon freshly ground black
   pepper
Russian dressing

Shell the eggs, cut them in halves and remove the yolks. Mash these well and combine with the caviar, chives or onion, parsley, mayonnaise or sour cream, and pepper. When the mixture is thoroughly whipped together, heap it into the whites with a spoon or pipe it in using the rosette end of a pastry tube. Serve the halves on greens and topped with Russian dressing.

Red-Caviar Dip

1 pint sour cream
¼ cup cream or milk
1½ cups red caviar
1 small grated onion

1 teaspoon freshly ground pepper
1 tablespoon lemon juice
1 chopped hard-cooked egg

Dilute the sour cream with the cream or milk. Add the caviar, grated onion, ground pepper and lemon juice. Heap in a bowl and sprinkle the top with chopped hard-cooked egg. Serve with raw vegetables, toast or bread sticks.

Poor Man's Caviar
Baklazhannaya Ikra

To make about 3 cups

1 large eggplant, about 2 pounds
1 cup finely chopped onions
6 tablespoons olive oil
½ cup finely chopped green pepper
1 teaspoon finely chopped garlic
2 large ripe tomatoes, peeled, seeded
   and finely chopped, or ¼ cup

canned tomato purée
½ teaspoon sugar
2 teaspoons salt
Freshly ground black pepper
2 to 3 tablespoons lemon juice
Pumpernickel bread or sesame seed
   crackers

Preheat the oven to 425°. Bake the eggplant on a rack in the center of the oven for about an hour, turning it over once or twice until the eggplant is soft and its skin is charred and blistered.

Meanwhile, cook the onions in 4 tablespoons of the oil over moderate heat for 6 to 8 minutes until they are soft but not brown. Stir in the green pepper and garlic and cook, stirring occasionally, for 5 minutes longer. Scrape the entire contents of the skillet into a mixing bowl.

Remove the skin from the baked eggplant with a small sharp knife, then chop the eggplant finely, almost to a purée. Add it to the mixing bowl and stir in the tomatoes or tomato purée, the sugar, salt and a few grindings of black pepper. Mix together thoroughly. Heat the remaining oil in the skillet over moderate heat and pour in the eggplant mixture. Bring to a boil, stirring constantly, then turn the heat low, cover the skillet and simmer for about an hour. Remove the cover and cook an additional half hour, stirring frequently, until all the moisture in the pan has evaporated and the mixture is thick enough to hold its shape in a spoon. Stir in 2 tablespoons of the lemon juice and taste for seasoning, adding more salt, freshly ground black pepper and lemon juice to taste. Transfer the "caviar" to a mixing bowl and chill, covered with plastic wrap, until ready to serve. Spread on squares of pumpernickel bread or sesame seed crackers.

Eggplant Spread

Melitzanes Salata

To serve 8

2 large eggplants
½ cup grated onion
1 cup tomatoes, peeled and diced
3 tablespoons chopped parsley

¾ cup olive or vegetable oil
3 tablespoons vinegar
1½ teaspoons salt
¼ teaspoon black pepper

Wash the eggplants and place them on a baking pan. Bake in a 400° oven 50 minutes, or until they are tender. Dip the eggplants in cold water, then, holding them by the stems, remove the skins. Discard the stems and skins.

Chop the eggplants, then add the onion, tomatoes and parsley. Continue chopping until they are all very fine. Gradually add the olive oil, beating constantly with a wooden spoon. Beat in the vinegar, salt and pepper. Taste for seasoning. Chill. Spread on Greek bread, crackers or thin French bread.

Liptauer Cheese

Liptovský Sýr

To make approximately 2 cups

8 ounces cottage cheese
8 tablespoons (1 quarter-pound stick) unsalted butter, softened
1 tablespoon sweet Hungarian paprika
Freshly ground black pepper

¼ teaspoon salt
2 teaspoons caraway seeds
1 teaspoon dry mustard
1 teaspoon chopped capers
1 tablespoon finely chopped onions
½ cup sour cream (plus ¼ cup if a dip is desired)
3 tablespoons finely chopped chives

With a wooden spoon rub the cottage cheese through a sieve into a mixing bowl. Cream the butter by beating it against the side of a mixing bowl with a wooden spoon. Beat in the cheese, the paprika, a generous grinding of black pepper, the salt, caraway seeds, mustard, capers, onions and sour cream.

Continue beating vigorously with a wooden spoon or by using an electric mixer at medium speed until the mixture forms a smooth paste.

If the Liptauer cheese is to be used as a spread, shape it into a mound and decorate it with the chives, or shape it into a ball that may be rolled in the chives. Refrigerate it for 2 hours, or until it is firm.

To make a Liptauer dip, stir the extra sour cream into the paste with a wooden spoon or beat it in with an electric mixer. Sprinkle the chives over the dip after it has been poured into a serving bowl.

Humus, a popular spread from the Middle East, is a purée of chick-peas that is subtly flavored with lemon juice and chopped garlic, parsley and mint.

Chick-Pea Spread
Humus

To make 3 cups

2 cups cooked chick-peas
  freshly cooked or canned
1½ teaspoons salt
3 cloves garlic, finely chopped

½ to ¾ cup vegetable oil
¼ cup fresh lemon juice
2 tablespoons coarsely chopped
  parsley, flat-leaf type preferably, or
2 tablespoons chopped mint

If the chick-peas are canned, drain them through a sieve and wash them under cold running water until the water runs clear. Spread them on paper towels and pat them dry. Freshly cooked chick-peas need only be drained and cooled.

To make the *humus* in a blender, place the chick-peas, salt, garlic, ½ cup of oil and ¼ cup of lemon juice in the container and blend at high speed for 10 seconds. Stop the blender and scrape down the sides with a rubber spatula. Blend again at high speed, adding as much oil as you need to prevent the blender from clogging. The finished *humus* should be a very smooth purée, just thick enough to hold its shape in a spoon. Taste for seasoning and add more salt and lemon juice if you like.

To make the *humus* by hand, force the chick-peas through a sieve with the back of a large spoon or purée them in a food mill. Add the salt and garlic and, beating constantly, slowly pour in as much oil and lemon juice as necessary to form a smooth, thick purée. Taste for seasoning.

Transfer the *humus* to a serving dish and sprinkle it with the parsley or mint. Serve this Middle Eastern spread on pieces of flat Arabic bread, if available, or on sesame seed crackers.

Chopped Chicken Liver

To serve 8

1½ pounds chicken livers
½ cup rendered chicken fat
1½ cups diced onions

4 hard-cooked eggs
1½ teaspoons salt
½ teaspoon black pepper
Lettuce leaves

Wash and drain the livers, removing any discolored spots. Heat half the fat in a skillet; add the onions and cook over a low heat for 10 minutes, stirring frequently. Remove the onions.

Heat the remaining fat in the skillet and cook the livers 5 minutes, or until they are barely pink inside when cut. Put the livers, onions and eggs through the fine blade of a food chopper, or chop very fine. Season with the salt and pepper. Chill, form into balls and serve them on lettuce leaves.

Hot Crabmeat Canapés
Varm Krabbsmörgås

To make 24 hors d'oeuvre

½ pound fresh, frozen or canned
  crabmeat, drained and picked
  clean of shell and cartilage
1 tablespoon dry sherry
1 teaspoon salt
⅛ teaspoon white pepper

1 tablespoon chopped fresh dill
1 tablespoon butter
1 tablespoon flour
1 egg yolk
1 cup light cream
6 slices home-style white bread

In a large mixing bowl, combine the crabmeat, sherry, salt, pepper and dill and set aside. Melt the tablespoon of butter without browning it in a small, heavy saucepan, remove from the heat and stir in the flour. In a small bowl, beat the egg yolk with the cream, and briskly stir this mixture into the butter-flour *roux* with a wire whisk. Return the pan to the heat and cook slowly, whisking constantly for a minute or two until the mixture thickens; do not let it boil. Pour the sauce over the crabmeat mixture in the bowl and stir together with a spoon until the ingredients are well combined. Taste for seasoning.

Cut four rounds from each slice of bread, using a small cookie cutter or glass. Toast the bread rounds on one side only under a moderately hot broiler. Remove and spread the untoasted side of each round generously with the crabmeat mixture, mounding it slightly. These may be prepared in advance up to this point and then refrigerated. Just before serving, place under a hot broiler for a minute or so until the canapés brown slightly. Serve very hot.

Dutch Meatballs

Bitterballen

To make 60 balls

3 tablespoons butter
4 tablespoons flour
1 cup milk
1 tablespoon grated onion
1 teaspoon Worcestershire sauce
1 teaspoon salt
½ teaspoon nutmeg

1 tablespoon chopped parsley
1½ cups ground cooked meat
1 cup dry bread crumbs
2 eggs
Water
Fat for deep frying
Dutch-style mustard

Melt the butter in a saucepan; stir in the flour, then the milk, stirring steadily until sauce thickens. Add the onion, Worcestershire sauce, salt, nutmeg, parsley and meat. Simmer 5 minutes, stirring frequently. Spread on a plate or board until cool, then shape into ½-inch balls. Roll the balls in the bread crumbs, then in the eggs beaten with a little water, and again in the bread crumbs. Let stand 1 hour.

Heat deep fat to 370°. Drop the balls into it, not too many at once, and fry until browned. Drain, put a cocktail pick into each, and arrange around a small bowl of mustard.

Russian Beef Crescents

Pirozhki

To make 24 crescents

2 cups sifted flour
½ teaspoon baking powder
1½ teaspoons salt
¾ cup shortening
1 egg yolk
4 tablespoons ice water

4 tablespoons butter
¾ cup chopped onions
½ pound ground beef
¼ teaspoon black pepper
1 tablespoon chopped dill or parsley
1 hard-cooked egg, chopped

Preheat the oven to 400°. Sift together the flour, baking powder and ½ teaspoon of the salt. Cut in the shortening. Beat the yolk and water together, then add to the flour mixture, tossing until a ball of dough is formed.

Melt the butter in a skillet; sauté the onions 5 minutes, stirring frequently. Add the beef and cook, stirring almost constantly, until the meat browns. Season with the pepper and remaining salt. Cool, then mix in the dill and chopped egg.

Roll out the dough on a lightly floured surface until it is ⅛ inch thick; cut into 3-inch circles. Place a tablespoon of the filling on each round, fold over into a half-moon and press the edges together with a little water. Arrange on a greased baking sheet. Bake for 15 minutes or until browned.

Chilean Beef Pastries
Empanadas

To make about 40 pastries

1 pound ground chuck steak
2 tablespoons vegetable oil
2 cups chopped onions
½ cup boiling water
1 tablespoon Spanish paprika
1 teaspoon ground cumin
2 teaspoons salt
3 cups sifted flour

1½ teaspoons baking powder
½ cup shortening
1 egg, beaten
½ cup ice water
½ cup seedless raisins
½ cup pitted black olives
3 hard-cooked eggs, chopped
Fat for deep frying

Have the chuck steak ground through a coarse blade. Heat the oil in a skillet; add the onion and the beef. Cook over medium heat, stirring frequently, until it is browned. Mix in the boiling water, paprika, cumin and 1½ teaspoons of the salt. Cook for 10 minutes. Taste for seasoning, then chill.

Sift the flour, baking powder and remaining salt into a bowl. Cut in the shortening with a pastry blender or two knives. Add the egg and water, tossing until a ball of dough is formed.

Add the raisins, olives and chopped eggs to the chilled filling. Roll out the dough very thin and cut into 3-inch circles. Put a teaspoonful of the meat mixture on each and fold over into a half-moon, sealing the edges with a little water or egg white. Flute the edges.

Heat the fat to 370° and fry a few *empanadas* at a time until they are browned. Drain and serve hot.

Ground Beef Triangles
Samosas

To make 24 triangles

2 cups flour
1½ teaspoons salt
¼ cup melted butter
¼ cup yoghurt
1 tablespoon vegetable oil

½ pound ground beef
1½ cups chopped onions
2 green chilies, minced
¼ teaspoon minced fresh or
    preserved ginger root
Vegetable oil for deep frying

Sift the flour and ¾ teaspoon of the salt into a bowl; stir in the melted butter and yoghurt until a smooth dough is formed. Cover the dough and let it stand while preparing the filling.

Heat the oil in a skillet. Add the beef, onions, chilies, ginger and remaining salt. Cover and cook over low heat for 15 minutes, stirring frequently. Remove from the heat and let the mixture cool.

On a lightly floured surface roll out the dough until it is very thin, then cut it into 3-inch squares. Put a little filling in the center of each square, then fold it over to form a triangle, sealing the edges with a little water or egg white.

Heat the frying oil to 370°. Drop the triangles in, a few at a time, and fry until they are golden brown. Drain on paper towels and serve hot.

Mushroom tidbits are stuffed with crabmeat *(far left)*, spinach *(center)* or chopped mushrooms *(right)*.

Cold Baked Herring

4 large tomatoes, peeled and seeded
3 medium onions
2 cloves garlic
6 tablespoons olive oil
4 or 5 pimientos, cut in strips
1 teaspoon fresh basil
1 teaspoon salt

1 teaspoon freshly ground pepper
¼ cup tomato purée
8 small herring
Lemon slices
Capers
Chopped parsley

Chop the tomatoes, onions and garlic, and sauté them in the olive oil until soft. Add the pimientos, the basil, salt, pepper and tomato purée. Oil a baking dish, arrange the herring in it, top with the sauce, and cover tightly. Bake at 425° for 20 minutes. Let the fish cool in the sauce. Serve cold on greens with lemon slices, capers and chopped parsley.

Mushrooms with Crabmeat Stuffing

Champignons Farcis au Crabe

1½ cups lump crabmeat, fresh, frozen
   or canned
2 tablespoons butter
4 tablespoons finely chopped shallots
   or scallions

1 cup *béchamel* sauce
¼ to ½ teaspoon lemon juice
Salt
White pepper
18 to 24 two-inch mushroom caps

Preheat the oven to 350°. Carefully inspect the crabmeat and remove any bits of cartilage, then shred the lumps with a fork. In a heavy 8- to 10-inch skillet, melt 2 tablespoons of butter over moderate heat and in it cook the shallots, stirring constantly, for 2 minutes, or until they are soft. Stir in the crabmeat and toss it with the shallots for 10 seconds or so. With a rubber spatula, transfer the mixture to a large bowl.

Stir in the 1 cup *béchamel* sauce, then season to taste with lemon juice, salt and white pepper. Lightly butter a shallow baking dish or roasting pan large enough to hold the mushroom caps in one layer. Sprinkle the inside of the caps with salt, spoon in the crab filling and arrange the caps in the pan. Bake in the upper third of the oven for 10 to 15 minutes, or until the mushrooms are tender when pierced with the tip of a sharp knife and the filling is bubbly. Serve on a large heated platter.

BÉCHAMEL SAUCE
2 tablespoons butter
3 tablespoons flour

1 cup hot milk
Salt
White pepper

17

In a heavy 2- to 3-quart saucepan, melt 2 tablespoons of butter over moderate heat, and very gradually stir in the flour. Cook, stirring constantly, for 2 minutes. Do not let this *roux* brown. Remove the pan from the heat and blend in the hot milk. Then return to high heat and cook, stirring constantly, until the sauce comes to a boil. Reduce the heat and simmer, still stirring, for 2 or 3 minutes, or until the sauce is thick enough to coat a spoon heavily. Remove the pan from the heat, season with salt and white pepper to taste. Set aside.

Mushrooms with Minced Mushroom Stuffing
Champignons Farcis Duxelles

3/4 pound fresh mushrooms, finely chopped

4 tablespoons finely chopped shallots or scallions

2 tablespoons butter

1 cup *béchamel* sauce *(page 17)*

1 teaspoon finely chopped parsley

Salt

Freshly ground black pepper

18 to 24 two-inch mushroom caps

2 tablespoons fine dry bread crumbs

1 tablespoon grated, imported Swiss cheese

2 tablespoons butter, cut in tiny pieces

Taking a handful at a time, squeeze the chopped mushrooms in the corner of a towel to extract as much juice as possible. Preheat the oven to 350°. In a heavy 8- to 10-inch skillet, cook the shallots in 2 tablespoons of butter over moderate heat, stirring constantly, for 2 minutes, or until they are soft. Add the chopped mushrooms and cook, stirring occasionally, for 8 to 10 minutes, or until all the moisture has evaporated and they are beginning to brown lightly. With a rubber spatula, transfer the mixture to a large bowl; stir in the 1 cup *béchamel* sauce and parsley, and season to taste with salt and pepper. Butter a large, shallow baking dish or roasting pan; salt the mushroom caps and spoon the filling into them. Mix the bread crumbs and grated cheese, then sprinkle them over the filling. Arrange the caps in the pan and dot them with butter. Bake in the upper third of the oven for 10 to 15 minutes, or until the mushrooms are tender and the filling is lightly browned. Serve hot or cold.

Mushrooms with Spinach Stuffing

Champignons Farcis aux Épinards

½ cup finely chopped shallots or
    scallions
3 tablespoons butter
¾ cup finely chopped, squeezed and
    firmly packed cooked fresh spinach
    (about ¾ pound) or 1 ten-ounce
    package frozen, chopped spinach,
defrosted and squeezed dry
¾ cup finely chopped boiled ham
1 cup *béchamel* sauce *(page 17)*
Salt
Freshly ground black pepper
18 to 24 two-inch mushroom caps
2 tablespoons butter, cut in tiny
    pieces

First preheat the oven to 350°. Then in a heavy 8- to 10-inch skillet, cook the shallots in 3 tablespoons of butter over moderate heat, stirring constantly, for 2 minutes, or until soft. Add the spinach and toss it in the skillet for 3 to 4 minutes. With a rubber spatula, transfer the mixture to a large bowl. Stir in the ham and 1 cup *béchamel* sauce, and season with salt and pepper. Butter a large, shallow baking dish or roasting pan; sprinkle the caps with salt and spoon the filling into them. Arrange the caps in the pan and dot them with butter. Bake in the upper third of the oven for 10 to 15 minutes, or until the mushrooms are tender and the filling is lightly browned. Serve on a heated platter.

Italian Marinated Mushrooms

Funghi Marinati

To make about 2 cups

⅔ cup olive oil
½ cup water
Juice of about 2 lemons
1 bay leaf
2 garlic cloves, bruised with the flat
    of a knife
6 whole peppercorns
½ teaspoon salt
1 pound small whole fresh
    mushrooms

Combine the ⅔ cup of olive oil, ½ cup of water, juice of 2 lemons, bay leaf, bruised garlic cloves, peppercorns and salt in a 10- to 12-inch enameled or stainless-steel skillet, and bring to a boil over moderate heat. Reduce the heat, cover and simmer for 15 minutes. Strain this marinade through a sieve and return it to the skillet; bring to a simmer over low heat. Drop the mushrooms into the marinade and simmer, turning them over from time to time, for 5 minutes.

Let the mushrooms cool in the marinade. Serve them at room temperature or, after they have cooled, refrigerate them and serve them cold. (The mushrooms will keep in the refrigerator at least 2 days.) Before serving, lift the mushrooms out of the marinade with a slotted spoon, draining them carefully, and arrange them on a platter or in a serving bowl.

Mushrooms with Cream-Cheese Stuffing

36 small white mushrooms, each about 1 inch in diameter (about 1 pound)
An 8-ounce package of cream cheese

2 tablespoons anchovy paste
1 teaspoon lemon juice
1 teaspoon finely grated onion
2 tablespoons finely cut fresh chives

One at a time, remove the stems from the mushrooms by holding their caps securely, and gently bending back the stems until they snap free. With a small sharp knife, cut away any part of the stem that adheres to the center of the mushroom. It is not necessary to wash the mushrooms; merely wipe them clean with a damp cloth.

In a small mixing bowl, beat the cream cheese with a large spoon until smooth. Beat in the anchovy paste, lemon juice and grated onion. Taste for seasoning. Then use a small spoon to fill the mushrooms with the cheese mixture, mounding it slightly. Sprinkle lightly with the chives and refrigerate the mushrooms until ready to serve.

Oysters Rockefeller

To make 24 appetizers

¼ cup chopped shallot or green onion
¼ cup chopped celery
1 teaspoon chopped chervil
⅓ cup chopped fennel
⅓ cup chopped parsley
½ pound butter

2 cups watercress
⅓ cup bread crumbs
⅓ cup Pernod or anisette
Salt
Black pepper
Cayenne pepper
2 dozen oysters on the half shell .

Sauté the onion, celery, chervil, fennel and parsley in 3 tablespoons of butter for 3 minutes. Add the watercress and let it wilt. Put this mixture with the rest of the butter, the bread crumbs and the Pernod or anisette in the electric blender. Season to taste with salt, black pepper and a few grains of cayenne. Blend for 1 minute. Put about 1 tablespoon of this on each oyster, place the oysters on beds of rock salt in individual containers and dampen the salt slightly. Bake at 450° to 475° for about 4 minutes, or until the butter is melted and the oysters heated through.

Oysters Rockefeller with Sour Cream

6 oysters on the half shell
3/4 cup sour cream
3 cloves garlic, crushed
Salt
Pepper

1 cup chopped raw spinach
3 tablespoons grated cheese
Bread crumbs
1 tablespoon butter
1/2 cup whipped cream

Remove the oysters from their shells, mix 1/4 cup sour cream with a little crushed garlic, salt and pepper and put a teaspoon of the mixture in the bottom of each oyster shell. Cover with an oyster and cover the oyster with spinach, which has been mixed with the rest of the sour cream, a little garlic, salt and pepper. Sprinkle with grated cheese and bread crumbs and dot with butter. Brown under the broiler; remove and top each oyster with a tablespoon of whipped cream. Brown again.

Danish Pork-Liver Pâté
Leverpostej

To serve 12 to 16

2 tablespoons butter
2 tablespoons flour
1 cup milk
1 cup heavy cream
1 pound fresh pork liver
3/4 pound fresh pork fat
1 onion, coarsely chopped (1/2 cup)

3 flat anchovy fillets, drained
2 eggs
1 1/2 teaspoons salt
3/4 teaspoon white pepper
1/2 teaspoon allspice
1/4 teaspoon ground cloves
3/4 pound fresh pork fat, sliced into
    long, 1/8-inch-thick strips or sheets

Melt the butter in a saucepan, remove from the heat, and stir in the flour. Add the milk and cream and bring to a boil over high heat, beating constantly with a whisk until the sauce is smooth and thick. Let it simmer for a minute, then set aside to cool. Cut the liver into chunks. Roughly chop the pork fat and mix both with the chopped onion and anchovies. Divide the mixture into thirds. Purée each batch in an electric blender set at high speed, adding enough sauce to keep the mixture from clogging the blender. Transfer the batches, as completed, to a large bowl and beat in any remaining cream sauce. (To make by hand, first have the butcher grind the liver and pork fat together 3 times very fine, then combine with the cream sauce, beating them together thoroughly.) Beat the eggs well with the salt, pepper, allspice and cloves and mix thoroughly into the liver mixture. The blender mixture will be considerably more fluid than the one made by hand.

Preheat the oven to 350°. Line a 1-quart loaf pan or mold with the strips of pork fat. Arrange the strips lengthwise or crosswise, making sure they overlap slightly and cover the bottom and sides of the pan. If long enough, let them hang over the sides; otherwise, save enough strips to cover the top. Spoon the liver mixture into the loaf pan and fold the overhanging strips (or extra strips) of pork fat over the top. Cover with a double thickness of aluminum foil, sealing the edges tightly, and place in a large baking pan. Pour into the baking pan enough boiling water to reach at least halfway up the side of the loaf pan and bake the liver paste in the center of the oven for 1½ hours. Remove from the oven and lift off the foil. When it cools to room temperature, re-cover with foil and chill thoroughly.

Sardine Puffs

1 can skinned and boned sardines
2 tablespoons onion juice
⅔ cup grated Gruyère or Cheddar
  cheese

1 teaspoon freshly ground black
  pepper
2 egg whites, stiffly beaten
Bread slices

Mash the sardines with a fork. Add the onion juice, cheese and pepper and blend thoroughly. Fold in the beaten egg whites. Toast slices of bread on one side. Spread the sardine mixture on the untoasted side and place under the broiler flame or in a 450° oven. Cook until they puff and brown lightly. Serve hot.

Broiled Barbecued Shrimp

2 pounds shrimp

1 cup olive oil

1 teaspoon salt

3 tablespoons chopped parsley

1 tablespoon basil

2 cloves garlic

1 tablespoon tomato or chili sauce

1 teaspoon freshly ground pepper

1 tablespoon wine vinegar

Shell and devein the shrimp, but leave the tails on. Make a sauce by mixing all the other ingredients together. Arrange the shrimp in a shallow pan—9 by 14 inches—and pour the sauce over them. Marinate for several hours. Broil for 5 to 8 minutes under a brisk flame. Arrange the shrimp on a serving dish or serve them in the broiling pan. You eat them by picking them up by the tail and dipping them into the hot sauce, so plates and plenty of paper napkins are needed with this dish.

Butterfly Shrimp

2 pounds shrimp

2 eggs, beaten

¾ cup milk

Bread crumbs

Soy sauce

Hot mustard

Kumquat chutney

Heat the fat in a French fryer to 360°. Shell and devein the shrimp, leaving the tails on. Split them almost in two and flatten them out. Beat the eggs with the milk. Dip the shrimp in the eggs and milk, then in the crumbs, and fry 2½ to 3 minutes, or until brown. Drain on absorbent paper. Serve with bowls of soy sauce, hot mustard and kumquat chutney.

Spinach Pie

Spanakopita

To serve 8

2 pounds spinach

½ cup chopped parsley

½ cup chopped dill

2 cups chopped green onions

1½ teaspoons salt

¼ cup olive oil

3 cups chopped onions

¼ teaspoon black pepper

½ pound Feta cheese, crumbled

12 *filo* or strudel leaves

¾ cup melted butter

Wash and clean the spinach; discard the stems. Drain and cut the leaves into fine shreds. Combine the spinach, parsley, dill, green onions and salt in a bowl. Let stand for 10 minutes, then press out all the liquid.

Heat the oil in a skillet; sauté the chopped onions 10 minutes. Add to the spinach mixture, with the pepper and cheese. Mix well.

Brush an 11-by-14-inch baking pan with butter, then in it put 6 layers of pastry leaves, brushing each layer with melted butter. Spread the filling evenly on top, then cover with the remaining pastry leaves. Brush each layer with melted butter, brushing the top layer heavily. With a sharp knife, trace the top layer into squares. Bake in a preheated 375° oven 30 minutes, or until golden brown. Cut through the squares and serve hot.

NOTE: *Filo* leaves can be purchased in Middle East food shops, and strudel leaves are available frozen in many markets. Keep the pastry leaves covered until ready to use.

Steak-and-Scallion Rolls
Gyuniku Negimaki

To make 8 rolls

A ¼-pound slice (about ¼ inch thick) of sirloin steak
2 scallions, including 3 inches of the green stems, cut in half lengthwise, then cut into 4-inch pieces
¼ cup *teriyaki* sauce

PREPARE AHEAD: Place the steak between sheets of wax paper and, with a meat pounder or the flat of a cleaver, pound it to a ⅛-inch thickness. Cut the steak in half crosswise. Arrange a strip of scallions down the length of each piece of the meat, then, starting with the wide sides of the meat, roll the pieces into tight cylinders. Secure the seams with toothpicks.

TERIYAKI SAUCE
1 cup sweet *sake*, or substitute 1 cup less 2 tablespoons pale dry sherry
1 cup Japanese soy sauce
1 cup chicken stock, fresh or canned

To make the *teriyaki* sauce, first warm the *sake* or sherry in a 1½- to 2-quart enameled or stainless-steel saucepan over moderate heat. Off the heat ignite the *sake* with a match, and shake the pan back and forth until the flame dies out. Then stir in the soy sauce and chicken stock, and bring to a boil. Pour the sauce into a bowl and cool to room temperature.

TO COOK: Preheat the broiler (or light a charcoal grill or hibachi) With chopsticks or tongs, dip the rolls into the *teriyaki* sauce, and then broil them 3 inches from the heat for about 3 minutes. Dip them again into the sauce, and broil the other side for a minute. Remove the toothpicks, trim the ends of the rolls neatly with a sharp knife, and cut the rolls into 1-inch pieces. Stand each piece on end, to expose the scallions, and serve at once.

Steak Tartare Balls

To make about 2 dozen

1 pound lean top round beef, ground
1 tablespoon Worcestershire sauce
½ teaspoon salt

Freshly ground black pepper
¼ cup finely chopped chives or
  green stems of scallions
2 tablespoons black caviar (optional)

In a small mixing bowl, thoroughly combine the beef, Worcestershire sauce, salt and a few grindings of pepper. Taste for seasoning, then shape the mixture into balls about 1 inch in diameter. Roll the balls in the chopped chives or scallions so that the herbs adhere to the surface of the meat. Make a small indentation in each ball and fill with about ¼ teaspoon of caviar, arrange them caviar side up on an attractive platter and chill before serving.

Vegetables with Sour-Cream Dip

To make 3 cups

VEGETABLES
4 cucumbers, peeled, seeded and cut
  into 2-by-½-inch strips
4 carrots, peeled and cut into 2-by-
  ½-inch strips

2 green peppers, seeded and cut into
  2-by-½-inch strips
4 celery stalks, cut into 2-by-½-inch
  strips
1 bunch scallions, trimmed and cut
  into 2-inch lengths
12 cherry tomatoes

Soak the vegetable strips in a bowl of ice water for an hour to crisp them. Pat dry with paper towels and arrange on a platter with the tomatoes. Cover with plastic wrap and refrigerate.

SOUR-CREAM DIP
1 pint sour cream
2 tablespoons finely chopped fresh
  dill
2 tablespoons finely chopped

scallions, green stems only
½ teaspoon lemon juice
Pinch of cayenne pepper
8 ounces red caviar
1 tablespoon finely chopped parsley

Combine in a deep, attractive bowl the sour cream, dill, parsley, chopped scallions, lemon juice and cayenne. Gently fold in the caviar with a rubber spatula without crushing the fragile eggs. Taste for seasoning, then chill until ready to serve.

Serve cold, accompanied by the platter of cold vegetables.

Vegetables with Hot Anchovy Dip

Bagna Cauda

To serve 6

1 cucumber, peeled, seeded and cut
    into 2-by-½-inch strips
2 carrots, peeled and cut into
    2-by-½-inch strips
1 sweet red pepper, seeded and cut
    into 2-by-½-inch strips
1 green pepper, seeded and cut into
    2-by-½-inch strips
4 celery stalks, cut into 2-by-½-inch
    strips
1 bunch scallions, trimmed and cut
    into 2-inch lengths

A small head of romaine, broken into
    separate leaves
12 cherry tomatoes
¼ pound fresh mushrooms, whole if
    small, quartered if large
Italian bread sticks

2 cups heavy cream
4 tablespoons butter
8 flat anchovy fillets, drained, rinsed
    and finely chopped
1 teaspoon finely chopped garlic
1 canned white truffle, finely chopped
    (optional)

Soak the vegetable strips in a bowl of ice cubes and water for an hour to crisp them. Pat dry with paper towels and arrange on a platter with the romaine leaves, tomatoes and mushrooms. Cover with plastic wrap and refrigerate. Arrange the bread sticks on a separate plate and set aside.

In a heavy 1-quart enameled or stainless-steel saucepan, bring the cream to a boil and cook it, stirring frequently, for about 15 to 20 minutes, or until it has thickened and has reduced to about 1 cup.

Choose a 3- or 4-cup enameled or flameproof earthenware casserole that fits over a candle warmer, spirit lamp or electric hot tray. On the stove, melt the butter in the casserole over low heat; do not let it brown. Add the anchovies and garlic, then the reduced cream and the optional truffle, and bring the sauce to a simmer, stirring constantly. Do not let it boil. Serve the *bagna cauda* at once, accompanied by the cold vegetables and the bread sticks. To eat, pick up a vegetable or bread stick with your fingers and dip it into the hot sauce. If the butter and cream separate as the sauce stands, beat with a wire whisk. (You may substitute almost any raw vegetable you like for *bagna cauda*: fennel sticks, cauliflower or broccoli flowerets, white turnip wedges, or red or white radishes.)

Marinated Vegetables
Légumes à la Grecque

To serve 8 to 10

MARINADE
3 cups chicken stock, fresh or canned
1 cup dry white wine
1 cup olive oil

½ cup lemon juice
6 parsley sprigs
2 large garlic cloves, cut up
½ teaspoon dried thyme
10 peppercorns
1 teaspoon salt

Stir the ingredients together in a 3- to 4-quart enameled or stainless-steel saucepan, bring to a boil, partially cover the pan and simmer slowly for 45 minutes. Using a fine sieve, strain the marinade into a large bowl, pressing the ingredients to squeeze out their juices before discarding them. Return the marinade to the saucepan.

VEGETABLES
24 white onions, 1 inch in diameter, peeled
1 pound small zucchini, unpeeled, sliced 1 inch thick
1 pound small yellow squash,

unpeeled, sliced 1 inch thick
3 medium green peppers, seeded and cut lengthwise into ½-inch strips
½ pound whole green string beans, trimmed
2 lemons, cut into ¼-inch slices

Bring the marinade to a boil and add the onions; cover and cook over moderate heat for 20 to 30 minutes or until the onions are just tender when pierced with the tip of a sharp knife. With a slotted spoon, remove the onions to a large glass or stainless-steel baking dish.

Add the slices of zucchini and yellow squash to the simmering marinade and cook slowly uncovered for 10 to 15 minutes or until they are barely done, then put them in the baking dish with the onions. Finally, add the green-pepper strips and string beans to the marinade and cook them slowly uncovered for 8 to 10 minutes, or until they are just tender. The vegetables must not be overcooked because they will soften as they cool and marinate. Add the green peppers and string beans to the other vegetables. Taste and season the marinade and pour it over the vegetables, making sure that they are all at least partly covered with the hot liquid.

Place in the refrigerator to cool. Then cover the dish tightly with aluminum foil or plastic wrap and let the vegetables marinate in the refrigerator for at least 4 hours. To serve, lift the vegetables out of the marinade with a slotted spoon and arrange them attractively on a serving platter. Moisten the vegetables with a little marinade and garnish them with lemon slices.

NOTE: Other firm vegetables may be used in the recipe, such as mushrooms, celery hearts, leeks, cucumbers, red peppers and artichoke hearts.

27

Soups & Broths

Belgian Asparagus Soup
Crème d'Asperges
To serve 6 to 8

1½ pounds asparagus
1½ quarts chicken stock

3 egg yolks
1 cup light cream
3 tablespoons minced parsley

If possible, buy white asparagus, the type used in Belgium. If only the green type is available, peel off the outer green portions. Cut off about 16 tips and reserve them. Cut the remaining asparagus into small pieces and combine it with the stock. Bring to a boil and cook over low heat for 30 minutes. Purée the mixture in an electric blender, then strain it or force it through a sieve. Cook the reserved asparagus tips for 10 minutes and drain them. Beat the egg yolks in a bowl, then mix in the cream. Gradually add the hot soup, stirring steadily to prevent the egg from curdling. Return the soup to the saucepan, add the asparagus tips, and heat, but do not let it boil. Taste for seasoning, sprinkle with the parsley, and serve.

Avocado Cream Soup
Sopa de Aguacate

To serve 8

3 large ripe avocados, peeled, halved,
   seeded and diced
1½ cups heavy cream
6 cups chicken stock, fresh or canned

¼ cup pale dry sherry (optional)
1 teaspoon salt
½ teaspoon ground white pepper
1 ripe avocado, peeled and thinly
   sliced

Purée the diced avocados in 3 batches, combining ⅓ of the dice and ½ cup of cream at a time in the jar of a blender and blending at high speed for 30 seconds. (To make the purée by hand, force the diced avocados—with the back of a large spoon—through a sieve set over a bowl. Beat the cream into the purée, a few tablespoons at a time.) In a 3-quart enameled or stainless-steel saucepan, bring the stock to a boil over high heat, reduce the heat to low, and when the stock is simmering, stir in the avocado purée. Add the sherry, salt and pepper, and taste for seasoning. To serve the soup hot, pour it into a tureen and strew the top with avocado slices. Or refrigerate and serve it cold.

28

Black Bean Soup

To serve 6 to 8

1 pound black turtle beans (2 cups)
1 cup coarsely chopped onion
1 cup coarsely chopped celery with
   leaves
1 bay leaf
3 smoked ham hocks
10 cups water
½ to 1 cup water or chicken stock,

fresh or canned (optional)
Salt
Freshly ground black pepper
4 hard-cooked eggs, coarsely
   chopped
2 tablespoons red-wine vinegar
Lemon slices
Parsley sprigs

Wash the beans in a sieve under cold running water. When the water runs clear, transfer the beans to a large soup pot. Add the onion, celery, bay leaf and ham hocks. Pour in the 10 cups of water and bring to a boil over high heat. Skim off any scum that rises to the surface, half cover the pot and reduce the heat to low. Simmer the soup for 2½ to 3 hours, or until the beans are soft enough to be crushed easily with a fork. Remove the ham hocks and the bay leaf, and purée the soup through a food mill or sieve. Do not use an electric blender. Return the purée and all its liquid to the soup pot. If it seems too thick, thin it with as much chicken stock or water as you think it needs. Taste for seasoning, and add salt and a few grindings of black pepper. Bring the soup to a simmer. Just before serving, stir in the hard-cooked eggs and the vinegar. Garnish each portion with a slice of lemon topped with a small sprig of parsley.

Beet Soup

Borshch

To serve 12

3 pounds brisket of beef
Marrow bone
3½ quarts boiling water
4 cups shredded cabbage
2 bay leaves
6 peppercorns
6 tablespoons butter
1½ cups sliced onions
1 cup sliced carrots

½ cup sliced celery
1 tablespoon salt
10 beets, peeled and cut in julienne
   strips, or 2 cans julienne beets,
   drained
1 tablespoon vinegar
1 tablespoon flour
2 cups peeled, diced tomatoes
Sour cream

Wash the beef and the marrow bone and combine them in a large saucepan with 3 quarts of the boiling water, the cabbage, bay leaves and peppercorns.

Bring to a boil, then cook over low heat while preparing the vegetables.

Melt 2 tablespoons of the butter in a skillet, add the onions, carrots and celery, and cook, stirring frequently, until they are lightly browned. Add them and the salt to the soup. Melt the remaining butter in a skillet. Add the beets, vinegar and ½ cup of the remaining water, and cook over low heat for 20 minutes. Blend in the flour, then add the mixture to the soup, along with the remaining 1½ cups of water. Cook for 1½ hours, then add the tomatoes and cook 15 minutes longer. Taste for seasoning. Serve in individual soup plates with a heaping tablespoon of sour cream in each.

Cold Yoghurt and Cucumber Soup
Cacik

To serve 2 to 4

1 medium-sized cucumber (about ½ pound)
2 cups yoghurt
2 teaspoons distilled white vinegar
1 teaspoon olive oil

2 teaspoons finely cut fresh mint leaves or 1 teaspoon dried mint
½ teaspoon finely cut fresh dill leaves or ¼ teaspoon dried dill weed
1 teaspoon salt

With a small, sharp knife, peel the·cucumber and slice it lengthwise into halves. Scoop out the seeds by running the tip of a teaspoon down the center of each half. Discard the seeds, and grate the cucumber coarsely. There should be about 1 cup.

In a deep bowl, stir the yoghurt with a whisk or large spoon until it is completely smooth. Gently but thoroughly beat in the grated cucumber, vinegar, olive oil, mint, dill and salt. Do not overbeat. Taste for seasoning, adding more salt if necessary, and refrigerate the soup for at least 2 hours, or until it is thoroughly chilled.

Serve the *cacik* in chilled individual soup plates, and add an ice cube to each portion if you like.

Cream of Mushroom Soup
Potage Crème de Champignons

To serve 4 to 6

1½ pounds fresh mushrooms	6 cups chicken stock, fresh or canned
9 tablespoons butter (1 quarter-pound stick plus 1 tablespoon)	2 egg yolks
	¾ cup heavy cream
2 finely chopped shallots or scallions	Salt
6 tablespoons flour	White pepper

Separate the mushroom caps and stems. Then slice half the mushroom caps about ⅛ inch thick and coarsely chop the remaining caps and all the stems. In an 8- to 10-inch enameled or stainless-steel skillet (iron or aluminum will discolor the mushrooms), melt 2 tablespoons of the butter over moderate heat.

When the foam subsides, add the sliced mushrooms and cook them, tossing them constantly with a wooden spoon, for 2 minutes or until they are lightly colored. With a slotted spoon, transfer them to a bowl and set them aside. Melt an additional 2 tablespoons of butter in the same skillet and cook the chopped mushroom caps and stems and the shallots for 2 minutes. Set them aside in the skillet.

In a heavy 4- to 6-quart saucepan, melt the remaining 5 tablespoons of butter over moderate heat. Remove the pan from the heat and stir in the 6 tablespoons of flour, then cook over low heat, stirring constantly, for 1 or 2 minutes. Do not let this *roux* brown. Remove the pan from the heat, let cool a few seconds, then pour in the chicken stock, beating constantly with a wire whisk to blend stock and *roux*. Return to heat and stir until this cream soup base comes to a boil, thickens and is perfectly smooth. Then add the chopped mushrooms and shallots and simmer, stirring occasionally, for 15 minutes.

Purée the soup through a food mill into a mixing bowl and then again through a fine sieve back into the saucepan. With a wire whisk, blend the egg yolks and the cream together in a bowl. Whisk in the hot puréed soup, 2 tablespoons at a time, until ½ cup has been added. Then reverse the process and slowly whisk the now-warm egg-yolk-and-cream mixture into the soup.

Bring to a boil, and boil for 30 seconds, stirring constantly. Remove the pan from the heat. Taste and season with salt and white pepper. Add the reserved sliced mushrooms and serve the soup from a tureen or individual soup bowls.

French Onion Soup
Soupe à l'Oignon

To serve 6 to 8

4 tablespoons butter	1 teaspoon salt
2 tablespoons vegetable oil	3 tablespoons flour
2 pounds onions, thinly sliced	2 quarts beef stock, fresh or canned,
(about 7 cups)	or beef and chicken stock combined

In a heavy 4- to 5-quart saucepan or a soup kettle, melt the butter with the oil over moderate heat. Stir in the onions and 1 teaspoon salt, and cook uncovered over low heat, stirring occasionally, for 20 to 30 minutes, or until the onions are a rich golden brown. Sprinkle flour over the onions and cook, stirring, for 2 or 3 minutes. Remove the pan from the heat. In a separate saucepan, bring the stock to a simmer, then stir the hot stock into the onions. Return the soup to low heat and simmer, partially covered, for another 30 or 40 minutes, occasionally skimming off the fat. Taste for seasoning, and add salt and pepper if needed.

CROÛTES	1 garlic clove, cut
12 to 16 one-inch-thick slices of	1 cup grated, imported Swiss cheese
French bread	or Swiss and freshly grated
2 teaspoons olive oil	Parmesan cheese combined

While the soup simmers, make the *croûtes*. Preheat the oven to 325°. Spread the slices of bread in one layer on a baking sheet and bake for 15 minutes. With a pastry brush, lightly coat both sides of each slice with olive oil. Then turn the slices over and bake for another 15 minutes, or until the bread is completely dry and lightly browned. Rub each slice with the cut garlic clove and set aside.

To serve, place the *croûtes* in a large tureen or individual soup bowls and ladle the soup over them. Pass the grated cheese separately.

ALTERNATIVE: To make onion soup *gratinée,* preheat the oven to 375°. Ladle the soup into an ovenproof tureen or individual soup bowls, top with *croûtes,* and spread the grated cheese on top. Sprinkle the cheese with a little melted butter or olive oil. Bake for 10 to 20 minutes, or until the cheese has melted, then slide the soup under a hot broiler for a minute or two to brown the top if desired.

Leek and Potato Soup
Potage Parmentier; Vichyssoise

To serve 6 to 8

4 cups peeled and coarsely chopped
  potatoes
3 cups thinly sliced leeks (white part
  plus 2 inches of green) or substitute
  3 cups thinly sliced onions
2 quarts chicken stock, fresh or

canned, or substitute water or a
  combination of chicken stock and
  water
1 teaspoon salt
Freshly ground black pepper
½ cup heavy cream
3 tablespoons finely cut fresh chives
  or finely chopped fresh parsley

In a heavy 6-quart saucepan or a soup kettle, simmer the potatoes, leeks, chicken stock and salt partially covered for 40 to 50 minutes or until the vegetables are tender. Force the soup through a food mill or sieve into a mixing bowl and then pour back into the pan. Season the soup with salt and a few grindings of pepper, and stir in the cream. Before serving, return the soup to low heat and bring it to a simmer. Ladle the soup into a tureen or individual soup bowls. Serve garnished with fresh chives or fresh parsley.

VICHYSSOISE: When Louis Diat was chef at the Ritz-Carlton Hotel in New York City half a century ago, he devised vichyssoise—a cold version of *potage Parmentier*. To make it, force the soup through a food mill or sieve, then through a fine sieve back into the pan. Season and stir in 1½ cups of heavy cream. (Do not use a blender; the mixture will be too smooth.) Chill the soup until it is very cold. Serve it garnished with finely cut fresh chives.

Cream of Green Pea Soup
Erbsensuppe
To serve 8 to 10

4 pounds green peas, shelled, or 3
  packages frozen peas
2 cups water
4 tablespoons butter
4 tablespoons flour

6 cups chicken stock
½ cup sliced onion
1 cup shredded lettuce
2 sprigs parsley
2 egg yolks
1 cup light cream

Cook the fresh peas in the water for 25 minutes, then drain, reserving ½ cup of the liquid. Melt the butter in a large saucepan and blend in the flour until it is golden. Add the reserved liquid and the stock, stirring steadily until it boils. Add the onion, lettuce and parsley, and cook over low heat for 20 minutes. Purée the soup in an electric blender or force it through a sieve. Beat the egg yolks and cream together, then gradually add a little of the hot soup, stirring steadily to prevent the mixture from curdling. Stir it into the soup and taste for seasoning. Heat before serving, but do not boil the soup.

Yellow Pea Soup
Ärter med Fläsk

To serve 4 to 6

1 pound (2 cups) dried yellow Swedish peas or substitute domestic yellow split peas
5 cups cold water
2 finely chopped medium onions

1 whole onion, peeled, studded with 2 cloves
1 pound lean salt pork, in 1 piece
1 teaspoon leaf marjoram or ¼ teaspoon powdered marjoram
½ teaspoon thyme
Salt

Wash the dried peas in cold running water and place them in a 2- to 3-quart saucepan. Cover with 5 cups of cold water and bring to a boil over high heat. Boil briskly for 2 or 3 minutes, then turn off the heat and let the peas soak in the water for an hour.

Skim off any pea husks that may have risen to the surface, add the finely chopped onion, the whole onion, salt pork, marjoram and thyme and again bring to a boil. Immediately lower the heat and simmer with the pot partially covered for about 1¼ hours, or until the peas are quite tender but have not all fallen apart. Remove the whole onion and the salt pork from the soup and cut the pork in slices about ¼ inch thick. Place a few slices of pork in individual serving bowls. Season the hot soup with salt to taste, and ladle it over the pork.

Italian Vegetable Soup

Minestrone

To serve 8

½ cup dry white beans
4 tablespoons butter
1 cup fresh green peas (about 1 pound
    unshelled)
1 cup diced unpeeled but scrubbed
    zucchini (about ½ pound)
1 cup diced carrots
1 cup diced potatoes
⅓ cup thinly sliced celery
2 ounces salt pork, diced
2 tablespoons finely chopped onions
½ cup finely chopped leeks
2 cups drained canned whole-pack

tomatoes, coarsely chopped
2 quarts chicken stock, fresh or canned
1 bay leaf and 2 parsley sprigs, tied
    together
1 teaspoon salt
Freshly ground black pepper
½ cup plain white raw rice

GARNISH

1 tablespoon finely cut fresh basil or
    1 teaspoon dried basil, crumbled
1 tablespoon finely chopped fresh
    parsley
½ teaspoon finely chopped garlic
½ cup freshly grated imported
    Parmesan cheese

Bring 1 quart of water to a bubbling boil in a heavy 3- to 4-quart saucepan. Add the ½ cup of beans (either marrow, Great Northern, white kidney or navy) and boil them briskly for 2 minutes. Remove the pan from the heat and let the beans soak undisturbed in the water for 1 hour. Then return the pan to the stove, and over low heat simmer the beans uncovered for 1 to 1½ hours, or until they are barely tender. Drain the beans thoroughly and set them aside in a bowl.

Melt the butter over moderate heat in a heavy 10- to 12-inch skillet. When the foam subsides, add the peas, zucchini, carrots, potatoes and celery. Tossing constantly with a wooden spoon, cook 2 or 3 minutes, until they are lightly coated with butter but not browned. Set aside.

Render the salt pork dice by frying them in a 6- to 8-quart soup pot or kettle over moderate heat, stirring frequently. When the pork dice are crisp and brown, lift them out with a slotted spoon and set them aside to drain on paper towels. Stir the onions and leeks (or if leeks are unavailable, substitute another ½ cup of onions) into the fat remaining in the pot and cook, stirring constantly, for about 5 minutes until the vegetables are soft and lightly browned. Stir in the coarsely chopped tomatoes, the vegetables from the skillet, the chicken stock, the bay leaf and parsley sprigs, salt and a few grindings of pepper. Bring the soup to a boil over high heat, reduce the heat and simmer partially covered for 25 minutes.

Remove and discard the bay leaf and parsley sprigs, add the rice, white beans and salt pork dice and cook for about 15 to 20 minutes longer, or until the rice is tender. Taste the soup and season it with salt and pepper if needed. Serve, sprinkled with the herb and garlic garnish. Pass a bowl of the grated cheese separately.

Cold Vegetable Soup

Gazpacho

To serve 6 to 8

SOUP*
2 medium-sized cucumbers, peeled
and coarsely chopped
5 medium-sized tomatoes, peeled
and coarsely chopped
1 large onion, coarsely chopped
1 medium-sized green pepper,
deribbed, seeded and coarsely
chopped
2 teaspoons finely chopped garlic
4 cups coarsely crumbled French or
Italian bread, trimmed of crusts
4 cups cold water
¼ cup red wine vinegar
4 teaspoons salt
4 tablespoons olive oil
1 tablespoon tomato paste

In a deep bowl, combine the coarsely chopped cucumbers, tomatoes, onion and green pepper, garlic and crumbled bread, and mix together thoroughly. Then stir in the water, vinegar and salt. Ladle the mixture, about 2 cups at a time, into the jar of a blender and blend at high speed for 1 minute, or until reduced to a smooth purée. Pour the purée into a bowl and with a whisk beat in the olive oil and tomato paste.

Cover the bowl tightly with foil or plastic wrap and refrigerate for at least 2 hours, or until thoroughly chilled. Just before serving, whisk or stir the soup lightly to recombine it. Then ladle it into a large chilled tureen or individual soup plates.

GARNISH
1 cup ¼-inch bread cubes, trimmed
of crusts
½ cup finely chopped onions
½ cup peeled and finely chopped
cucumbers
½ cup finely chopped green peppers

Accompany the *gazpacho* with the bread cubes and the vegetable garnishes presented in separate serving bowls to be added to the soup at the discretion of each diner.

NOTE: If you prefer crisp croutons for the garnish, fry the bread cubes. In a 6- to 8-inch skillet, heat ¼ cup of olive oil over moderate heat until a light haze forms above it. Drop in the bread cubes and, turning them frequently, cook them until they are crisp and golden brown on all sides. Drain on paper towels and cool.

Beef and Chicken Stocks
Fonds de Cuisine

To make 3 to 4 quarts

2 pounds beef shank and 4 pounds
   beef bones or 6 pounds chicken
   backs and necks
4 to 5 quarts cold water
2 onions, peeled

2 carrots, peeled
2 celery stalks with leaves, cut up
Bouquet garni, made of 6 parsley
   sprigs, 1 bay leaf, 2 garlic cloves
   and ½ teaspoon dried thyme,
   wrapped together in cheesecloth
1 tablespoon salt

Good soups depend on good stocks—and so do stews, casseroles, braised meats and vegetables, and many sauces. Here are recipes for three stocks (or *fonds de cuisine*) that are basic to French cooking.

SIMPLE STOCK: Place the beef and bones, or the chicken backs and necks in a soup pot or kettle, and add enough cold water to cover them by 1 inch. Bring to a boil over high heat, skimming off the scum that rises to the surface. Add the vegetables, *bouquet garni* and salt. Bring to a simmer, skimming if necessary, then partially cover and cook very slowly for 4 hours. Remove the bones and strain the stock through a fine sieve into a large bowl, pressing down hard on the vegetables and herbs before discarding them. Taste and season. Skim any fat from the surface or refrigerate until the fat solidifies on the top and can be removed. The stock will keep refrigerated for 3 or 4 days or can be frozen for future use. For richer taste boil down the strained and degreased stock until its flavor has concentrated.

BROWN BEEF STOCK: Preheat the oven to 450°. Roast the beef bones, onions and carrots in a shallow pan for 30 to 40 minutes, turning them occasionally. Transfer the bones and vegetables to a soup pot. Then discard the fat from the roasting pan, add 2 cups of water and bring to a boil over high heat, scraping in any browned bits clinging to the pan. Pour this into the soup pot and add the celery, *bouquet garni,* salt and cold water to cover. Proceed with the stock, following the directions above.

BROWN POULTRY STOCK: Over high heat, brown the chicken backs and necks in 2 tablespoons of vegetable oil in a large skillet. Transfer them to the soup pot and deglaze the skillet with a little water. Add this to the soup pot with the onions, carrots, celery, *bouquet garni,* salt and cold water to cover. Proceed with the stock, following the directions for simple stock.

Oxtail Soup
Potage Queue de Boeuf

To serve 4

3 tablespoons butter
1 tablespoon vegetable oil
2 pounds oxtail, cut in 1-inch
  sections
1 onion, thinly sliced
1 carrot, thinly sliced
2 tablespoons flour
2 quarts beef stock, fresh or canned

Bouquet garni made of 2 parsley
  sprigs, 2 celery stalks and 1 leek,
  tied together
1 teaspoon dried thyme
4 or 5 peppercorns
Salt
Freshly ground black pepper
½ cup finely diced carrots
½ cup finely diced turnips
1 to 2 tablespoons dry Madeira or port

In a heavy 4- to 6-quart saucepan or soup pot, melt 1 tablespoon of the butter with the oil over moderate heat. Add the oxtail and cook, turning frequently, until the pieces are golden brown on all sides. Using kitchen tongs, transfer the oxtail to a plate. Cook the sliced onion and carrot in the fat remaining in the pan for 8 to 10 minutes, or until they are soft and lightly browned. Stir in the flour and cook, stirring constantly, until the flour has browned. Remove the pan from the heat and let it cool slightly. Gradually beat in the beef stock, whisking vigorously. Bring to a boil and cook, stirring, until the soup is smooth and has begun to thicken. Return the oxtail to the pan together with the *bouquet garni*, thyme and peppercorns, and bring to a boil over high heat. Skim the fat from the surface, reduce the heat and simmer the soup, partially covered, for 3½ hours, skimming frequently. Lift out the oxtail with a slotted spoon and strain the soup through a fine sieve into a large mixing bowl. Let it settle for a few minutes, then skim off the surface fat. Taste the strained soup, season it with salt and pepper, and return it to the pan. Melt 2 tablespoons of butter in a 6- to 8-inch skillet and in it cook the diced carrots and turnips, stirring frequently, for 1 or 2 minutes or until they are coated with butter. Add the diced carrots and turnips and the oxtail to the soup and simmer the soup for 30 minutes, skimming the fat from the surface as necessary. To serve, ladle the soup into a tureen and stir in the wine.

Chicken Soup with Lemon and Mint
Canja

To serve 6

A 3½- to 4-pound stewing fowl,
  securely trussed
The fowl's giblets—heart, gizzard
  and liver—finely chopped
2 quarts water

1 cup finely chopped onions
1½ teaspoons salt
3 tablespoons raw medium or long-
  grain regular-milled rice, or
  imported short grain rice
¼ cup fresh lemon juice
6 tablespoons finely cut fresh mint

Place the chicken and its giblets in a heavy 3- to 4-quart casserole. Pour in the water and bring to a boil over high heat, meanwhile skimming off the foam and scum as they rise to the surface. Add the onions and salt and reduce the heat to low. Simmer partially covered for 2½ hours, then add the rice and simmer for 30 minutes or until the chicken and rice are tender.

Remove the casserole from the heat and transfer the chicken to a plate. When the bird is cool enough to handle, remove the skin with a small knife or your fingers. Cut or pull the meat away from the bones. Discard the skin and bones, and cut the meat into strips about ⅛ inch wide and 1 inch long.

Just before serving, return the chicken to the casserole, add the lemon juice and taste for seasoning. Bring to a simmer and cook only long enough to heat the chicken through. Place a tablespoon of the cut mint in each of six individual serving bowls, ladle the soup over it and serve at once.

Chick-Pea Soup with Garlic and Mint
Sopa da Panela

To serve 4

1 cup dried chick-peas, or substitute
  1½ cups canned chick-peas
½ cup olive oil
2 slices homemade-type white bread,
  trimmed of crusts and cut into ½-
  inch squares
2 teaspoons finely chopped garlic

½ teaspoon salt, preferably coarse salt
⅓ cup finely chopped fresh mint
  leaves
¼ cup finely chopped fresh parsley
1 quart chicken stock, fresh or
  canned
4 mint sprigs

Starting a day ahead, wash the dried chick-peas in a sieve under cold running water, place them in a large bowl or pan, and add enough cold water to cover them by 2 inches. Soak at room temperature for at least 8 hours. Drain the peas and place them in a heavy 2- to 3-quart saucepan. Add enough fresh water to cover them completely and bring to a boil over high heat. Reduce the heat to low and simmer partially covered for 2 to 2½ hours, or until the peas are tender but still intact. Replenish the liquid with boiling water from time to time if necessary. (Canned chick-peas need only be drained and rinsed under cold running water.)

Meanwhile, in a heavy 8- to 10-inch skillet, heat ¼ cup of the olive oil over high heat until a light haze forms above it. Add the bread squares, lower the heat to moderate and cook, turning them frequently, until they are golden brown on all sides. With a slotted spoon, transfer the croutons to a double thickness of paper towels to drain.

With a mortar and pestle or the back of a large spoon, mash the garlic and salt to a paste in the bottom of a heavy mixing bowl. Beat in the mint, parsley, and then the remaining ¼ cup of olive oil, 1 tablespoon at a time. Continue to beat until the oil is thoroughly absorbed. Bring the stock to a boil in a large saucepan. Add the chick-peas, reduce the heat and simmer for 3 or 4 minutes to heat them through.

To serve, transfer the garlic mixture to a heated tureen. Pour the soup into the tureen, stir with a large spoon to distribute the garlic mixture evenly, and scatter the croutons on top. Garnish with mint.

Egg and Lemon Soup
Soupa Avgolemono

To serve 4 to 6

6 cups chicken stock, fresh or canned
⅓ cup uncooked long- or medium-
    grain rice

4 eggs
3 tablespoons fresh lemon juice
Salt
2 tablespoons finely cut fresh mint
    or 1 tablespoon dried mint

In a 3- to 4-quart saucepan, bring the chicken stock to a boil over high heat. Pour in the rice, reduce the heat to low and simmer partially uncovered for about 15 minutes, or until the grains are just tender but still slightly resistant to the bite. Reduce the heat to low.

Beat the eggs with a whisk or a rotary beater until frothy. Beat in the lemon juice and stir in about ¼ cup of the simmering chicken broth. Then slowly pour the mixture into the broth, stirring constantly. Cook over low heat for 3 to 5 minutes, or until the soup thickens enough to coat the spoon lightly. Do not let the soup come to a boil or the eggs will curdle. Add salt to taste and serve at once, garnished with mint.

Court Bouillon

2 pounds fish heads, bones and
    trimmings
6 cups water
1 cup dry white wine
2 onions, thinly sliced
2 leeks, white part only, thinly sliced
    (optional)

2 tablespoons wine vinegar,
    preferably white
2 three-inch strips fresh orange peel
2 bay leaves
1 teaspoon fennel seeds
2 teaspoons salt

In a 4- to 6-quart saucepan, bring the court bouillon ingredients to a boil, partially cover the pan, and cook over low heat for 30 minutes.

Strain the court bouillon through a sieve into a bowl, pressing down hard on the vegetables and trimmings with a spoon before discarding them.

This stock may be used in fish soups, sauces and aspics. It may be stored in the refrigerator in a tightly covered jar for several days, or it may be frozen and kept in the freezer for a month.

Fish Soup with Garlic Mayonnaise
Bourride

To serve 8 to 10

Court bouillon (*above*)
12 *croûtes* (see French onion
    soup, page 31)

AÏOLI
1 tablespoon fine, dry bread crumbs
1 tablespoon wine vinegar
6 garlic cloves, coarsely chopped
7 egg yolks
½ teaspoon salt

⅛ teaspoon white pepper
1½ cups olive oil
1 tablespoon lemon juice

FISH
2 pounds each of three kinds of firm,
    white fish fillets or steaks such as
    haddock, porgy, cod, sole, perch,
    rockfish, pollack or halibut, cut in
    2-inch serving pieces

Prepare the court bouillon according to the recipe above, and the *croûtes* according to the recipe for French onion soup on page 31. In the meantime, make the *aïoli*. Soak the bread crumbs in 1 tablespoon of wine vinegar for 5 minutes, then squeeze the crumbs dry in the corner of a towel. With a large mortar and pestle or a small, heavy mixing bowl and wooden spoon, vigorously mash the crumbs and garlic to a smooth paste. Beat in 3 egg yolks, one at a time and, along with the third yolk, add the salt and pepper. When the mixture is thick and sticky, begin to beat in the olive oil a few drops at a time. As soon as the mixture resembles thick cream, transfer it to a large mixing bowl. With a wire whisk, rotary or electric beater, beat in the rest of the oil, 1 teaspoon at a time. The sauce will be like a thick mayonnaise. Season it with lemon juice, salt and pepper if

41

needed. Spoon ⅔ cup of *aïoli* into a small sauceboat and cover with plastic wrap. Put the rest of the sauce (about 1⅓ cups) into a 3- to 4-quart saucepan.

Add the fish to the court bouillon, bring to a boil and simmer uncovered for 3 to 8 minutes, or until the fish is just firm to the touch. Watch the fish carefully; different kinds cook at different speeds. Transfer the pieces to a heated platter as they are done. Cover loosely to keep them warm.

Off the heat, beat the 4 remaining egg yolks, one at a time, into the *aïoli* in the saucepan. Add 1 cup of hot fish broth, beating constantly, then gradually beat in the remaining broth. Cook over low heat, stirring, until the soup is thick enough to coat the whisk lightly. Do not let it come to a boil. Season with salt, pepper, and lemon juice if needed.

To serve, pour the soup into a large tureen and bring it to the table with the platter of fish, the sauceboat of *aïoli,* and the *croûtes*. Place a *croûte* in the bottom of each individual soup bowl, lay one or several pieces of fish on top of the *croûte,* and ladle in the soup. Top with a dab of *aïoli* and pass the remaining sauce separately.

Fresh Clam Soup
Zuppa di Vongole

To serve 4

6 tablespoons olive oil
1 teaspoon finely chopped garlic
½ cup dry white wine
3 pounds firm ripe tomatoes, peeled, seeded, gently squeezed of excess juice, and coarsely chopped (about 3 to 4 cups)

2 dozen small hardshell clams in their shells
1 cup boiling water
4 tablespoons finely chopped fresh parsley, preferably the flat-leaf Italian type

Heat the olive oil in a heavy 2- to 3-quart saucepan. Add the garlic and cook, stirring, over moderate heat for about 30 seconds. Pour in the wine, add the tomatoes, and bring to a boil. Then reduce the heat and simmer the sauce, partially covered, for 10 minutes.

Meanwhile, scrub the clams thoroughly and drop them into about ⅛ inch of boiling water (approximately 1 cup) in a heavy 12- to 14-inch skillet. Cover tightly and steam the clams over high heat for 5 to 10 minutes, or until they open. With tongs or a slotted spoon, transfer the clams, still in their shells, to 4 large heated soup plates. Strain all the clam juice in the skillet through a fine sieve lined with cheesecloth into the simmering tomato sauce. Cook for 1 or 2 minutes, then pour the soup over the clams and sprinkle chopped parsley on top. Serve at once.

NOTE: If the amount of liquid called for in the ingredients sounds insufficient, do not worry. The shellfish produce their own liquid in the cooking.

Oyster Bisque

To serve 4 to 6

2/3 cup rice
1 pint oysters
1 small onion stuck with cloves
Bouquet garni of thyme, parsley,
 celery or fennel, tied in cheesecloth

1 cup oyster liquid, or oyster liquid
 mixed with white wine
1 pint cream
Salt
Pepper
Paprika

Cook the rice in boiling salted water until it is very soft, then drain. Chop the oysters fine and reserve all their juice. In a saucepan, combine the minced oysters with the onion, *bouquet garni* and oyster liquid. Bring it to the boiling point and simmer for 10 minutes. Remove the *bouquet garni*. Add the drained rice, mix well, then put the soup through a fine sieve. Add the cream, and season to taste with salt and pepper. Bring the soup to the boiling point and serve, with a dash of paprika on each bowlful.

Mediterranean Fisherman's Soup

Bouillabaisse

To serve 8 to 10

COURT BOUILLON
2 cups thinly sliced onions
1 cup thinly sliced leeks
3/4 cup olive oil
8 cups water or 2 cups dry white wine
 and 6 cups water
2 pounds fish heads, bones and
 trimmings
3 pounds ripe tomatoes, coarsely
chopped (about 6 cups)
1/2 cup fresh fennel or 1/2 teaspoon dried
 fennel seeds, crushed
1 teaspoon finely chopped garlic
1 three-inch strip fresh orange peel
1 teaspoon dried thyme
2 parsley sprigs
1 bay leaf
1/4 teaspoon crushed saffron threads
Salt
Freshly ground black pepper

In a heavy 4- to 6-quart saucepan, cook the onions and leeks in the oil over low heat, stirring frequently, for 5 minutes, or until they are tender but not brown (additional onions may be substituted for the leeks). Add the water or wine and water, the fish trimmings, tomatoes, herbs and seasonings, and cook uncovered over moderate heat for 30 minutes.

ROUILLE

2 small green peppers, seeded and cut in small squares	2 canned pimientos, drained and dried
1 dry chili pepper or a few drops of Tabasco added to the finished sauce	4 garlic cloves, coarsely chopped
	6 tablespoons olive oil
1 cup water	1 to 3 tablespoons fine dry bread crumbs

THE ROUILLE: Meanwhile, prepare the *rouille*. In a 1½- to 2-quart saucepan, simmer the green peppers and chili pepper in 1 cup of water for 10 minutes, or until they are tender. Drain them thoroughly and dry them with paper towels. Then, with a large mortar and pestle, or a mixing bowl and wooden spoon, mash the peppers, pimiento and garlic to a smooth paste. Slowly beat in the olive oil and add enough bread crumbs to make the sauce thick enough to hold its shape in a spoon. Taste and season with Tabasco if you have omitted the chili pepper.

A quicker but less authentic way to make *rouille* is to combine the simmered peppers, the pimiento, garlic and the olive oil in an electric blender. Blend at low speed until they are smooth, adding more oil if the blender clogs. With a rubber spatula, transfer the sauce to a bowl and stir in enough bread crumbs to make it thick enough to hold its shape in a spoon. Taste and season with Tabasco if you have omitted the chili pepper. Set aside.

FISH AND SEAFOOD

2 two-pound live lobsters, cut up and cracked	hake, cod, yellow pike, lake trout, whitefish, rockfish
1½ pounds each of three kinds of firm, white fish cut into 2-inch serving pieces: halibut, red snapper, bass, haddock, pollack,	1 eel, cut in 2-inch pieces (optional)
	2 pounds live mussels (optional)
	2 pounds fresh or frozen sea scallops, cut in halves or quarters (optional)
	12 *croûtes* (*see French onion soup, page 31*)

ASSEMBLING THE SOUP: When the court bouillon is done, strain it through a large fine sieve into a soup pot or kettle, pressing down hard on the fish trimmings and vegetables with the back of a spoon to extract their juices before discarding them. Bring the strained stock to a boil over high heat and add the lobster. Boil briskly for 5 minutes, then add the fish (and the eel, if you wish) and cook another 5 minutes. Finally, add the mussels and scallops (optional) and boil 5 minutes longer. Taste for seasoning.

To serve, remove the fish and seafood from the soup with a slotted spoon and arrange them on a heated platter. Ladle the soup into a large tureen. Thin the *rouille* with 2 or 3 tablespoons of soup and pour it into a sauceboat. At the table, place a *croûte* in each individual soup bowl, ladle in the soup over it, and arrange fish and seafood on top. Pass the *rouille* separately.

Cold Buttermilk Soup
Kaernemaelkskoldskaal

The flavor of commercial buttermilk varies enormously from dairy to dairy. Natural fresh buttermilk, if available, would be ideal for this unusual summer luncheon or dessert soup, but cultured buttermilk of good flavor will do almost as well.

To serve 6 to 8

3 egg yolks
½ cup sugar
½ teaspoon grated lemon rind

1 teaspoon lemon juice
1 teaspoon vanilla (optional)
1 quart buttermilk
¼ cup whipped heavy cream
  (optional)

With an electric beater or a wire whisk, beat the egg yolks in a large bowl. Gradually add the sugar, beating until the eggs fall back into the bowl in a lazy ribbon when the beater is lifted. Add the grated lemon rind and juice and the optional vanilla. Slowly beat in the buttermilk, continuing to beat until the soup is smooth. Serve in chilled bowls and float a spoonful of unsweetened whipped cream on the surface of each serving if you like.

Cold Sour-Cherry Soup
Hideg Meggyleves

To serve 6

3 cups cold water
1 cup sugar
1 cinnamon stick

4 cups pitted sour cherries or drained
  canned sour cherries
1 tablespoon arrowroot
¼ cup heavy cream, chilled
¾ cup dry red wine, chilled

In a 2-quart saucepan, combine the water, sugar and cinnamon stick. Bring to a boil and add the cherries. Partially cover and simmer over low heat for 35 to 40 minutes if the cherries are fresh or 10 minutes if they are canned. Remove the cinnamon stick.

Mix the arrowroot and 2 tablespoons of cold water into a paste, then beat into the cherry soup. Stirring constantly, bring the soup almost to a boil. Reduce the heat and simmer about 2 minutes, or until clear and slightly thickened. Pour into a shallow glass or stainless-steel bowl, and refrigerate until chilled. Before serving—preferably in soup bowls that have been pre-chilled—stir in the cream and wine.

Beef

Standing Rib Roast with Yorkshire Pudding

To serve 6 to 8

A 6-pound standing rib roast

Preheat the oven to 500° (it will take about 15 minutes for most ovens to reach this temperature). For the most predictable results, insert a meat thermometer into the thickest part of the beef, being careful not to let the tip of the thermometer touch any fat or bone.

Place the beef, fat side up, in a large shallow roasting pan. (It is unnecessary to use a rack, since the ribs of the roast form a natural rack.)

Roast the beef undisturbed in the middle of the oven for 20 minutes. Reduce the heat to 350° and continue to roast, without basting, for about 1 hour, or until the beef is cooked to your taste. A meat thermometer will register 130° to 140° when the beef is rare, 150° to 160° when medium, and 160° to 170° when it is well done. If you are not using a thermometer, start timing the roast after you reduce the heat to 350°. You can estimate approximately 20 minutes per pound for rare beef, 25 minutes per pound for medium, and 30 minutes per pound for well done.

Transfer the beef to a heated platter and let it rest for at least 15 minutes for easier carving. If you plan to accompany the beef with Yorkshire pud-

46

ding *(recipe below)*, increase the oven heat to 400° as soon as the beef is cooked. Transfer the roast from the oven to a heated platter, drape foil loosely over it, and set aside in a warm place while the pudding bakes. If you have two ovens, time the pudding to finish cooking during the 15 minutes that the roast rests.

To carve, first remove a thin slice of beef from the large end of the roast so that it will stand firmly on this end. Insert a large fork below the top rib and carve slices of beef from the top, separating each slice from the bone as you proceed. Serve with its own juice and a horseradish sauce *(below)*.

YORKSHIRE PUDDING

2 eggs

½ teaspoon salt

1 cup all-purpose flour

1 cup milk

2 tablespoons roast beef drippings, or substitute 2 tablespoons lard

To make the batter in a blender, combine the eggs, salt, flour and milk in the blender jar, and blend at high speed for 2 or 3 seconds. Turn off the machine, scrape down the sides of the jar, and blend again for 40 seconds. (To make the batter by hand, beat the eggs and salt with a whisk or a rotary or electric beater until frothy. Slowly add the flour, beating constantly. Then pour in the milk in a thin stream and beat until the mixture is smooth and creamy.) Refrigerate for at least 1 hour.

Preheat the oven to 400°. In a 10-by-15-by-2½-inch roasting pan, heat the fat over moderate heat until it splutters. Briefly beat the batter again and pour it into the pan. Bake in the middle of the oven for 15 minutes, reduce the heat to 375°, and bake for 15 minutes longer, or until the pudding has risen over the top of the pan and is crisp and brown. With a sharp knife, divide the pudding into portions, and serve immediately.

HORSERADISH SAUCE

¼ cup bottled horseradish, drained and squeezed dry in a kitchen towel

1 tablespoon white wine vinegar

1 teaspoon sugar

¼ teaspoon dry English mustard

½ teaspoon salt

½ teaspoon white pepper

½ cup chilled heavy cream

In a small bowl, stir the horseradish, vinegar, sugar, mustard, salt and white pepper together until well blended. Beat the cream with a whisk or a rotary or electric beater until stiff enough to form unwavering peaks on the beater when it is lifted from the bowl. Pour the horseradish mixture over the cream and, with a spatula, fold together lightly but thoroughly. Taste for seasoning. Serve the sauce from a sauceboat as an accompaniment to the beef.

Marinated Pot Roast
Sauerbraten

To serve 6 to 8

½ cup dry red wine
½ cup red wine vinegar
2 cups cold water
1 medium-sized onion, peeled and
  thinly sliced
5 black peppercorns and 4 whole
  juniper berries coarsely crushed
  with a mortar and pestle
2 small bay leaves
4 pounds boneless beef roast,

preferably top or bottom round
  or rump, trimmed of fat
3 tablespoons lard
½ cup finely chopped onions
½ cup finely chopped carrots
¼ cup finely chopped celery
2 tablespoons flour
½ cup water
½ cup gingersnap or
  honey-cake crumbs

In a 2- to 3-quart saucepan, combine the wine, vinegar, water, sliced onion, crushed peppercorns and juniper berries, and bay leaves. Bring this marinade to a boil over high heat, then remove it from the heat and let it cool to room temperature. Place the beef in a deep crock or a deep stainless-steel or enameled pot just large enough to hold it comfortably and pour the marinade over it. The marinade should come at least halfway up the sides of the meat; if necessary, add more wine. Turn the meat in the marinade to moisten it on all sides. Then cover the pan tightly with foil or plastic wrap and refrigerate for 2 to 3 days, turning the meat over at least twice a day.

Remove the meat from the marinade and pat it completely dry with paper towels. Strain the marinade through a fine sieve set over a bowl and reserve the liquid. Discard the spices and onions.

In a heavy 5-quart flameproof casserole, melt the lard over high heat until it begins to splutter. Add the meat and brown it on all sides, turning it frequently and regulating the heat so that it browns deeply and evenly without burning. This should take about 15 minutes. Transfer the meat to a platter, and pour off and discard all but about 2 tablespoons of the fat from the casserole. Add the chopped onions, carrots and celery to the fat in the casserole and cook them over moderate heat, stirring frequently, for 5 to 8 minutes, or until they are soft and light brown. Sprinkle 2 tablespoons of flour over the vegetables and cook, stirring constantly, for 2 or 3 minutes longer, or until the flour begins to color. Pour in 2 cups of the reserved marinade and ½ cup of water and bring to a boil over high heat. Return the meat to the casserole. Cover tightly and simmer over low heat for 2 hours, or until the meat shows no resistance when pierced with the tip of a sharp knife. Transfer the meat to a heated platter and cover it with aluminum foil to keep it warm while you make the sauce.

Pour the liquid left in the casserole into a large measuring cup and skim the fat from the surface. You will need 2½ cups of liquid for the sauce. If you have more, boil it briskly over high heat until it is reduced to that amount; if you have less, add some of the reserved marinade. Combine the liquid and the gingersnap or honey-cake crumbs in a small saucepan, and cook over moderate heat, stirring frequently, for 10 minutes. The crumbs will disintegrate in the sauce and thicken it slightly. Strain the sauce through a fine sieve, pressing down hard with a wooden spoon to force as much of the vegetables and crumbs through as possible. Return the sauce to the pan, taste for seasoning and let it simmer over a low heat until ready to serve.

To serve, carve the meat into ¼-inch-thick slices, arrange them in overlapping layers on a heated platter, and moisten with a few tablespoons of the sauce. Pass the remaining sauce separately in a sauceboat.

NOTE: If you prefer, you may cook the *Sauerbraten* in the oven rather than on top of the stove. Bring the casserole to a boil over high heat, cover tightly and cook in a preheated 350° oven for about 2 hours.

A tenderizing and flavoring marinade of wine, onions, bay leaves, juniper berries and pepper transforms a boneless beef roast into savory *Sauerbraten*.

Venezuelan Pot Roast
Asado Antiguo a la Venezolana Mechado

To serve 8 to 10

6 to 8 strips larding pork, cut ⅛
    inch wide and 2 inches longer than
    length of the meat
4 pounds bottom round of beef, in
    one piece
3 tablespoons capers, drained and
    rinsed
2 tablespoons white distilled vinegar

¼ cup finely grated onions
½ teaspoon finely chopped garlic
1 teaspoon salt
¼ teaspoon freshly ground black
    pepper
¼ cup olive oil
1 tablespoon dark brown sugar
2 cups water

Lard the beef in the following fashion: Chill the pork strips in the freezer for 10 minutes or so to stiffen them. First make a hole by inserting the point of the larding needle 2 inches into one short end of the meat; pull the needle back an inch or so and lay a pork strip in its groove. Then gradually force the needle through the length of the beef roast until the pork strip emerges from the other end. Pressing the end of the strip where it entered the meat, carefully pull out the needle, leaving the pork in the meat. Repeat with the rest of the pork strips, spacing them at about 2-inch intervals. Trim off the protruding ends of the larding strips. Then, with the tip of a small skewer or knife, push one caper at a time into the beef around the strips of pork at both ends.

Combine the vinegar, grated onion, garlic, salt and pepper, and press and rub the mixture firmly into the outside surfaces of the beef. Cover with foil, and let it stand at room temperature for at least 6 hours—or overnight in the refrigerator. When you are ready to cook the meat, heat the olive oil over high heat in a heavy 4- to 6-quart casserole until a light haze forms above it. Then sprinkle the meat evenly with the dark brown sugar and press the sugar into the meat with the fingers. Place the meat in the pot. Regulate the heat so that the meat colors quickly and evenly without burning, turning it every few minutes to brown it on all sides. When the meat is a deep-mahogany color, pour the water into the pan and bring it to a boil, scraping up any brown sediment clinging to the bottom and sides of the pan. Cover the casserole tightly, reduce the heat to its lowest point and simmer the meat for about 2 hours, or until it shows no resistance when pierced with the tip of a small, sharp knife.

To serve, remove the meat from the casserole and carve it against the grain into neat ¼-inch slices, each of which should be patterned with tiny bits of larding pork. Arrange the slices on a heated platter and cover it with foil to keep the meat warm. Bring the cooking liquid in the casserole to a vigorous boil and boil it rapidly, uncovered, until it thickens to the desired consistency. Taste the sauce for seasoning and either pour it over the sliced meat or serve it separately.

Portuguese Steak
Bife à Portuguésa

To serve 4

4 large peeled garlic cloves, 2 crushed with a cleaver or knife and 2 cut lengthwise into halves
1 tablespoon red wine vinegar
1 teaspoon salt
Freshly ground black pepper
4 beef tenderloin steaks, sliced about 3/4 inch thick
2 tablespoons olive oil

2 tablespoons butter
1 large bay leaf, crumbled
8 thin slices *presunto* ham or prosciutto or other lean smoked ham
1/4 cup dry red wine
1 teaspoon fresh lemon juice
2 teaspoons finely chopped parsley
1 lemon cut into 8 wedges

Preheat the oven to 250°. Mash the crushed garlic, vinegar, salt and a few grindings of pepper to a smooth paste with a mortar and pestle or in a bowl with the back of a spoon. With your fingers, rub the paste into the steaks, pressing it firmly into both sides of the meat.

In a heavy 10- to 12-inch skillet, melt the butter in the olive oil over moderate heat. When the foam has almost subsided, add the garlic halves and bay leaf and cook for 1 minute, stirring constantly. Then with a slotted spoon, remove and discard the garlic and bay leaf. Add the steaks and cook for 2 or 3 minutes on each side, turning them with tongs, and regulating the heat so that they color quickly and evenly. The steaks should be well browned, but still pink inside.

Transfer the steaks to individual baking dishes or fairly deep plates and keep them warm in the oven. Add the slices of ham to the fat remaining in the skillet and cook over high heat, turning them frequently for 1 or 2 minutes. With the tongs, place 2 slices of ham on each steak. Pour off all but a thin film of fat from the skillet, add the wine and lemon juice and bring to a boil over high heat, meanwhile scraping in any brown particles clinging to the bottom and sides of the pan. Pour the sauce over the steaks, sprinkle them with parsley and garnish each serving with lemon wedges. Serve at once.

51

Steaks Eszterházy

Eszterházy Rostélyos

To serve 6

Salt
Freshly ground black pepper
2 pounds top round steak ½ inch
   thick, cut into 6 equal portions
Flour
3 tablespoons lard
1½ cups finely chopped onions
½ teaspoon finely chopped garlic
½ cup finely chopped carrots
3 tablespoons flour
3 cups beef stock, fresh or canned
3 whole allspice or ⅛ teaspoon
   ground allspice
3 medium-size bay leaves

4 peppercorns
⅛ teaspoon thyme
⅛-inch-wide strip lemon peel
4 slices lean bacon, coarsely chopped
   (⅓ cup)
2 tablespoons finely chopped parsley
¼ cup white wine vinegar
¾ cup heavy cream
1 teaspoon fresh lemon juice

THE GARNISH
2 parsnips, scraped and cut into 3-by-
   ½-inch julienne strips
1 medium-sized carrot, cut into 3-by-
   ½-inch julienne strips
4 sour gherkin pickles, cut into 3-by-
   ½-inch julienne strips

Salt and pepper the steaks, then dip them in flour and shake them to remove the excess. Heat the lard in a 12-inch skillet until a light haze forms over it, then brown the steaks over high heat for about 3 minutes on each side. Remove them to a platter and reduce the heat to medium.

Add the onions, garlic and carrots and cook for about 8 minutes, stirring frequently, until the vegetables are lightly colored.

Off the heat, stir in the 3 tablespoons of flour, continuing to stir until all the flour is absorbed. Return the skillet to the heat, add the stock and bring it to a boil, stirring constantly with a whisk until the sauce is smooth and thick. Add the allspice, bay leaves, peppercorns, thyme, lemon peel, bacon, parsley and vinegar. Return the meat to the skillet and bring the stock to a boil again. Reduce the heat to low, partially cover the pan and simmer for 50 minutes to an hour, or until the steaks show no resistance when pierced with the tip of a small sharp knife.

Drop the parsnip and carrot strips into a saucepan of boiling, lightly salted water. Boil uncovered for 2 or 3 minutes, or until the vegetables are slightly tender, then drain in a colander or sieve. Arrange the steaks on a platter and keep them warm in a 200° oven while you prepare the sauce.

Strain the contents of the frying pan, pressing hard on the vegetables before discarding them. Skim off the surface fat from the sauce. Whisk the cream and lemon juice into the sauce and add the carrot, parsnip and gherkin strips. Simmer 2 or 3 minutes. Taste for seasoning. Pour the vegetables and the sauce over the steaks and serve at once.

Steak with Red Wine Sauce

Bifteck Marchand de Vins

To serve 6

MARCHAND DE VINS SAUCE
2 tablespoons butter
½ cup finely chopped shallots or
    scallions
1½ cups dry red wine
½ bay leaf
¼ teaspoon dried thyme

4 parsley sprigs
2 teaspoons meat extract combined
    with 3 tablespoons hot water
12 tablespoons soft butter (1½
    quarter-pound sticks)
1 tablespoon lemon juice
1 teaspoon flour
2 tablespoons finely chopped fresh
    parsley

In a 1- to 2-quart enameled saucepan, melt 2 tablespoons of butter over moderate heat. When the foam subsides, cook the shallots, stirring constantly, for 2 minutes, or until they are soft. Pour in the wine, add the bay leaf, thyme and parsley sprigs and simmer over moderate heat until reduced to ¾ cup. Strain the reduced wine through a fine sieve into a small bowl, pressing down hard on the shallots and herbs with the back of a spoon before discarding them. Return the wine to the saucepan, add the thinned meat extract and bring to a boil. Set the pan aside.

Cream 12 tablespoons of soft butter, beating it vigorously against the side of a small bowl with a wooden spoon until it is fluffy. Beat in the lemon juice, flour and parsley. Set the bowl aside.

THE STEAK
A 3- to 3½-pound sirloin, porterhouse
    or T-bone steak, cut 1 to 1¼
    inch thick and trimmed of excess
    fat

1 tablespoon butter
2 tablespoons vegetable oil
Salt
Freshly ground black pepper

Pat the trimmed steak thoroughly dry with paper towels. Cut small incisions every inch or so around the outside of the steak so the fat won't curl as it cooks. In a heavy 12- or 14-inch skillet or sauté pan, melt 1 tablespoon of butter with the 2 tablespoons of vegetable oil over high heat. Add the steak and brown it quickly for 1 or 2 minutes on each side, turning it with tongs. Then reduce the heat to moderate and sauté the steak for about 5 minutes on each side, or until it is done to a medium-rare degree.

Experts test a steak by pressing it with a finger. It should be slightly resilient, neither soft nor firm. If that method seems tricky, make a small incision near the bone with the tip of a sharp knife and judge by the meat's color. Transfer to a heated platter and season with salt and pepper.

Pour the reduced wine mixture into the skillet and bring it to a boil over moderate heat, stirring constantly and scraping in any browned bits that cling to the bottom and sides of the pan. Remove from the heat and blend in the creamed butter mixture, 2 tablespoons at a time. To serve, slice the steak and offer the sauce separately.

Steak with Sour-Cream Sauce
Zwiebelfleisch

To serve 4 to 6

2 tablespoons vegetable oil
2 tablespoons butter
2 pounds beef tenderloin or other
   tender cut of beefsteak, cut
   into strips 2 inches long, 1 inch
   wide and ¼ inch thick

1¼ cups finely chopped onions
½ teaspoon finely chopped garlic
½ teaspoon caraway seeds
⅛ teaspoon marjoram
Freshly ground black pepper
2 tablespoons white vinegar
1 cup beef stock, fresh or canned

In a heavy 10- or 12-inch skillet, heat the oil and butter. When the foam subsides, add the meat and brown it on both sides—about 5 minutes in all. Remove it to a platter.

Pour off most of the fat, leaving only a thin film on the bottom of the skillet. Add the onions and cook them, stirring occasionally, for 8 to 10 minutes, or until they are lightly colored, then add the garlic and cook for about 3 minutes longer.

Stir in the caraway seeds, the marjoram and a generous grinding of pepper. Add the vinegar and boil for 1 minute. Pour in the stock and bring to a boil, stirring in any brown bits that cling to the bottom and sides of the pan.

Return the meat to the pan and bring the beef stock to a boil again. Turn the heat to low and simmer the meat for 15 minutes or longer until it is tender.

THE SAUCE
1 tablespoon flour

1 cup sour cream

In the meanwhile with a wire whisk, beat the flour into the sour cream in a small mixing bowl. With a large spoon stir the mixture into the skillet, then turn the heat to its lowest point and simmer for 10 minutes without letting the sauce reach the boiling point. Mask the steak with some of the sauce and serve the rest in a sauceboat.

Beef Stroganov

Created in the late 19th Century for a Russian count, "bef Stroganov" has become one of the world's famous dishes. The recipe that follows is the classic Russian version. The numerous European and American variations called beef Stroganov do not in any sense reproduce the dish as it was originally made.

To serve 4 to 6

1 tablespoon powdered mustard
1 tablespoon sugar
2 teaspoons salt
4 to 5 tablespoons vegetable oil
4 cups thinly sliced onions separated
    into rings

1 pound fresh mushrooms, thinly
    sliced lengthwise
2 pounds fillet of beef, trimmed of
    all fat
1 teaspoon freshly ground black
    pepper
1 pint sour cream

In a small bowl combine the mustard, 1½ teaspoons of the sugar, a pinch of the salt and enough hot water (perhaps a tablespoon) to form a thick paste. Let the mustard rest at room temperature for about 15 minutes.

Heat 2 tablespoons of the oil in a heavy 10- to 12-inch skillet over high heat until a light haze forms above it. Drop in the onions and mushrooms, cover the pan, and reduce the heat to low. Stirring from time to time, simmer 20 to 30 minutes, or until the vegetables are soft. Drain them in a sieve, discard the liquid and return the mixture to the skillet.

With a large, sharp knife cut the fillet across the grain into ¼-inch-wide rounds. Lay each round on a board and slice it with the grain into ¼-inch-wide strips. Heat 2 tablespoons of oil in another heavy 10- to 12-inch skillet over high heat until very hot but not smoking. Drop in half the meat and, tossing the strips constantly with a large spoon, fry for 2 minutes or so until the meat is lightly browned. With a slotted spoon transfer the meat to the vegetables in the other skillet and fry the remaining meat similarly, adding additional oil if necessary. When all the meat has been combined with the vegetables, stir in the remaining salt, pepper and the mustard paste. Stir in the sour cream, a tablespoon at a time, then add the remaining ½ teaspoon of sugar and reduce the heat to low. Cover the pan and simmer 2 or 3 minutes, or until the sauce is heated through. Taste for seasoning.

To serve *bef Stroganov,* transfer the contents of the pan to a heated serving platter and, if you like, scatter straw potatoes (see *Index*) over the top.

Viennese Steaks
Wiener Rostbraten

To serve 6

6 medium-sized onions, peeled and
  thinly sliced
4 tablespoons butter
3 pounds boneless beef sirloin, cut
  ½ inch thick, then pounded to ¼

inch thick
3 tablespoons vegetable oil
2 tablespoons butter
Salt
Freshly ground black pepper
½ cup beef stock, fresh or canned
  (optional)

Cut the sliced onions into strips ⅛ to ¼ inch wide. In a heavy 8- or 10-inch skillet over medium heat, melt the 4 tablespoons of butter, and when the foam subsides, add the onions. Stirring occasionally, cook them for 8 to 10 minutes, or until they are colored and crisp. Add more butter if necessary while the onions are frying—they must not burn. Set the onions aside, uncovered, in the skillet.

Cut the steak into 6 equal portions. In a 10- or 12-inch heavy skillet, heat the oil and 2 tablespoons of butter over medium heat. When the butter foam subsides, add the steaks. Raise the heat to moderately high and cook the steaks briskly for 2 to 4 minutes, depending upon the degree of doneness you prefer.

Arrange the steaks on a heated platter and sprinkle them with salt and a few grindings of pepper.

Reheat the onions over high heat for a minute or so to restore their crispness. Serve the steaks with a mound of the onions placed on each one.

If you prefer a light sauce, add the stock to the skillet in which the steaks were cooked, and bring it to a boil, stirring in any brown bits clinging to the pan, then pour the sauce over the steaks before you place the onions on top. *Wiener Rostbraten* may be served with chopped parsley and crumbled bacon sprinkled over the onions.

Beef Strips with Onions and Peppers
Borsos Bélszíntokány

To serve 6

3 tablespoons lard
2½ to 3 pounds fillet of beef, cut
  into ¼-by-¼-by-3-inch strips
1 cup thinly sliced onions
¼ teaspoon finely chopped garlic

1 teaspoon sweet Hungarian paprika
½ cup chopped mushrooms (⅛
  pound)
2 large green peppers with seeds and
  ribs removed, cut into strips ⅛
  inch wide and 2½ inches long

Heat 2 tablespoons of the lard in a heavy 10-inch skillet over high heat until a light haze forms over it. Add the meat strips and toss them about for 3 to 5 minutes, or until they are browned on all sides.

Remove the meat to a platter and add the remaining tablespoon of lard to the skillet. Turn the heat to medium and add the onions and garlic. Cook for 8 to 10 minutes, or until the onions are lightly colored. Off the heat, stir in the paprika, continuing to stir until the onions are well coated. Return the meat to the skillet and gently stir in the mushrooms and peppers. Place the pan on high heat, and when it begins to sizzle, turn the heat to its lowest point and cover the pan tightly. Simmer for 25 to 30 minutes, or until the meat shows no resistance when pierced with the point of a sharp knife. Taste for seasoning.

Tip the skillet and skim off any of the surface fat. Arrange the strips on a platter, pour the pan juices over them and serve. *Borsos Bélszíntokány* is usually served with rice and sour pickles.

Beef Slices with Sweet Glaze
Gyuniku Teriyaki

To serve 4

1½ pounds lean boneless beef, preferably tenderloin or boneless sirloin, cut in 12 slices ¼ inch thick

TERIYAKI SAUCE

1 cup *mirin* (sweet *sake*), or substitute 1 cup less 2 tablespoons pale dry sherry
1 cup Japanese all-purpose soy sauce
1 cup chicken stock, fresh or canned

TERIYAKI GLAZE

¼ cup *teriyaki* sauce
1 tablespoon sugar
2 teaspoons cornstarch mixed with 1 tablespoon cold water

GARNISH

4 teaspoons powdered mustard, mixed with just enough hot water to make a thick paste and set aside to rest for 15 minutes
12 sprigs fresh parsley

PREPARE AHEAD: 1. To make the sauce, warm the *mirin* or sherry in a 1½- to 2-quart enameled or stainless-steel saucepan over moderate heat. Off the heat ignite the *mirin* with a match, and shake the pan back and forth until the flame dies out. Then stir in the soy sauce and chicken stock, and bring to a boil. Pour the sauce into a bowl and cool to room temperature.

2. To make the glaze, combine ¼ cup of the *teriyaki* sauce and 1 tablespoon of sugar in an enameled or stainless-steel saucepan. Bring almost to a boil over moderate heat, then reduce the heat to low. Stir the combined cornstarch and water into the sauce. Cook, stirring constantly, until it thickens to a clear syrupy glaze. Immediately pour into a dish and set aside.

TO COOK: Preheat the broiler to its highest point, or light a hibachi or charcoal grill. Dip the beef, one slice at a time, into the *teriyaki* sauce. Broil 2 inches from the heat for 1 minute on each side, or until lightly brown. For well-done meat broil an additional minute.

TO SERVE: Slice the meat into 1-inch-wide strips and place them on individual serving plates. Spoon a little of the glaze over each serving, and garnish each plate with a dab of the mustard and a sprig of parsley. If you prefer, mix the mustard into the glaze before pouring it over the meat.

NOTE: Any leftover *teriyaki* sauce may be stored in tightly closed jars and refrigerated for as long as one month. Before using, bring to a boil and skim the surface of any scum.

Pepper Steak

Ching-chiao-ch'ao-niu-jou

To serve 2 to 4

1 pound flank steak, trimmed of all
    fat
1 tablespoon Chinese rice wine, or
    pale dry sherry
3 tablespoons soy sauce
1 teaspoon sugar
2 teaspoons cornstarch

2 medium-sized green peppers,
    seeded, deribbed and cut into ½-
    inch squares
4 slices peeled fresh ginger root,
    about 1 inch in diameter and ⅛ inch
    thick
¼ cup peanut oil, or flavorless
    vegetable oil

PREPARE AHEAD: 1. With a cleaver or sharp knife, cut the flank steak lengthwise into strips 1½ inches wide, then crosswise into ¼-inch slices.

2. In a large bowl, mix the wine, soy sauce, sugar and cornstarch. Add the steak slices and toss with a large spoon to coat them thoroughly. The steak may be cooked at once, or marinated for as long as 6 hours.

3. Place the peppers, ginger root and oil within easy reach.

TO COOK: Set a 12-inch wok or 10-inch skillet over high heat for about 30 seconds. Pour in a tablespoon of the oil, swirl it about in the pan and heat for another 30 seconds, turning the heat down to moderate if the oil begins to smoke. Immediately add the pepper squares and stir-fry for 3 minutes, or until they are tender but still crisp. Scoop them out with a slotted spoon and reserve. Pour 3 more tablespoons of oil into the pan and heat almost to the smoking point. Add the ginger, stir for a few seconds, then drop in the steak mixture. Stir-fry over high heat for about 2 minutes, or until the meat shows no sign of pink. Discard the ginger. Add the pepper and cook for a minute, stirring, then transfer the contents of the pan to a heated platter and serve.

Fried Steak with Cellophane Noodles

Kan-shao-nu-jou-ssŭ

To serve 2

Half of a 2-ounce package of
  cellophane noodles
½ pound flank steak
2 tablespoons soy sauce
1 teaspoon cornstarch
½ teaspoon sugar
2 cups peanut oil, or flavorless
  vegetable oil

1 green pepper, seeded, deribbed and
  shredded into strips 1½ to 2
  inches long and ⅛ inch wide
1 teaspoon finely chopped fresh
  ginger root
¼ to ½ teaspoon cayenne pepper,
  according to taste

PREPARE AHEAD: 1. With a sharp knife or a pair of scissors, cut the cellophane noodles into 4-inch lengths, separating any noodles that cling together.

2. With a cleaver or sharp, heavy knife, trim off and discard the fat from the flank steak. To shred the steak, put it in the freezer for 30 minutes or so to firm the meat and make it easier to slice. Then lay the steak flat on a chopping board and slice the meat horizontally (with the grain) as thin as possible. Cut these slices into pieces 1½ to 2 inches long and ⅛ inch wide.

3. In a small bowl combine the soy sauce, cornstarch and sugar. Add the shredded steak and toss it about in the bowl until it is well coated with the mixture.

4. Have the noodles, steak, oil, green pepper, ginger and cayenne pepper within easy reach.

TO COOK: Set a 12-inch wok or 10-inch skillet over high heat and pour in the 2 cups of oil. Heat the oil until it smokes, or it registers 450° on a deep-frying thermometer. Drop in half of the noodles and let them deep-fry for one second. As soon as they puff up, lift them out with a slotted spoon and spread them on a double thickness of paper towels to drain. Then fry the other half of the noodles. Pour off the oil and set it aside in a small mixing bowl.

Return the wok or skillet to the heat and return 1 tablespoon of the oil to the pan. Swirl it about in the pan and let it heat for 30 seconds, turning the heat down to moderate if the oil begins to smoke. Drop in the green pepper and stir-fry for 2 minutes until it begins to darken in color. With a slotted spoon, transfer the green pepper to a plate. Add another 2 tablespoons of oil to the pan and let it heat for 30 seconds. Add the ginger root, and stir it about for 1 or 2 seconds, then add the shredded flank steak and cayenne pepper, and stir-fry for 1 to 2 minutes, until the beef is lightly browned and any liquid which may have accumulated in the pan has completely evaporated. Return the green pepper to the pan and heat it through, stirring constantly.

To serve, place the beef and pepper mixture in the center of a large heated platter and arrange the fried cellophane noodles around the outside.

Braised Stuffed Beef Rolls
Rouladen

To serve 6

3 pounds top round steak, sliced
  ½ inch thick, trimmed of all fat.
  and pounded ¼ inch thick
6 teaspoons Düsseldorf-style
  prepared mustard, or substitute
  6 teaspoons other hot prepared
  mustard
¼ cup finely chopped onions
6 slices lean bacon, each about
  8 inches long
3 dill pickles, rinsed in cold water

and cut lengthwise into halves
3 tablespoons lard
2 cups water
1 cup coarsely chopped celery
¼ cup thinly sliced leeks, white
  part only
1 tablespoon finely chopped scraped
  parsnip
3 parsley sprigs
1 teaspoon salt
1 tablespoon butter
2 tablespoons flour

Cut the steak into 6 rectangular pieces about 4 inches wide and 8 inches long. Spread each rectangle with a teaspoon of mustard, sprinkle it with 2 teaspoons of onions, and place a slice of bacon down the center. Lay a strip of pickle across the narrow end of each piece and roll the meat around it, jelly-roll fashion, into a cylinder. Tie the rolls at each end with kitchen cord.

In a heavy 10- to 12-inch skillet melt the lard over moderate heat until it begins to splutter. Add the beef rolls, and brown them on all sides, regulating the heat so they color quickly and evenly without burning. Transfer the rolls to a plate, pour the water into the skillet and bring it to a boil, meanwhile scraping in any brown particles clinging to the bottom and sides of the pan. Add the celery, leeks, parsnip, parsley and salt, and return the beef rolls to the skillet. Cover, reduce the heat to low, and simmer for 1 hour, or until the meat shows no resistance when pierced with a fork. Turn the rolls once or twice during the cooking period. Transfer the rolls to a heated platter, and cover with foil to keep them warm while you make the sauce.

Strain the cooking liquid left in the skillet through a fine sieve, pressing down hard on the vegetables before discarding them. Measure the liquid, return it to the skillet, and boil briskly until it is reduced to 2 cups. Remove from the heat. Melt the butter in a small saucepan over moderate heat and, when the foam subsides, sprinkle in the flour. Lower the heat and cook, stirring constantly, until the flour turns a golden brown. Be careful not to let it burn. Gradually add the reduced cooking liquid, beating vigorously with a whisk until the sauce is smooth and thick. Taste for seasoning and return the sauce and the *Rouladen* to the skillet. Simmer over low heat only long enough to heat the rolls through. Serve the rolls on a heated platter and pour the sauce over them. *Rouladen* are often accompanied by red cabbage and dumplings or boiled potatoes.

Matambre, an Argentine beef roll (recipe on page 62), dates from stagecoach days when travelers took them along to eat while crossing the Pampa.

Stuffed Flank-Steak Roll

Matambre

To serve 8 to 10

2 two-pound flank steaks
½ cup red wine vinegar
1 teaspoon finely chopped garlic
1 teaspoon dried thyme

THE STUFFING
½ pound fresh spinach
8 scraped cooked whole carrots, about
   6 to 8 inches long and no more
   than 1 inch in diameter

4 hard-cooked eggs, cut lengthwise
   into quarters
1 large onion, sliced ⅛ inch thick
   and divided into rings
¼ cup finely chopped fresh parsley
1 teaspoon crumbled *pequín* chili or
   crushed, seeded, dried *hontaka* chili
1 tablespoon coarse salt
3 cups beef stock, fresh or canned
1 to 3 cups cold water

Ask your butcher to butterfly the steaks, or do it yourself in the following fashion: With a long, very sharp knife slit the steaks horizontally from one long side to within ½ inch of the other side. Open the steaks, place them between 2 sheets of wax paper, and pound them with the side of a cleaver to flatten them further. Trim away all gristle and fat.

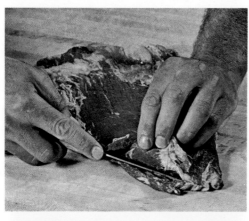

*A Sharp Knife and Sure Touch
to Butterfly Steaks*

1 To butterfly steaks for *matambre*, slice into each one horizontally from one side, using your sharpest knife.

2 Continuing to slice horizontally, slit the steak almost in half, cutting to within ½ inch of the far side.

3 Open the steak out flat when you finish the cutting—its shape will be similar to that of a butterfly.

Lay one steak, cut side up, on a 12-by-18-inch jelly-roll pan. Sprinkle it with half the vinegar, then scatter half the garlic and thyme over it. Cover the meat with the other steak, also cut side up, and sprinkle it with the remaining vinegar, garlic and thyme. Cover the pan and let the steaks marinate for 6 hours at room temperature or overnight refrigerated.

Preheat the oven to 375°. Lay the steaks end to end, cut side up, so that they overlap by about 2 inches. Pound the joined ends together with the flat of a cleaver to seal them securely. Wash the spinach under running water, drain it and trim off the stems. Spread the leaves evenly over the meat, and arrange the carrots across the grain of the meat in parallel rows about 3 inches apart. Place the eggs between the rows of carrots. Scatter the onion rings over them and sprinkle the surface evenly with parsley, chili and salt. Carefully roll the steaks with the grain, jelly-roll fashion, into a thick, long cylinder. To tie the *matambre*, cut a kitchen cord into a 10-foot length. Wrap one end of the cord around the steaks

Filling, Rolling and Tying the Steaks

4 After marinating the butterflied steaks, place them end to end, overlapping them by about 2 inches.

63

5 Spread both steaks with the *matambre* stuffing: spinach leaves, carrots, hard-cooked eggs, onion rings, parsley, chili and salt. Then, beginning at either of the short ends, roll the steaks with the grain, jelly-roll fashion.

about 1 inch from the edge of the roll and knot it securely. Then, holding the cord in a loop near the knot, wrap the remaining length of cord around the steaks about 2 inches from the edge of the roll and feed it through the loop. Now tighten the cord to keep the loop in place. Repeat until the roll is tied in loops at intervals of about 1 inch. Bring the remaining cord across the length of the bottom of the roll (catching it in one or two loops) and up over the opposite end. Tie it securely around the first loop. Trim off any excess cord.

Place the *matambre* in a 12-quart casserole or roasting pan and pour in the stock. Add enough cold water to come a third of the way up the roll. Then cover tightly and place in the middle of the oven for 1 hour. To serve hot, remove the *matambre* from the pan to a board and let it rest for 10 minutes. With a sharp knife remove the strings and cut the *matambre* into ¼-inch slices. Arrange the slices on a heated platter and moisten them with a little pan liquid before serving. Or the *matambre* may be thoroughly chilled, and served in similarly cut slices. In Argentina, the *matambre* is generally poached in stock or water to cover it completely; it is then removed from the pot, pressed under weights until the juices drain off, refrigerated and served cold.

64

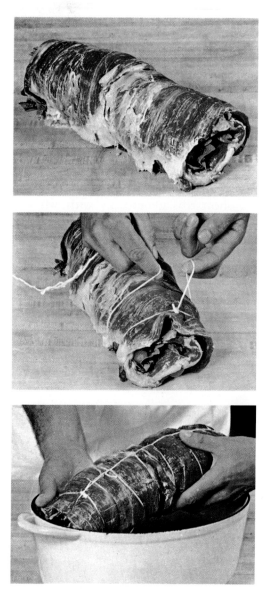

6 Roll the steaks together carefully and as compactly as possible until they form a long, thick cylinder.

7 Tie the rolled steaks with one long cord, looping it at 1-inch intervals (*see recipe, opposite page*).

8 Cook the *matambre* in a heavy casserole or roasting pan just large enough to hold it snugly.

Braised Short Ribs

To serve 6 to 8

5 to 6 pounds lean short ribs of beef,
   cut into 3- to 4-inch pieces
Salt
Freshly ground black pepper
½ cup flour
2 tablespoons butter

1 cup coarsely chopped onion
1 cup coarsely chopped, scraped
   carrot
½ teaspoon finely chopped garlic
⅛ teaspoon thyme
1 cup beef stock, fresh or canned
2 small bay leaves

Preheat the oven to 500°. Season the short ribs generously with salt and a few grindings of black pepper. Dip them in flour, vigorously shaking off any excess, then arrange them side by side on a rack in a shallow roasting pan. Brown them in the middle of the oven for 20 to 25 minutes, checking periodically to make sure they do not burn.

Meanwhile, melt the 2 tablespoons of butter over moderate heat in a heavy, 6-quart, flameproof casserole. When the foam subsides, add the onion, carrot, garlic and thyme, and, stirring frequently, cook for 6 to 8 minutes until the vegetables are lightly colored. Place the browned ribs, preferably in one layer, on top of the vegetables, add the stock to the roasting pan and stir into it any brown bits clinging to the pan. Then pour it over the ribs in the casserole. Bring to a boil on top of the stove, add the bay leaves and cover the casserole tightly. Reduce the oven heat to 325°. Braise the short ribs in the middle of the oven for about an hour until the meat shows no resistance when pierced with a fork.

To serve, arrange the short ribs on a heated platter. Strain the braising juices through a fine sieve into a saucepan, pressing down on the vegetables to extract all their juices before discarding them. Skim the fat from the surface, taste the sauce for seasoning and pour over the meat.

Deviled Short Ribs

To serve 3 to 4

6 tablespoons butter, softened
1 tablespoon Worcestershire sauce
1 teaspoon dry English mustard
1 teaspoon curry powder (preferably
   imported Madras curry powder)

Freshly ground black pepper
¼ teaspoon cayenne pepper
1 teaspoon salt
2½ to 3 pounds lean short ribs of
   beef, each 4 to 5 inches long
½ cup flour

Preheat the oven to 450°. With a pastry brush and 2 tablespoons of the softened butter, coat the bottom and sides of a shallow roasting pan large enough to hold the short ribs in one layer. In a small bowl, cream the remaining 4 tablespoons of softened butter by beating and mashing it against the sides of the bowl with a large spoon until it is light and fluffy. Then beat in the Worcestershire sauce, mustard, curry powder, 1 teaspoon of black pepper, cayenne pepper and ½ teaspoon of the salt. Set aside.

With a small, sharp knife, make ¼-inch-deep crisscrossing cuts about 1 inch apart on the meaty surface of the ribs. Then coat them with the flour and shake them vigorously to remove any excess. Sprinkle the ribs with the remaining ½ teaspoon of salt and a few grindings of pepper and arrange them fat side up in a single layer in the roasting pan. Roast in the middle of the oven for 10 minutes. Using a pastry brush coat the ribs evenly with the seasoned butter, reduce the heat to 400°, and roast for 1 hour and 15 minutes, or until the meat is tender and shows no resistance when pierced with the tip of a fork. Arrange the ribs on a large platter and serve at once.

Short Ribs with Lemon Sauce
Westfälischer Pfefferpotthast

To serve 4

2 pounds beef short ribs, cut into
   2-inch pieces
Salt
Freshly ground black pepper
2 tablespoons lard
6 medium-sized onions (about 2
   pounds), sliced ⅛ inch thick
1 small bay leaf

¼ teaspoon ground cloves
4 cups cold water
3 tablespoons fresh rye bread
   crumbs, made in a blender from
   1 slice fresh dark rye bread
2 teaspoons capers, drained and
   rinsed in cold water
2 tablespoons fresh lemon juice
½ teaspoon finely grated fresh
   lemon peel

Sprinkle the short ribs with salt and pepper. In a 3- to 4-quart flameproof casserole or Dutch oven, heat the lard over high heat, until it begins to splutter. Add the short ribs and brown them on all sides, regulating the heat so that the ribs brown quickly and evenly without burning. Remove the meat to a platter. Add the onions to the fat remaining in the casserole, and cook, stirring occasionally, for 5 minutes, or until they are soft and transparent but not brown. Add the bay leaf and cloves and pour in the water. Bring to a boil over high heat, scraping in any brown bits clinging to the bottom and sides of the pan.

Return the ribs to the casserole, cover and reduce the heat to its lowest point. Simmer for 1½ hours, or until the meat shows no resistance when pierced with the tip of a small, sharp knife. Then transfer the short ribs to a deep heated platter and cover with foil to keep them warm. Discard the bay leaf, and skim off the fat from the liquid remaining in the casserole. Stir in the bread crumbs, capers, lemon juice and lemon peel, and bring to a boil over high heat. Reduce the heat; simmer uncovered, for a minute or two. Taste for seasoning. The sauce should be quite peppery; add more pepper to taste if necessary. Then pour the sauce over the meat and serve at once.

Beef Stew with Red Wine
Boeuf Bourguignon

To serve 6 to 8

THE ONIONS
½ pound lean salt pork, cut into strips about 1½ inches long and ¼ inch in diameter

1 quart water
1 tablespoon butter
18 to 24 peeled white onions, about 1 inch in diameter

To ensure that no one element in your *boeuf bourguignon* is overdone, cook the onions, mushrooms and beef separately before finally combining them. Although the different steps may be taken simultaneously, it is easier to deal with them one at a time.

THE ONIONS: Preheat the oven to 350°. To remove excess saltiness, the salt pork should be blanched by simmering it in 1 quart of water for 5 minutes; drain on paper towels and pat dry. In a heavy 8- to 10-inch skillet, melt 1 tablespoon of butter over moderate heat, and in it brown the pork, stirring the pieces frequently, until they are crisp and golden. Remove them with a slotted spoon and set aside to drain on paper towels. In the rendered fat left in the skillet, brown the onions lightly over moderately high heat, shaking the pan occasionally to roll them around and color them as evenly as possible. Transfer the onions to a shallow baking dish large enough to hold them in one layer, and sprinkle them with 3 tablespoons of pork fat. (Set the skillet aside, leaving the rest of the fat in it.) Bake the onions uncovered, turning them once or twice, for 30 minutes or until they are barely tender when pierced with the tip of a sharp knife. Remove from the oven and set aside.

THE MUSHROOMS
3 tablespoons butter

¾ pound fresh mushrooms, whole if small, quartered or sliced if large

THE MUSHROOMS: While the onions are baking or after they are done, melt 3 tablespoons of butter over moderate heat in an 8- to 10-inch enameled or stainless-steel skillet. When the foam subsides, cook the mushrooms, tossing and turning them frequently, for 2 or 3 minutes, or until they are slightly soft. Add the mushrooms to the onions and set aside.

3 pounds lean boneless beef chuck or rump, cut in 2-inch chunks

Bouquet garni made of 4 parsley sprigs and 1 bay leaf, tied together

2 tablespoons finely chopped shallots or scallions

¼ cup very finely chopped carrots

3 tablespoons flour

1 cup hot beef stock, fresh or canned

2 cups red Burgundy or other dry red wine

1 tablespoon tomato paste

1 teaspoon finely chopped garlic

1 teaspoon dried thyme

1 teaspoon salt

Freshly ground black pepper

2 tablespoons finely chopped fresh parsley

THE BEEF: Make sure the oven is preheated to 350°. Pour almost all of the rendered pork fat from the skillet in which the onions browned into a small bowl, leaving just enough to make a thin film about ¹⁄₁₆ inch deep on the bottom of the pan. Over moderately high heat, bring the fat almost to the smoking point. Dry the beef with paper towels, then brown it in the fat, 4 or 5 chunks at a time to avoid crowding the skillet. Add more pork fat as needed. When the chunks are brown on all sides, remove them with kitchen tongs to a heavy, flameproof 4- to 6-quart casserole. Bury the *bouquet garni* in the meat.

After all the beef is browned, add the chopped shallots and carrots to the fat remaining in the pan and cook them over low heat, stirring frequently, until they are lightly colored. Stir in the flour. (If the mixture looks dry, add a little more pork fat.) Return the skillet to low heat and cook, stirring constantly, until the flour begins to brown lightly, but be careful it doesn't burn. Remove from the heat, let cool a moment, then pour in the hot beef stock, blending vigorously with a wire whisk. Blend in the wine and the tomato paste and bring to a boil, whisking constantly as the sauce thickens. Mix in the garlic, thyme, sautéed pork strips, salt and a few grindings of black pepper, and pour the sauce over the beef, stirring gently to moisten it thoroughly. The sauce should almost, but not quite, cover the meat; add more wine or beef stock if needed. Bring to a boil on top of the stove, cover tightly, and place the casserole in the lower third of the oven. Let the beef cook, regulating the oven heat so the meat simmers slowly, for 2 to 3 hours, or until the meat is tender when pierced with the tip of a sharp knife. Then gently stir the browned onions and mushrooms, together with any juices that may have accumulated under them, into the casserole. With a large spoon, gently mix the beef and vegetables with the sauce in the casserole. Continue baking for another 15 minutes. To serve, remove the *bouquet garni* and skim off any fat from the surface. Taste the sauce and season it with salt and pepper if needed. Sprinkle the beef with parsley and serve it directly from the casserole, or for more formal occasions, transfer it to a deep, heated platter.

Beef and Vegetable Stew
Cocido Bogotano

To serve 6 to 8

2 tablespoons olive oil
½ cup coarsely chopped onions
2 medium tomatoes, peeled, seeded
    and coarsely chopped, or substitute
    ⅔ cup chopped, drained, canned
    Italian plum tomatoes
2 pounds lean boneless stewing beef,
    preferably chuck, cut into 1½-
    inch cubes
1 large bay leaf
1 teaspoon ground cumin seeds
½ teaspoon dried oregano
¼ teaspoon turmeric
½ teaspoon finely chopped garlic
2 teaspoons salt

6 whole black peppercorns
3 cups cold water
2 teaspoons cider vinegar
3 medium potatoes (1 pound), peeled
    and cut lengthwise into ¼-inch
    slices and then into ½-inch-wide
    strips
4 medium carrots, cut lengthwise into
    ¼-inch slices and then into
    ½-inch-long strips
4 trimmed celery stalks, washed and
    cut into 2-inch lengths
1 pound fresh green peas, shelled, or
    1 cup thoroughly defrosted frozen
    peas
4 ears corn, shucked and cut into
    2-inch lengths

In a heavy 3- to 4-quart flameproof casserole, heat the oil over moderate heat, tipping the casserole to coat the bottom evenly. Add the onions and cook, stirring constantly, for 4 or 5 minutes, or until they are soft and transparent but not brown. Stir in the tomatoes, cook for 3 minutes, then add the meat, bay leaf, cumin, oregano, turmeric, garlic, salt and peppercorns, and pour in the water and vinegar. Reduce the heat to its lowest point, cover the casserole, and simmer for 30 minutes. Add the potatoes, carrots and celery, turning them about in the liquid to moisten them well. Cover the casserole and cook for 20 minutes longer. Drop in the peas and corn, cover again, and cook for an additional 10 minutes, or until the meat is tender when pierced with the tip of a knife and the vegetables are done. Taste for seasoning, and serve directly from the casserole.

Hunter's Stew
Lovački Djuveč

To serve 4 to 6

8 slices bacon, chopped
1½ cups finely chopped onions
1 teaspoon finely chopped garlic
1 cup scraped and sliced carrots
2 cups water
¼ cup red wine vinegar
3 pounds boneless beef chuck, cut
 into 2-inch cubes

½ teaspoon salt
Freshly ground black pepper
1 cup converted rice
2 medium-sized green peppers, with
 seeds and ribs removed and cut
 into slices ¼ inch wide and 2
 inches long (about 1½ cups)
1¼ cups beef stock
Salt

In a 10- or 12-inch skillet, cook the bacon over medium heat for 6 to 8 minutes, or until it has rendered most of its fat and is slightly crisp. Remove the bacon with a slotted spoon, reserve it and pour off all but a thin film of the fat from the skillet.

Add the onions and, stirring occasionally, cook them for 3 or 4 minutes, or until they are slightly translucent, then add the garlic and carrots and cook for 5 or 6 minutes longer.

Return the reserved bacon to the skillet, stir in the water and vinegar, and add the beef cubes, the salt, and a few grindings of black pepper. Reduce the heat to its lowest point and simmer, covered, for about 1 hour, or until the beef shows only a slight resistance when it is pierced with the tip of a small sharp knife.

Gradually stir in the rice and add the sliced peppers and 1 cup of the beef stock. Bring the liquid to a boil, then reduce the heat to low, cover and simmer for 20 minutes, or until the rice is tender but not mushy. Taste for seasoning. If at any point the rice becomes too dry or shows signs of sticking to the bottom of the pan, add the remaining beef stock.

Kettle Goulash
Bogrács Gulyás

To serve 4 to 6

2 tablespoons lard
1 cup finely chopped onions
½ teaspoon finely chopped garlic
3 tablespoons sweet Hungarian
    paprika
2 pounds shin beef, cut into 1½-
    inch cubes
½ teaspoon caraway seeds
4 cups chicken or beef stock

fresh or canned, or 4 cups water
½ teaspoon salt
Freshly ground black pepper
2 medium-size boiling potatoes
1 pound tomatoes, peeled, seeded and
    finely chopped (about 1½ cups)
2 medium-size green peppers, with
    seeds and ribs removed, finely
    chopped
½ teaspoon marjoram

Heat the lard in a 4- or 5-quart heavy saucepan until a light haze forms over it, then reduce the heat to medium and add the onions and garlic. Cook them 8 to 10 minutes, or until the onions are lightly colored. Off the heat, stir in the paprika. Stir until the onions are well coated.

Add the beef cubes, caraway seeds and stock or water to the pan and season with the salt and pepper. Bring the liquid to a boil and partially cover the pan. Simmer for 1 hour, or until the beef is almost tender.

Parboil the potatoes in boiling water for 8 to 10 minutes, or until they can be easily penetrated with the point of a sharp knife for ¼ inch or so. Peel them, cut them into 1½-inch cubes and add them, the tomatoes, the peppers and marjoram to the pan. Partially cover again and cook over medium heat for 25 to 35 minutes, or until the potatoes are done and the beef is tender. Skim off the surface fat and taste for seasoning.

Beef and Onions Braised in Beer
Carbonades de Boeuf à la Flamande

To serve 6 to 8

¼ pound salt pork, diced
2 cups water
5 tablespoons butter
7 cups thinly sliced onions (about 2
    pounds)
3 pounds lean boneless beef chuck
    or rump, cut in 2-inch chunks
Bouquet garni made of 4 parsley
    sprigs and 1 bay leaf, tied together

3 tablespoons flour
2 cups beer
1½ cups beef stock, fresh or canned
1½ teaspoons sugar
1 tablespoon vinegar
1 teaspoon finely chopped garlic
1 teaspoon dried thyme, crumbled
Salt
Freshly ground black pepper
2 tablespoons finely chopped fresh
    parsley

To remove excess saltiness, blanch the pork dice by simmering them in 2 cups of water for 5 minutes, drain on paper towels and pat dry. In a heavy 10- to 12-inch skillet, melt 1 tablespoon of the butter over moderate heat, and in it brown the pork dice, stirring them or shaking the pan frequently, until they are crisp and golden. Remove them with a slotted spoon and set them aside to drain on paper towels. Pour off almost all the rendered fat from the skillet into a small bowl, leaving just enough in the skillet to make a thin film about 1/16 inch deep on the bottom. Set the bowl of fat and the skillet aside.

In another heavy 10- to 12-inch skillet, melt 4 tablespoons of butter over moderate heat. When the foam subsides, add the sliced onions and cook them over low heat, turning them frequently with a wide metal spatula, for 20 to 30 minutes, or until they become limp and lightly colored.

While the onions are cooking, heat the fat in the first skillet over moderate heat until it almost smokes. Dry the beef with paper towels, then brown it in the hot oil 4 or 5 chunks at a time to avoid crowding the skillet, adding more pork fat as needed. When the chunks are a rich brown on all sides, remove them with kitchen tongs to a Dutch oven or a heavy, flameproof casserole about 9 to 10 inches in diameter and at least 3 inches deep. Bury the *bouquet garni* in the meat.

Preheat the oven to 350°. After all the meat is browned, remove the skillet from the heat and stir the flour into the fat remaining in it. If the mixture seems dry, add a little more pork fat (or vegetable oil). Return to very low heat and cook, stirring constantly, until the *roux* is amber color: be careful it doesn't burn. Remove from heat, pour in the beer and beef stock, and beat vigorously with a wire whisk until the *roux* and liquid are blended. Bring to a boil over moderate heat, whisking constantly as the sauce thickens. Boil for 1 minute, then mix in the sugar, vinegar, garlic and thyme, and simmer over low heat for 2 or 3 minutes. Taste the sauce and season it with salt and pepper if needed.

When the onions are done, add them to the casserole, and pour the sauce over the onions and meat, stirring the mixture gently. The sauce should nearly cover the meat; add more beer if needed. Bring the casserole to a boil on top of the stove, cover it tightly and place it in the lower third of the oven. Cook, regulating the oven heat so that the meat simmers slowly for 1½ to 2 hours, or until the meat is tender when pierced with the tip of a sharp knife. Before serving, let the *carbonades* cool for a few minutes. Then skim off the surface fat, discard the *bouquet garni* and taste the sauce for seasoning. Sprinkle the *carbonades* with the crisp pork bits and garnish with chopped parsley.

Braised Beef with White Wine
Manzo alla Sarda

To serve 6 to 8

MARINADE
3 cups dry white wine
¼ cup olive oil
¼ cup finely chopped parsley,
   preferably the flat-leaf Italian type
1 bay leaf, crumbled
⅛ teaspoon ground allspice
⅛ teaspoon ground nutmeg
1 tablespoon salt

A 4-pound boneless beef chuck or
   bottom round roast at least 4 inches in diameter, trimmed, rolled and
tied securely in 3 or 4 places
2 tablespoons butter
2 tablespoons olive oil
1 cup dry white wine
2 cups beef stock, fresh or canned
2 tablespoons finely chopped fresh
   parsley
1 flat anchovy fillet, drained, rinsed
   and finely chopped
¼ teaspoon lemon juice
Salt
Freshly ground black pepper

In a large glass, porcelain or stainless-steel bowl, combine the 3 cups of white wine, ¼ cup of olive oil, ¼ cup of finely chopped parsley, bay leaf, ground allspice and nutmeg, and salt. Place the rolled and securely tied beef in the mixing bowl and turn it over in the marinade until it has become thoroughly moistened on all sides. Marinate the beef for at least 6 hours at room temperature or for about 12 hours in the refrigerator, turning the beef occasionally.

Preheat the oven to 350°. Remove the beef from the marinade and pat it completely dry with paper towels, but do not discard the marinade; set it aside to be used again later. Over moderately high heat, melt the butter with the oil in a flameproof casserole that is just large enough to hold the beef comfortably. When the foam subsides, add the beef and brown it on all sides, turning it with 2 wooden spoons. Transfer the browned meat to a plate and discard all but a thin film of the browned fat from the casserole. Pour in the marinade and boil it briskly over high heat until it has reduced to about 1 cup, meanwhile using a wooden spoon or rubber spatula to scrape in any browned bits clinging to the bottom and sides of the pan. Return the beef to the casserole and add 1 cup of white wine and the 2 cups of beef stock. The combined liquid should come about ⅓ of the way up the side of the meat; add more beef stock if necessary. Bring the casserole to a boil over high heat, cover, and place in the middle of the oven. Braise the beef for 2 to 2½ hours, turning it over in the casserole 2 or 3 times. When it is tender enough to be easily pierced with the tip of a sharp knife, transfer the roast to a cutting board.

Pour the braising liquid through a fine sieve into a 1½- to 2-quart saucepan. Let it settle for a minute or so, then with a large spoon skim off as much surface fat as possible. Boil the braising liquid briskly over high heat, stirring occasionally, until it has reduced to about 2 cups. Stir in 2 table-spoons of finely chopped parsley, the chopped anchovy and lemon juice. Taste the sauce and season it with salt and pepper if needed. Cut the strings off the beef and carve the roast into thin, even slices.

Arrange the slices of beef, slightly overlapping, in a row on a heated platter. Moisten them with a few tablespoons of the hot sauce and pass the rest separately, in a sauceboat.

Boiled Beef with Chive Sauce
Rindfleisch mit Schnittlauchsosse

To serve 4 to 6

3 pounds lean boneless beef chuck or lean brisket of beef	5 whole black peppercorns
	2 teaspoons salt
2 medium-sized carrots, scraped	4 tablespoons butter
2 celery stalks, with their leaves	3 tablespoons flour
1 leek, white part only	½ cup light cream
1 large onion, peeled	¼ cup finely chopped fresh chives, or substitute ¼ cup green scallion tops, finely chopped
4 parsley sprigs	¼ teaspoon ground nutmeg

Place the beef in a heavy 4- to 5-quart flameproof casserole or Dutch oven, and pour in enough water to cover the beef by about 2 inches. Bring to a boil over high heat, meanwhile skimming off any scum that rises to the surface. Add the carrots, celery stalks, leek, onion, parsley sprigs, peppercorns and salt, then reduce the heat to its lowest point, partially cover the casserole, and simmer for 2½ to 3 hours, or until the meat shows no resistance when pierced with a fork. Transfer the meat to a heated plate and cover it with aluminum foil to keep it warm. Strain the cooking stock into a bowl and discard the vegetables. Skim as much of the surface fat from the stock as you can.

In a heavy 8- to 10-inch skillet, melt the butter over moderate heat, and when the foam subsides, add the flour. Stirring constantly, cook the mixture for 1 or 2 minutes. Do not let the flour brown. Slowly pour in 2 cups of the strained stock and then the cream. Bring the sauce to a boil, beating constantly with a whisk until it is thick and smooth. Reduce the heat to low and simmer for 10 minutes. Add the chives and nutmeg and taste for seasoning. If the sauce is too thick for your taste, thin with a few tablespoons of the reserved stock.

To serve, carve the meat into thin slices and arrange them slightly overlapping on a large, heated platter. Spoon a few tablespoons of the sauce over the meat and pass the rest separately in a sauceboat.

New England Boiled Dinner

To serve 6

4 pounds corned beef
2 pounds green cabbage, cored and
    quartered
12 to 16 new potatoes, about 1½

inches in diameter, peeled
6 small carrots, scraped
12 small white onions, about 1 inch
    in diameter, peeled and trimmed
6 medium-sized beets
2 tablespoons finely chopped parsley

Before cooking the corned beef, ask your butcher whether it should be soaked in water to remove some of the salt. If it has been mildly cured, soaking will not be necessary.

Place the corned beef in a 5- or 6-quart pot and cover it with enough cold water to rise at least 2 inches above the top of the meat. Bring to a boil, skimming off any scum that rises to the surface. Half cover the pot, turn the heat to its lowest point (the liquid should barely simmer) and cook the beef from 4 to 6 hours, or until tender. If necessary, add more hot water to the pot from time to time to keep the meat constantly covered.

Cook the cabbage separately in boiling salted water for about 15 minutes. The potatoes, carrots and onions may be cooked together in a pot of salted boiling water of their own. The beets, however, require different treatment. Scrub them thoroughly, then cut off their tops, leaving 1 inch of stem. Cover them with boiling water and bring to a boil. Simmer the beets from ½ to 1½ hours, or until they are tender. Let them cool a bit, then slip off their skins.

To serve the dinner in the traditional way, slice the corned beef and arrange it along the center of a large heated platter. Surround the meat with the vegetables and sprinkle the vegetables with chopped parsley. Horseradish, mustard and a variety of pickles make excellent accompaniments to this hearty meal.

Beef Pie with Peaches
Pastel de Cambraye

To serve 4 to 6

THE PASTRY
4 cups flour
1 cup sugar
1½ cups (3 quarter-pound sticks)

butter, cut into small pieces
4 egg yolks
1 cup muscatel
1 egg yolk beaten with 1 teaspoon
    water

THE PASTRY: In a large mixing bowl, combine the flour, sugar and butter, and with your fingers or a spoon mix them together thoroughly until the dough resembles coarse meal. Add the egg yolks 1 at a time and, when they have all been absorbed, mix in the muscatel, ¼ cup at a time. Shape the dough into a compact ball, wrap it in wax paper or foil, and refrigerate it for 30 minutes to an hour, or until thoroughly chilled.

THE FILLING
½ cup seedless raisins
1 cup hot water
2 tablespoons olive oil
2 pounds lean top sirloin of beef, cut into ¼-inch cubes
1 cup coarsely chopped onions
½ cup dry white wine
⅓ cup sugar
½ teaspoon ground cinnamon
½ teaspoon ground cloves
½ teaspoon dried oregano
½ small bay leaf
1 teaspoon salt
¼ teaspoon freshly ground black pepper
1 tablespoon fresh bread crumbs
6 fresh peaches, peeled, halved and pitted, or 12 canned peach halves, thoroughly drained

THE FILLING: Soak the raisins in 1 cup of hot water for 30 minutes.

In a heavy 10- to 12-inch skillet, heat the olive oil over high heat. Add the beef and brown it well on all sides, stirring constantly and regulating the heat to brown it as quickly as possible without burning. Add the onions, lower the heat to moderate, and cook, stirring constantly, until they are soft. Then stir in the white wine, sugar, cinnamon, cloves, oregano, bay leaf, salt and pepper. Bring to a boil and cover the skillet. Reduce the heat to its lowest point and simmer for 25 minutes. Drain the raisins and stir them into the meat mixture. Remove the bay leaf. Transfer the entire contents of the pan to a bowl and cool to room temperature.

Preheat the oven to 375°. Remove the dough from the refrigerator and cut it in half. On a lightly floured board, roll the halves one at a time into 2 rough rectangles about 12 inches wide, 16 inches long and ⅛ inch thick. Drape one rectangle of dough loosely over a lightly buttered shallow 8-by-12-inch baking dish, and gently press the dough against the bottom and sides of the dish. Pour in the cooled meat filling, spreading it out evenly with a spatula or the back of a spoon. Sprinkle the meat with bread crumbs and then place the peach halves side by side on top of the meat. Cover with the second rectangle of dough, letting it sink to about ½ inch below the top rim of the dish. With the tines of a table fork, press the edges of the dough together all around the rim of the dish, then neatly cut off all the excess. Brush the top of the crust with the beaten egg yolk and water, and bake in the middle of the oven for 30 minutes, until the crust is golden brown. Then remove the pie from the oven and increase the heat to 425°.

THE MERINGUE
4 egg whites
¼ cup sugar

THE MERINGUE: In a large bowl, beat the egg whites with a whisk or a rotary or electric beater until they are stiff enough to form soft peaks on the beater when it is lifted from the bowl. Then beat in ¼ cup of sugar and continue beating until the meringue is firm and glossy. With a spatula, spread the meringue thickly over the pie top and swirl it decoratively if you like. Return the pie to the oven and bake for about 5 minutes, or until the meringue is a light golden brown. Serve at once.

Steak and Kidney Pudding

To serve 4 to 6

2 pounds lean boneless beef chuck
   or top round, cut into 1-inch cubes
1 pound veal or lamb kidneys, peeled
   and trimmed of fat, and cut into
   1-inch cubes
⅔ cup flour
¼ teaspoon ground nutmeg
1½ teaspoons salt

¼ teaspoon freshly ground black
   pepper
¼ pound large fresh mushrooms,
   trimmed and cut into quarters,
   including the stems
½ cup coarsely chopped onions
¼ cup finely chopped parsley
Suet pastry
1½ cups boiling water

Place the cubes of beef and kidney in a large mixing bowl. Combine ⅓ cup of the flour with the nutmeg, salt and pepper, and sift it over the meat. Then toss together with a large spoon to coat the pieces evenly. Stir in the mushrooms, onions and parsley. Set aside.

On a lightly floured surface, roll out about two thirds of the suet pastry into a rough circle 14 inches in diameter and ¼ inch thick. Drape the pastry over the rolling pin and unfold it slackly over a 6-cup English pudding basin or a plain 6-cup mold about 7 inches in diameter and 4 inches deep. Gently press the pastry into the basin, being careful not to stretch it. Roll out the remaining pastry into an 8-inch circle, and set it aside.

Ladle the beef-and-kidney mixture into the mold, filling it to within ½ inch of the top. Mound the meat in the center, and pour in the water.

With a sharp knife, trim the excess pastry from the rim of the mold and lightly moisten the rim with a pastry brush dipped in cold water. Carefully place the 8-inch circle of pastry over the mold and trim the edges again. Then crimp the pastry all around the rim with your fingers or the tines of a fork to seal it tightly. Lay a lightly buttered 10-inch circle of parchment paper or foil over the top of the pudding, turning the edges down all around its circumference to hold it in place.

Now dampen a cloth kitchen towel with cold water and wring it dry. Spread the towel flat, sprinkle it evenly with the remaining ⅓ cup of flour, and shake it vigorously to dislodge the excess flour. Spread the towel, floured side down, over the top of the pudding. Bring the ends of the towel down around the sides of the basin or mold and tie them in place about 1½ to 2 inches down the side (just below the rim if you are using a pudding basin) with

Steak and kidney pudding can be
steamed in a pudding basin or
in any plain mold. First press the
pastry lining into the mold. Fill
with beefsteak and kidney and trim
the rim (1). Top the pudding with a
circle of pastry (2), and cover that
with buttered paper. To ensure a
tight seal, spread a kitchen towel
across the mold (3), bring it down
around the sides, and tie it in place
with string. Lift two diagonally
opposite corners of the towel and tie
them over the mold (4). Then tie the
two other corners above the first
knot (5).

The finished pudding shown above has been turned out and the crust cut away to display its contents.

a long length of kitchen cord. Bring up two diagonally opposite corners of the towel and tie them together on top of the pudding. Then bring the remaining corners together and tie them similarly.

Place the pudding in a large pot and pour in enough boiling water to come three fourths of the way up the side of the mold. Bring to a boil, cover the pot tightly, reduce the heat to its lowest point, and steam for 5 hours. From time to time replenish the water in the pot with additional boiling water.

To serve, lift the pudding out of the water (holding it by the looped cloth if you are using a basin with a rim) and remove the towel and paper or foil. Wipe the mold completely dry and wrap it in a clean linen napkin. Serve at the table directly from the basin or mold.

SUET PASTRY

½ pound finely chopped beef suet, thoroughly chilled
4 cups all-purpose flour

1 teaspoon salt
Freshly ground black pepper
6 to 8 tablespoons ice water

In a large chilled mixing bowl, combine the suet, flour, salt and a few grindings of pepper. With your fingertips rub the flour and fat together until they look like flakes of coarse meal. Pour 6 tablespoons of ice water over the mixture all at once, knead together vigorously and gather the dough into a ball. If the dough crumbles, add up to 2 more tablespoons of ice water, 1 teaspoon at a time, until the particles adhere.

Gather the dough into a ball and place it on a lightly floured surface. Knead, pressing the dough flat, pushing it forward and folding it back on itself for 6 to 8 minutes, or until it is smooth and satiny. Dust the suet pastry with a little flour and wrap it in wax paper. Refrigerate at least 1 hour before using.

Chili con Carne

To serve 6 to 8

3 pounds top round, cut into ½-inch cubes	1 teaspoon red-pepper flakes
6 tablespoons vegetable oil	1 six-ounce can tomato paste
2 cups coarsely chopped onion	4 cups beef stock, fresh or canned
2 tablespoons finely chopped garlic	1 teaspoon salt
4 tablespoons chili powder	Freshly ground black pepper
1 teaspoon oregano	1½ cups freshly cooked red kidney beans or drained canned kidney beans (optional)
1 teaspoon ground cumin	

Pat the meat dry with paper towels. Then, in a 12-inch heavy skillet, heat 4 tablespoons of the oil until a light haze forms above it. Add the meat and cook over high heat for 2 to 3 minutes, stirring, until the meat is lightly browned. With a slotted spoon transfer it to a 4-quart heavy flameproof casserole. Add the remaining 2 tablespoons of oil to the skillet and in it cook the onion and garlic for 4 to 5 minutes, stirring frequently.

Remove the skillet from the heat, add the 4 tablespoons chili powder, or to taste, oregano, cumin and pepper flakes, and stir until the onions are well coated with the mixture. Then add the tomato paste, pour in the beef stock and with a large spoon mix the ingredients together thoroughly before adding them to the meat in the casserole. Add the salt and a few grindings of black pepper. Bring to a boil, stirring once or twice, then half cover the pot, turn the heat to low and simmer for 1 to 1½ hours, or until the meat is tender.

Continued on the next page

If you plan to use the beans, add them to the casserole 15 minutes or so before the meat is done. Before serving the chili, skim off as much of the surface fat as you can. If the chili is refrigerated overnight, the fat will rise to the surface and can be easily skimmed off before reheating.

NOTE: Chili con carne is often made with coarsely ground chuck in place of the cubed round steak. Follow the above recipe, but be sure to break up the ground chuck with a fork as you brown it.

Meat Loaf in Sour-Cream Pastry
Lihamurekepiiras

To serve 6 to 8

PASTRY
2¼ cups flour
1 teaspoon salt

12 tablespoons chilled unsalted butter,
    cut into ¼-inch bits
1 egg
½ cup sour cream
1 tablespoon soft butter

SOUR CREAM PASTRY: Sift the flour and salt together into a large chilled bowl. Drop the ¼-inch bits of butter into the bowl. Working quickly, use your fingertips to rub the flour and butter together until they have the appearance of flakes of coarse meal. In a separate bowl, mix together the egg and sour cream and stir into this the flour-butter mixture, working with your fingers until you can gather the dough into a soft, pliable ball. Wrap in wax paper and refrigerate 1 hour. Cut the chilled dough in half and roll out each half to rectangles of 6 by 14 inches each, setting aside any scraps.

Butter the bottom of a jelly-roll pan with 1 tablespoon of soft butter. Lift 1 sheet of the pastry over the rolling pin and unroll it into the pan.

MEAT FILLING

4 tablespoons butter
¾ cup finely chopped mushrooms
    (about ¼ pound fresh mushrooms)
3 pounds finely ground meat (beef,
    pork, ham, lamb or veal or a
    combination of any of these), or
    4 cups cooked ground or finely
    chopped meat

⅓ cup finely chopped onions
¼ cup finely chopped parsley
1 cup freshly grated cheddar or
    Switzerland cheese
½ cup milk
1 egg combined with 2 tablespoons
    milk

MEAT FILLING: Melt the 4 tablespoons of butter in a 10- to 12-inch skillet. When the foam subsides, add the chopped mushrooms and cook them over moderate heat, stirring frequently, for 6 to 8 minutes, or until they are lightly colored. If you are using ground raw meat, add it to the skillet and cook, stirring occasionally, for another 8 to 10 minutes, or until the meat loses its red color and any accumulated liquid in the pan cooks completely away. Scrape the meat mixture from the skillet (or the mushrooms and already cooked meat) into a large mixing bowl and stir in the chopped onions, parsley, cheese and milk. Now gather this meat mixture into a ball and place it in the center of the dough in the pan. With your hands, pat the meat into a narrow loaf extending across the center of the dough from one end to the other. Lift the second sheet of pastry over the pin and gently drape it on top of the meat loaf; press the edges of the 2 sheets together. Dip a pastry brush into the combined egg and milk mixture and moisten the edges of the dough. Press down on the edges all around the loaf with the back of a fork (the tines will seal the edges securely). Prick the top of the loaf in several places with a fork to allow steam to escape.

Preheat the oven to 375°. Gather together into a ball all of the excess scraps of dough and roll it out to a thin rectangle. With a pastry wheel or small, sharp knife, cut this dough into long, narrow strips. Brush the loaf with more of the egg and milk mixture and crisscross the pastry strips over the top of the loaf in an attractive pattern. Now brush the strips with the milk and egg mixture and set the jelly-roll pan in the center of the oven. Bake for 45 minutes, or until the loaf has turned a golden brown. Serve the meat loaf cut in thick slices.

Baked Ground Beef with Okra

Bamia

To serve 4

1½ pounds fresh okra
4 tablespoons butter plus 1 tablespoon softened butter
½ cup finely chopped onions
1 pound ground lean beef, preferably chuck

1 teaspoon finely chopped garlic
6 tablespoons canned tomato purée
1½ to 2 cups beef stock, fresh or canned
1 teaspoon salt
Freshly ground black pepper
Lemon wedges

Wash the fresh okra under cold running water, and with a small, sharp knife, scrape the skin lightly to remove any surface fuzz. Cut ⅛ inch off the stem at the narrow end of each pod.

In a heavy 10- to 12-inch skillet, melt 2 tablespoons of butter over moderate heat. When the foam subsides, add the okra and, stirring frequently, cook for about 5 minutes until it stops "roping," or producing thin white threads. With a slotted spoon, transfer the okra to paper towels to drain.

Pour off the fat remaining in the skillet, add 2 more tablespoons of butter and melt it over moderate heat. Drop in the onions and cook for 8 to 10 minutes, or until they are soft and lightly browned. Add the meat, mashing it with the back of the spoon to break up any lumps, and cook until all traces of pink disappear. Stir in the garlic, tomato purée, 1 cup of the stock, the salt and a few grindings of pepper. Cook briskly uncovered until most of the liquid in the pan has evaporated and the mixture is thick enough to hold its shape almost solidly in the spoon. Remove from the heat.

Preheat the oven to 325°. With a pastry brush coat the bottom and sides of a circular baking dish 7 or 8 inches in diameter and about 3 inches deep with the tablespoon of softened butter. Spoon half the meat mixture into the casserole, smoothing and spreading it to the edges with a spatula. Arrange the okra over the meat, placing the pieces closely together side by side in a spokelike pattern with the cut ends facing out. Spread the remaining meat mixture evenly over the okra, masking it completely, and sprinkle over it ½ cup of the stock.

Bring to a boil over moderate heat, cover tightly with a lid or foil and bake in the middle of the oven for about 1 hour. (Check the casserole occasionally, and if the top seems dry pour in up to ½ cup more stock, a few tablespoons at a time.) Cool the *bamia* uncovered for 5 minutes, then unmold it in the following fashion: Run a long, sharp knife around the inside edges of the casserole, place a heated serving plate upside down over the top and, grasping the casserole and plate together firmly, invert them. The *bamia* should slide out easily. Serve garnished with lemon wedges.

Italian Meatballs with Tomato Sauce
Polpette alla Casalinga

To serve 4 to 6

2 slices French or Italian bread, torn
   into small pieces
½ cup milk
1 pound beef chuck, ground twice
¼ pound sweet Italian sausage,
   removed from casing
6 tablespoons freshly grated imported
   Parmesan cheese
2 tablespoons finely chopped fresh
parsley, preferably the flat-leaf
   Italian type
1 tablespoon olive oil
2 teaspoons finely chopped garlic
1 teaspoon grated lemon peel
¼ teaspoon ground allspice
1 teaspoon salt
Freshly ground black pepper
1 egg, lightly beaten
Olive or vegetable oil
1½ cups tomato sauce

Soak the pieces of bread in ½ cup milk for 5 minutes, then squeeze them dry and discard the milk. In a large mixing bowl, combine the soaked bread, the beaten egg, 1 pound of ground beef, ¼ pound of Italian sausage meat, grated Parmesan cheese, finely chopped parsley, 1 tablespoon of olive oil, garlic, lemon peel, allspice, salt and a few grindings of black pepper. Knead the mixture vigorously with both hands or beat with a wooden spoon until all of the ingredients are well blended and the mixture is smooth and fluffy.

Shape the mixture into small balls about 1½ inches in diameter. Lay the meatballs out in one layer on a flat tray or baking sheet, cover them with plastic wrap and chill for at least 1 hour.

Heat ¼ cup of olive or vegetable oil in a heavy 10- to 12-inch skillet until a light haze forms over it. Fry the meatballs 5 or 6 at a time over moderately high heat, shaking the pan constantly to roll the balls and help keep them round. In 8 to 10 minutes the meatballs should be brown outside and show no trace of pink inside. Add more olive or vegetable oil to the skillet as it is needed.

Serve the meatballs hot with the heated tomato sauce poured over them.

Swedish Meatballs with Cream Sauce
Små Köttbullar

To serve 6 to 8 (about 50 meatballs)

1 tablespoon butter
4 tablespoons finely chopped onion
1 large boiled potato, mashed (1 cup)
3 tablespoons fine dry bread crumbs
1 pound lean ground beef
⅓ cup heavy cream
1 teaspoon salt

1 egg
1 tablespoon finely chopped fresh
   parsley (optional)
2 tablespoons butter
2 tablespoons vegetable oil
1 tablespoon flour
¾ cup light or heavy cream

In a small frying pan, melt the tablespoon of butter over moderate heat. When the foam subsides, add the onions and cook for about 5 minutes, until they are soft and translucent but not brown.

In a large bowl, combine the onions, mashed potato, bread crumbs, meat, cream, salt, egg and optional parsley. Knead vigorously with both hands or beat with a wooden spoon until all of the ingredients are well blended and the mixture is smooth and fluffy. Shape into small balls about 1 inch in diameter. Arrange the meatballs in one layer on a baking sheet or a flat tray, cover them with plastic wrap and chill for at least 1 hour before cooking.

Over high heat, melt the 2 tablespoons of butter and 2 tablespoons of oil in a heavy 10- to 12-inch skillet. When the foam subsides, add the meatballs, 8 to 10 at a time. Reduce the heat to moderate and fry the balls on all sides, shaking the pan almost constantly to roll the balls around in the hot fat to help keep their shape. In 8 to 10 minutes the meatballs should be brown outside and show no trace of pink inside when one is broken open with a knife. Add more butter and oil to the skillet as needed, and transfer each finished batch to a casserole or baking dish and keep warm in a 200° oven.

To make a sauce with the pan juice, remove from the heat, pour off all of the fat from the pan, and stir in 1 tablespoon of flour. Quickly stir in ¾ cup of light or heavy cream and boil the sauce over moderate heat for 2 or 3 minutes, stirring constantly, until it is thick and smooth. Pour over the meatballs and serve.

Chilies Stuffed with Beef

Chiles en Nogada

To serve 6

6 fresh *poblano* chilies, or substitute

6 fresh green peppers, each about
4 inches in diameter

NOTE: Wear rubber gloves when handling *poblano* chilies.

Roast the chilies or peppers by impaling them, one at a time, on the tines of a long-handled fork, and turning them over a gas flame until the skin blisters and darkens. Or place the chilies on a baking sheet and broil them 3 inches from the heat for about 5 minutes, turning them so that they color on all sides. As the chilies are roasted, wrap them in a damp towel and let them rest for a few minutes. Rub them with the towel until the skins slip off. Cut out the stems and white membranes, discard the seeds.

THE FILLING

2 tablespoons lard
2 pounds ground beef, preferably
   chuck
1 cup coarsely chopped onions
½ teaspoon finely chopped garlic
5 medium tomatoes, peeled, seeded,
   and coarsely chopped, or substitute
   1⅔ cups chopped, drained, canned

Italian plum tomatoes
¾ cup seedless raisins
¼ cup distilled white vinegar
1½ teaspoons sugar
2 teaspoons cinnamon
½ teaspoon ground cloves
2 teaspoons salt
½ cup slivered blanched almonds

In a heavy 10- to 12-inch skillet, melt the lard over high heat. Add the beef and brown it lightly, stirring constantly with a fork to break up any lumps. Reduce the heat to moderate, add the onions and garlic, and cook 5 minutes. Stir in the tomatoes, raisins, vinegar, sugar, 2 teaspoons of cinnamon, cloves and 2 teaspoons of salt; then reduce the heat and simmer, uncovered, for 15 minutes. Add the slivered almonds.

THE TOPPING

2 cups heavy cream
½ cup shelled walnuts, ground in a
   blender or pulverized with a mortar
   and pestle
½ cup blanched almonds, ground
   in a blender or pulverized with a
   mortar and pestle

2 tablespoons finely chopped fresh
   parsley
½ teaspoon ground cinnamon
Pinch of salt
2 tablespoons fresh pomegranate
   seeds, or substitute 12 pimiento
   strips, 2 inches long and ⅛ inch wide
Fresh coriander leaves

Whip the cream with a whisk or a rotary or electric beater until it forms soft peaks. Fold in the ground nuts, parsley, ½ teaspoon of cinnamon and pinch of salt. (If you like, you may beat in a little sugar.)

To assemble, fill the roasted chilies with the warm beef mixture, packing it down and mounding it slightly on top. Spoon the whipped cream over the top of each pepper. Scatter a teaspoon of pomegranate seeds on the cream or arrange 2 strips of pimiento over it. Top with fresh coriander leaves and serve at once.

Peppers Stuffed with Beef
Dolmeh Felfel Sabz

To serve 8

8 green peppers	½ teaspoon ground cinnamon
2½ cups water	3 teaspoons salt
¼ cup dry yellow split peas	¾ teaspoon pepper
¼ cup raw rice	¼ cup chopped green onions
4 tablespoons butter	3 tablespoons minced parsley
¾ cup minced yellow onions	2 cups peeled chopped tomatoes
1 pound ground beef	Yoghurt

Wash the peppers, cut a half-inch slice from the stem ends and reserve. Scoop out the seeds and fibers from the peppers. Cover the peppers with water, bring to a boil and cook over low heat for 5 minutes, then drain.

Bring 2½ cups of water to a boil. Add the split peas and rice. Cook them for 25 minutes, stirring occasionally, then drain the peas and rice.

Melt 2 tablespoons of the butter in a skillet. Add the yellow onions and beef. Cook them over medium heat for 10 minutes, stirring frequently. Mix in the cinnamon, 1½ teaspoons of the salt, ½ teaspoon of the pepper, the green onions, parsley and cooked split peas and rice. Stuff the peppers with this mixture and replace the reserved tops.

Melt the remaining butter in a deep skillet or casserole. Arrange the stuffed peppers in it in an upright position. Mix the tomatoes with the remaining salt and pepper; pour over the peppers. Bring to a boil, cover and cook over low heat for 35 minutes, or until the peppers are tender. Top with yoghurt and serve immediately.

Veal

Marinated Veal Roast
Trouxa de Vitela

To serve 6 to 8

1 cup olive oil
⅓ cup white wine vinegar
1 large red onion, peeled and finely
 chopped
½ teaspoon finely chopped garlic
2 tablespoons finely chopped parsley
¼ teaspoon crushed dried hot red

pepper
2 teaspoons salt
½ teaspoon freshly ground black
 pepper
A 3½- to 4-pound boneless veal
 roast, preferably cut from the leg
 or rump and securely tied

For the marinade, combine ¾ cup of the oil, the vinegar, onion, garlic, parsley, red pepper, salt and black pepper in a small bowl and stir well. Place the
veal in a deep bowl just large enough to hold it comfortably, and pour in
the marinade, turning the veal about with a large spoon until it is moistened
on all sides. Marinate at room temperature for 4 hours or in the refrigerator
for at least 8 hours, turning it over two or three times as it marinates.

Preheat the oven to 450°. Remove the veal from the marinade, brush off
any bits of onion or spice clinging to it, and place it on a rack in a shallow
roasting pan. Set the marinade aside in a small saucepan. Roast the veal in
the middle of the oven for 20 minutes. Then baste it with a tablespoon or so
of olive oil and reduce the heat to 350°. Basting two or three more times
with the remaining olive oil, continue to roast for about 1½ hours longer,
or until the veal is tender.

Then bring the reserved marinade to a boil over high heat, reduce the
heat to low and simmer for 5 minutes. To serve, carve the veal into ¼-inch
slices, arrange them attractively on a large heated platter and pour the simmering marinade over them. Serve at once.

Casserole-roasted Veal
Veau Braisé en Casserole

To serve 6

2 tablespoons butter
2 tablespoons vegetable oil
A 3-pound boneless veal rump,
  shoulder or loin roast, wrapped in
  a thin layer of fat and tied
2 carrots, thinly sliced

2 onions, thinly sliced
½ teaspoon salt
Freshly ground black pepper
Bouquet garni made of 4 parsley sprigs
  and 1 bay leaf, tied together
½ teaspoon dried thyme, crumbled
½ cup hot chicken stock, fresh or
  canned (optional)

Preheat the oven to 325°. In a heavy casserole that is just large enough to hold the veal and has a cover, melt the butter with the oil over moderate heat. When the foam subsides, brown the veal lightly on all sides. Remove the veal to a plate and stir the vegetables into the fat remaining in the casserole. (If the fat has burned, discard it and use 3 tablespoons of fresh butter instead.) Cook the vegetables over low heat for 5 to 10 minutes, stirring occasionally, until they are tender but not brown.

Return the veal to the casserole, sprinkle it with salt and a few grindings of pepper, and add the *bouquet garni* and the thyme. Cover the casserole and bring it to a sizzle on top of the stove, then place it in the lower third of the oven. Using a bulb baster or large spoon, baste the veal every 20 or 30 minutes with the juices that will accumulate in the pan. In the unlikely event the casserole is dry, add the hot chicken stock. After 1½ hours test the veal for doneness by piercing it with the tip of a sharp knife—the juices should run clear yellow. Transfer the veal to a heated platter and cut off the strings. Strain the juices remaining in the casserole through a fine sieve into a small saucepan, pressing down hard on the vegetables and herbs with a spoon to extract their juices before discarding them. Skim the fat from the top and boil the liquid down to about half its original volume, or until it reaches the intensity of flavor desired. Taste for seasoning. Carve the veal into ¼-inch slices, moisten each slice with a little of the roasting juices and pass the rest in a warm sauceboat.

Black olives, parsley, capers and lemon slices adorn this dish of cold veal in creamy tuna fish sauce. It may be refrigerated overnight before serving.

Cold Veal with Tuna Sauce
Vitello Tonnato

To serve 6 to 8

A 3- to 3½-pound boneless veal roast, securely tied	2 cups dry white wine
	2 cups water
3 flat anchovy fillets, cut into 1-inch lengths	2 onions, quartered
	2 carrots, cut up
1 to 2 garlic cloves, cut into thin slivers	3 celery stalks, cut up
	2 bay leaves
1 quart chicken stock, fresh or canned	6 parsley sprigs
	10 whole peppercorns

With a small sharp knife, make deep incisions along the length of the veal and insert a 1-inch piece of anchovy and a sliver of garlic in each one. Blanch the veal in a large pot by covering it with cold water and boiling it over high heat for 1 minute. Pour off the water and quickly rinse the meat of its scum in cold water.

Place the veal in a heavy saucepan or pot just large enough to hold it comfortably. Add the chicken stock, wine, water, onions, carrots, celery, bay leaves, parsley and peppercorns. If the liquid does not quite cover the meat completely, add more chicken stock or water. Bring to a boil, reduce

91

the heat and simmer the veal slowly, partially covered, for about 1 hour and 40 minutes, or until the veal is tender when pierced with the tip of a sharp knife. Remove the pan from the heat and let the veal cool in the stock. Ladle out about ½ cup of the stock, strain it through a fine sieve, and set it aside in a cup or bowl to cool.

TUNA SAUCE
¾ cup olive oil
1 egg yolk
1 three-ounce can tuna fish, preferably
   Italian tuna packed in olive oil
4 flat anchovy fillets, drained and
   soaked in water for 10 minutes, then
   cut into small pieces
2 tablespoons lemon juice
¼ cup heavy cream
¼ to ½ cup cooled, strained
   veal-braising stock (*from above*)
2 tablespoons capers, thoroughly
   washed and drained
Salt
White pepper

Meanwhile, prepare the tuna sauce. If you have a blender, all you need to do is to combine all of the olive oil, the egg yolk, tuna fish, 4 anchovy fillets and lemon juice in the jar of the blender and whirl the ingredients at high speed for no more than 10 seconds, or until the mixture is a purée. Transter it to a small mixing bowl and stir in the cream gradually. Add the cooled. strained braising stock from the veal 2 tablespoons at a time until the sauce is thinned to the consistency of heavy cream. You probably will need about 4 tablespoons of the braising stock in all. Stir in the capers. Taste the sauce for seasoning.

When the veal is cool, transfer it to a carving board. Strain the braising stock and refrigerate for use in soups or sauces. Trim the veal of any fat or gristle and cut the meat into thin, even slices. Spread a thin film of tuna sauce in the bottom of a large platter or baking dish and arrange the veal in the sauce, laying the slices side by side. Pour the rest of the sauce over the veal, smoothing it with a spatula to mask each slice. Cover the platter with plastic wrap and refrigerate the *vitello tonnato* for at least 2 or 3 hours—overnight, or longer, if possible.

GARNISH
2 tablespoons finely chopped fresh
   parsley, preferably the flat-leaf
   Italian type
2 lemons, sliced
2 tablespoons capers
12 black olives, preferably
   Mediterranean style

About 1 hour before serving, remove the veal from the refrigerator and allow it to come to room temperature. Arrange the slices so that they over-lap as neatly as possible in a circle on a large serving platter. Spoon all of the sauce over them. Sprinkle the veal and sauce with the chopped parsley, and garnish the platter with lemon slices, capers and black olives.

92

Braised Stuffed Veal Roll
Kalbsrolle

To serve 6 to 8

POACHING STOCK

The bones from a leg or breast of
  veal, sawed into 2-inch lengths
4 cups water

½ cup coarsely chopped onions
½ cup coarsely chopped celery,
  including the leaves
6 whole black peppercorns
1 small bay leaf

In a heavy 3- to 4-quart saucepan, bring the veal bones and water to a boil over high heat, skimming off any foam and scum that rise to the surface. Add the ½ cup of coarsely chopped onions, the celery, peppercorns and bay leaf, reduce the heat to low and partially cover the pan. Simmer, undisturbed, for 1 hour. Strain the stock through a fine sieve set over a bowl, discarding the bones, vegetables and spices. Set the stock aside.

STUFFING

2 slices homemade type fresh white
  bread
⅓ cup milk
1 tablespoon butter
½ cup finely chopped onions
½ pound ground beef chuck
½ pound fresh sausage meat
1 egg, lightly beaten

3 tablespoons finely chopped parsley
⅛ teaspoon ground nutmeg
Salt
Freshly ground black pepper

A 4- to 4½-pound breast of veal,
  boned and trimmed
3 tablespoons lard

Tear the slices of bread into small pieces and soak them in the milk for 5 minutes, then gently squeeze them and set them aside in a large mixing bowl. In a small skillet, melt the butter over moderate heat. When the foam subsides add ½ cup of finely chopped onions and cook, stirring frequently, for 5 minutes, or until they are soft and transparent but not brown. With a rubber spatula, scrape the contents of the skillet into the bowl with the bread, and add the beef, sausage meat, egg, parsley, nutmeg, ¼ teaspoon of salt and a few grindings of pepper. Knead the mixture with your hands or beat with a large spoon until all the ingredients are well blended.

Preheat the oven to 325°. Place the boned veal flat side down on a board or table, sprinkle it with salt and a few grindings of pepper and, with a knife or spatula, spread the ground-meat stuffing mixture evenly over the veal. Beginning with a wide side, roll up the veal jelly-roll fashion into a thick cylinder. Tie the roll at both ends and in the center with 8-inch lengths of white kitchen cord.

In a heavy flameproof casserole just large enough to hold the roll comfortably, melt the lard over high heat until a light haze forms above it. Add the veal roll and brown it on all sides, regulating the heat so that it browns quickly and evenly without burning. Pour in the reserved stock and bring it to a boil over high heat.

Cover the casserole and transfer it to the middle of the oven. Cook for 1¾ hours, turning the roll over after the first hour. Then remove the cover and cook, basting occasionally with the pan juices, for 30 minutes longer, or until the veal is tender and shows no resistance when pierced with the tip of a small, sharp knife.

To serve hot, carve the veal into ¼-inch slices and arrange them attractively in overlapping layers on a heated platter. Skim and discard the fat from the juices in the casserole, taste for seasoning, and either pour over the veal or serve separately in a sauceboat. (If you would like to make a sauce, measure the skimmed juices. If there is more than 2 cups, boil briskly to reduce it; if there is less, add water. Melt 2 tablespoons of butter over moderate heat and, when the foam subsides, stir in 3 tablespoons of flour. Cook, stirring, over low heat until the flour browns lightly. Gradually add the pan juices, beating vigorously with a whisk until the sauce is smooth and thick. Taste for seasoning.)

To serve cold, transfer the veal roll to a loaf pan and pour the degreased cooking juices over it. Cool to room temperature, then refrigerate overnight. When cold, the juices should jell into a light aspic. Serve the veal cut into thin slices.

Sautéed Veal Scallops with Cream Sauce
Escalopes de Veau à la Savoyarde

To serve 4

8 veal scallops, cut ½ inch thick and pounded ¼ inch thick (1½ to 2 pounds)	3 tablespoons butter
	1 tablespoon vegetable oil
	2 tablespoons finely chopped shallots or scallions
Salt	½ cup dry white wine
Freshly ground black pepper	½ cup heavy cream
Flour	A few drops of lemon juice
	Fresh parsley sprigs

Season the scallops with salt and a few grindings of pepper. Dip them in flour and then shake them vigorously to remove all but a light dusting. In a 10- to 12-inch enameled or stainless-steel skillet, melt the butter with the oil over moderate heat. When the foam subsides, brown the scallops for 3 or 4 minutes on each side, or until they are a light golden color. Remove them from the pan and set aside. Pour off almost all the fat from the skillet, leaving just enough to make a thin film on the bottom. Stir in the shallots and cook slowly for a moment. Pour in the wine and bring it to a boil over high heat, stirring and scraping in any browned bits that cling to the bottom or sides of the pan. Boil for 2 or 3 minutes until the wine has been reduced to about ¼ cup. Reduce the heat, stir in the cream and simmer, stirring constantly, for 3 to 5 minutes, or until the sauce thickens. Taste and season with a few drops of lemon juice, salt and pepper. Return the scallops to the skillet, baste with the sauce and cook just long enough to heat the scallops through. Arrange the scallops, overlapping them slightly, down the center of a heated serving platter, pour the sauce over them, decorate with parsley and serve at once.

Sautéed Veal Scallops with Lemon
Scaloppine al Limone

To serve 4

1½ pounds veal scallops, cut ⅜ inch
   thick and pounded until ¼ inch
   thick
Salt
Freshly ground black pepper

Flour
2 tablespoons butter
3 tablespoons olive oil
¾ cup beef stock, fresh or canned
6 paper-thin lemon slices
1 tablespoon lemon juice
2 tablespoons soft butter

Season the veal scallops with salt and pepper, then dip them in flour and shake off the excess. In a heavy 10- to 12-inch skillet, melt 2 tablespoons of butter with the 3 tablespoons of oil over moderate heat. When the foam subsides, add the veal, 4 or 5 scallops at a time, and sauté them for about 2 minutes on each side, or until they are golden brown. With tongs, transfer the veal scallops to a plate. Now pour off almost all the fat from the skillet, leaving a thin film on the bottom. Add ½ cup of beef stock and boil it briskly for 1 or 2 minutes, stirring constantly and scraping in any browned bits clinging to the bottom and sides of the pan. Return the veal to the skillet and arrange the lemon slices on top. Cover the skillet and simmer over low heat for 10 to 15 minutes, or until the veal is tender when pierced with the tip of a sharp knife.

To serve, transfer the scallops to a heated platter and surround with the lemon slices. Add the ¼ cup of remaining beef stock to the juices in the skillet and boil briskly until the stock is reduced to a syrupy glaze. Add the lemon juice and cook, stirring, for 1 minute. Remove the pan from the heat, swirl in 2 tablespoons of soft butter and pour the sauce over the scallops.

Sautéed Veal Scallops with Marsala Sauce
Scaloppine al Marsala

To serve 4

1½ pounds veal scallops, sliced ⅜
   inch thick and pounded to ¼ inch
Salt
Freshly ground black pepper
Flour

2 tablespoons butter
3 tablespoons olive oil
½ cup dry Marsala
½ cup chicken or beef stock, fresh
   or canned
2 tablespoons soft butter

Season the veal scallops with salt and pepper, then dip them in flour and vigorously shake off the excess. In a heavy 10- to 12-inch skillet, melt 2 tablespoons of butter with the 3 tablespoons of oil over moderate heat. When the foam subsides, add the scallops, 3 or 4 at a time, and brown them for about 3 minutes on each side. Transfer them to a plate.

Pour off most of the fat from the skillet, leaving a thin film on the bottom. Add the Marsala and ¼ cup of chicken or beef stock and boil the liquid briskly over high heat for 1 or 2 minutes. Scrape in any browned fragments clinging to the bottom and sides of the pan. Return the veal to the skillet, cover the pan and simmer over low heat for 10 to 15 minutes, basting the veal now and then with the pan juices.

To serve, transfer the scallops to a heated platter. Add ¼ cup of stock to the sauce remaining in the skillet and boil briskly, scraping in the browned bits sticking to the bottom and sides of the pan. When the sauce has reduced considerably, and has the consistency of a syrupy glaze, taste it for seasoning. Remove the pan from the heat, stir in 2 tablespoons of soft butter, and pour the sauce over the scallops.

Veal Scallops with Prosciutto and Cheese
Cuscinetti di Vitello

To serve 4

16 thin 4-inch-square veal scallops
8 thin 3½-inch-square slices Fontina
   or Gruyère cheese
8 thin 3-inch-square slices prosciutto
Salt

Freshly ground black pepper
Flour
2 tablespoons butter
3 tablespoons olive oil
½ cup dry white wine
¾ cup chicken or beef stock, fresh or
   canned

Place a square slice of cheese and a square of prosciutto on each one of eight veal scallops and top with the remaining scallops. The veal should cover the cheese and ham completely. Press the edges of the veal together and seal them by pounding with the flat of a cleaver or the bottom of a heavy bottle. Season with salt and pepper; dip them in flour and shake off the excess. In a heavy 10- to 12-inch skillet, melt the butter with the oil over moderate heat. When the foam subsides, add the *cuscinetti* 3 or 4 at a time and cook in the hot fat, turning gently with a slotted spoon or spatula until they are golden brown on both sides. Transfer them to a platter.

Discard most of the fat from the skillet, leaving a thin film on the bottom. Pour in the wine and boil it briskly, stirring and scraping in any browned bits that cling to the skillet. Continue to boil until the wine has been reduced to about ¼ cup. Add ½ cup of stock and bring it to a simmer. Then return the veal to the skillet, cover, and simmer 20 minutes over low heat, turning the *cuscinetti* over after 10 minutes. Transfer the *cuscinetti* to a heated serving platter, and add the remaining ¼ cup of stock to the skillet. Bring the stock and the pan juices to a boil, and let them cook briskly for a minute or so. Taste and season with salt and pepper, then pour over the veal.

Sautéed Veal Scallops in Tomato Sauce
Ternera a la Sevillana

To serve 6

12 pitted green Spanish olives
1 cup olive oil
2 cups finely chopped onions
1 tablespoon finely chopped garlic
2 small green peppers, deribbed, seeded and finely chopped
¼ pound fresh mushrooms, sliced ⅛ inch thick (about 2 cups sliced)
4 medium-sized tomatoes peeled, seeded, and finely chopped
½ cup finely diced *serrano* ham, or

substitute ⅛ pound prosciutto or other lean smoked ham
2 tablespoons blanched almonds, pulverized in a blender or with a nut grinder or mortar and pestle
Salt
Freshly ground black pepper
1 cup flour
6 veal scallops, cut about ⅜ inch thick and pounded ¼ inch thick
½ cup pale dry sherry
½ cup water

In a small glass, enameled, or stainless-steel saucepan, bring 2 cups of water to a boil over high heat. Drop in the olives, reduce the heat to low and simmer for 2 minutes. Drain the olives in a sieve or colander and run cold water over them to stop their cooking. Set aside.

For the *sofrito,* heat ½ cup of the olive oil in a heavy 10- to 12-inch skillet over moderate heat until a light haze forms above it. Add the onions, garlic and green pepper and stirring frequently, cook for 5 minutes, or until the vegetables are soft but not brown. Add the mushrooms, tomatoes, olives, ham and pulverized almonds, and bring to a boil, stirring constantly. Cook briskly until most of the liquid in the pan evaporates and the mixture is thick enough to hold its shape lightly in a spoon. Set aside.

Sprinkle the veal scallops liberally with salt and a few grindings of pepper. Dip them in the flour and shake them vigorously to remove all but a light dusting. Heat the remaining ½ cup of oil in another 10- to 12-inch skillet until a light haze forms above it. Cook the scallops (in two batches if necessary) for 3 or 4 minutes on each side, turning them with tongs and regulating the heat so that they brown quickly and evenly without burning.

As they brown, transfer the scallops to a plate. Discard the oil remaining in the pan and in its place pour in the sherry and water. Bring to a boil over high heat, meanwhile scraping in any brown particles clinging to the bottom and sides of the skillet. Then add the reserved *sofrito* and stir together thoroughly. Taste the sauce for seasoning.

Return the veal to the skillet, lower the heat, cover tightly and simmer for 4 or 5 minutes, or until the scallops are tender when pierced with a knife.

To serve, arrange the scallops attractively in a row down the center of a deep heated platter, overlapping them slightly, pour the sauce evenly over them and serve at once.

Rolled Veal Scallops with Chicken Liver Stuffing
Involtini alla Cacciatora

To serve 4 to 6

2 tablespoons butter
¼ pound chicken livers
1 ounce prosciutto, cut in tiny pieces
1 green scallion stem, finely chopped
2 teaspoons finely chopped fresh parsley
⅛ teaspoon sage leaves, crumbled
⅛ teaspoon salt
Freshly ground black pepper

1 pound veal scallops, sliced ⅜ inch thick and pounded ¼ inch thick, then cut into 4-by-4-inch squares (about 12 squares)
Flour
2 tablespoons butter
3 tablespoons olive oil
½ cup dry Marsala
1 cup chicken stock, fresh or canned

Over moderate heat melt 2 tablespoons of butter in a heavy 8- to 10-inch skillet. When the foam subsides, add the livers and cook them, turning frequently, for 4 or 5 minutes, or until they stiffen and are lightly browned. Cut them into ¼-inch cubes and place them in a large bowl. Sauté the prosciutto and scallions in the same skillet for about 2 minutes, adding more butter if necessary. Then, with a rubber spatula, scrape them into the bowl of livers, and add the parsley, sage, salt and a few grindings of pepper. Stir together gently and taste for seasoning.

Place about 2 tablespoons of the chicken-liver mixture on the bottom third of each veal scallop. Roll up the scallops and tie both ends with soft string. Dip the rolls in flour, then shake off the excess. Melt 2 tablespoons of butter with the oil in a heavy 10- to 12-inch skillet. When the foam sub-sides, add the veal rolls, 4 or 5 at a time, and cook over moderate heat, turning them frequently, until they are golden brown on all sides, transfer-ring them to a plate when done. Now discard almost all of the fat from the skillet, leaving a thin film on the bottom. Pour in the wine and ¾ cup of chicken stock, and boil briskly for 1 or 2 minutes, scraping in any browned fragments clinging to the pan.

Return the veal to the skillet, reduce the heat, cover and simmer, basting once or twice with pan juices, for 15 minutes, or until the veal is tender when pierced with the tip of a sharp knife. With tongs, transfer the veal to a heated serving platter. Pour the remaining stock into the skillet and boil briskly, until the liquid has reduced to ½ cup and thickened slightly. Pour it over the veal rolls and serve.

Breaded Veal Cutlets
Wiener Schnitzel

To serve 4

2 eggs	
2 tablespoons water	Freshly ground black pepper
2 pounds leg of veal, cut into slices	¼ cup flour
¼ inch thick	1 cup fine bread crumbs
Salt	1½ cups lard

Beat the eggs with the water only long enough to combine them. Sprinkle the veal slices liberally with salt and pepper, dip them in flour and shake off the excess; next dip them in the beaten eggs and finally in the bread crumbs. Gently shake any excess crumbs from the cutlets and refrigerate for at least 20 minutes.

Heat the lard in a heavy 12-inch skillet until a light haze forms over it, then add the cutlets. Cook over medium heat 3 to 4 minutes on each side, or until they are brown, using tongs to turn them. Serve immediately, gar-nished with lemon wedges or anchovy butter sauce.

NOTE: *Schnitzel* is common in Germany as well as Austria. To prepare a classic German version, *Schnitzel à la Holstein*, cook the cutlets as described above. Then top each cutlet with a fried egg garnished with anchovy fillets and sprinkled with a few capers. If you wish, you may surround the cutlets with small portions of several of the following: smoked salmon, caviar, crayfish tails, lobster salad, sardines in oil, mushrooms, green beans or truffles.

Veal Cutlets with Cream-and-Mushroom Sauce
Rahm Schnitzel

To serve 4 to 6

2 pounds veal cutlets, cut into slices
   ¼ inch thick
1 cup lemon juice
Salt

Freshly ground black pepper
Flour
4 tablespoons butter
4 tablespoons vegetable oil
1 cup fresh mushrooms, sliced
½ cup heavy cream

In a glass, stainless-steel or enameled baking dish, marinate the cutlets in the lemon juice for 1 hour, turning them every 20 minutes or so. Remove them from the lemon juice and pat them dry with paper towels. Salt and pepper them generously, then dip them in flour and shake off the excess.

In a heavy 12-inch skillet, heat the butter and oil over high heat. When the foam subsides, add the cutlets. Cook them for 1 or 2 minutes on each side over high heat, using tongs to turn them. Then lower the heat to medium and cook for 5 to 6 minutes longer on each side. Arrange them on a platter and set them in a 200° oven to keep warm.

Pour off all but a thin film of fat, add the mushrooms to the skillet and cook them for 3 or 4 minutes over medium heat. Pour in the cream and bring it to a boil, stirring in any brown bits that cling to the pan. Cook briskly until the cream thickens enough to coat a spoon lightly. Taste for seasoning, then pour the sauce over the cutlets and serve.

Veal Cutlets with Paprika and Sour Cream
Paprika Schnitzel

To serve 4 to 6

2 pounds leg of veal, cut into slices
   ¼ inch thick
1 cup fresh lemon juice
Salt
Flour
3 tablespoons lard

3 tablespoons butter
1 cup finely chopped onions
1½ tablespoons sweet Hungarian
   paprika
½ cup chicken stock, fresh or canned
2 tablespoons flour
1 cup sour cream

In a glass, stainless-steel or enameled baking dish, marinate the cutlets in the lemon juice for 1 hour, turning them every 20 minutes or so. Pat them dry with paper towels, salt them, then dip them in flour and shake off the excess.

In a heavy 12-inch skillet, heat the lard until a light haze forms over it, then add the cutlets. Over medium heat, cook them for 3 or 4 minutes on each side, or until lightly browned, using tongs to turn them. Arrange them on a serving platter, cover lightly with foil, and set them in a 200° oven to keep them warm.

Pour off all the fat from the skillet and replace it with the butter. Melt it over medium heat, then reduce the heat to low and add the onions. Cook them for 8 to 10 minutes, or until they are lightly colored. Remove the skillet from the heat and stir in the paprika, continuing to stir until the onions are well coated. Return the skillet to medium heat and add the chicken stock. Bring it to a boil, stirring in any brown bits clinging to the bottom and sides of the pan.

In a mixing bowl, stir the 2 tablespoons of flour into the sour cream with a wire whisk. Whisking constantly, add the sour-cream mixture to the stock in the skillet. Simmer for 2 or 3 minutes, or until the sauce is well heated. Pour the sauce over the cutlets and serve.

Veal Chops in Cream Sauce
Côtes de Veau à la Crème

To serve 4

	1 cup veal stock or water
4 veal chops	1 cup heavy cream
4 tablespoons butter	Salt
2 tablespoons brandy	Pepper
1 small clove garlic, crushed	1 bay leaf
¼ pound mushrooms, sliced	¼ teaspoon dried thyme
½ teaspoon meat extract	2 tablespoons grated Parmesan
3 tablespoons flour	cheese

Brown the chops quickly on both sides in 2 tablespoons of hot butter. Heat the brandy in a small pan, ignite it and pour it over the chops, then remove them from the pan. Add 1 tablespoon of butter to the pan, then the garlic, and cook for ½ minute. Add the sliced mushrooms and cook for another 2 to 3 minutes. Off the heat, blend in the meat extract and the flour. Pour in the veal stock or water and stir, over the heat, until the mixture comes to a boil. Still stirring constantly, slowly add the heavy cream. Return the chops to the sauce. Add salt and pepper to taste, the bay leaf and the thyme. Cover and simmer for 40 to 50 minutes, or until the chops are tender.

To serve, arrange the chops on a hot, ovenproof serving dish and cover them with the sauce. Sprinkle the top with Parmesan cheese and dot with the remaining tablespoon of butter, then brown under the broiler.

Veal Chop and Vegetable Casserole

Côtes de Veau à la Bonne Femme

To serve 4

4 lean veal chops
1 small clove garlic, crushed
4 tablespoons butter
12 very small white onions, peeled
10 very small new potatoes, peeled
¼ pound salt pork, diced

2 tablespoons dry white wine
½ teaspoon meat extract
½ cup veal or chicken stock
Salt
Freshly ground pepper
½ teaspoon lemon juice
1 tablespoon chopped parsley

Rub the veal chops with crushed garlic. Heat 1 tablespoon of butter in an ovenproof casserole dish and, when the butter is very hot, brown the chops quickly on both sides. Remove chops from the casserole. Melt another 3 tablespoons of butter in the casserole and add the white onions, potatoes and diced salt pork. Brown very slowly for 10 to 15 minutes. Add 2 tablespoons of dry white wine and mix well.

Blend in, off the fire, the meat extract, stock, salt, pepper and lemon juice. Bring slowly to a boil. Add the chops, cover and bake in a moderate oven at 350° for 30 to 40 minutes. Sprinkle with a tablespoon of finely chopped parsley just before serving.

Veal Ragout with Caraway Seeds

Dušené Telecí na Kmíně

To serve 4

2 pounds boneless shoulder of veal
   cut into 1-inch cubes
Salt
Freshly ground black pepper

3 tablespoons butter
½ cup finely chopped onions
2 tablespoons flour
1½ tablespoons caraway seeds
1½ cups chicken stock
1 cup thinly sliced fresh mushrooms

Sprinkle the veal cubes with salt and a few grindings of pepper. Over medium heat in a 10- or 12-inch skillet, melt the butter. When the foam subsides, add the onions and cook them 6 to 8 minutes, or until translucent. Stir in the veal cubes and sprinkle the flour and caraway seeds over them. Stir again to coat the veal evenly with the mixture. Cover tightly and cook over very low heat for 10 minutes, shaking the pan every now and then to keep the veal from sticking. Stir in the stock, bring to a boil and reduce the heat to low. Add the mushrooms, cover and simmer for 1 hour, or until the veal is tender. Add more stock by the tablespoon if the veal seems too dry or the stock too thick. Taste for seasoning.

This veal ragout is a Czech dish made with caraway seeds and mushrooms. It is customarily served with buttered noodles sprinkled with toasted bread crumbs.

103

Veal Stew with Cream Sauce
Blanquette de Veau à l'Ancienne

To serve 6

3 to 3½ pounds boneless veal shoulder
  cut into 2-inch chunks
6⅔ cups chicken stock, fresh or
  canned
2 carrots, peeled and cut in chunks
1 large whole peeled onion
2 celery tops
1 leek, white part plus 2 inches of
  green (optional)
1 teaspoon dried thyme
1 bay leaf
4 parsley sprigs

1 teaspoon salt
5 tablespoons butter
18 peeled white onions, about 1 inch
  in diameter
1 pound fresh mushrooms, whole if
  small, quartered or sliced if large
1 teaspoon lemon juice
3 tablespoons flour
2 egg yolks
1 cup heavy cream
White pepper
2 tablespoons finely chopped
fresh parsley

In a heavy 4- to 6-quart casserole, blanch the veal by covering it with cold water, bringing it to a boil over high heat and boiling it briskly for 1 minute. Drain the veal immediately. Under cold running water, wash away any accumulated scum. Wash the casserole and return the veal to it. Add 6 cups of the chicken stock, carrots, onion, celery, leek, herbs and salt. The meat should be completely covered with liquid; add more stock or water if needed. Bring to a boil over moderate heat, skimming off any scum. Reduce the heat to low and simmer the veal, partially covered, for 1 to 1½ hours, or until it is tender when pierced with a sharp knife.

While the veal is simmering, combine the remaining ⅔ cup chicken stock, 2 tablespoons of the butter, and the onions in a 10- to 12-inch enameled or stainless-steel skillet. Bring to a boil, cover and simmer, stirring occasionally, for 15 to 20 minutes, or until the onions are tender. With a slotted spoon, transfer them to a bowl. Stir the mushrooms and lemon juice into the stock remaining in the skillet. Bring to a boil, cover and simmer for 5 minutes. Remove them from the pan and add them to the onions. Pour the liquid in the skillet into the casserole.

When the veal is tender, transfer it to a bowl with a slotted spoon. Strain the stock from the casserole through a fine sieve into a 2- to 3-quart saucepan, pressing down hard on the vegetables and herbs with the back of a spoon before discarding them. Skim off the surface fat. Over high heat, boil the stock down until it has been reduced to about half.

In a small saucepan, melt the remaining 3 tablespoons of butter over moderate heat, and stir in the flour. Return to low heat and cook, stirring constantly, for 2 minutes. Do not let this *roux* brown. Remove from heat, pour in 2 cups of reduced stock and blend vigorously with a wire whisk. Then return to high heat and cook the sauce, stirring constantly, until it thickens and comes to a boil. Reduce the heat and simmer for about 10

104

minutes, skimming off any scum.

Remove from the heat. With a wire whisk, blend the egg yolks and cream together in a bowl. Whisk in the hot sauce, 2 tablespoons at a time, until ½ cup has been added; then reverse the process and whisk the egg-yolk-and-cream mixture back into the remaining hot sauce. Bring it to a boil, stirring constantly; then boil slowly for 30 seconds. Taste and season with salt, white pepper and a few drops of lemon juice.

Drain the veal, onions and mushrooms of any juices that may have accumulated in their bowls. Wash the casserole and spread the veal and vegetables in it. Pour the sauce over them and gently stir to coat every piece. Simmer over moderate heat for 5 to 10 minutes. Do not let the sauce boil again. Sprinkle with parsley and serve.

Veal Stew with Tomatoes and Green Peppers
Borjúpörkölt

To serve 4 to 6

2 pounds of veal shoulder, cut into
   1½-inch cubes
4 tablespoons lard
2 cups finely chopped onions
½ teaspoon finely chopped garlic
1 tablespoon sweet Hungarian
   paprika

3 medium fresh ripe tomatoes, peeled,
   seeded and coarsely chopped,
   or an equivalent amount of
   canned drained tomatoes
1 medium green pepper, with
   seeds and ribs removed, coarsely
   chopped (about ¼ cup)
Salt

In a heavy 4- or 5-quart saucepan, melt the lard over medium heat, then add the onions and garlic. Cook them for 8 to 10 minutes, or until the onions are lightly colored. Off the heat, stir in the paprika, continuing to stir until the onions are well coated, then stir in the veal. Cover tightly, turn the heat to its lowest point and simmer for ½ hour.

Stir in the tomatoes and cook, covered for ½ hour longer, stirring occasionally. Then add the green peppers. Cook, covered, ½ hour more, again stirring occasionally, or until the veal is tender. The tomatoes will provide sufficient liquid. Taste for seasoning.

Succulent cubes of veal and pork, divided by bay leaves, are broiled on skewers in this Serbian dish. The meat is marinated for 3 hours in oil and onions.

Veal and Pork Barbecue
Ražnjići

To serve 4 to 6

1 pound boneless veal, cut into
   1½-inch cubes
1 pound lean boneless pork, cut into
   1½-inch cubes

Salt
Freshly ground black pepper
2 tablespoons vegetable oil
1 cup thinly sliced onions
15 small bay leaves, broken in half
2 tablespoons finely chopped onions

Pat the veal and pork cubes dry with paper towels, sprinkle them with salt and a few grindings of pepper and mix them well with the oil and onions in a large bowl. Cover and refrigerate for at least 3 hours, stirring them every now and then. Remove the cubes to a plate and reserve the marinade for later use.

To prepare *ražnjići* for cooking, arrange the veal and pork cubes alternately on skewers—either small bamboo skewers or 6- to 8-inch trussing skewers—with half a bay leaf separating each pair of cubes. Broil *ražnjići* in a preheated oven broiler, 4 to 6 inches from the flame, or on an outdoor grill, for 10 minutes on each side, or until the cubes show no pink in the center when one is cut into. The pork should not be undercooked. With either method, baste the *ražnjići* with the marinade while they are broiling.

Ražnjići may be removed from the skewers before they are served, or served on the skewers. Sprinkle the chopped onions over them just before serving.

106

Braised Veal Shanks
Osso Buco

To serve 6 to 8

4 tablespoons butter
1½ cups finely chopped onions
½ cup finely chopped carrots
½ cup finely chopped celery
1 teaspoon finely chopped garlic
6 to 7 pounds veal shank or shin,
   sawed—not chopped—into 8
   pieces, each 2½ inches long, and tied
   with string around their
   circumference
Salt
Freshly ground black pepper
Flour

½ cup olive oil
1 cup dry white wine
½ teaspoon dried basil
¾ cup beef or chicken stock, fresh
   or canned
½ teaspoon dried thyme
3 cups drained canned whole
   tomatoes, coarsely chopped
6 parsley sprigs
2 bay leaves

GREMOLATA
1 tablespoon grated lemon peel
1 teaspoon finely chopped garlic
3 tablespoons finely chopped parsley

Choose a heavy shallow casserole or Dutch oven that has a tight cover and is just large enough to snugly hold the pieces of veal standing up in 1 layer. Melt the butter in the casserole over moderate heat and when the foam subsides, add the chopped onions, carrots, celery and garlic. Cook, stirring occasionally, for 10 to 15 minutes, or until the vegetables are lightly colored. Remove the casserole from the heat.

Season the pieces of veal with salt and pepper, then roll them in flour and shake off the excess. In a heavy 10- to 12-inch skillet, heat 6 tablespoons of olive oil until a haze forms over it. Brown the veal in the oil over moderately high heat, 4 or 5 pieces at a time, adding more oil as needed. Transfer the browned pieces to the casserole and stand them side by side on top of the vegetables.

Preheat the oven to 350°. Now discard almost all of the fat from the skillet, leaving just a film on the bottom. Pour in the wine and boil it briskly over high heat until it is reduced to about ½ cup. Scrape in any browned bits clinging to the pan. Stir in the beef stock, basil, thyme, tomatoes, parsley sprigs and bay leaves and bring to a boil, then pour it all over the veal. The liquid should come halfway up the side of the veal; if it does not, add more stock. Bring the casserole to a boil on top of the stove. Cover and bake in the lower third of the oven, basting occasionally and regulating the oven heat to keep the casserole simmering gently. In about 1 hour and 15 minutes the veal should be tender; test it by piercing the meat with the tip of a sharp knife. To serve, arrange the pieces of veal on a heated platter and spoon the sauce and vegetables from the casserole around them. Sprinkle the top with *gremolata*—a piquant garnish made by mixing the grated lemon rind and chopped garlic and parsley together.

English Veal and Ham Pie

To serve 6 to 8

2 tablespoons butter, softened
2 pounds lean boneless veal, cut
    into ¼-inch cubes
1 pound lean smoked ham, cut into
    ¼-inch cubes
¼ cup finely chopped parsley
6 tablespoons brandy
6 tablespoons fresh or canned
    chicken or beef stock
2 tablespoons fresh lemon juice
1 teaspoon finely grated lemon peel

1 teaspoon crumbled dried sage leaves
2 teaspoons salt
¼ teaspoon freshly ground black
    pepper
Hot-water pastry (*below*)
4 hard-cooked eggs
8 to 10 pickled walnuts (optional)
1 egg yolk combined with 1
    tablespoon heavy cream
1 envelope unflavored gelatin
2 cups chicken stock, fresh or canned

Preheat the oven to 350°. Using a pastry brush, coat the bottom and sides of a 10-by-5-by-4-inch loaf mold with the butter. Set aside. In a large bowl, combine the veal, ham, parsley, brandy, stock, lemon juice, peel, sage, salt and pepper. Toss the ingredients about with a spoon until thoroughly mixed.

Break off about one third of the hot-water pastry and set it aside. On a lightly floured surface, roll out the remaining pastry into a rectangle about 20 inches long, 10 inches wide and ¼ inch thick. Drape the pastry over the rolling pin, lift it up, and unroll it slackly over the mold. Gently press the pastry into the mold. Roll the pin over the rim to trim off the excess pastry.

Spoon enough of the veal and ham mixture into the pastry shell to fill it a little less than half full. Arrange the hard-cooked eggs in a single row down the center of the mold, and line up the pickled walnuts, if you are using them, on both sides of the eggs. Cover the eggs with the remaining meat mixture, filling the shell to within 1 inch of the top.

Roll the reserved pastry into a 4-by-13-inch rectangle ¼ inch thick. Lift it up on the pin and drape it over the top of the mold. Trim off the excess with a small knife and, with the tines of a fork or your fingers, crimp the pastry to secure it to the rim of the mold. Then cut a 1-inch round hole in the center of the pie. Roll out the scraps of pastry and cut them into leaf and flower shapes. Moisten their bottom sides with the egg-and-cream mixture and arrange on the pie. Brush the entire surface with the egg-and-cream mixture.

Bake the pie in the middle of the oven for 2 hours, or until the top is a deep golden brown. Remove from the oven and cool for 15 minutes.

Meanwhile, in a 1- to 1½-quart saucepan, sprinkle the gelatin over 2 cups of cold chicken stock and let it soften for 2 or 3 minutes. Then set the pan over low heat and cook, stirring constantly, until the gelatin dissolves completely. Pour the gelatin through a funnel into the opening of the pie. Cool the pie to room temperature, then refrigerate it for at least 6 hours, or until

1 To assemble a veal and ham pie, line a large loaf mold with hot-water pastry, then fill it half full of the meat mixture. Arrange hard-cooked eggs in a row down the center and add the rest of the meat, patting the filling gently to spread it and smooth the top.

2 Cover the pie with pastry and trim the excess from the rim of the mold with a small knife. Crimp the edge of the pastry by pinching it between your thumb and forefinger to make a rope-like scallop all around the pie. This also seals the pastry shell securely.

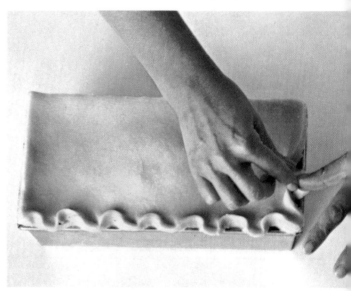

the aspic is set. Ideally the pie should be removed from the refrigerator about 30 minutes before being served.

To unmold and serve the pie, run the blade of a sharp knife around the inside edges of the mold and dip the bottom of the mold in hot water. Wipe the mold dry, place an inverted serving plate over it and, grasping mold and plate together firmly, quickly turn them over. Rap the plate on a table and the pie should slide out easily. Turn the pie over and serve, cut into ½-inch-thick slices.

3 Cut a hole in the top and trim it with flower petals cut from scraps of pastry. Then brush the pie with the egg-and-milk mixture and bake it. After aspic is poured in the hole and the pie chilled, serve it in thick slices; they will look like the cross section below.

HOT-WATER PASTRY
5 cups all-purpose flour
½ teaspoon salt
10 tablespoons lard

6 tablespoons milk
2 tablespoons water

In a deep bowl, combine the flour and salt. Warm the lard, milk and water in a saucepan over moderate heat, and stir until the lard melts. Beat the mixture, a few tablespoons at a time, into the flour, and continue to beat until the dough can be gathered into a compact ball. On a lightly floured surface, knead the dough for 2 or 3 minutes by pressing it down, pushing it forward, and folding it back on itself until it is smooth and elastic. Again gather it into a ball. Place it in a bowl and drape a dampened kitchen towel over it. Let the dough rest for 30 minutes before using.

Veal Pies
Talaş Kebabi

To serve 4

16 tablespoons butter (½ pound),
   cut into ¼-inch bits and clarified
½ cup finely chopped onions
1 tablespoon finely chopped parsley,
   preferably flat-leaf parsley
1 teaspoon tomato paste
1 teaspoon salt
Freshly ground black pepper

½ cup water
1½ pounds lean boneless veal, cut
   into ½-inch dice
8 sheets *filo* pastry, each about 16
   inches long and 12 inches wide,
   thoroughly defrosted if frozen
1 egg yolk, lightly beaten
4 fresh mushroom caps, each about
   2 inches in diameter, cut crosswise
   into ⅛-inch-thick slices

In a heavy 10- to 12-inch skillet, heat 4 tablespoons of the butter over moderate heat until a drop of water flicked into it sputters instantly. Add the onions and, stirring constantly, cook for 5 minutes, or until they are soft and transparent but not brown. Add the parsley, tomato paste, salt, a few grindings of pepper and ¼ cup of the water and bring to a boil over high heat. Drop in the veal, turning the pieces about with a spoon until they are thoroughly moistened. Reduce the heat to low, and simmer partially covered for about 30 minutes, or until the veal is tender and almost all of the liquid in the pan has evaporated. Then increase the heat to high and, stirring constantly, cook briskly until the veal browns lightly. Be careful that it does not burn. With a slotted spoon, transfer the veal to a bowl and set it aside to drain. Pour the remaining ¼ cup of water into the skillet and bring to a boil over high heat, meanwhile scraping in any brown particles clinging to the bottom and sides of the pan. Set aside.

    Preheat the oven to 400°. With a pastry brush, coat a large baking sheet with 1 tablespoon of the butter. To assemble each veal pie, lay a sheet of *filo* flat and brush the top evenly with about 1 tablespoon of butter. Cover with a second sheet of *filo*, and fold the two in half crosswise to make a four-layered rectangle about 8 inches wide and 12 inches long. Place about ½ cup of the veal in the center of the pastry and, with a knife or metal spatula, spread the filling into a rectangle about 2 inches wide and 4 inches long. Fold one long edge of the *filo* completely across the filling and bring the opposite side over the first fold to make a packet about 2½ inches wide. Brush the top with 1 more teaspoon of butter. Turn both ends of the packet up, overlapping them slightly, to enclose the filling securely. The finished pie will be about 4½ inches long.

Place the pies, seam sides down, on the baking sheet and brush them with beaten egg yolk. Bake in the middle of the oven for 15 to 20 minutes until the pastry is crisp and delicately browned.

Meanwhile, heat the remaining 2 tablespoons of butter in an 8- to 10-inch skillet. Add the mushrooms and cook over moderate heat for 2 minutes, or until they brown lightly. Add the reserved veal cooking sauce and bring to a boil, then reduce the heat to low. Cover and simmer for 5 minutes.

To serve, arrange the pies on a heated serving platter, place a row of overlapping mushroom slices on the top of each, and moisten with the sauce remaining in the skillet.

Lamb

Crown Roast of Lamb

To serve 6 to 8

A crown roast of lamb, consisting of
16 to 18 chops and weighing about
4½ pounds
1 clove garlic, cut into tiny slivers
(optional)
2 teaspoons salt
1 teaspoon freshly ground black
pepper

1 teaspoon crushed dried rosemary
16 to 18 peeled new potatoes, all
about 1½ inches in diameter
3 cups cooked fresh or frozen peas
2 tablespoons melted butter
6 to 8 sprigs of fresh mint

Preheat the oven to 475°. With the point of a small, sharp knife make
small incisions a few inches apart in the meaty portions of the lamb, and insert in them the slivers of garlic, if you are using it. Combine the salt,
pepper and rosemary, and with your fingers pat the mixture all over the bottom and sides of the crown. To help keep its shape, stuff the crown with
a crumpled sheet of foil and wrap the ends of the chop bones in strips of
foil to prevent them from charring and snapping off. Place the crown of
lamb on a small rack set in a shallow roasting pan just large enough to
hold it comfortably and roast it in the center of the oven for about 20 minutes. Then turn down the heat to 400° and surround the crown with the
new potatoes, basting them with the pan drippings and sprinkling them
lightly with salt. Continue to roast the lamb (basting the lamb is unnecessary, but baste the potatoes every 15 minutes or so) for about an
hour to an hour and 15 minutes, depending upon how well done you prefer your lamb. Ideally, it should be served when it is still somewhat pink,
and should register 140° to 150° on a meat thermometer.

When the crown is done, carefully transfer it to a large circular platter, remove the foil and let the lamb rest about 10 minutes to make carving
easier. Meanwhile, combine the peas with the melted butter and season

them with as much salt as is necessary. Fill the hollow of the crown with as many of the peas as it will hold and serve any remaining peas separately. Put a paper frill on the end of each chop bone and surround the crown with the roasted potatoes. Garnish with mint and serve at once.

To carve the lamb, insert a large fork in the side of the crown to steady it and with a large, sharp knife cut down through each rib to detach the chops. Two rib chops per person is a customary portion.

Roast Leg of Lamb
Gigot d'Agneau Rôti
To serve 6 to 8

A 5- to 6-pound leg of lamb trimmed of excess fat but with the fell (or parchmentlike covering) left on
1 garlic clove, cut in slivers
3 tablespoons vegetable oil
2 tablespoons salt

2 onions, thinly sliced
2 carrots, thinly sliced
1½ cups fresh or canned beef or chicken stock
½ teaspoon lemon juice
Salt
Freshly ground black pepper

Preheat the oven to 500°. Make 6 or 8 quarter-inch incisions on the fatty side of the lamb, and insert a sliver of garlic in each cut. Brush the leg with oil and pat salt all over it. Insert a meat thermometer into the thickest part of the leg, being careful not to touch a bone. Place the leg, fat side up, on a rack in a shallow roasting pan and roast it uncovered for 20 minutes on the middle shelf of the oven. Then reduce the heat to 375°, scatter the vegetables around the rack and roast the lamb for another 40 to 60 minutes, or until done to your liking. For rare lamb, roast it until the meat thermometer reads 130° to 140°, for medium, 140° to 150°; for well done, 150° to 160°. Transfer the lamb to a heated platter and remove the thermometer; let it rest 10 minutes before carving.

Meanwhile, skim off the fat from the roasting pan, add the stock to the vegetables and boil briskly on top of the stove for 4 or 5 minutes, scraping in any browned bits clinging to the pan. When the sauce has reached the intensity of flavor desired, strain it through a fine sieve into a saucepan, pressing down hard on the vegetables before discarding them. Skim the sauce of its surface fat; taste the sauce and season it with lemon juice, salt and pepper. Reheat the sauce and serve it with the lamb.

Roast Leg of Lamb with Mint Sauce

To serve 6 to 8

MINT SAUCE
¼ cup water
1 tablespoon sugar

¼ cup finely chopped fresh mint
   leaves
½ cup malt vinegar

Make the mint sauce in advance. Combine the water and sugar in a 1- to 1½-quart saucepan, and bring to a boil over high heat, stirring until the sugar dissolves completely.

Remove the pan from the heat, and stir in the mint leaves and vinegar. Taste and add up to 1 more tablespoon of sugar if desired. Set aside at room temperature for 2 or 3 hours.

MEAT
2 tablespoons salt
1 teaspoon finely ground black
   pepper
1 tablespoon finely cut fresh
   rosemary or 2 teaspoons dried

crushed rosemary
A 5- to 6-pound leg of lamb,
   trimmed of excess fat, but with
   the fell (the parchmentlike
   covering) left on

Preheat the oven to 500° (it will take about 15 minutes for most ovens to reach this temperature). Combine the salt, pepper and rosemary in a small bowl, and with your fingers press the mixture firmly into the lamb, coating the entire surface as evenly as possible. For the most predictable results, insert a meat thermometer into the thickest part of the leg, being careful not to touch a bone.

Place the leg, fat side up, on a rack in a shallow roasting pan, and roast it uncovered in the middle of the oven for 20 minutes. Reduce the heat to 375° and roast for another 40 to 60 minutes, or until the lamb is cooked to your taste (basting is unnecessary). A meat thermometer will register 130° to 140° when the lamb is rare, 140° to 150° when medium, and 150° to 160° when well done.

Transfer the lamb to a heated platter, and let the roast rest for 15 minutes for easier carving. Stir the mint sauce once or twice, pour it into a sauceboat and serve it separately with the lamb.

Roast Leg of Lamb with Orzo
Giouvetsi

To serve 8

A 6½- to 7-pound leg of lamb, trimmed of excess fat but with the fell (the parchmentlike covering) left on
1 large garlic clove, peeled and cut lengthwise into 8 thin slivers
1 teaspoon oregano, crumbled
2 teaspoons salt
Freshly ground black pepper

6 tablespoons fresh lemon juice
2 medium-sized onions, peeled and thinly sliced
1 cup boiling water
2 cups (about 1 pound) *orzo* (rice-shaped pasta)
½ cup canned tomato purée
Freshly grated *kefalotiri* or imported Parmesan cheese

Preheat the oven to 450°. With the tip of a small, sharp knife, make 8 quarter-inch-deep incisions on the fat side of the lamb and insert a sliver of garlic in each. Combine the oregano, 1 teaspoon of the salt, and a few grindings of pepper and press the mixture firmly all over the surface of the lamb. For the most predictable results, insert a meat thermometer into the thickest part of the leg, being careful not to let the tip touch any fat or bone.

Place the leg, fat side up, on a rack in a shallow roasting pan and roast it un-covered in the middle of the oven for 20 minutes. Reduce the heat to 350°, baste the leg with a tablespoon or so of lemon juice, and scatter the onions in the bottom of the pan. Roast for 15 minutes more, then baste the lamb again with another tablespoon of lemon juice and pour the cup of boiling water over the onions. Basting periodically with the remaining lemon juice, continue roasting for another 40 to 60 minutes, or until the lamb is done to your taste. A meat thermometer will register 130° to 140° for rare, 140° to 150° for medium, and 150° to 160° for well done.

Meanwhile, bring 2 quarts of water and the remaining teaspoon of salt to a boil over high heat. Pour in the *orzo* in a slow thin stream so that the water does not stop boiling, and cook briskly for about 10 minutes until the *orzo* is tender but still slightly resistant to the bite. Drain in a sieve or colander.

When the leg of lamb is done, place it on a large heated platter and let it rest at room temperature for 10 or 15 minutes for easier carving.

Meanwhile, pour off all but a thin film of fat from the roasting pan. Stir the tomato purée into the onions, scraping in any brown particles clinging to the bottom and sides of the pan. Stir in the *orzo*, return the pan to the middle shelf of the oven and bake uncovered for 10 to 15 minutes until the *orzo* is heated through. Taste for seasoning.

To serve, mound the *orzo* around the leg of lamb and pass the grated cheese separately to be sprinkled over the pasta.

Roast Leg of Lamb with Sherry

To serve 6

A 5-pound leg of lamb
3 garlic cloves, slivered
2 teaspoons salt
½ teaspoon black pepper
½ teaspoon rosemary

3 tablespoons butter
2 sliced celery stalks
1 grated carrot
¾ cup chopped onions
¾ cup water
¾ cup dry sherry

Preheat the oven to 300°. Make several shallow cuts in the lamb and into them insert the garlic slivers. Season the lamb with the salt, pepper and rosemary. Place it in a roasting pan then dot it with the butter. Surround the lamb with the celery, carrot and onions. Pour the water into the pan. Roast in the oven, allowing 25 minutes per pound. Baste and turn frequently. Add the sherry 30 minutes before the end of the roasting time. Pour off the pan juices and skim the fat. Serve the sauce with the carved lamb.

Marinated Leg of Lamb
Jagnjeći But

To serve 6 to 8

A 7-pound leg of lamb, boned and tied
1 teaspoon salt
1 cup vinegar
2 cups water
3 bay leaves
2 cups sliced onions

6 peppercorns
2 sprigs parsley
½ teaspoon thyme
2 tablespoons lard
4 large fresh tomatoes, coarsely chopped,
    or 1 large can tomatoes, drained
3 slices bacon
Salt

Rub the leg of lamb with the salt and put it in an earthenware or enameled casserole. In a saucepan, combine the vinegar, water, bay leaves, onions, peppercorns, parsley and thyme. Over high heat, bring to a boil, cool to lukewarm, then pour over the lamb. Marinate the lamb, uncovered, in the refrigerator for 6 to 24 hours, turning it every couple of hours.

Preheat the oven to 350°. Remove the lamb from the marinade and pat it dry with paper towels. Heat the lard in a heavy 12-inch skillet until a light haze forms over it, then add the lamb. Cook it for 15 to 20 minutes, or until it is brown, turning it every 5 minutes with two wooden spoons. Place it in a casserole or roasting pan just large enough to hold it. Strain the marinade into a bowl and add the contents of the strainer, 1½ cups of the marinade and the tomatoes to the casserole. Lay the bacon slices over the lamb. Bring the liquid to a boil on top of the

117

stove, then cook, covered, in the middle of the oven for about 2 hours, checking occasionally to see that the liquid is barely bubbling. (Reduce the heat if necessary.) When the meat shows no resistance when pierced with the point of a small sharp knife, remove it to a platter. Strain the cooking juices through a sieve into a saucepan, pressing down hard on the vegetables before discarding them. Skim the surface fat and bring the juices to a boil on top of the stove. Taste for seasoning. To serve, slice the lamb, and arrange it on a serving platter. Mask the slices with some of the sauce and serve the rest in a sauceboat.

Spiced Leg of Lamb
Raan

To serve 6 to 8

2 tablespoons scraped, finely
    chopped fresh ginger root
6 medium-sized garlic cloves, peeled
    and coarsely chopped
The seeds of 2 cardamom pods or
    1/8 teaspoon cardamom seeds
A 1-inch piece of stick cinnamon,
    coarsely crushed with a rolling
    pin or mallet
8 whole cloves
1 teaspoon cumin seeds
1 teaspoon turmeric
1 teaspoon ground hot red pepper

4 teaspoons salt
1/4 cup fresh lemon juice
A 5- to 6-pound leg of lamb,
    trimmed of all fell (parchmentlike
    outer covering) and any excess
    fat
1/2 cup unsalted, unroasted pistachios
1/2 cup seedless raisins
1/4 cup slivered, blanched almonds
1 cup unflavored yoghurt
1/4 cup honey
1/2 teaspoon saffron threads
3 tablespoons plus 1 cup boiling
    water

Combine the ginger, garlic, cardamom, cinnamon, cloves, cumin, turmeric, hot red pepper, salt and lemon juice in the jar of an electric blender. Blend at high speed for 30 seconds, then turn off the machine and scrape down the sides of the jar with a rubber spatula. Blend again until the mixture becomes a smooth purée.

With a small, sharp knife, make about a dozen slashes 1 inch long and 2 inches deep on each side of the leg of lamb. Rub the spice purée over the entire outer surface of the leg, pressing it as deeply into the slashes as possible. Place the lamb in a heavy casserole large enough to hold it comfortably and set it aside to marinate for 30 minutes at room temperature.

Meanwhile purée the pistachios, raisins, almonds and yoghurt in the blender jar, and spread the mixture evenly over the lamb. Drip the honey on top of the leg, cover the casserole tightly, and marinate the lamb in a cool place for about 24 hours, or in the refrigerator for at least 48 hours.

118

Preheat the oven to 350°. Drop the saffron threads into a small bowl, add 3 tablespoons of boiling water, and let them soak for 15 minutes. Pour the saffron and its soaking water over the leg of lamb, and pour the remaining cup of water down the sides of the casserole.

Bring to a boil over high heat, cover tightly, and bake the lamb in the middle of the oven for 1½ hours. Then reduce the heat to 250° and bake 30 minutes longer, or until the lamb is tender and shows no resistance when pierced with the point of a small, sharp knife.

Remove the casserole from the oven, uncover it, and let the lamb cool in the sauce for 1 hour before serving.

Lamb in Dill Sauce
Dillkött på Lamm

To serve 6 to 8

4 pounds breast or shoulder of lamb, cut in 2-inch cubes	Bouquet of 1 bay leaf, 5 sprigs dill and 5 sprigs parsley, tied together with a string
4 to 5 cups water	1 tablespoon salt
	4 whole peppercorns, white if possible

In a heavy 4- to 6-quart casserole that is equipped with a cover, cover the lamb with 4 to 5 cups of cold water and bring it to a boil, uncovered, over high heat. Lower the heat to moderate and with a large spoon skim off and discard the scum as it rises to the surface. Add the bouquet and the salt and peppercorns to the pot. Partially cover the pot and simmer the lamb very slowly for about 1½ hours, or until the meat is tender when pierced with the tip of a sharp knife. With a slotted spoon, remove the lamb to a deep heated platter or casserole, cover with foil and keep warm in a 200° oven.

DILL SAUCE	
2 tablespoons butter	2 teaspoons sugar
2 tablespoons flour	½ teaspoon salt
2½ cups reduced lamb stock *(from above)*	½ teaspoon lemon juice
	Pepper
3 tablespoons chopped fresh dill	1 egg yolk, lightly beaten
1 tablespoon white vinegar	Dill sprigs
	Lemon slices

To make the sauce, strain the lamb stock from the casserole through a fine sieve into a 1½- to 2-quart shallow saucepan and boil it down rapidly over high heat until it is reduced to 2½ cups. Meanwhile, in another 1-quart saucepan, melt the 2 tablespoons of butter. Remove this pan from the heat, stir in the 2 tablespoons of flour, then add all of the reduced lamb stock at once, stirring it rapidly with a wire whisk. Return the pan to the heat and bring the sauce to a boil, whisking constantly, until it is smooth

119

and thick. Simmer the sauce over low heat for about 5 minutes, stirring frequently. Add the chopped dill, vinegar, sugar, salt and lemon juice. Stir a couple of tablespoons of the hot sauce into the beaten egg yolk, then pour this mixture slowly back into the sauce, beating constantly with a wire whisk. Heat through again, but do not let the sauce boil. Taste for seasoning, add salt and pepper if necessary, and strain the sauce through a fine sieve over the lamb. Garnish the platter with additional sprigs of dill and lemon slices, and serve with boiled buttered new potatoes or rice.

Broiled Skewered Lamb
Şiş Kebabi

To serve 4

1 large onion, peeled and cut into 1/8-inch-thick slices and separated into rings
2 tablespoons olive oil
4 tablespoons fresh lemon juice
2 tablespoons salt
1/2 teaspoon freshly ground black pepper

2 pounds lean boneless lamb, preferably from the leg, trimmed of excess fat and cut into 2-inch cubes
1 large, firm, ripe tomato, cut crosswise into four slices
1 large green pepper, cut into quarters, seeded and deribbed
2 tablespoons heavy cream

Drop the onion rings into a deep bowl and sprinkle them with the olive oil, lemon juice, salt and pepper. Add the lamb and turn the pieces about with a spoon to coat them well. Marinate at room temperature for at least 2 hours, or in the refrigerator for 4 hours, turning the lamb occasionally.

Light a layer of coals in a charcoal broiler and let them burn until a white ash appears on the surface, or preheat a stove broiler to its highest point.

Remove the lamb from the marinade and string the cubes tightly on 3 or 4 long skewers, pressing them firmly together. Thread the tomato slices and green pepper quarters alternately on a separate skewer. If you are broiling the lamb in a stove, suspend the skewers side by side across the length of a roasting pan deep enough to allow a 1-inch space below the meat.

Brush the meat evenly on all sides with the cream. Broil 4 inches from the heat, turning the skewers occasionally, until the vegetables brown richly and the lamb is done to your taste. For pink lamb, allow about 10 minutes; for well-done lamb, allow about 15 minutes. Watch the vegetables carefully; they will take less time to cook than the lamb. Slide the lamb off the skewers onto heated individual plates. Serve with the broiled tomato and green pepper.

Broiled skewered lamb, the traditional shish kebab, is varied by adding swordfish and tomatoes with peppers. A delicious flavored rice accompanies.

Braised Lamb and Eggplant
Khoresh Bademjan

To serve 4

1 medium-sized eggplant (about 1 to 1½ pounds)
¼ cup plus 1 teaspoon salt
½ to ¾ cup olive oil
1 medium-sized onion, peeled and cut into ¼-inch-thick slices
1½ pounds lean boneless lamb shoulder, cut into 2-inch cubes
2 cups beef stock, fresh or canned, or 2 cups water
2 tablespoons tomato paste
½ teaspoon turmeric
Freshly ground black pepper
1 medium-sized tomato, cut crosswise into 4 slices
2 tablespoons fresh lemon juice
1 tablespoon bottled pomegranate syrup (optional)

With a large, sharp knife peel the eggplant and cut off its stem end. Slice the eggplant lengthwise into quarters, then cut the quarters lengthwise in half to make 8 long strips. Combine 1 quart of water and ¼ cup of the salt in a shallow bowl or baking dish, add the eggplant and turn the strips about with a spoon to moisten them thoroughly with the brine. Soak at room temperature for about 10 minutes.

Meanwhile, in a heavy 12-inch skillet, heat ½ cup of olive oil over moderate heat until a light haze forms above it. Add the onions and, stirring frequently, cook for about 10 minutes, or until they are deeply browned. Then transfer them with a slotted spoon to a plate and set aside.

Drain the eggplant strips through a sieve and pat them dry with paper towels. Heat the oil remaining in the skillet over high heat. Add the eggplant strips and brown them thoroughly on both sides, adding more oil to the pan if necessary. Transfer the strips to a plate and set them aside. Brown the lamb cubes well in the same pan, again adding more oil if needed. Then add the stock or water, tomato paste, turmeric, the remaining teaspoon of salt, and a few grindings of pepper. Bring to a boil over high heat, meanwhile scraping in the brown particles clinging to the bottom and sides of the pan. Add the reserved onions, reduce the heat to low, and simmer tightly covered for 45 minutes.

Arrange the strips of eggplant side by side on top of the lamb and place the tomato slices over them. Pour in the lemon juice and the pomegranate syrup, if you are using it. Cover tightly again and simmer for about 45 minutes longer, or until the eggplant and lamb are tender.

Taste for seasoning and serve at once from a deep heated platter or bowl.

Braised Lamb with Lemon Sauce

Abbacchio Brodettatto

To serve 6

2 ounces fresh pork fat, diced
  (about ½ cup)
2 pounds boneless lamb shoulder,
  cut in 1½-inch chunks
½ teaspoon salt
Freshly ground black pepper
3 tablespoons flour

½ teaspoon finely chopped garlic
½ cup dry white wine
3 cups beef stock, fresh or canned
1 bay leaf
2 egg yolks
1 tablespoon lemon juice
2 tablespoons finely chopped fresh
  parsley

Preheat the oven to 500°. Fry the diced pork fat in a heavy 10- to 12-inch skillet over high heat, stirring frequently, until the dice are crisp and brown. Remove them with a slotted spoon and discard them. In the fat remaining in the skillet, brown the lamb, 4 or 5 chunks at a time. As the chunks become golden brown on all sides, transfer them to a heavy 2½- to 3-quart flameproof casserole. Then pour off all but a thin film of fat from the skillet and set the pan aside; it will be used again.

Sprinkle the lamb with salt and a few grindings of pepper, and add the flour, tossing the meat with a wooden spoon to coat the chunks as evenly as possible with the seasoning and flour. Place the casserole in the upper third of the oven and brown the lamb uncovered, turning it 2 or 3 times, for about 10 minutes, or until no trace of gummy flour remains and the chunks are lightly crusted. Remove from the oven, and reduce the heat to 350°.

In the fat remaining in the skillet, cook the garlic over moderate heat, stirring constantly for 1 minute. Pour in the wine and boil briskly until it is reduced to ¼ cup. Scrape in any browned bits clinging to the bottom and sides of the skillet. Stir in the stock and bring to a boil, then pour the entire contents of the skillet over the chunks of lamb in the casserole. Bring the casserole to a boil on top of the stove. Add the bay leaf, cover the casserole and cook in the middle of the oven for 1½ hours, or until the lamb is tender. Transfer the lamb to a heated platter, and cover it lightly with foil to keep it warm. Strain the braising stock through a fine sieve into a small saucepan. Let the stock settle, then skim the fat from the surface. In a small bowl, beat the egg yolks and lemon juice together with a whisk, and stir in 2 tablespoons of the hot stock. Add 2 more tablespoons of stock, stirring constantly, then whisk the now warmed egg-yolk-and-lemon mixture into the stock remaining in the pan. Over moderate heat, bring this sauce to a boil, stirring constantly, and cook it for 30 seconds, or until it is thick enough to coat the wires of the whisk lightly. Taste for seasoning. Pour the sauce over the lamb, sprinkle with parsley and serve.

Fricassee of Lamb with Lemon and Garlic
Cochifrito

To serve 4

2 pounds lean boneless shoulder of
   lamb, cut into 1-inch cubes
Salt
Freshly ground black pepper
¼ cup olive oil

1 cup finely chopped onions
½ teaspoon finely chopped garlic
1 tablespoon paprika
2 tablespoons finely chopped parsley
2 tablespoons fresh lemon juice

Sprinkle the lamb liberally with salt and a few grindings of pepper. In a heavy 10- to 12-inch skillet, heat the olive oil over high heat until a light haze forms above it. Add the lamb and brown it well, turning the pieces with tongs and regulating the heat so that the meat colors evenly without burning. With a slotted spoon, transfer the lamb to a plate.

Add the onions and garlic to the fat remaining in the skillet and, stirring frequently, cook for about 5 minutes, or until the onions are soft and transparent but not brown. Stir in the paprika, then return the lamb and any juices that have collected around it to the skillet. Add the parsley and lemon juice and reduce the heat to low. Cover tightly and simmer for about 1 hour, or until the lamb is tender and shows no resistance when pierced with the point of a small, sharp knife. Taste for seasoning and serve at once.

Lamb with String Beans
Lubya Khadra Billahma

To serve 4

2 pounds green string beans,
   trimmed and cut into 2-inch
   lengths
3 tablespoons olive oil
1 pound boneless stewing lamb, cut
   into 1-inch cubes
1 cup finely chopped onions
6 medium-sized, fresh, ripe
   tomatoes, peeled, seeded and

   coarsely chopped, or substitute
   2 cups chopped, drained, canned
   tomatoes
1 teaspoon salt
Freshly ground black pepper
½ teaspoon ground nutmeg,
   preferably freshly grated
½ teaspoon ground allspice

Spread the beans evenly in the bottom of a heavy 4- to 6-quart casserole, and set aside. In a heavy 10- to 12-inch skillet, heat the oil over moderate heat until a light haze forms above it. Add the lamb and brown it, turning the pieces frequently with a spoon and regulating the heat so they color deeply and evenly without burning. As they brown, transfer the pieces of lamb to the casserole, placing them on top of the beans.

Pour off all but a thin film of fat from the skillet, and in it cook the onions over moderate heat for 5 minutes, or until they are soft and transparent but not brown. Spread the onions over the lamb and cover them with the tomatoes. Sprinkle the top with salt, a few grindings of the pepper, the nutmeg and allspice. Place the casserole over low heat, cover tightly, and simmer without stirring for 1 hour, or until the beans and meat are tender. Serve at once.

Lamb, Chick-Pea and Bean Casserole
Dizi

To serve 4

1 cup chick-peas (garbanzos),
    preferably the small imported
    Italian chick-peas
1 cup dried broad beans (favas), or
    substitute other small dried beans
2 pounds lean boneless lamb
    shoulder, cut into 2-inch cubes
1 pound lamb bones, sawed, not
    chopped, into 1-inch-long pieces
2 medium-sized onions, peeled and

quartered
1 quart water
1 tablespoon salt
Freshly ground black pepper
1 medium-sized fresh, ripe tomato,
    peeled, seeded and finely chopped
    or ⅓ cup chopped, drained,
    canned tomatoes
2 tablespoons fresh lemon juice
½ teaspoon turmeric
¼ cup finely chopped onions

Starting a day ahead, wash the chick-peas in a sieve under cold running water, then place them in a large bowl or pan and add enough water to cover them by 2 inches. Soak at room temperature for at least 12 hours. Drain the peas in a sieve or colander.

In a heavy 2- to 3-quart saucepan, bring 1 quart of water to a boil over high heat. Drop in the beans and boil briskly for 2 minutes. Turn off the heat and let the beans soak for 1 hour. Drain and set the beans aside.

Spread out the lamb and lamb bones on the bottom of a heavy 3- to 4-quart casserole, arrange the onion quarters on top, and cover them with the chick-peas and the beans. Add 1 quart of fresh water, the salt and a few grindings of pepper. Bring to a boil over high heat, meanwhile skimming off the scum and foam as they rise to the surface. Reduce the heat to low, cover tightly and simmer for 1 hour. Stir in the tomato, lemon juice, and turmeric and simmer tightly covered for about 1½ hours longer, or until the chick-peas and beans are tender but still intact. (Check the casserole from time to time and add more water when necessary; the ingredients should be covered with liquid throughout the cooking period.) Taste for seasoning.

To serve, discard the bones, and transfer the meat to a plate. Strain the broth into a tureen, place the beans in a bowl and, with the back of a spoon, mash them to a purée. Stir in the chopped onions, then spread the purée on a deep heated platter and scatter meat over it. Traditionally, the broth is served first, followed by the beans and meat as a separate course.

A rich and pungent Iranian stew, *dizi* is made with lamb, chick-peas, tomato, onions, turmeric and fava beans.

Lamb and Vegetable Stew

Cazuela de Cordero

To serve 6

2 tablespoons vegetable oil
2 teaspoons paprika
6 shoulder lamb chops, or 3 lamb
    shanks sawed in half lengthwise
6 cups water
6 medium boiling potatoes, peeled
2 large carrots, scraped and cut
    crosswise into 2- to 3-inch pieces
1 onion, peeled and quartered
1½ pounds unpeeled winter squash,
    scrubbed and cut into 6 pieces
1 large garlic clove, peeled

½ teaspoon freshly ground black
    pepper
⅛ teaspoon dried oregano
1 cup fresh string beans, trimmed,
    washed and cut into 2-inch lengths
3 tablespoons raw long-grain rice
3 ears corn, shucked and cut in half
    crosswise
½ pound fresh green peas, shelled,
    or ½ cup thoroughly defrosted
    frozen peas
2 teaspoons salt
1 tablespoon finely chopped fresh
    parsley

In a heavy 5-quart casserole, heat the oil over high heat, tipping the casserole to coat the bottom evenly, and turning the heat down to moderate if the oil begins to smoke. Stir in the paprika, then add the lamb and brown it well on all sides, turning the pieces frequently with tongs. Pour in the water, and bring it to a boil, then add the potatoes, carrots, onion, squash, garlic, black pepper and oregano. Reduce the heat to low, cover the casserole and simmer undisturbed for 15 minutes. Add the string beans and rice, stirring gently once or twice, and cook covered for 30 minutes. Add the corn, peas and salt. Cook covered for 5 minutes more. Sprinkle the stew with chopped parsley and serve directly from the casserole.

Lamb Chops in Wine

To serve 4

3 tablespoons butter
4 thick loin lamb chops
8 small white onions
8 small pieces of carrot

½ cup water
½ pound sliced mushrooms
½ cup white wine
Salt
Pepper
Lemon juice

Heat 1 tablespoon of the butter in a large skillet, add the chops and brown them on both sides. Remove the chops, melt the remaining 2 tablespoons of butter in the pan, and brown the onions and carrot pieces over a moderate fire, shaking the pan often to brown them evenly. Stir in the water, scraping the pan to blend in all the particles. Put back the chops, add the sliced mushrooms, white wine, and salt and pepper to taste. Cover and simmer for 30 minutes. Just before serving sprinkle the chops with a little lemon juice.

Make a bed of the vegetables and sauce on a hot serving dish. Arrange the chops down the center of the dish and serve immediately.

Braised Lamb Shanks

To serve 4

	2 tablespoons olive oil
3 tablespoons flour	1 large onion, thinly sliced
Salt	¾ cup red wine
Paprika	1¼ cups water
4 lamb shanks, about 1 pound each	¼ teaspoon chopped fresh rosemary
2 tablespoons butter	Pepper

Preheat the oven to 375°. Season 1 tablespoon of the flour with salt and a little paprika and lightly dust the shanks. Heat the butter and olive oil in a deep heavy saucepan and brown the shanks all over. Remove them from the pan and lightly brown the onion in the pan juices. Return the meat to the pan, adding the wine, ¾ cup of water and the chopped fresh rosemary. Season with salt and pepper. Cover and cook in the oven for about 2 hours, or until the meat is tender enough to be easily pierced with a fork.

Remove the lamb shanks. Blend the remaining flour with the remaining ½ cup of water, add to the pan liquid and stir over the fire until the gravy thickens and comes to a boil. Simmer for 2 to 3 minutes, then strain.

The shanks can be served as they are on a hot platter, with the gravy in a separate gravy boat; or the meat can be cut from the bones and arranged on a hot serving dish, spooning a little of the gravy over the meat and serving the rest separately.

Roast Lamb Shanks and Lentils

To serve 4

	2 tablespoons butter
2 cloves garlic cut into paper-thin slivers	½ cup finely chopped onion
	2½ cups beef stock, fresh or canned
4 meaty lamb shanks (about 1 pound each)	2½ cups lentils, thoroughly washed and drained
Salt	1 bay leaf
Freshly ground black pepper	½ cup chopped scallions
3 tablespoons vegetable oil	¼ cup chopped fresh parsley

Preheat the oven to 350°. With the point of a small, sharp knife, insert 2 or 3 garlic slivers into the meaty portion of each lamb shank. Then sprinkle the shanks generously with salt and a few grindings of black pepper. In a 12-inch heavy skillet, heat the oil over high heat until a light haze forms over it. Add the shanks, and then, over moderate heat, cook them on all sides for about 10 minutes, turning them with tongs. When the shanks are a deep golden brown, transfer them to a rack set in a shallow roasting pan. Roast them in the middle of the oven for about an hour, or until the shanks are tender. Basting is unnecessary.

While the shanks are roasting, melt 2 tablespoons of butter over moderate heat in a 2- to 4-quart saucepan. When the foam subsides add the onions and cook them for about 6 minutes, stirring frequently until they are transparent but not brown. Pour in the stock and add the lentils, bay leaf, salt and a few grindings of black pepper. Bring to a boil. Cover the pot and reduce the heat to its lowest point. Simmer the lentils, stirring occasionally, for about 30 minutes, or until they are very tender.

To serve, stir into the lentils 2 tablespoons of drippings from the roasting pan and ½ cup of chopped scallions. Taste for seasoning. Arrange the lamb and lentils on a heated platter and sprinkle with parsley.

Lamb Shanks with Tomato Sauce
Lahma Bisalsat Tamatim

To serve 4

1 tablespoon olive oil	Freshly ground black pepper
4 lean, meaty lamb shanks, each about ¾ pound	A pinch of cayenne pepper
2 medium-sized onions, cut into ¼-inch-thick slices	9 medium-sized, fresh, ripe tomatoes, peeled, seeded and finely chopped, or substitute 3
1 teaspoon allspice	cups chopped, drained, canned
½ teaspoon ground nutmeg	tomatoes
1 teaspoon salt	3 cups water

Preheat the oven to 450°. Using a pastry brush apply the tablespoon of olive oil to the bottom of a baking dish large enough to hold the lamb shanks comfortably in one layer. Place the shanks in the dish and bake in the middle of the oven for 30 minutes, turning the pieces occasionally so that they color evenly on all sides.

Remove the dish from the oven and spread the onion slices over the lamb. Sprinkle them with the allspice, nutmeg, salt, a few grindings of black pepper, cayenne, and spread the tomatoes on top. Pour in the water and bring to a boil on top of the stove. Bake on the lowest shelf of the oven for 1 hour, or until the lamb is tender and shows no resistance when pierced with the point of a small, sharp knife. Serve directly from the baking dish or arrange the shanks on a heated platter and pour the sauce over them.

Lancashire Hot Pot

To serve 6

1 tablespoon butter, softened, plus 1 tablespoon butter, cut into ¼-inch bits
6 medium-sized potatoes, peeled and cut crosswise into ¼-inch slices
6 lean shoulder lamb chops (about 2 pounds), each cut about 1 inch thick and trimmed of all fat
1 teaspoon salt
Freshly ground black pepper
6 lamb kidneys, membranes removed, trimmed of all fat, and cut crosswise into ¼-inch slices
6 shucked oysters (optional)
½ pound fresh mushrooms, including stems, cut lengthwise into ¼-inch slices
3 medium-sized onions (about 1 pound), peeled and cut crosswise into ⅛-inch slices
2 cups water
1 tablespoon finely chopped parsley

Preheat the oven to 350°. Using a pastry brush, coat the bottom and sides of a 4- to 5-quart casserole at least 6 inches deep with the 1 tablespoon of softened butter. Spread about one third of the potato slices evenly over the bottom of the casserole, and place 3 lamb chops side by side on top. Sprinkle the chops with ½ teaspoon of the salt and a few grindings of pepper. Add half the kidneys, 3 oysters, half the mushrooms and half the onions, and cover with another third of the potatoes. Place the 3 remaining chops on the potatoes and sprinkle them with the remaining salt and a few grindings of pepper. Add the remaining kidneys, oysters, mushrooms and onions, and spread the rest of the potatoes evenly over the top. Pour in the water. Dot with the bits of butter. Cover and bake in the middle of the oven for 1½ hours. Remove the cover and bake for 30 minutes longer, or until the top is brown. Sprinkle with parsley and serve directly from the casserole.

Lamb and Beef Rolls
Ćevapčići

To serve 6

1 tablespoon lard
½ cup finely chopped onions
½ teaspoon finely chopped garlic
1 pound ground lamb
1 pound ground beef chuck

1 egg white, lightly beaten
1 teaspoon salt
1 tablespoon sweet Hungarian
   paprika
2 tablespoons lard (optional)
2 tablespoons very finely chopped
   onions

Heat the lard in an 8-inch skillet over high heat until a light haze forms over it. Reduce the heat to medium, add the onions and garlic and, stirring occasionally, cook them for 6 to 8 minutes, or until the onions are lightly colored. Scrape them into a large mixing bowl.

Add the lamb, beef, egg white, salt and paprika. Mix well with your hands or a wooden spoon.

Shape the mixture into small cylinders approximately 1 inch in diameter and 2 inches long and arrange them on a plate. Cover the plate with wax paper or plastic wrap and then refrigerate it for at least an hour before cooking, or until the meat mixture has become firm.

Arrange the cylinders on 6- to 10-inch metal skewers, 4 or 5 to a skewer, leaving at least ¼ inch space between them and running the skewers through the sides, not the ends, of the cylinders.

Like most other meats cooked on skewers (kabobs) this Yugoslav favorite can be cooked in one of three ways.

Broil the *ćevapčići* on a charcoal grill or in a preheated oven broiler that is 4 to 6 inches from the flame. Another method is to fry them over high heat in a heavy 12-inch skillet in which 2 tablespoons of lard have been heated to the smoking point. If the *ćevapčići* are broiled on a grill or in an oven broiler, cook them about 8 minutes on each side, or until they are dark brown on the outside and well done on the inside. If *ćevapčići* are cooked in a skillet, they should be turned every so often, a skewerful at a time, with a wide metal spatula.

Ćevapčići may be served on the skewers so that the diners may remove them or they may be removed from the skewers before serving. Sprinkle the meat sausage rolls with the finely chopped onion just before serving.

Lamb Pies

Sfeeha

To make about 16 pies

DOUGH

2¼ to 2¾ cups lukewarm water (110° to 115°)

2 packages active dry yeast

A pinch of sugar

8 cups all-purpose flour

2 teaspoons salt

¼ cup olive oil

Make the dough in the following fashion: Pour ¼ cup of the lukewarm water into a small, shallow bowl and sprinkle it with the yeast and sugar. Let the mixture rest for 2 or 3 minutes, then stir to dissolve the yeast completely. Set the bowl in a warm, draft-free place (such as a turned-off oven) for about 5 minutes, or until the mixture almost doubles in volume.

In a deep mixing bowl, combine the flour and the 2 teaspoons of salt, make a well in the center and into it pour the yeast mixture, the ¼ cup of olive oil, and 2 cups of the remaining lukewarm water. Gently stir the center ingredients together with a large spoon, then slowly incorporate the flour and continue to beat until the ingredients are well combined. Add up to ½ cup more water, beating it in a tablespoon at a time, and using as much as necessary to form a dough that can be gathered into a compact ball.

Place the dough on a lightly floured surface and knead it by pressing it down, pushing it forward several times with the heel of your hand and folding it back on itself. Repeat for about 20 minutes, or until the dough is smooth and elastic. Sprinkle it from time to time with a little flour to prevent it from sticking to the board.

Shape the dough into a ball and place it in a lightly oiled bowl. Drape loosely with a kitchen towel and set aside in the warm, draft-free place for 45 minutes to 1 hour, or until the dough doubles in bulk. Punch the dough down with a single blow of your fist and divide it into 16 equal pieces. Roll each piece into a ball, cover with a towel and let them rest for 30 minutes.

Meanwhile, prepare the filling. Drop the onions into a deep bowl and sprinkle them with 1 tablespoon of the salt, turning them about with a spoon to coat them evenly. Let the onions rest at room temperature for at least 30 minutes, then squeeze them dry and return them to the bowl.

FILLING

2 cups finely chopped onions

1 tablespoon plus 2 teaspoons salt

4 tablespoons olive oil

½ cup pine nuts (pignolia)

2 pounds lean boneless lamb, coarsely ground

2 medium-sized fresh, ripe tomatoes, peeled, seeded and finely chopped

½ cup finely chopped green pepper

½ cup finely chopped parsley, preferably flat-leaf parsley

½ cup fresh lemon juice

¼ cup red wine vinegar

1 tablespoon tomato paste

1 teaspoon cayenne pepper

1 teaspoon allspice

2 teaspoons salt

Freshly ground black pepper

In a small skillet or saucepan, heat 1 tablespoon of olive oil until a light haze forms above it. Add the pine nuts and, stirring constantly, brown them lightly. Add them to the bowl of onions, along with the lamb, tomatoes, green pepper, parsley, lemon juice, vinegar, tomato paste, cayenne pepper, allspice, 2 teaspoons of salt and a liberal grinding of black pepper. Knead the mixture vigorously with both hands, then beat with a wooden spoon until the mixture is smooth and fluffy. Taste for seasoning.

Preheat the oven to 500°. With a pastry brush, coat 3 large baking sheets or jelly-roll pans with the remaining 3 tablespoons of oil.

On a lightly floured surface, roll each of the balls into a round about 4 inches in diameter and no more than ⅛ inch thick. To make open-faced pies, spoon about ½ cup of the lamb filling mixture on the center of each round. Then spread the filling to about ½ inch of the edge.

To make closed pies, spoon about ½ cup of the filling on the center of each round. Pull up the edge from 3 equally distant points to make a roughly triangular-shaped pie and pinch the dough securely together at the top.

With a metal spatula, arrange the pies on the baking sheets. Bake in the lower third of the oven for 30 minutes, or until the pastry is lightly browned. Serve hot, or at room temperature, accompanied, if you like, with yoghurt.

Pork & Ham

Crown Roast of Pork

To serve 10 to 12

STUFFING
3 tablespoons butter
¾ cup finely chopped onion
¼ cup finely chopped celery
½ cup peeled, cored and coarsely diced tart apples
½ cup fresh bread crumbs
1 pound ground pork (the crown roast trimmings plus extra pork, if necessary)

½ pound well-seasoned sausage meat
½ cup finely chopped parsley
½ teaspoon sage
1½ teaspoons salt
Freshly ground black pepper

A crown roast of pork, consisting of 22 chops and weighing 8 to 9 pounds

Preheat the oven to 350°. For the stuffing, melt the butter over moderate heat in an 8- to 10-inch skillet. When the foam subsides, add the onion and cook, stirring frequently, for about 5 minutes, then add the celery and apples. Cook without browning about 5 minutes longer. Scrape the contents of the pan into a large mixing bowl. Add the bread crumbs, ground pork, sausage meat, parsley, sage, salt and a few grindings of black pepper. With a large spoon, mix all the ingredients together.

Fill the center of the crown with the stuffing, mounding it slightly. Cover it with a round of foil and wrap the ends of the chop bones in strips of foil to prevent them from charring and snapping off. Place the crown on a rack in a shallow roasting pan just about large enough to hold it comfortably, and roast it in the center of the oven, undisturbed, for about 3 hours, or until a meat thermometer, if you have used one, reads 170° to 175°. One half hour before the pork is done, remove the circle of foil from the top of the stuffing to allow the top to brown.

Carefully transfer the crown to a large, heated, circular platter, strip the foil from the ends of the chops and replace it with paper frills. Let the crown rest for about 10 minutes before carving and serving.

134

Glazed Roast Loin of Pork

Rôti de Porc Boulangère

To serve 6

2 teaspoons salt

1 teaspoon coarsely ground black
  pepper

2 teaspoons finely cut fresh rosemary
  or 1½ teaspoons dried rosemary,
  crumbled

A 3-pound center-cut pork loin with
  the chine bone (backbone) sawed
  through but still attached, and
  circumference of loin tied in 2 or 3
  places

3 onions, coarsely chopped

2 carrots, cut in 1-inch chunks

Bouquet garni made of

4 parsley sprigs and
  1 bay leaf, tied together

2 tablespoons butter

2 medium onions, thinly sliced

6 large firm boiling-type potatoes,
  cut in ¼-inch slices

Salt

Freshly ground black pepper

½ cup heated chicken stock, fresh
  or canned

1½ cups hot beef or chicken stock,
  fresh or canned, or a combination
  of both

2 tablespoons finely chopped fresh
  parsley

Preheat the oven to 475°. Combine the salt, pepper and rosemary, and press the mixture firmly into the pork roast. Place the seasoned pork, fat side up, in a heavy casserole just large enough to hold the pork. Roast uncovered on the middle shelf of the oven, turning the meat over 2 or 3 times, for 20 to 30 minutes, or until the pork is lightly browned. Then reduce the oven to 325°. Scatter the chopped onions, carrots and the *bouquet garni* around the pork, cover the casserole, and roast for 40 minutes longer, basting the pork every 10 minutes with the pan juices.

Meanwhile butter the bottom and sides of a shallow baking-and-serving dish about 12 inches long and 1½ to 2 inches deep. Melt 2 tablespoons of butter in an 8- to 10-inch skillet, and in it cook the onions over moderate heat, stirring frequently, for 10 minutes, or until they are limp and lightly colored. When the pork is ready, spread the potato slices over the bottom of the baking dish and season with salt and pepper. Scatter the onions over the potato slices and pour in the heated stock. Place the pork loin on top and moisten both the pork and the potatoes with 2 or 3 tablespoons of fat skimmed from the drippings in the casserole. Roast uncovered in the bottom third of the oven for another 1¼ hours, or until the pork is crusty and glazed, and the vegetables are tender and brown.

While the pork is roasting, add 1½ cups of stock to the drippings left in the casserole. Bring to a boil over high heat and cook for 5 minutes, stirring frequently and scraping in any browned bits that cling to the bottom and sides of the pan. Strain the mixture through a fine sieve into a saucepan, pressing down hard on the vegetables before discarding them. Skim off the surface fat. Season with salt and pepper. Set aside in the pan.

135

To serve, transfer the roast to a carving board, cut off the strings and slice the roast into 8 chops. Reheat the sauce made from the casserole drippings. Return the chops to the baking dish and arrange them in a line over the potatoes and onions. Moisten the pork with a little sauce and dust the potatoes with parsley. Serve the remaining sauce in a sauceboat.

Pork Loin Stuffed with Prunes and Apples
Mørbrad med Svedsker og Aebler

To serve 6 to 8

	Salt
4½- to 5-pound boned loin of pork, center cut	Freshly ground black pepper
	3 tablespoons butter
12 medium-sized pitted prunes	3 tablespoons vegetable oil
1 large tart apple, peeled, cored and cut into 1-inch cubes	¾ cup dry white wine
	¾ cup heavy cream
1 teaspoon lemon juice	1 tablespoon red currant jelly

Place the prunes in a saucepan, cover with cold water, and bring to a boil. Remove from the heat and let the prunes soak in the water for 30 minutes. Then drain, pat dry with paper towels, and set aside. Sprinkle the cubed apple with lemon juice to prevent discoloring. With a strong, sharp knife, make a pocket in the pork by cutting a deep slit down the length of the loin, going to within ½ inch of the two ends and to within 1 inch of the other side. Season the pocket lightly with salt and pepper and stuff it with the prunes and apples, sewing up the opening with strong kitchen thread. Tie the loin at 1-inch intervals to keep its shape while cooking. An alternative method of stuffing the loin is described opposite.

Preheat the oven to 350°. In a casserole equipped with a cover and just large enough to hold the loin of pork comfortably, melt the butter and oil over moderate heat. When the foam subsides, add the loin, turning it from time to time with 2 wooden spoons. It should take about 20 minutes to brown the loin evenly on all sides. With a bulb baster or large spoon, remove all the fat from the pan. Pour in the wine, stir in the heavy cream, whisking briskly, and bring to a simmer on top of the stove. Cover the pan and cook in the center of the oven for 1½ hours, or until the meat shows no resistance when pierced with the tip of a sharp knife.

Remove the loin from the pan and let it rest on a heated platter while you finish the sauce. Skim the fat from the liquid in the pan and bring the liquid to a boil. When it has reduced to about 1 cup, stir in the red currant jelly, reduce the heat and, stirring constantly, simmer briefly until the sauce is smooth. Taste for seasoning and pour into a heated sauceboat. Cut away the strings from the loin, then carve the meat into 1-inch slices. Each slice of meat will surround a portion of the stuffing. Pass the sauce separately.

136

Pierce a loin of pork with a long, sharp
tool—here, a steel knife sharpener.

Fill the tunnel you have made in the
loin with prunes and apples.

Pack in the fruit tightly with a blunt,
round tool, such as a wooden-spoon
handle.

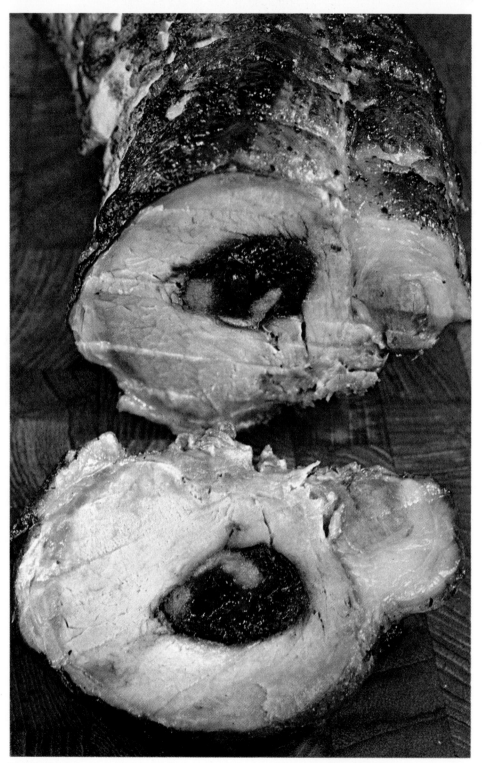

Each slice of the roasted loin has its own built-in decorative core of prunes and apples.

The sweetness of peppers melds with pungent garlic-marinated pork and lemon in the Portuguese dish called *lombo de porco com pimentos vermelhos doces.*

Pork Loin with Sweet Red Peppers
Lombo de Porco com Pimentos Vermelhos Doces

To serve 4 to 6

1 tablespoon finely chopped garlic
1 teaspoon salt, preferably coarse
   salt
½ teaspoon freshly ground black
   pepper
2 pounds boneless pork loin, cut
   into ¼-inch-thick slices
¼ cup lard
4 medium-sized sweet red peppers,

seeded, deribbed and cut
   lengthwise into ½-inch-wide
   strips, or substitute 1½ cups
   drained, canned pimientos, cut
   lengthwise into ½-inch strips
1 cup dry white wine
½ cup chicken stock, fresh or canned
1 lemon, cut lengthwise into 8
   wedges

With a mortar and pestle or the back of a large heavy spoon, mash the garlic, salt and pepper together to a smooth paste. Lightly spread the pork slices with the paste, place them in a bowl and toss with a spoon. Cover tightly and marinate at room temperature for 2 or 3 hours, or in the refrigerator for 6 hours, turning the pork about in the bowl from time to time.

In a heavy 10- to 12-inch skillet, melt the lard over high heat. Brown the pork in the hot fat (in two or three batches if necessary), turning the slices with tongs and regulating the heat so that the slices color quickly and evenly on both sides without burning. As they brown, transfer them to a plate.

Add the red peppers to the fat remaining in the pan and, stirring frequently, cook them for about 5 minutes, or until they are well coated with the fat but not brown. (The canned pimiento strips need only be cooked until they are coated with fat.) Transfer the peppers to the plate with the meat. Pour off all but a thin film of fat from the skillet and add the wine and stock. Bring to a boil over high heat, meanwhile scraping into the liquid any brown particles clinging to the bottom and sides of the pan.

Return the pork and peppers to the skillet, cover tightly, and reduce the heat to low. Simmer for about 25 minutes, or until the pork is tender and shows no resistance when pierced with the point of a small, sharp knife.

With a slotted spoon, transfer the pork and peppers to a deep, heated platter. Bring the liquid remaining in the skillet to a boil over high heat, stirring constantly and cook briskly until it thickens lightly. Taste for seasoning, then pour the sauce over the meat. Serve garnished with lemon wedges.

Transylvanian Goulash
Székely Gulyás

To serve 4 to 6

1 pound sauerkraut, fresh, canned or packaged	3 cups chicken stock or water
2 tablespoons lard	2 pounds boneless shoulder of pork, cut into 1-inch cubes
1 cup finely chopped onions	1½ teaspoons caraway seeds
¼ teaspoon finely chopped garlic	¼ cup tomato purée
2 tablespoons sweet Hungarian paprika	Salt
	½ cup sour cream
	½ cup heavy cream
	2 tablespoons flour

Wash the sauerkraut thoroughly under cold running water, then soak it in cold water for 10 to 20 minutes to reduce its sourness.

Melt the lard in a 5-quart casserole and add the onions. Cook them over moderate heat, stirring occasionally, for 6 to 8 minutes, or until they are lightly colored, then add the garlic and cook a minute or 2 longer. Off the heat, stir in the paprika, continuing to stir until the onions are well coated. Pour in ½ cup of the stock or water and bring it to a boil, then add the pork cubes.

Now spread the sauerkraut over the pork and sprinkle it with the caraway seeds. In a small bowl, combine the tomato purée and the rest of the stock or water, and pour the mixture over the sauerkraut. Bring the liquid to a boil once more, then reduce the heat to its lowest point, cover the casserole tightly and simmer for 1 hour. Check every now and then to make sure the liquid has not cooked away. Add a little stock or water if it has; the sauerkraut should be moist.

When the pork is tender, combine the sour cream and heavy cream in a mixing bowl. Beat the flour into the cream with a wire whisk, then carefully stir this mixture into the casserole. Simmer for 10 minutes longer. Taste for seasoning. Serve Transylvanian goulash in deep individual plates, accompanied by a bowl of sour cream.

Sweet-and-Sour Pork

T'ien-suan-ku-lao-jou

To serve 2 to 4

1 pound lean boneless pork,
    preferably butt
1 egg, lightly beaten
1 teaspoon salt
¼ cup cornstarch
¼ cup flour
¼ cup chicken stock, fresh or canned
3 cups peanut oil, or flavorless
    vegetable oil

SAUCE
1 tablespoon peanut oil, or flavorless
    vegetable oil

1 teaspoon finely chopped garlic
1 large green pepper, seeded, deribbed
    and cut into ½ inch squares
1 medium carrot, scraped and sliced
    into 2-inch strips ¼ inch wide and
    ¼ inch thick
½ cup chicken stock, fresh or canned
4 tablespoons sugar
4 tablespoons red-wine vinegar
1 teaspoon soy sauce
1 tablespoon cornstarch dissolved in
    2 tablespoons cold water

PREPARE AHEAD: 1. Trim the pork of any excess fat and, with a cleaver or sharp knife, cut the meat into 1-inch cubes.

2. In a large bowl, mix together the egg, ¼ cup cornstarch, ¼ cup flour, ¼ cup chicken stock and salt. Set aside.

3. For the sauce, have the oil, garlic, green pepper, carrot, chicken stock, sugar, vinegar, soy sauce and cornstarch mixture within easy reach.

TO COOK: Just before cooking, add the pork cubes to the egg and flour mixture, and stir until each piece of meat is well coated. Preheat the oven to 250°. Pour the 3 cups of oil into a wok and set it over high heat. When the oil almost begins to smoke or reaches 375° on a deep-frying thermometer, drop in half of the coated pork cubes one by one. Fry

Sweet-and-sour pork—a photograph of which is superimposed here on an old Chinese painting—is made with pork, green pepper, carrot, sugar and vinegar.

for 5 to 6 minutes, regulating the heat so that the pork turns a crisp, golden brown in that period without burning. Remove the pork with a strainer or slotted spoon to a small baking dish and keep it warm in the oven. Fry the other half and add to the first batch.

To make the sauce, pour off any oil remaining in the wok or use a 10-inch skillet. Set the pan over high heat for about 30 seconds. Pour in the tablespoon of oil, swirl it about in the pan and heat for another 30 seconds, turning the heat down to moderate if the oil begins to smoke. Add the garlic, then the green pepper and carrot, and stir-fry for 2 to 3 minutes until the pepper and carrot darken somewhat in color. Be careful not to let them burn. Pour in the ½ cup of chicken stock, the sugar, vinegar and soy sauce, and bring to a boil. Boil rapidly for about 1 minute, or until the sugar has thoroughly dissolved. Immediately give the cornstarch mixture a quick stir to recombine it and add it to the pan. Cook a moment longer, stirring constantly. When the sauce is thick and clear, pour the entire contents of the pan over the fried pork and serve at once.

VARIATION: Sweet-and-sour shrimp is made in precisely the same way—with identical batter and sauce. Shell and devein 1 pound of fresh or defrosted frozen shrimp and substitute them for the pork in this recipe.

Pork and Veal Stew with Green Tomatoes
Tinga de Cerdo y Ternera

To serve 6

3 tablespoons lard
1½ pounds lean boneless veal, cut into 2-inch cubes
1½ pounds lean boneless pork, cut into 2-inch cubes
2 cups chicken stock, fresh or canned
½ cup coarsely chopped onions
¼ teaspoon finely chopped garlic

A 10-ounce can Mexican green tomatoes, drained
3 canned *chipotle* chilies, rinsed in cold water and cut lengthwise into ⅛-inch strips
½ teaspoon thyme
½ teaspoon marjoram
1 teaspoon salt
¼ teaspoon freshly ground black pepper

In a heavy 10- to 12-inch skillet, melt 2 tablespoons of the lard over moderate heat until a light haze forms above it. Add the veal cubes and brown them, turning the pieces frequently and regulating the heat so that the cubes brown quickly and evenly without burning. Transfer them to a heavy 3-quart flameproof casserole and brown the pork in the fat remaining in the skillet. Drain the pork and add it to the veal in the casserole; set the skillet aside. Pour the 2 cups of stock over the meat, bring it to a boil over high heat, then reduce the heat to low. Cover the pan and simmer the meat undisturbed for 45 minutes. Pour all the cooking juices from the casserole into a bowl; set the casserole of meat aside.

Over moderate heat, melt the remaining tablespoon of lard in the skillet, add the onions and garlic, and cook, stirring frequently, for 5 minutes, or until the onions are transparent but not brown. Pour in 1½ cups of the reserved cooking juices and add the tomatoes, chilies, thyme, marjoram, salt and pepper. Cook over low heat for 15 minutes, meanwhile stirring and crushing the tomatoes with a large spoon. Pour the sauce over the meat in the casserole and cook it, uncovered, for about 10 minutes over low heat, stirring occasionally. Taste for seasoning.

Pork Chops with Mustard Sauce
Côtes de Porc Braisées à la Moutarde

To serve 6

6 center cut loin pork chops, cut 1½
  inches thick
Salt
Freshly ground black pepper
Flour
2 tablespoons butter
3 tablespoons vegetable oil
1½ cups thinly sliced onions

3 tablespoons wine vinegar
  (preferably white)
Bouquet garni made of 2 parsley
  sprigs and 1 bay leaf, tied together
¾ cup heavy cream
2 teaspoons Dijon-style prepared
  mustard
A few drops of lemon juice
Fresh parsley sprigs

Preheat the oven to 325°. Season the chops generously with salt and pepper, dip them in flour, then vigorously shake off all but a light dusting. In a heavy 10- to 12-inch skillet, melt the butter with the oil over moderate heat. When the foam subsides, brown the chops for about 3 minutes on each side, or until they are a rich golden color. As the chops brown, remove them from the skillet with tongs and place them in a shallow flameproof casserole large enough to hold them all, preferably in one layer.

After the chops are browned, pour off all but a thin film of fat from the skillet. Add the onions and cook them over moderate heat, stirring frequently, for 5 minutes, or until they are soft and lightly browned. Stir in the wine vinegar, bring it to a boil and scrape up any browned bits that cling to the bottom and sides of the skillet. Cook the vinegar almost completely away, then spoon the onions and juices over the chops, and add the *bouquet garni.*

Bring the casserole to a sizzle on top of the stove, cover it tightly and bake it on the middle shelf of the oven for 10 minutes. With a bulb baster or large spoon, baste the chops with the juices that have accumulated in the casserole or, if there is not enough of these, with 2 or 3 tablespoons of heated chicken stock. Bake for 10 minutes longer, then turn the chops over and baste them again. After another 10 minutes, test the chops by piercing

144

one near the bone with the tip of a sharp knife; if the juices that run out are yellow with no traces of pink, the chops are done. With tongs, transfer the chops to a heated platter and cover or set in a 200° oven to keep warm.

Tip the casserole and skim as much fat as possible from the surface of the drippings. Pour in the cream and bring the sauce to a boil over high heat, stirring constantly. When the sauce has thickened sufficiently to coat the back of a spoon lightly, remove the casserole from the heat and stir in the mustard and lemon juice. Strain the sauce through a fine sieve directly over the chops, pressing down hard on the onions with the back of a spoon before discarding them. Garnish the chops with parsley and serve at once.

Pork Chops with Tomato and Garlic Sauce
Costolette di Maiale alla Pizzaiola

To serve 6

4 tablespoons olive oil
6 center-cut loin pork chops, cut
    1 to 1½ inches thick
1 teaspoon finely chopped garlic
½ teaspoon dried oregano, crumbled
¼ teaspoon dried thyme, crumbled
½ bay leaf
½ teaspoon salt

½ cup dry red wine
1 cup drained canned tomatoes,
    puréed through a sieve or food mill
1 tablespoon tomato paste
½ pound green peppers, seeded and
    cut in 2-by-¼-inch strips (about
    1½ cups)
½ pound fresh mushrooms, whole if
    small, quartered or sliced if large

In a heavy 10- to 12-inch skillet, heat 2 tablespoons of olive oil until a light haze forms over it. Brown the chops in this oil for 2 or 3 minutes on each side and transfer them to a plate. Pour off almost all of the fat. In it cook the garlic, oregano, thyme, bay leaf and salt for 30 seconds, stirring constantly. Add the wine and boil briskly to reduce it to about ¼ cup, scraping in any bits of meat or herbs in the pan. Stir in the tomatoes and tomato paste and return the chops to the skillet. Baste with the sauce, cover, and simmer over low heat, basting once or twice, for 40 minutes.

Meanwhile, heat the remaining oil in another large skillet. Fry the green peppers in the oil for about 5 minutes, stirring frequently. Add the mushrooms and toss them with the peppers for a minute or two, then transfer them to the pan with the pork chops. Cover and simmer for 5 minutes. Simmer uncovered, stirring occasionally, for 10 minutes longer, until the pork and vegetables are tender and the sauce is thick. To serve, arrange the chops on a heated platter and spoon the vegetables and sauce over them.

Baked Pork Chops and Cabbage
Côtes de Porc à l'Auvergnate

To serve 4

6 quarts water
Salt
3 pounds cabbage, finely chopped
   (about 12 cups)
3 tablespoons butter
½ cup finely chopped onions
½ teaspoon finely chopped garlic
Freshly ground black pepper

8 center-cut loin pork chops, about
   ¾ inch thick
3 tablespoons oil
½ cup dry white wine
1 cup heavy cream
1 bay leaf
4 teaspoons freshly grated Parmesan
   cheese mixed with 2 teaspoons
   fine, dry bread crumbs

In a soup pot or kettle, bring the water and 3 tablespoons of salt to a bubbling boil. Drop in the cabbage and boil for 5 minutes. Drain the cabbage thoroughly in a sieve or colander. In a 10- to 12-inch skillet, melt 2 tablespoons of the butter over moderate heat. When the foam subsides, cook the onions and garlic, stirring constantly, for 3 or 4 minutes, or until they are soft but not brown. Stir in the cabbage, ½ teaspoon salt and a few grindings of pepper, and cook, stirring frequently, for 5 minutes, or until almost all of the moisture in the pan has evaporated. With a rubber spatula, transfer the contents of the skillet to a bowl; set aside.

Pat the pork chops dry with paper towels, and season them with salt and a few grindings of black pepper. In the skillet, melt the remaining 1 tablespoon of butter with the oil over moderate heat. When the foam subsides, brown the chops for about 3 minutes on each side, or until they are a rich golden color. Remove them from the skillet with tongs and set them aside. Pour off almost all the fat from the skillet, leaving only a thin film on the bottom. Add the wine and boil rapidly, stirring frequently and scraping in any brown bits that cling to the bottom and sides of the pan, until the wine is reduced to ¼ cup. Mix the reduced wine into the cabbage. Spread about ⅓ of the cabbage in the bottom of a heavy flameproof casserole at least 4 inches deep, and large enough to hold 4 chops in a single layer. Lay 4 chops on top of the cabbage, then add another layer of cabbage, 4 more chops, and finish with the rest of the cabbage. The casserole should be firmly packed. Preheat the oven to 350°.

In a small saucepan, scald the cream by heating it over moderate heat until tiny bubbles form around the edge of the pan. Pour the hot cream into the casserole and place a bay leaf on top of the cabbage. Bring the casserole to a simmer on top of the stove, then set it into a larger pan to catch any juices that may spill over during cooking, cover it tightly, and bake it on the middle shelf of the oven for 1½ hours. Remove the cover, discard the bay leaf and check the seasoning. Sprinkle the cabbage with cheese and crumbs. Bake the casserole for 30 minutes longer, or until the top is browned and crusty. Serve directly from the casserole.

Pork Chops Braised in White Wine
Costolette di Maiale alla Modenese

To serve 4

1 teaspoon dried sage leaves, crumbled	4 center-cut loin pork chops, about 1 inch thick
1 teaspoon dried rosemary leaves, crumbled	2 tablespoons butter
1 teaspoon finely chopped garlic	1 tablespoon olive oil
1 teaspoon salt	¾ cup dry white wine
Freshly ground black pepper	1 tablespoon finely chopped fresh parsley, preferably the flat-leaf Italian type

Combine the sage, rosemary, garlic, salt and a few grindings of pepper and press a little of this mixture firmly into both sides of each pork chop. In a heavy 10- to 12-inch skillet, melt the butter with the olive oil over moderate heat. When the foam subsides, place the chops in the hot fat and brown them for 2 or 3 minutes on each side, turning them carefully with tongs. When the chops are golden brown, remove them from the pan to a platter. Pour off all but a thin film of fat from the pan, add ½ cup of the wine and bring it to a boil. Return the chops to the pan, cover and reduce the heat to the barest simmer. Basting with the pan juices occasionally, cook the chops for 25 to 30 minutes, or until they are tender when pierced with the tip of a sharp knife. Transfer the chops to a heated serving platter and pour into the skillet the remaining ¼ cup of wine. Boil it briskly over high heat, stirring and scraping in any browned bits that cling to the bottom and sides of the pan, until it has reduced to a few tablespoons of syrupy glaze. Remove the skillet from the heat. Taste for seasoning and stir in the parsley. Pour the sauce over the pork chops and serve.

Barbecued Spareribs

To serve 4 to 6

¼ cup vegetable oil
1 teaspoon garlic, minced
2 medium onions, finely chopped
1 six-ounce can tomato paste
¼ cup white vinegar
1 teaspoon salt

1 teaspoon basil or thyme
¼ cup strained honey
½ cup beef stock
½ cup Worcestershire sauce
1 teaspoon dry mustard
4 pounds spareribs

Heat the vegetable oil over high heat in a 10- or 12-inch skillet. When a light haze forms above it, add the garlic and onions, and cook, stirring frequently, for 3 to 4 minutes without letting the onions brown. Combine the tomato paste and the vinegar, and then add it to the skillet. Stir in the salt, basil or thyme, the honey, beef stock, Worcestershire sauce and mustard. Mix thoroughly and simmer uncovered over low heat for 10 to 15 minutes. Remove from heat. Preheat the oven to 400°. Place the spareribs fat side up on a rack set in a shallow roasting pan and with a pastry brush thoroughly coat the surface of the meat with the barbecue sauce. Bake in the middle of the oven for 45 minutes to 1 hour, basting thoroughly with the barbecue sauce every 10 minutes or so. When the spareribs are brown and crisp, cut into individual portions and serve at once.

Chinese Barbecued Spareribs
K'ao-pai-ku

To serve 4 to 6

2 pounds spareribs in one piece

MARINADE
¼ cup soy sauce
2 tablespoons honey
2 tablespoons *hoisin* sauce
2 tablespoons white vinegar

1 tablespoon Chinese rice wine, or
   pale dry sherry
1 teaspoon finely chopped garlic
1 teaspoon sugar
2 tablespoons chicken stock, fresh or
   canned
Canned plum sauce

PREPARE AHEAD: 1. With a cleaver or large, sharp knife, trim any excess fat from the spareribs. If the breastbone is still attached, use a cleaver to chop it away from the ribs and discard it. Place the spareribs in a long, shallow dish, large enough to hold them comfortably.

2. In a small bowl, combine the soy sauce, honey, *hoisin* sauce, vinegar, wine, garlic, sugar and chicken stock. Stir until they are well mixed. Pour

the sauce over the spareribs, baste them thoroughly and let them marinate for 3 hours at room temperature (6 hours if refrigerated), turning them over in the marinade and basting them every hour or so.

TO COOK: Preheat the oven to 375°. To catch the drippings of the spareribs as they roast, and to prevent the oven from smoking as well, fill a large shallow roasting pan or baking dish with water and place it on the lowest rack of the oven. Insert the curved tips of two or three S-shaped hooks—such as curtain hooks or 5-inch lengths of heavy-duty wire or even unpainted coat hangers bent into shape—at each end of the spareribs. As if hanging a hammock, use the curved ends of the hooks to suspend the ribs from the uppermost rack of the oven directly above the pan of water. Roast the ribs undisturbed for 45 minutes. Then raise the oven heat to 450° and roast about 15 minutes longer, or until the spareribs are crisp and a deep, golden brown.

To serve, place the ribs on a chopping board and, with a cleaver, separate the strip into individual ribs. If the ribs are large, chop them each in half crosswise. Serve hot or cold with plum sauce.

Danish Meat Patties
Frikadeller

Makes 8 to 10 patties

	1½ cups club soda
½ pound boneless veal	1 egg, well beaten
½ pound boneless pork	1 teaspoon salt
1 medium onion, coarsely chopped or grated (½ cup)	¼ teaspoon pepper
	4 tablespoons butter
3 tablespoons flour	2 tablespoons vegetable oil

Put the veal, pork and chopped onion twice through the finest blade of a meat grinder, or have the butcher grind the meats together and then grate in the onion yourself.

In a large mixing bowl, vigorously beat the flour into the ground meat mixture with a wooden spoon, or use an electric mixer equipped with a pastry arm or paddle. Gradually beat in the club soda, a few tablespoons at a time, and continue to beat until the meat is light and fluffy. Now thoroughly beat in the egg, salt and pepper. Cover the bowl with aluminum foil or plastic wrap and refrigerate for 1 hour; this will make the meat mixture firmer and easier to handle.

Shape the mixture into oblongs about 4 inches long, 2 inches wide and 1 inch thick. Melt the butter and oil over high heat in a heavy 10- to 12-inch skillet. When the foam subsides, lower the heat to moderate and add the meat patties, 4 or 5 at a time, taking care not to crowd them. Cook about 6 to 8 minutes on each side, turning the patties with a wide spatula or two wooden spoons. When they are a rich mahogany brown, remove them from the pan and set them aside on a heated platter. Continue with the remaining patties. Because *frikadeller* contain pork, they should never be served rare. To be certain they are cooked through, puncture one with the tip of a small knife. The juices should run clear and show no tinge of pink.

Frikadeller are traditionally accompanied by boiled potatoes and pickled beets, cucumber salad or red cabbage.

Pork-Stuffed Cabbage Rolls

Töltött Káposzta

To serve 4 to 6

2 pounds sauerkraut, fresh, canned
  or packaged
1 large head green cabbage (2 to 3
  pounds)
2 tablespoons lard or bacon fat
1 cup finely chopped onions
¼ teaspoon finely chopped garlic
1 pound ground lean pork

¼ cup rice, cooked in boiling salted
  water (¾ cup cooked)
2 lightly beaten eggs
2 tablespoons sweet Hungarian
  paprika
⅛ teaspoon marjoram
1 teaspoon salt
Freshly ground black pepper
1 cup water mixed with 1 cup tomato
  purée

Wash the sauerkraut in cold water, then soak in cold water 10 to 20 minutes to reduce sourness. Squeeze dry and set aside. In a large saucepan, bring to a boil enough salted water to cover the cabbage. Add the cabbage, turn the heat to low and simmer 8 minutes. Remove the cabbage and let it drain while it cools enough to handle. Pull off the large unbroken leaves and lay them on paper towels to drain and cool further.

In a 10-inch skillet, heat the lard or bacon fat on high heat until a light haze forms over it. Add the onions and garlic and cook them, stirring occasionally, until lightly colored. In a mixing bowl, combine the pork, rice, eggs, paprika, marjoram, the onion-garlic mixture, salt and a few grindings of black pepper. Mix well with a fork or wooden spoon.

Place 2 tablespoons of the stuffing in the center of one of the wilted cabbage leaves and, beginning with the thick end of the leaf, fold over the sides, then roll the whole leaf tightly, as you would a small bundle. Repeat with more leaves until all the stuffing has been used.

Spread the sauerkraut on the bottom of a 5-quart casserole and arrange the cabbage rolls on top of it. Add the water mixed with the tomato purée. Bring the liquid to a boil, then cover the pan tightly and cook the stuffed cabbage over low heat for 1 hour. Transfer the rolls from the casserole to a warm platter.

THE SAUCE   2 tablespoons flour
3 tablespoons unsalted butter   1 cup sour cream

THE SAUCE: In a small saucepan on medium heat, melt the butter and stir in the flour. Continue to stir until the flour browns slightly. Gradually stir in the cream, continuing to stir until the sauce is thick and smooth. Stir the sauce into the sauerkraut and simmer 5 to 10 minutes longer. With a fork or slotted spoon, lift the sauerkraut onto a serving platter. Arrange the cabbage rolls on the sauerkraut and pour some of the sauce over them. Serve the rest of the sauce in a sauceboat.

Pork and Ham Balls

To make 32 meatballs

1 cup fresh bread crumbs
3 tablespoons milk
1 pound fresh lean pork, finely
   ground, combined with ½ pound
   cooked smoked ham, finely ground
1 tablespoon prepared mustard

1 tablespoon finely chopped fresh
   parsley
1 egg, lightly beaten
Freshly ground black pepper
2 tablespoons butter
2 tablespoons vegetable oil
¾ cup dry red wine

Soak the bread crumbs in the milk for about 5 minutes, then combine them with the ground pork and ham in a large mixing bowl. Add the mustard, parsley, lightly beaten egg and a few grindings of black pepper, and with a large spoon mix them thoroughly together. Form the mixture into small balls about 1 inch in diameter and chill for at least ½ hour.

Preheat the oven to 350°. Over high heat, melt the butter with the oil in a large, heavy skillet. When the foam subsides, add the ham balls. To help keep their shape as they brown, roll the balls around in the hot fat by shaking the pan back and forth over the burner. When the ham balls are well browned on all sides (this should take about 5 minutes), transfer them with a slotted spoon to a 2-quart casserole. Pour off all but a thin film of fat from the skillet and pour in the wine. Bring it to a boil over high heat, scraping and stirring into it any brown bits clinging to the bottom and sides of the pan. Cook briskly for about a minute, then pour the wine into the casserole. Cover tightly and bake in the middle of the oven for about 30 minutes, basting the ham balls after 15 minutes with the wine. Serve either directly from the casserole or arrange the balls on a heated platter and pour the sauce over them.

Braised Fresh Ham
Falscher Wildschweinbraten

To serve 6 to 8

2 cups dry red wine
½ cup red wine vinegar
1 cup finely grated onions
15 whole juniper berries, crushed
    with a mortar and pestle or
    wrapped in a towel and crushed
    with a rolling pin
2 tablespoons grated fresh lemon
    peel
6 small bay leaves, coarsely crushed
2 teaspoons dried tarragon

1 teaspoon ground cloves
1 teaspoon ground allspice
1 teaspoon ground ginger
1 teaspoon freshly ground black
    pepper
A 5- to 6-pound fresh ham, rind
    removed and the ham trimmed of
    fat
1 tablespoon salt
2 tablespoons lard
2 cups water
3 tablespoons flour
3 tablespoons cold water

For the marinade pour the wine and vinegar into a mixing bowl and stir in the grated onions, juniper berries, grated lemon peel, bay leaves, tarragon, cloves, allspice, ginger and black pepper. Place the ham in a deep dish just large enough to hold it comfortably and pour the marinade over it. Cover with foil and marinate in the refrigerator for two days, turning it over once or twice a day.

Preheat the oven to 325°. Remove the ham from the marinade, and dry it thoroughly with paper towels, brushing off any bits of onion or herbs clinging to it. Rub the salt evenly into its surface. Strain the marinade into a bowl or saucepan, pressing down hard with a spoon on the solid ingredients to extract all their liquid before throwing them away.

In a heavy casserole or Dutch oven just large enough to hold the ham comfortably, melt the lard over high heat until a light haze forms above it. Add the ham and brown it well on all sides, turning the ham frequently and regulating the heat so the meat colors quickly and evenly without burning. Transfer the ham to a plate. Combine the strained marinade with 2 cups of water and pour the mixture into the casserole. Bring the liquid to a boil over high heat, meanwhile scraping in any brown bits clinging to the bottom and sides of the casserole.

Return the ham to the casserole, cover tightly, and bake in the middle of the oven for about 2 hours, basting it every 30 minutes or so with the cooking liquid. The ham is done when it can easily be pierced with the tip of a sharp knife. (You may use a meat thermometer, if you like, for more predictable results. After the ham is browned, insert the thermometer into the thickest part without letting the tip touch any bone. Roast until the thermometer reads 170° to 175°.) Transfer the ham to a heated platter and set it aside to rest for 10 to 15 minutes for easier carving.

Meanwhile, strain the cooking liquid into a small saucepan and skim off as much fat as possible from the surface. Measure the liquid, then boil it briskly to reduce it to 2 cups. Reduce the heat to low. Make a smooth paste of the flour and 3 tablespoons of cold water and, with a whisk or spoon, stir it gradually into the simmering liquid. Cook, stirring frequently, for about 10 minutes, or until the sauce thickens slightly. Taste for seasoning.

To serve, carve the ham into ¼-inch slices and arrange the slices attractively in overlapping layers on a large heated platter. Serve the sauce separately in a sauceboat.

Fresh Ham Braised in Marsala

Prosciutto Fresco Brasato al Marsala

To serve 6

1 cup dry Marsala
¼ cup olive oil
2 teaspoons lemon juice
2 bay leaves, crumbled
A 4- to 6-pound half of fresh
    ham
½ cup coarsely chopped onions

¼ cup coarsely chopped carrots
¼ cup coarsely chopped celery
¼ cup olive oil
2 cups beef stock, fresh or canned
1 tablespoon arrowroot
2 tablespoons dry Marsala
Salt
Freshly ground black pepper

Combine 1 cup of Marsala, ¼ cup of olive oil, the lemon juice and bay leaves in a large glass or stainless-steel bowl. Turn the fresh ham in this marinade until it is thoroughly moistened. Marinate at room temperature for at least 6 hours or in the refrigerator for at least 12 hours—turning the ham 2 or 3 times.

Preheat the oven to 350°. Remove the ham from the marinade and pat it dry with paper towels. Strain the marinade into a small bowl. Combine the onions, carrots and celery and chop them together into very small pieces. (This chopped mixture is called a *battuto*, which is called a *soffritto* after it is cooked.) Heat 2 tablespoons of olive oil in a heavy 4- to 6-quart flameproof casserole just large enough to hold the ham comfortably. Add the *battuto* and cook over moderate heat, stirring frequently, for about 10 minutes, or until it is lightly colored. Heat the remaining 2 tablespoons of oil in a heavy 10- to 12-inch skillet until a light haze forms over the oil. Brown the ham in the skillet, starting it fat side down and turning it with 2 wooden spoons. When it is a golden-brown color all over, place the ham on top of the *soffritto* in the casserole and insert a meat thermometer deep into the thickest part of the meat.

Discard almost all of the fat from the skillet, leaving just a film on the bottom. Pour in the strained marinade and boil it briskly over high heat, stirring and scraping in any browned bits that cling to the pan. When the marinade has reduced to about half its original quantity, add it to the casserole along with the beef stock. If the liquid does not come ⅓ of the way up the side of the ham, add more stock. Bring the casserole to a boil on top of the stove, cover and place on the middle shelf of the oven. Braise the ham until the thermometer reaches 185°—which should take 3 to 3½ hours. Transfer the ham to a heated platter, and let it rest for about 15 minutes to make carving easier.

Strain the sauce from the casserole through a fine sieve into a 1½- to 2-quart saucepan, pressing down hard on the vegetables to extract all their juices before discarding them. Skim the surface of fat, then bring the sauce to a simmer over moderate heat. Mix the arrowroot with 2 additional table-spoons of Marsala and, when the arrowroot has dissolved, stir it into the simmering sauce. Continue cooking, stirring constantly, until the sauce thickens and clears. Do not let it boil. Taste the sauce for seasoning. Carve the ham into thin slices and arrange the slices in a row on a heated serving platter. Pour a few tablespoons of the sauce over the ham before serving it, and pass the rest separately.

Roast Fresh Ham with Crackling
Flaeskesteg med Svaer

To serve 8 to 10

½ fresh ham (butt or shank) weighing about 6 pounds or 6 pounds shoulder of pork with the rind on

Coarse salt or substitute regular salt

Freshly ground black pepper

Preheat the oven to 300°. Using a sharp, heavy knife, cut deeply through the rind and fat until you reach the meat, making the incisions ½ inch apart lengthwise and crosswise. Rub salt and pepper liberally into these gashes. Insert a meat thermometer into the thickest part of the ham and place it on a rack set in a shallow roasting pan just large enough to hold the meat comfortably. Roast slowly 4 to 4½ hours, or until the meat thermometer reads 180°. Do not baste the meat. When roasted, the meat should be moist and tender, and the rind (or crackling) very crisp. Let the roast rest outside the oven for 10 to 15 minutes for easier carving. A little of the crackling should be included in each serving of meat.

Ham Braised in Burgundy
Schinken in Burgunder

To serve 6 to 8

Half a precooked smoked ham, butt
  or shank end, about 5 to 6 pounds
2 cups water
2 cups red Burgundy or other dry
  red wine
1 medium-sized onion, peeled and

thinly sliced
1 medium-sized tomato, peeled,
  seeded and coarsely chopped
1 whole clove, crushed with a mortar
  and pestle
1 small bay leaf
1 tablespoon butter, softened
1 tablespoon flour

Preheat the oven to 350°. With a small, sharp knife, separate the rind from
the ham and place the rind in a 1- to 2-quart saucepan. Trim the ham of all
but a ¼-inch layer of fat. Pour 2 cups of water over the rind, bring to a boil
over high heat, then reduce the heat to low and simmer uncovered for 20 minutes. Strain the liquid through a sieve into a bowl and discard the rind.

Pour 1 cup of the rind stock into a shallow roasting pan just large enough
to hold the ham comfortably. Add 1 cup of the wine, and the onion, tomato, clove and bay leaf. Place the ham, fat side up, in the pan and bake uncovered in the middle of the oven for about 1 hour. Baste the ham thoroughly
every 20 minutes with the pan liquid. The ham is done when it can easily be
pierced with a fork. Transfer the ham to a heated platter and let it rest for easier carving while you prepare the sauce.

Skim and discard all the fat from the pan liquid and stir in the remaining
1 cup of wine. Bring to a boil over high heat, meanwhile scraping in any
brown bits clinging to the bottom or sides of the pan, and boil briskly for a
minute or two. In a small bowl, make a paste of the butter and flour, and stir
it bit by bit into the pan. Cook over low heat, stirring constantly, for 5 minutes, or until the sauce is smooth and slightly thickened. Strain it through a
fine sieve into a small saucepan and taste for seasoning.

To serve, carve the ham into ¼-inch slices and arrange the slices attractively, in overlapping layers, on a large heated platter. Moisten the slices
with a few spoonfuls of the Burgundy sauce, and serve the remaining sauce
separately in a sauceboat.

Baked Bourbon-glazed Ham

To serve 12 to 14

A 12- to 14-pound smoked ham,
  processed, precooked variety
¾ cup bourbon whiskey

2 cups dark brown sugar
1 tablespoon dry mustard
¾ cup whole cloves
2 navel oranges, peeled and sectioned

Preheat the oven to 325°. Place the ham fat side up on a rack set in a shallow roasting pan large enough to hold the ham comfortably. Bake in the middle of the oven, without basting, for two hours, or until the meat can be easily pierced with a fork. For greater cooking certainty, insert a meat thermometer in the fleshiest part of the ham before baking it. It should register between 130° and 140° when the ham is done.

When the ham is cool enough to handle comfortably, cut away the rind with a large, sharp knife. Then score the ham by cutting deeply through the fat until you reach the meat, making the incisions ½ inch apart lengthwise and crosswise. Return the ham to the rack in the pan and raise the oven heat to 450°. With a pastry brush, paint the ham on all sides with ½ cup of the whiskey. Then combine the sugar and mustard and ¼ cup of whiskey, and pat the mixture firmly into the scored fat. Stud the fat at the intersections or in the center of each diamond with a whole clove, and arrange the orange sections as decoratively as you can on the top of the ham with toothpicks or small skewers to secure them. Baste lightly with the drippings on the bottom of the pan and bake the ham undisturbed in the hot oven for 15 to 20 minutes, or until the sugar has melted and formed a brilliant glaze.

Smoked Bacon with Onions and Apples
Äppel-Fläsk

To serve 4

2 to 4 tablespoons butter
1 pound Canadian bacon
2 large onions, thinly sliced

2 large red, tart cooking apples,
  unpeeled, cored and cut in
  ½-inch-thick rings
Freshly ground black pepper

Melt 2 tablespoons of butter in a heavy 10- to 12-inch skillet, and when the foam subsides, add the bacon. Fry 5 to 10 minutes, or until the bacon is lightly browned. Remove from the skillet with a slotted spatula and set aside on paper towels to drain.

Fry the onion slices for 6 to 8 minutes in the fat remaining in the skillet, adding more butter if necessary. When the onions are soft and transparent, add the apple rings and cover the pan. Simmer over low heat for 5 to 10 minutes, shaking the pan gently at intervals to prevent the apples from sticking.

When the apple rings are sufficiently cooked (they should offer little or no resistance when pierced with the tip of a sharp knife), return the drained bacon to the skillet. Cover the pan and simmer an additional 3 to 5 minutes, or until the bacon is heated through. Grind black pepper liberally over the top and serve the *äppel-fläsk* directly from the pan as a luncheon entrée or Sunday night supper.

Bratwurst in Sweet-Sour Sauce
Süss-saure Bratwurst

To serve 4

8 bratwurst, separated	2 cups cold water
1 tablespoon dried black currants	1 tablespoon butter
4 whole allspice, pulverized with a mortar and pestle	2 tablespoons flour
	2 teaspoons sugar
	½ teaspoon salt
	1 tablespoon fresh lemon juice

Place the bratwurst, currants and allspice in a 2- to 3-quart saucepan and pour in the water. Bring to a boil over high heat, reduce the heat to low and cover the pan. Simmer for 20 minutes, then set the sausages aside on a plate and cover with foil to keep them warm. Let the cooking liquid settle for a minute or two, and skim as much of the fat from the surface as possible.

In a heavy 8- to 10-inch skillet, melt the butter over moderate heat. Stir in the flour and cook, stirring constantly, for 3 to 4 minutes, or until the mixture colors lightly. Be careful it doesn't burn. Pour in 1 cup of the reserved cooking liquid including the currants. Stirring constantly with a whisk, bring the sauce to a boil. When it is thick and smooth, reduce the heat to low, stir in the sugar and salt and simmer for 3 to 4 minutes. Slice the sausages into ¼-inch rounds, add them to the sauce and simmer only long enough to heat them through. Just before serving, stir in the lemon juice and taste for seasoning. Transfer the entire contents of the skillet to a large, deep serving platter and serve at once.

Specialty Cuts

Calf's Liver with Apples and Onion Rings
Gebratene Kalbsleber auf Berliner Art

To serve 3 or 4

8 tablespoons butter
2 medium-sized onions, cut into ⅛-
  inch slices and separated into rings
Salt
Freshly ground black pepper

5 medium-sized cooking apples
  (about 1½ pounds), peeled, cored
  and sliced crosswise into ¼-inch
  rings
1 pound calf's liver, cut into ¼-
  inch slices
Flour

Preheat the oven to 250°. In a heavy 10- to 12-inch skillet, melt 2 table-spoons of the butter over moderate heat. When the foam subsides, add the onion rings, a little salt and a few grindings of pepper. Stirring occasionally, cook the onion rings for about 10 minutes, or until they are light brown. With a slotted spoon, transfer them to a heatproof plate, cover them loosely with aluminum foil and place them in the preheated oven. Add 2 tablespoons of butter to the skillet and drop in half of the apple rings. Cook them until they are golden on both sides, add them to the plate with the onion rings and cook the remaining apple slices similarly in another 2 tablespoons of but-ter. Keep the apples and onions warm in the oven while you cook the liver.

Season the liver slices with salt and a few grindings of pepper. Dip the slices in flour, then vigorously shake off any excess. Add the remaining 2 ta-blespoons of butter to the skillet and melt the butter over moderate heat. When the foam subsides add the liver and cook it for 2 minutes on each side, or until the slices are light brown, turning them with kitchen tongs. Do not overcook. Remove the liver to a heated platter and scatter the apple and onion rings over it and serve at once.

158

Sautéed Calf's Liver

To serve 6

6 slices of calf's liver, cut ½ inch
   thick (about 1½ pounds)
Salt
Freshly ground black pepper
Flour
4 tablespoons butter

2 tablespoons vegetable oil
½ cup beef or chicken stock, fresh or
   canned
1 tablespoon soft butter
A few drops of lemon juice
2 tablespoons finely chopped, fresh
   parsley

Season the liver slices with salt and a few grindings of pepper. Dip the slices in flour, then vigorously shake off all but a fine dusting. In a heavy 12-inch skillet or sauté pan, melt the butter with the oil over high heat. When the foam subsides, sauté the liver quickly for 2 or 3 minutes on each side, turning the slices with kitchen tongs. Remove the liver to a heated platter and cover loosely to keep warm.

Working quickly, pour off almost all the fat from the skillet, leaving just enough to film the bottom. Add the chicken stock and cook over high heat, stirring constantly and scraping in any bits that cling to the pan.

Continue to cook until the stock is syrupy and has been reduced to about ¼ cup. Remove the pan from the heat and swirl in 1 tablespoon of soft butter and a few drops of lemon juice. Pour the sauce over the liver, sprinkle with parsley and serve at once.

Sautéed Calf's Liver with Onions

Fegato alla Veneziana

To serve 4

4 tablespoons olive oil
1 cup thinly sliced onions
¼ teaspoon dried sage leaves
1 pound calf's liver, cut crosswise
   into ¼-inch strips

Salt
Freshly ground black pepper
2 tablespoons wine vinegar, preferably
   white
2 tablespoons finely chopped fresh
   parsley

Heat 2 tablespoons of olive oil in a heavy 8- to 10-inch skillet. Add the onions and cook over moderate heat, stirring frequently, for 7 or 8 minutes. Then stir in the sage and cook 2 or 3 minutes longer, or until the onions are limp and lightly colored. Set the skillet aside, off the heat.

Pat the liver strips dry with paper towels and season them with salt and a few grindings of pepper. In another large heavy skillet, heat the remaining 2 tablespoons of olive oil until a light haze forms over it. Drop in the liver

159

strips and sauté them, turning them frequently, for 2 or 3 minutes, or until they are lightly browned on all sides. Stir in the onions and cook with the liver for 1 or 2 minutes. Transfer the liver and onions to a heated platter. Immediately pour the white wine vinegar into the skillet and boil this mixture briskly for a minute or 2, meanwhile scraping in any browned bits clinging to the pan. Pour the sauce over the liver and onions and sprinkle with the chopped parsley. Serve immediately.

Marinated Liver in Wine
Iscas

To serve 4

	Freshly ground black pepper
¾ cup dry red wine	1 pound calf's or beef liver, cut
2 tablespoons red wine vinegar	into ⅛-inch-thick slices
1 teaspoon finely chopped garlic	3 tablespoons olive oil
½ bay leaf, crumbled	3 bacon slices, coarsely chopped
½ teaspoon salt	2 tablespoons finely chopped parsley

Combine the wine, vinegar, garlic, bay leaf, salt and a few grindings of pepper in a glass, enamel or stainless-steel bowl or baking dish. Add the liver, turning the slices about with a spoon until they are evenly coated. Marinate at room temperature for about 2 hours.

In a heavy 10- to 12-inch skillet, heat the olive oil over moderate heat until a light haze forms above it. Add the bacon and cook, stirring frequently, until golden brown and crisp. Drain on a double thickness of paper towels. Remove the liver slices from the marinade and pat them dry with paper towels. Reserve the marinade. Heat the bacon fat remaining in the skillet until it splutters. Add the liver and cook the slices about 2 minutes on each side, regulating the heat so they brown quickly and evenly without burning. Remove the liver to a heated platter. Quickly pour the reserved marinade into the skillet and boil it uncovered over high heat until it has reduced to about half, meanwhile scraping in any browned bits clinging to the bottom and sides of the pan. Taste for seasoning. Scatter the bacon pieces over the liver, pour the sauce over it and sprinkle with parsley. Serve at once.

Sautéed Kidneys with Mustard Sauce

Rognons en Casserole

To serve 4 to 6

6 tablespoons butter

3 or 4 whole veal kidneys or 12 whole lamb kidneys, peeled and trimmed of fat

2 tablespoons finely chopped shallots or scallions

¾ cup dry white wine

4 tablespoons soft butter

2 tablespoons Dijon-style prepared mustard

½ teaspoon salt

Freshly ground black pepper

2 teaspoons lemon juice

3 tablespoons finely chopped fresh parsley

In a heavy, shallow flameproof casserole about 10 inches across, or in a chafing dish, melt the 6 tablespoons of butter over moderate heat. When the foam subsides, sauté the kidneys in the butter, uncovered, turning them frequently, until they are lightly browned. (Sauté veal kidneys for 10 minutes, lamb kidneys for 4 to 5.) With tongs, transfer the kidneys to a heated platter and cover loosely to keep them warm.

Stir the shallots into the butter remaining in the casserole and cook, stirring, for 1 minute. Then add the wine and bring to a boil, stirring constantly and scraping in any brown bits or coagulated juices that cling to the pan. Boil briskly for 4 to 5 minutes or until the wine is reduced to ¼ cup. Remove the casserole from the heat. Cream the butter by beating it vigorously with a wooden spoon until it is fluffy, then beat in the mustard, salt and a few grindings of pepper. Off the heat, swirl spoonfuls of the seasoned butter into the casserole.

Working quickly, cut the kidneys into crosswise slices ⅛ inch thick. Return them to the casserole, sprinkle with lemon juice and parsley, and toss over low heat for 1 or 2 minutes to heat them through. Serve at once.

Sautéed Kidneys with Sherry Sauce
Riñones al Jerez

To serve 6

6 tablespoons olive oil
1 cup finely chopped onions
1 teaspoon finely chopped garlic
1 small bay leaf
2 tablespoons flour
½ cup beef or chicken stock, fresh
   or canned

2 tablespoons finely chopped parsley
2 pounds veal kidneys, split
   lengthwise in half, trimmed of all
   fat, and cut into 1-inch cubes
Salt
Freshly ground black pepper
½ cup pale dry sherry

In a heavy 8- to 10-inch skillet, heat 4 tablespoons of the olive oil over moderate heat until a light haze forms above it. Add the onions, garlic and bay leaf. Stirring frequently, cook for 5 minutes, or until the onions are soft and transparent but not brown. Add the flour and mix thoroughly. Pour in the stock and, stirring constantly, cook over high heat until the mixture thickens heavily and comes to a boil. Add the parsley, reduce the heat to low, and simmer for about 3 minutes. Set aside.

Heat the remaining 2 tablespoons of olive oil in a heavy 10- to 12-inch skillet. Sprinkle the kidneys liberally with salt and a few grindings of pepper. Then cook them in the hot oil for 4 or 5 minutes, turning them about with a large spoon and regulating the heat so that they brown quickly on all sides without burning.

Transfer the kidneys to a plate and pour the sherry into the pan. Bring to a boil over high heat, meanwhile scraping in any brown particles clinging to the bottom and sides of the pan. Return the kidneys to the pan, stir in the reserved onion sauce and bring to a boil. Reduce the heat to low, simmer a minute or two and taste for seasoning.

Skewered Lamb Kidneys
Rognons en Brochette

To serve 4

8 lamb kidneys
8 slices bacon
½ pound boiled ham
8 mushroom caps
8 baby white onions

4 tablespoons butter
2 green peppers
1 clove garlic, crushed
Salt
Pepper
1 bunch watercress

Cut the kidneys in half and remove the center white cores. Cut the bacon in half crosswise and wrap each piece of kidney in half a slice of bacon. Cut the ham in ½-inch cubes. Sauté the mushroom caps. Slowly brown the onions in 1 tablespoon of butter. Core and seed the peppers, and cut them into pieces the same size as the ham. Thread all these ingredients on skewers, alternating a piece of meat with a vegetable. Melt the remaining 3 tablespoons of butter in the pan the onions were cooked in. Add the garlic and cook for 1 minute. Place the skewers on a cookie sheet. Pour the butter over them and season with salt and pepper. Broil them for 5 minutes on each side in a preheated broiler. Serve on the skewers, garnished with watercress.

Pork Kidneys and Sea Scallops

Hsien-kan-pei-yao-hua

To serve 4

4 pork kidneys
½ pound fresh or thoroughly
   defrosted frozen sea scallops
¼ cup peanut oil, or flavorless
   vegetable oil
1 tablespoon Chinese rice wine, or
   pale dry sherry
1 teaspoon finely chopped, peeled

fresh ginger root
1 scallion, including the green top,
   finely chopped
2 tablespoons soy sauce
½ teaspoon salt
1 teaspoon sugar
1 teaspoon cornstarch dissolved in 1
   tablespoon chicken stock, fresh or
   canned, or cold water

PREPARE AHEAD: 1. Peel off the thin outer membrane covering the kidneys, if the butcher has not already removed it, with a cleaver or sharp knife. Split the kidneys in half lengthwise and cut away the small knobs of fat and any tough membrane surrounding them. Place the kidney halves flat side down on a chopping board and score their surfaces diagonally to create a crisscross pattern, cutting about two thirds of the way down into them and spacing the cuts about ¼ inch apart. Then cut the kidneys crosswise into 1-inch slices, and the slices into strips 2 inches long.

2. Wash the scallops under cold running water, pat them dry with paper towels and cut them horizontally into slices ¼ inch thick.

3. Have the above ingredients, and the oil, wine, ginger, scallions, soy sauce, salt, sugar and the cornstarch mixture within easy reach.

TO COOK: Set a 12-inch wok or 10-inch skillet over high heat for 30 seconds. Pour in 2 tablespoons of oil, swirl it about in the pan and heat for another 30 seconds, turning the heat down to moderate if the oil begins to smoke. Add the scallops and stir-fry for only 1 minute, or until they turn white but not too firm. Immediately pour in the wine and add the salt, stir well, and, with a large spoon, transfer the scallops to a plate. Pour the remaining 2 tablespoons of oil into the pan, heat for about 30 seconds, and add the ginger and scallions. Stir for a few seconds and drop

163

in the kidneys. Stir-fry over high heat for 2 minutes, or until their edges begin to curl. Then add the soy sauce and sugar. Return the scallops and their accumulated juices to the pan, and mix with the kidneys for a few seconds. Give the cornstarch mixture a quick stir to recombine it and add it to the pan. When the kidneys and scallops are coated with a light, clear glaze—this will take no more than a few seconds—transfer the entire contents of the pan to a heated platter and serve at once.

Brains or Sweetbreads in Brown Butter Sauce
Ris de Veau ou Cervelles au Beurre Noir

To serve 6

1½ pounds calf's sweetbreads or brains	¼ cup wine vinegar or lemon juice
Water	Freshly ground black pepper
Vinegar	Flour
Salt	3 tablespoons butter
Lemon juice	1 tablespoon vegetable oil
15 tablespoons butter (almost ½ pound)	2 tablespoons finely chopped fresh parsley

Soak the sweetbreads or brains in several changes of cold water for 2 hours; then soak them for another hour in acidulated cold water, using one tablespoon of vinegar for each quart of water. Gently pull off as much of the outside membrane as possible without tearing the brains or sweetbreads. Trim the sweetbreads by cutting the two lobes from the tube between them with a small sharp knife; discard the tubes. Trim the brains by cutting off the white, opaque bits at the base. Place the sweetbreads or brains in an enameled saucepan with enough water to cover by 2 inches, add the salt (1 teaspoon per quart of water) and lemon juice (1 tablespoon per quart of water), and cook uncovered just below a simmer for 15 to 20 minutes. Spread the sweetbreads or brains on paper towels to dry.

Clarify 12 tablespoons of the butter in a small heavy saucepan or skillet by melting it slowly, skimming off the surface foam. Spoon the clear butter on top into a clean pan and discard the milky residue. Pour the vinegar into the pan in which the butter melted and boil it briskly until it has been reduced to 1 tablespoon. Over moderate heat, brown the clarified butter. Stir in the reduced vinegar, taste and season with salt and pepper.

If the sweetbreads or brains are to be served whole, add them to the brown butter sauce and, basting periodically, heat through. If they are to be sliced and sautéed, set the brown butter sauce aside. Dip the slices in flour, then shake off all but a fine dusting of flour. In a heavy 10- to 12-inch skillet or sauté pan, melt the remaining 3 tablespoons of butter with the oil over moderate heat. When the foam subsides, sauté the sliced sweet-

164

breads or brains 3 or 4 minutes on each side, or until lightly browned. If all the slices don't fit into the skillet easily, sauté them in two batches. Arrange the slices neatly on a heated platter. Reheat the brown butter and pour it over them. Sprinkle with chopped parsley and serve at once.

Sweetbreads and Ham under Glass

To serve 6

6 pairs sweetbreads, about 3 pounds
2 tablespoons lemon juice
2 teaspoons salt
2 cups water
2/3 cup sherry
6 tablespoons butter
12 unpeeled mushroom caps, 1 1/2 to
    2 inches in diameter, rubbed lightly
    with a damp paper towel

SAUCE
1/2 cup sherry

1 cup heavy cream
2 teaspoons lemon juice
Salt
White pepper

6 circles of white bread, 3 1/2 inches
    in diameter, lightly browned on
    both sides in 4 tablespoons of hot
    butter
6 slices cooked ham, 1/4 inch thick,
    cut into circles 3 1/2 inches in
    diameter

To prepare the sweetbreads for poaching, soak them for about 2 hours in enough cold water to cover them, changing the water every 45 minutes or so. Then soak again, for another hour, in 2 quarts of cold water mixed with 2 tablespoons of lemon juice and 2 teaspoons salt. Drain. Separate the sweetbread lobes, and cut away and discard the soft, white connecting tubes. With a small, sharp knife, pull off as much of the thin outside membrane as you can without tearing the delicate flesh.

Place the sweetbreads in a 2-quart enameled or stainless-steel saucepan, and add 2 cups of water and 2/3 cup of sherry. If the liquid doesn't quite cover the sweetbreads, add more water. Bring to a simmer over moderate heat, then lower the heat and cook as slowly as possible, uncovered, for about 15 minutes. Drain, plunge into cold water for 5 minutes, then drain again. Pat dry with paper towels.

Over moderate heat, melt 4 tablespoons of the butter in a 10-inch enameled or stainless-steel skillet, and when the foam subsides add the sweetbreads. Cook them on each side for about 3 minutes, or until they are a delicate brown. Remove to a platter. Melt the remaining butter in the skillet and cook the mushrooms briskly for a minute or two on each side to brown them lightly, then put them aside with the sweetbreads. Pour off all but a thin film of the butter from the pan and pour in the 1/2 cup of sherry. Over high heat, boil briskly for 2 minutes, then add the cream and boil rapidly for about 5 minutes, or until it thickens enough to coat a spoon. Add the lemon juice and season with as much salt and white pepper as you think it needs. Put it aside. Preheat the oven to 375°.

Arrange the toast rounds in individual 4- to 5-inch shallow ramekins. Top each round with a slice of ham, then a pair of sweetbreads and, finally, the mushroom caps. Pour equal amounts of the sauce over each cap and cover with individual glass bells. Heat in the middle of the oven for 12 to 15 minutes and serve at once.

Braised Tripe with Tomato Sauce
Trippa alla Fiorentina

To serve 4

¼ cup olive oil
¾ cup finely chopped onions
½ cup finely chopped celery
2 pounds fresh or defrosted frozen
   honeycomb tripe, cut into
   2-by-½-inch strips
3 tablespoons tomato paste
2 cups chicken or beef stock, fresh

or canned
2 tablespoons finely chopped fresh
   parsley, preferably the flat-leaf
   Italian type
½ teaspoon finely chopped garlic
¼ teaspoon dried marjoram,
   crumbled
½ teaspoon salt
½ cup freshly grated imported
   Parmesan cheese

In a heavy 3- to 4-quart saucepan or flameproof casserole that has a cover, heat the olive oil until a light haze forms over it. Add the onions and celery and cook over moderate heat for 8 to 10 minutes, stirring frequently, until the onions are soft and slightly golden. Add the tripe and toss it with the onions and celery until they are well combined. Dissolve the tomato paste in the stock and pour it over the tripe and vegetables. Add the parsley, garlic, marjoram and salt. Bring to a boil over high heat, then reduce the heat, cover the pan and simmer the tripe slowly, regulating the heat so that the surface of the sauce barely moves. If at any point the sauce becomes too thick, add a few tablespoons of stock. In 2½ to 3 hours, the tripe should be tender when pierced with the tip of a sharp knife. Serve as hot as possible on heated plates. Sprinkle each serving with grated cheese.

Game & Wildfowl

Danish Roast Venison
Dyreryg

To serve 8 to 10

6 pounds venison, saddle or rib
2 teaspoons salt
¼ teaspoon pepper

8 slices bacon
3 tablespoons butter
3 tablespoons flour
2 cups hot milk
1 cup red currant jelly
½ cup light cream

Preheat the oven to 375°. Have the venison tied up; rub with the salt and pepper, then cover with the bacon slices. Place the meat in a roasting pan and cook in the oven for 30 minutes. Set the meat aside, but keep it warm. Turn the oven down to 325°.

Melt the butter in a saucepan; blend in the flour, then add the milk, stirring steadily to the boiling point. Add the pan juices from the venison and cook over low heat 5 minutes. Taste for seasoning. Pour the sauce over the meat and roast in the oven 1½ hours, basting frequently.

Transfer the meat to a platter. Pour the gravy into a saucepan. Skim the fat. Stir the jelly into the gravy, then the cream. Cook 5 minutes. Serve the sauce in a separate sauceboat.

Venison Tenderloin in Brandy Sauce
Piquante Rehfiletschnitten

To serve 4

½ cup dry red wine
½ cup water
1 medium-sized onion, peeled and
    cut into ⅛-inch slices
2 tablespoons finely chopped
    shallots, or substitute 2
    tablespoons finely chopped
    scallions
A 2-inch piece of cinnamon stick
1 small bay leaf

1 whole clove
3 parsley sprigs
⅛ teaspoon thyme
½ teaspoon salt
Freshly ground black pepper
2 pounds venison tenderloin, cut
    into ¼-inch-thick slices
3 tablespoons butter
2 tablespoons flour
½ cup chicken stock
2 tablespoons brandy

In a small mixing bowl, combine the red wine, water, sliced onion, shallots, cinnamon, bay leaf, clove, parsley, thyme, salt and a few grindings of pepper. Arrange the venison slices in one layer in a shallow baking dish and pour the marinade over them, turning the steaks to moisten them thoroughly. Marinate at room temperature for at least 2 hours, turning the steaks once or twice.

Preheat the oven to 300°. Remove the steaks from the marinade and pat them thoroughly dry. Set the marinade aside. In a heavy 10- to 12-inch skillet, melt the butter over moderate heat. When the foam subsides, add the venison steaks and brown them for 2 or 3 minutes on each side, regulating the heat so they color quickly and evenly and without burning. Transfer the steaks to a shallow casserole or baking dish just large enough to hold them comfortably in one layer, and set them aside.

Strain the marinade through a fine sieve set over a bowl, pressing down hard on the vegetables with the back of a spoon before discarding them. Add the flour to the fat remaining in the skillet, and cook over moderate heat, stirring constantly, until the flour browns lightly. Gradually pour in the strained marinade, chicken stock and brandy. Stirring constantly with a whisk, bring it to a boil, continuing to stir until the sauce is smooth and slightly thickened. Taste for seasoning. Pour the sauce over the venison steaks and bake in the middle of the oven for 10 minutes, basting them occasionally with the pan juices. Serve at once, directly from the casserole, or on a large heated platter.

NOTE: In Germany the venison is browned in butter as described above. Because butter alone burns easily, you may prefer to use 2 tablespoons of butter combined with 1 tablespoon of vegetable oil.

Venison Cutlets with Mushrooms

Rehschnitzel mit Pilzen

To serve 6

10 whole juniper berries
5 whole black peppercorns
1 small bay leaf, crumbled
½ teaspoon salt
6 six-ounce venison cutlets,

preferably from the leg, cut ½
inch thick and pounded slightly
½ cup plus 1 tablespoon flour
4 tablespoons butter
1 cup thinly sliced fresh mushrooms
¾ cup light cream

With a mortar and pestle, pulverize the juniper berries, peppercorns, crumbled bay leaf and salt together. Then firmly press the mixture with your fingertips into both sides of the venison cutlets. Dip the cutlets in ½ cup of the flour and shake off any excess. In a heavy 12-inch skillet, melt the butter over moderate heat. When the foam subsides, add the cutlets (in two batches if they crowd the pan), and cook them for 2 or 3 minutes on each side, regulating the heat so that they color evenly without burning. Don't overcook; when done, the cutlets should be slightly pink inside. Place the cutlets on a heated platter and cover with foil while you prepare the sauce.

Add the sliced mushrooms to the fat remaining in the skillet and cook them over moderate heat, stirring frequently, for 3 or 4 minutes. Then stir in 1 tablespoon of flour and cook, stirring constantly, for a minute or two. Add the cream and cook, stirring until the sauce thickens slightly. Taste for seasoning. Pour the sauce over the cutlets and serve.

Dutch Marinated Rabbit

To serve 6 to 8

2 rabbits
1 cup vinegar
3 cups dry red wine
½ pound butter
2 onions, sliced
2 tablespoons flour

2 teaspoons sugar
1 teaspoon salt
½ teaspoon pepper
1 bay leaf
4 cloves
2 tablespoons soy sauce

Have the rabbits skinned, cleaned and cut into serving-sized pieces. Pour boiling water over them, drain and dry.

Combine the vinegar and wine in a large bowl; marinate the pieces in the mixture overnight in the refrigerator. Drain, reserving the marinade. Dry the pieces with paper towels.

Melt half the butter in a skillet; add the rabbit pieces and cook over medium heat until they are browned on all sides. Melt the remaining butter in a Dutch oven; brown the onions in it. Mix in the flour until lightly browned. Add the reserved marinade and bring to a boil, stirring. Add the sugar, salt, pepper, bay leaf, cloves, soy sauce and browned pieces of rabbit. Cover and simmer for about 3 hours, or until the meat is tender.

Rabbit with Mustard Sauce
Lapin Moutarde

To serve 4

A 4-pound rabbit, cut into serving
    pieces
2 tablespoons lemon juice or wine
    vinegar
8 tablespoons flour
Salt
Pepper
2 tablespoons butter
1 finely chopped onion
2 finely chopped garlic cloves
4 sliced mushrooms
1 teaspoon meat extract
1 teaspoon tomato paste
1½ cups chicken stock
½ cup white wine
2 tablespoons dry mustard
½ cup sour cream
2 sprigs tarragon
1 tablespoon finely chopped tarragon

Soak the rabbit in cold water with the lemon juice or vinegar for 2 hours. Drain and dry with paper towels. Dust the joints lightly with 5 tablespoons of the flour, salt and pepper and brown well in sizzling hot butter.

Remove the rabbit and add to the pan the onion and garlic. Cook a few minutes and add the mushrooms; cook for 2 minutes longer. Remove from the fire and add the remaining 3 tablespoons of flour, the meat extract and tomato paste. Stir until smooth; add the stock and wine and taste for seasoning. Stir over the fire until the mixture comes to a boil. Mix the mustard into the sour cream and stir into the gravy. Add the pieces of rabbit and the sprigs of tarragon. Cover and cook slowly for 1 hour, or until the rabbit is quite tender. Place the rabbit in a deep serving dish. If the gravy is too thin, boil it down until it is thick and pour it over the rabbit. Sprinkle with the chopped tarragon and serve.

Rabbit Stew with White Wine
Sauté de Lapin au Vin Blanc

To serve 4 to 6

A 2½- to 3-pound fresh rabbit or
    defrosted frozen rabbit, cut in
    serving pieces
1 cup dry white wine
2 tablespoons white wine vinegar
¼ cup olive oil
1 onion, thinly sliced
½ teaspoon dried thyme
1 bay leaf, crumbled
2 teaspoons finely chopped fresh
    parsley

½ teaspoon salt
Freshly ground black pepper
¼ pound lean salt pork, diced
2 cups water
1 tablespoon butter
12 to 16 peeled white onions, about
    1 inch in diameter
3 tablespoons finely chopped shallots
½ teaspoon finely chopped garlic
2 tablespoons flour
1½ cups beef stock, fresh or canned
Bouquet garni made of 4 parsley
    sprigs and 1 bay leaf, tied together

Wash the rabbit under running water and dry it with paper towels. Combine ½ cup of the wine, 1 tablespoon wine vinegar, olive oil, the sliced onion, thyme, bay leaf, parsley, salt and pepper for the marinade in a shallow baking dish or casserole. Marinate the rabbit 6 hours at room temperature, 12 to 24 hours refrigerated. Turn the pieces every few hours.

Simmer the pork dice in 2 cups of water for 5 minutes; drain and pat dry with paper towels. In a heavy 10- to 12-inch skillet, melt 1 tablespoon of butter over moderate heat and in it brown the pork dice until they are crisp and golden. Set the pork aside and pour most of the fat into a bowl, leaving just a film on the bottom of the skillet. Brown the onions in the fat left in the skillet, then transfer them to a bowl.

Remove the rabbit from the marinade and dry it with paper towels. Reserve the marinade. Brown the rabbit in the skillet, adding more fat as needed, then transfer the pieces to a heavy flameproof 2- to 3-quart casserole. Pour off almost all the fat from the skillet, add the shallots and garlic and cook, stirring constantly, for 2 minutes. Stir in the flour and cook, stirring over low heat 1 minute. Remove from heat and pour in the remaining ½ cup wine and stock, stirring constantly. Cook over moderate heat, stirring, until the sauce thickens. Then pour it over the rabbit and add the *bouquet garni*, reserved marinade and browned pork dice. Preheat the oven to 350°.

Bring the stew to a boil on top of the stove, cover, and cook on the middle shelf of the oven for 40 minutes. Gently stir in the onions and cook for another 20 minutes, or until the rabbit is tender when pierced with the tip of a sharp knife. Just before serving, stir the remaining 1 tablespoon of vinegar into the sauce and taste for seasoning. Serve the stew directly from the casserole.

Braised Rabbit in Wine Sauce
Hasenpfeffer

To serve 6

½ pound lean bacon, finely chopped
A 5- to 6-pound fresh rabbit or
 defrosted frozen mature rabbit, cut
 in serving pieces, or substitute two
 2½- to 3-pound fresh or defrosted
 frozen rabbits, cut in serving
 pieces
½ teaspoon salt
½ teaspoon freshly ground black
 pepper
½ cup flour

½ cup finely chopped shallots, or
 substitute ½ cup finely chopped
 onions
½ teaspoon finely chopped garlic
1 cup dry red wine
1 cup chicken stock, fresh or canned
2 tablespoons brandy
1 teaspoon currant jelly
1 small bay leaf
⅛ teaspoon dried rosemary
⅛ teaspoon dried thyme
2 teaspoons fresh lemon juice

In a heavy 5-quart flameproof casserole, cook the bacon over moderate heat, stirring and turning it frequently, until it is crisp. Spread the bacon out on a double thickness of paper towels to drain and set the casserole with the bacon fat aside.

Wash the rabbit quickly under cold running water and pat it thoroughly dry with paper towels. Sprinkle the pieces with salt and pepper, then dip them in flour and shake off any excess. Heat the bacon fat in the casserole over high heat until it splutters. Add the rabbit, a few pieces at a time, and brown them on all sides, regulating the heat so that they color quickly and evenly without burning. As they are done, transfer the rabbit pieces to a plate. Pour off all but 2 tablespoons of fat from the casserole and in it cook the shallots and garlic, stirring frequently, for 4 or 5 minutes, or until the shallots are soft and transparent but not brown. Pour in the wine and stock, and bring to a boil over high heat, meanwhile scraping in any brown bits clinging to the bottom and sides of the pan. Stir in the brandy, currant jelly, bay leaf, rosemary and thyme, and return the rabbit and any juices collected around it to the casserole. Add the drained bacon, cover the casserole tightly, and simmer over low heat for 1½ hours, or until the rabbit is tender but not falling apart. (If you are substituting small rabbits, they may cook much faster. Test them for doneness after about 1 hour of cooking.) Pick out the bay leaf, stir in the lemon juice and taste for seasoning. The sauce should be quite peppery; add more pepper, if necessary, to taste.

Serve the rabbit directly from the casserole, or arrange the pieces attractively on a deep heated platter and pour the sauce over them.

Roast Partridge with Grapes
Rebhühner mit Weintrauben

To serve 4

10 slices lean bacon
4 partridge hearts, gizzards and livers
4 one-pound oven-ready young
   partridges
Salt
Freshly ground black pepper
8 whole juniper berries, coarsely
   crushed with a mortar and pestle

2 cups seeded green or red grapes,
   or 2 cups green seedless grapes
8 canned grape leaves, or 8 washed
   fresh grape leaves
½ cup dry white or red wine
¾ cup chicken stock, fresh or
   canned
½ cup sour cream
3 or 4 small bunches of green or
   red grapes (optional)

Preheat the oven to 400°. Cook 2 of the bacon slices over low heat in a small skillet only until they are somewhat translucent and soft but not brown. Drain them on a double thickness of paper towels and then cut each strip into 6 equal pieces. Wash the hearts, gizzards and livers of the birds and pat them dry with paper towels. Then wrap them individually in small pieces of the cooked bacon, keeping the giblets for each bird aside separately.

Wash the partridges quickly under running water and dry them thoroughly inside and out with paper towels. Sprinkle the cavities of the birds with salt and a few grindings of pepper, then stuff each bird with its wrapped giblets together with 2 of the juniper berries and ½ cup of the grapes. Neatly truss the partridges with white kitchen string. Drape 2 uncooked slices of bacon across the breast and thighs of each bird, pressing the bacon snugly against the bird to keep it in place. Drape 2 grape leaves over each partridge.

Place the birds on their backs on a rack in a large, shallow roasting pan and roast them in the middle of the oven for 20 minutes, basting them every 10 minutes with 2 tablespoons of the wine. Reduce the heat to 350°, and carefully remove and discard the grape leaves and bacon from the birds. Continue roasting for 15 to 20 minutes, basting every 5 minutes or so with the remaining wine and then with the juices as they collect in the pan. The birds are done when they are a golden brown and the drumsticks feel tender to the touch. Remove the string, transfer the partridges to a heated platter and cover loosely with foil to keep them warm while you make the sauce.

Pour the pan juices through a fine sieve set over a mixing bowl. Measure the strained liquid, add enough chicken stock to make 1¼ cups and pour it into a small saucepan. Bring to a boil over high heat, reduce the heat to low and beat in the sour cream, a few tablespoonfuls at a time. Cook for a moment or two to heat the cream through. Do not let it boil. Taste and season with as much salt and pepper as you think it needs. Then spoon the sauce over the partridges and serve at once.

Partridge in Burgundy
Wildgeflügel mit Burgunder

To serve 4

4 one-pound, oven-ready young
    partridge, baby pheasant, quail,
    woodcock or grouse
Salt
Freshly ground black pepper
1 cup flour
7 tablespoons butter
¼ cup finely chopped shallots
2 cups thinly sliced mushrooms

(about ½ pound)
2 tablespoons finely chopped cooked
    ham
2 cups Burgundy or other dry red wine
2 tablespoons brandy
⅛ teaspoon dried thyme
⅛ teaspoon dried tarragon
½ small bay leaf
Pinch of ground nutmeg
2 tablespoons finely chopped parsley

Wash the birds quickly under running water and dry them inside and out with paper towels. Season the birds generously with salt and pepper, roll them in flour, then vigorously shake off the excess. In a heavy 10- to 12-inch skillet, melt 3 tablespoons of the butter over moderate heat. When the foam subsides, brown the birds, turning them frequently, until they are a light golden color on all sides. Remove the birds from the skillet and set aside. Melt 2 more tablespoons of butter in the skillet. Add 3 tablespoons of shallots and cook them over moderate heat, stirring frequently, for 4 or 5 minutes, then drop in the mushroom slices and chopped ham. Cook, stirring occasionally, for 3 to 4 minutes, until the mushrooms are lightly browned. With a rubber spatula, transfer the mixture to a bowl and set aside.

Melt the remaining 2 tablespoons of butter in the skillet and in it cook the remaining 1 tablespoon of shallots for 2 or 3 minutes, until they are soft and lightly colored. Add the wine and brandy, and bring to a boil over high heat, meanwhile scraping in any brown bits clinging to the bottom and sides of the pan. Add the thyme, tarragon, bay leaf, nutmeg, ½ teaspoon of salt and a few grindings of black pepper, stir, and then return the birds to the skillet. Baste the birds thoroughly, reduce the heat to low, cover the skillet and simmer for 20 to 30 minutes, or until the birds are tender. Test by pressing a drumstick with your finger; it should show no resistance when the bird is fully cooked. Transfer the birds to a heated platter and cover them with foil; let them rest while you prepare the sauce.

Bring the juices remaining in the skillet to a boil, and boil briskly until the liquid is reduced to about 1 cup. Remove the bay leaf, stir in the mushroom-ham mixture and simmer for a minute or two. Taste for seasoning, and stir in the parsley. Pour the sauce into a sauceboat and serve with the birds.

Partridge Braised in White Wine
Perdices Estofadas

To serve 2

2 one-pound oven-ready partridges	separated into individual cloves
1½ teaspoons salt	2 whole cloves
¼ teaspoon freshly ground black	1 small bay leaf
pepper	6 to 8 peeled white onions, each
½ cup flour	about 1 inch in diameter
2 slices lean bacon, coarsely chopped	2 medium-sized potatoes, peeled and
2 tablespoons olive oil	cut into 1-inch cubes
½ cup dry white wine	3 medium-sized carrots, scraped and
1 cup water	cut into 1-inch lengths
1 small whole head of garlic,	¼ cup fresh peas (¼ pound) or
trimmed of root fibers and dry	thoroughly defrosted frozen peas
outer casing, but not peeled or	1 tablespoon finely chopped parsley

Wash the partridges under cold running water and pat them completely dry with paper towels. Sprinkle them inside and out liberally with salt and a few grindings of pepper, then dip each bird in flour and shake it vigorously to remove any excess.

In a heavy 1½- to 2-quart casserole, cook the bacon in the olive oil over moderate heat, stirring occasionally, until crisp and golden. With a slotted spoon, transfer the pieces to paper towels to drain.

Heat the fat remaining in the casserole over high heat until it splutters. Add the partridges and brown them well on all sides, turning them with tongs and regulating the heat so they color quickly and evenly without burning. Transfer the birds to a plate. Pour off and discard the fat from the casserole and in its place add the wine and water. Bring to a boil over high heat, meanwhile scraping in any brown particles clinging to the bottom and sides of the casserole.

Return the partridges and bacon to the casserole and add the garlic, cloves and bay leaf. Cover tightly, reduce the heat to low and simmer undisturbed for 30 minutes. Add the onions, potatoes and carrots, cover again, and cook for 15 minutes longer. Then add the green peas and simmer covered for about 5 minutes more, or until the partridges and all of the vegetables are tender. Garnish with the parsley and serve at once, directly from the casserole, or if you prefer, transfer the partridges and vegetables to a heated platter.

Pheasant with Giblet Stuffing
Gefüllter Fasan

To serve 4 to 6

STUFFING
3 slices fresh white homemade-type
  bread
2 tablespoons butter
The heart, liver and gizzard of the
  pheasant
4 large chicken livers, about ¼
  pound

1 tablespoon finely chopped parsley
4 whole juniper berries and 3 whole
  black peppercorns, finely
  pulverized with a mortar and pestle
  or wrapped in a towel and crushed
  with a rolling pin
Pinch of ground allspice
Pinch of dried thyme
Pinch of dried marjoram

Preheat the oven to 350°. To make the stuffing, trim off the crusts and cut the bread into ¼-inch cubes. Spread the cubes on a baking sheet and toast in the middle of the oven for 10 minutes, turning them over once or twice. When golden brown, transfer the cubes to a mixing bowl and set aside.

In a heavy 8- to 10-inch skillet, melt 2 tablespoons of butter over moderate heat. When the foam subsides, add the pheasant giblets and the chicken livers, and cook for 2 or 3 minutes, stirring occasionally, until the giblets and liver are lightly browned. Then remove them to a board, chop them very fine and add them to the toasted bread. With a rubber spatula, scrape any fat remaining in the skillet into the bread and stir in the parsley, pulverized juniper berries and pepper, allspice, thyme and marjoram.

PHEASANT
A 3½-to 4-pound oven-ready
  pheasant
3 tablespoons butter, softened
1 tablespoon fresh lemon juice

1 teaspoon salt
4 slices lean bacon
1 cup chicken stock, fresh or canned
½ cup sour cream

Wash the pheasant quickly under cold running water and pat it thoroughly dry inside and out with paper towels. Beat the 3 tablespoons of butter, lemon juice and salt together with a spoon and rub it into the pheasant inside and out. Fill the cavity loosely with the stuffing, and close the opening by lacing it with skewers or sewing it with heavy white thread. Fasten the neck skin to the back of the pheasant with a skewer. Lay the bacon slices side by side across the bird and wrap them around it, pressing the slices snugly against the body to keep them in place.

Place the pheasant, breast side up, on a rack set in a shallow baking pan just large enough to hold the bird comfortably. Roast undisturbed in the middle of the oven for 30 minutes. Then increase the oven heat to 400°, remove the bacon slices and set them aside. Baste the pheasant with ¼ cup of chicken stock and roast for about 30 minutes longer, basting every 10 minutes or so with another ¼ cup of stock. To test for doneness, pierce the thigh of the bird with the tip of a small, sharp knife. The juice should spurt out a clear yellow; if it is slightly pink, roast for another 5 to 10 minutes.

Transfer the pheasant to a heated platter, drape the bacon slices over it, and let the bird rest covered with aluminum foil for 10 minutes before carving. Meanwhile, make the sauce by pouring any remaining stock into the pan, bringing it to a boil over high heat, and scraping in the brown bits clinging to the bottom and sides of the pan. Stir in the sour cream a few tablespoons at a time, and simmer long enough to heat it through. Taste for seasoning. Pour the sauce into a heated sauceboat and serve it with the pheasant.

Pheasant and Mushrooms
Fasan in Rotwein

To serve 4 to 6

A 3½- to 4-pound oven-ready
  pheasant
6 tablespoons butter, softened
Salt
Freshly ground black pepper
½ cup finely chopped onions

1 cup dry red wine
½ cup cold water or ½ cup chicken
  stock, fresh or canned
½ small bay leaf
2 slices lean bacon
1 cup thinly sliced fresh mushrooms
1 tablespoon flour
⅓ cup heavy cream

Wash the pheasant quickly under cold running water and pat it thoroughly dry inside and out with paper towels. Then rub the cavity of the bird with 1 tablespoon of the soft butter and sprinkle it liberally with salt and a few grindings of pepper. Truss the bird securely with white kitchen cord.

In a heavy 5-quart casserole or Dutch oven, heat 3 tablespoons of the butter over moderate heat, add the pheasant and brown it well on all sides, turning it frequently and regulating the heat so that the bird browns quickly without burning. Transfer the pheasant to a plate. Add the chopped onions to the casserole and cook over moderate heat for 5 to 8 minutes, stirring occasionally, until the onions are soft and light brown. Then pour in the wine and bring it to a boil, meanwhile scraping into it any brown bits clinging to the bottom and sides of the casserole. Stir in the water or stock, bay leaf, ½ teaspoon of salt and a few grindings of black pepper.

Return the pheasant and any juices that have accumulated around it to the casserole and drape 2 slices of bacon across the breast. Cover the casserole, reduce the heat to its lowest point and simmer the pheasant for about 45 minutes, or until it is tender. (A mature pheasant may take from 15 to 30 minutes longer.) In either case test for doneness by piercing the thigh with the tip of a small, sharp knife. The juice should spurt out a clear yellow. If tinged with pink, simmer for a few minutes longer. Remove the bird to a warm platter and let it rest, loosely covered with foil, while you make the sauce. Discard the bay leaf.

In a 10-inch skillet melt the remaining 2 tablespoons of butter over high heat. When the foam subsides, add the mushrooms and cook for 3 minutes, stirring occasionally. Add the flour and cook, stirring constantly, for a minute or so. With a rubber spatula, transfer the entire contents of the skillet to the casserole. Then stir in the heavy cream and simmer until the sauce thickens slightly. Taste for seasoning. Carve the pheasant into attractive serving pieces, pour the sauce over them and serve at once.

Roast Pigeon

To serve 4

4 pigeons or doves, approximately 1 pound each	½ teaspoon salt
4 tablespoons soft butter, unsalted	Freshly ground black pepper
½ teaspoon thyme	2 small onions, peeled and halved
2 teaspoons finely chopped fresh tarragon or ½ teaspoon dried tarragon	2 tablespoons butter
	2 tablespoons oil
	2 strips of bacon, cut in half
2 tablespoons finely chopped fresh parsley	4 tablespoons finely chopped onion
	2 cups chicken stock, fresh or canned
	6 green olives, blanched and sliced

Wash the birds under cold running water and dry them thoroughly with paper towels inside and out. In a mixing bowl, cream the butter by beating it against the side of the bowl with a wooden spoon until it is light and fluffy. Then beat in the thyme, tarragon, parsley, ½ teaspoon salt and pepper. Rub the cavities of the birds with salt and then with the butter mixture. Place ½ onion inside each bird and truss them securely.

Preheat the oven to 425°. In a heavy 12-inch skillet, heat the butter and oil over moderate heat. When the foam subsides add the birds to the skillet and brown them on all sides for about 10 minutes, turning them with tongs. Be careful not to let them burn. Then transfer them to a rack set in a shallow roasting pan large enough to hold them comfortably.

Tie ½ strip of bacon on the breast of each bird and roast in the middle of the oven for 20 minutes. Reduce the heat to 350° and roast for 20 minutes more, basting the birds every 5 minutes or so with the drippings in the pan.

When they are done, remove the trussing strings, transfer the birds to a heated platter and sprinkle them lightly with salt. Cover the platter loosely with a piece of foil to keep the birds warm while you make the sauce. Add the chopped onions to the drippings remaining in the roasting pan
178

and cook them over moderate heat on top of the stove for 2 to 3 minutes. Then pour in the chicken stock and bring to a boil, stirring in any brown bits clinging to the bottom and sides of the pan. Boil briskly until the sauce is reduced to about half its volume. Strain it into a saucepan. Skim the surface of as much fat as you can and stir in the sliced green olives. Cook for a minute or so until they are heated through, and serve in a gravy boat.

NOTE: To blanch the olives, cover them with cold water in a small saucepan and bring to a boil. Cook briskly for 2 minutes, or a few minutes longer if the olives seem too briny, then drain and run cold water over them.

Broiled Quail
Bildircin

To serve 12

24 quail, split
½ pound butter
4 teaspoons salt

1½ teaspoons pepper
2 cups fine bread crumbs
2 cups chopped mushrooms
½ cup dry red wine
24 sautéed bread rounds

Split the quail down the middle but not completely through, so that each bird remains in one piece. Finely chop or grind the quail livers and giblets and set aside. Wash and dry the birds. Melt all but 4 tablespoons of the butter and brush the quail on both sides with the melted butter, then season with the salt and pepper. Sprinkle the quail inside and out with the bread crumbs. Arrange them on a broiling pan and broil for 10 minutes on each side, basting frequently with the melted butter.

While the quail are broiling, melt the remaining 4 tablespoons of butter. Sauté the chopped livers, giblets and mushrooms in the butter for 5 minutes. Add the wine, and salt and pepper to taste, then cook over low heat for 10 minutes. Spread the mixture on the sautéed bread rounds and put a broiled quail on each.

Wild Turkey with Cornbread Stuffing

To serve 8 to 10

CORNBREAD STUFFING
10 tablespoons butter
1½ cups finely chopped onion
1 pound well-seasoned sausage meat
The turkey liver
6 cups coarsely crumbled cornbread

½ teaspoon salt
Freshly ground black pepper
2 teaspoons thyme
¼ cup finely chopped fresh parsley
¼ cup Madeira or sherry
¼ cup heavy cream

CORNBREAD STUFFING: Melt 8 tablespoons of the butter in a large, heavy skillet, add the chopped onions and cook over moderate heat for 6 to 8 minutes, or until they color lightly. Scrape them into a large mixing bowl. Add the sausage to the skillet, now set over medium heat, and break the meat up with a fork as it cooks. When the meat is lightly browned, transfer it to a sieve set over a small bowl and let the fat drain through. Meanwhile, again in the same pan, melt the remaining 2 tablespoons of butter and, when the foam subsides, add the turkey liver. Brown it over high heat for 2 to 3 minutes, then chop it coarsely and combine with the onions in the bowl. Add the drained sausage meat, cornbread crumbs, salt, a few grindings of black pepper, the thyme and parsley. With a large spoon, gently stir the ingredients together, then moisten the stuffing with the Madeira or sherry and cream. Taste for seasoning.

TURKEY
A 10- to 12-pound wild turkey
1 teaspoon salt
Freshly ground black pepper

12 tablespoons melted butter (1½ quarter-pound sticks)
½ cup coarsely chopped onion

TURKEY: Preheat the oven to 350°. Wash the turkey under cold running water and dry it thoroughly inside and out with paper towels. Rub the inside of the turkey with the salt and a few grindings of pepper, and fill the body and breast cavities loosely with the stuffing, closing the openings with skewers or sewing them with thread. Truss the bird securely. With a pastry brush or paper towel, brush the outside of the turkey with a few tablespoons of the melted butter and sprinkle it with salt. Place the bird on a rack in a shallow roasting pan and scatter the onions around it in the bottom of the pan. Roast the turkey uncovered in the middle of the oven for about 2 hours, basting it every 15 minutes or so with the rest of the melted butter and with the drippings that accumulate in the pan.

To test for doneness pierce the thigh of the bird with the tip of a small, sharp knife. The juice should spurt out a clear yellow; if it is slightly pink, roast the bird for another 5 to 10 minutes. Transfer the turkey to a heated platter and let it rest for 10 minutes before carving.

GRAVY

3 tablespoons flour	½ cup light cream
1 cup water or chicken stock,	White pepper
fresh or canned	Salt

While the turkey is resting, make the gravy. Pour off all but about 3 tablespoons of fat from the roasting pan and stir the flour into the pan. When the flour is thoroughly absorbed, add the cup of water or stock. Bring to a boil over high heat, stirring constantly with a wire whisk and incorporating into the liquid the brown sediment on the bottom and sides of the pan. When the sauce is quite thick, beat in the cream. If you prefer the gravy thinner, add a little more cream. Taste for seasoning and pour into a heated gravy boat. The gravy may be strained if you like.

NOTE: A domestic turkey may be stuffed and roasted in the same fashion as a wild turkey but may take 15 minutes or so longer to roast.

Chicken

Roast Chicken Stuffed with Shrimp
Gefüllte Hühner mit Krabben

To serve 4

A 4½- to 5-pound roasting chicken
1 teaspoon salt
½ teaspoon dried marjoram

THE STUFFING
8 slices day-old white bread
1 cup heavy cream
12 tablespoons (1½ quarter-pound sticks) unsalted butter, melted
2 egg yolks
8 large shrimp, cooked, shelled and coarsely chopped

4 large shrimp, uncooked, shelled and finely chopped or puréed in a blender
¼ cup finely chopped parsley
¼ cup cooked green peas, fresh, frozen or canned
½ teaspoon salt
Freshly ground black pepper
2 egg whites
½ cup chicken stock, fresh or canned (optional)

Preheat the oven to 350°. Wash the chicken quickly under cold running water, pat it dry with paper towels, then rub the inside of it with a mixture of the salt and the marjoram.

Toast the bread in the upper third of the oven for 5 to 8 minutes, or until it is dry but not brown. Crumble it and soak it in the cream in a mixing bowl for about 5 minutes.

In an 8-inch saucepan, combine the bread-and-cream mixture with 4 tablespoons of the melted butter, then, stirring constantly, simmer over low heat until the mixture is pasty and smooth, somewhat resembling a soft dough. Remove it from the heat, let it cool for about 10 minutes, then beat in the egg yolks, one at a time, thoroughly incorporating one before adding the other. Beat in the cooked shrimp, the raw shrimp purée, the parsley and the peas. Add the salt and a grinding of pepper.

182

With a wire whisk or rotary or electric beater, beat the egg whites, preferably in an unlined copper bowl, until they form stiff, unwavering peaks when the beater is lifted from the bowl. With a rubber spatula, fold the egg whites into the stuffing, using an under-and-over cutting motion rather than a mixing motion, until no trace of them remains. Fill the breast cavity of the chicken, but don't pack it tightly—the stuffing will expand as it cooks. Fold the neck skin under the chicken and secure it with several stitches of strong thread. Stuff the body cavity loosely—no more than ¾ full—and close it with trussing pins or with a needle and thread. Brush the chicken all over with some of the melted butter and place it on a rack in a roasting pan just large enough to hold it. Pour the rest of the butter over the breast. Roast the chicken in the middle of the oven for about 1½ hours, basting it frequently with the pan juices. Test for doneness by piercing a thigh with the point of a small sharp knife. If the juice that spurts out is yellow, the chicken is done. If it is pink, roast a few minutes longer and test again.

Remove the chicken to a heated serving platter and let it stand for about 10 minutes before carving it. Serve it, if you like, with the pan juices diluted with ½ cup of chicken stock that has been brought to a boil in the drippings.

French Roast Chicken
Poulet Rôti

To serve 4

	3 tablespoons melted butter
A 3½- to 4-pound roasting chicken	1 tablespoon vegetable oil
2 tablespoons soft butter	1 onion, sliced
½ teaspoon lemon juice	1 carrot, cut in ½-inch chunks
Salt	1 celery stalk, cut in ½-inch chunks
Freshly ground black pepper	1 cup chicken stock, fresh or canned

Preheat the oven to 450°. Wash the chicken quickly under cold running water and dry it thoroughly inside and out with paper towels. Cream the soft butter, beating it vigorously against the side of a small bowl with a wooden spoon until it is fluffy. Beat in the lemon juice, ¼ teaspoon salt and a few grindings of pepper. Spread the seasoned butter inside the chicken. Neatly truss the chicken with white kitchen string. Combine the melted butter and oil and brush about half of it over the outside of the chicken.

Place the chicken on its side on a rack in a shallow roasting pan just large enough to hold it comfortably—about 9 by 12 inches—and place on the middle shelf of the oven. After 10 minutes, turn the chicken onto its other side. Brush with butter and oil and roast for another 10 minutes. Reduce the oven heat to 350°. Turn the chicken on its back, brush it with butter and oil and salt it lightly. Spread the vegetables in the bottom of the pan. Roast the chicken, basting it every 10 minutes with butter and oil while they last, then use a bulb baster or spoon to baste it with pan juices. After 60 minutes, test the chicken for doneness by lifting it with a wooden spoon inserted in the tail opening. When the juices that run out are yellow, it is done. If they are pink, cook a few minutes longer. Transfer the bird to a carving board, cut off the trussing strings, and let it rest for 5 minutes or so before serving.

Meanwhile, make the sauce. Stir the chicken stock into the roasting pan and bring to a boil over high heat, stirring and scraping in any browned bits clinging to the bottom and sides of the pan. Boil briskly for 2 or 3 minutes until the sauce has the desired intensity of flavor. Strain through a sieve, pressing down hard on the vegetables with the back of a spoon before discarding them. Skim off as much surface fat as possible, and taste for seasoning. The chicken may be carved in the kitchen or at the table. Serve the sauce separately.

Casserole-roasted Chicken
Poulet en Cocotte Bonne Femme

To serve 4

A 3½- to 4-pound roasting chicken
4 tablespoons soft butter
¼ teaspoon finely chopped garlic
½ teaspoon dried thyme, crumbled
¼ pound salt pork, diced
2 cups water
5 tablespoons butter
16 peeled white onions, about 1 inch
in diameter
6 peeled carrots, cut in 2-inch cylinders or olive shapes
16 one-inch potato balls, or potatoes cut in 2-inch olive shapes
Salt
Freshly ground black pepper
Bouquet garni made of 4 parsley sprigs and 1 bay leaf, tied together

Preheat the oven to 350°. Wash the chicken quickly under cold running water and dry it thoroughly inside and out with paper towels. Cream 2 tablespoons of soft butter until it is fluffy, and beat in the garlic and thyme. Spread the seasoned butter inside the chicken. Truss the chicken and rub the outside with the remaining 2 tablespoons of soft butter.

Blanch the salt pork dice by simmering them in 2 cups of water for 5 minutes; drain on paper towels and pat dry. In a heavy, enameled oval casserole just large enough to hold the chicken comfortably, melt 1 tablespoon of the butter over moderate heat and in it brown the pork dice, stirring them or shaking the casserole frequently, until they are crisp and
184

golden. Remove them with a slotted spoon and set aside to drain on paper towels. In the rendered fat left in the casserole, brown the chicken on all sides. Remove from heat and pour off all but a thin film of fat from the casserole. Return the chicken and the browned pork dice to it and set aside.

In a heavy 10- to 12-inch skillet, melt the remaining 4 tablespoons of butter over moderate heat and in it cook the onions, carrots, and potatoes, stirring frequently, for 5 minutes, or until coated with butter and lightly colored. Remove the vegetables and arrange around the chicken. Season with salt and pepper, add the *bouquet garni,* and cover the casserole. If the cover isn't snug, drape a piece of foil over the chicken before covering it.

On top of the stove, heat the casserole until the fat begins to splutter. Cook the chicken on the middle shelf of the oven, basting it every 20 minutes with the juices that will accumulate in the casserole. After 1¼ hours, start testing the chicken by lifting it with a wooden spoon inserted in its tail opening. When the juices that run out are yellow, it is done.

To serve, transfer the chicken to a heated platter and arrange the vegetables attractively around it. Discard the *bouquet garni* and skim as much surface fat as possible from the sauce left in the casserole. Taste the sauce and correct the seasoning. The chicken may be carved in the kitchen or at the table. Serve the sauce separately.

Chicken Breasts with Prosciutto and Cheese
Petti di Pollo alla Bolognese

To serve 4

4 individual chicken breasts, ½ pound each, skinned and boned
Salt
Freshly ground black pepper
Flour
3 tablespoons butter

2 tablespoons oil
8 thin 2-by-4-inch slices prosciutto
8 thin 2-by-4-inch slices imported Fontina or Bel Paese cheese
4 teaspoons freshly grated imported Parmesan cheese
2 tablespoons chicken stock, fresh or canned

Preheat the oven to 350°. With a very sharp knife, carefully slice each chicken breast horizontally to make 8 thin slices. Lay them an inch or so apart on a long strip of wax paper and cover them with another strip of wax paper. Pound the chicken slices lightly with the flat of a cleaver or the bottom of a heavy bottle to flatten them somewhat. Strip off the paper. Season the slices with salt and a few grindings of pepper, then dip them in flour and shake off the excess. In a heavy 10- to 12-inch skillet, melt the butter with the oil over moderate heat. Brown the chicken to a light golden color in the hot fat, 3 or 4 slices at a time. Do not overcook them.

Transfer the chicken breasts to a shallow buttered baking-and-serving dish large enough to hold them comfortably. Place a slice of prosciutto and then a slice of cheese on each one. Sprinkle them with grated cheese and dribble the chicken stock over them. Bake uncovered in the oven for about 10 minutes, or until the cheese is melted and lightly browned. Serve at once.

Slice the filleted breasts
as indicated in the picture above.

Cover fillets with wax paper; pound
them thin with the flat of a cleaver.

After the fillets have been browned,

After the fillets have been browned,
cover them with prosciutto and cheese.

Sautéed Chicken with Artichoke Hearts
Poulet Sauté à la Bordelaise

To serve 4

A 2½- to 3-pound frying chicken,
  cut up
6 tablespoons butter
2 tablespoons vegetable oil
16 to 24 large whole peeled shallots,
  or 16 one-inch peeled white onions

Salt
Freshly ground black pepper
2 bay leaves
1 teaspoon lemon juice
1 nine-ounce package frozen
  artichoke hearts, defrosted and
  drained
½ cup chicken stock, fresh or canned

Wash the chicken quickly under cold running water and dry the pieces thoroughly with paper towels; if they are damp, they won't brown well. In a heavy 10- to 12-inch enameled or stainless-steel skillet or sauté pan, melt 4 tablespoons of the butter and the 2 tablespoons of oil over moderately high heat. When the foam begins to subside, brown the chicken a few pieces at a time, starting them skin side down and turning them with tongs. As the pieces become a rich golden brown, remove them to a plate.

First the chicken is browned, starting
each piece skin side down.

Next shallots are swirled in
the same skillet until they are golden.

Then the chicken and shallots
are combined, covered and simmered.

When all the chicken is browned, add the shallots or onions to the skillet and cook them, shaking the pan to color them lightly and as evenly as possible. Pour off all but a thin film of fat and return the chicken to the skillet. Season with salt and pepper, lay the bay leaves on top and cover the pan. Cook over high heat until the fat splutters. At once reduce the heat and cook the chicken slowly, using a bulb baster or spoon to baste it with pan juices every 7 or 8 minutes.

Meanwhile, melt the remaining 2 tablespoons of butter in an 8- to 10-inch enameled or stainless-steel skillet. When the foam subsides, stir in the lemon juice. Add the artichoke hearts and toss them in the lemon butter until they glisten. Season them with salt, cover the skillet, and cook

188

over low heat for 10 to 15 minutes or until the artichoke hearts are tender.

After the chicken has cooked for about 30 minutes it should be done, and its juices will run yellow when a thigh is pierced with the tip of a sharp knife. Remove the chicken from the skillet and arrange the pieces attractively on a large heated platter with the shallots or white onions and the artichoke hearts around them. Discard the bay leaves.

Pour the chicken stock into the juices remaining in the skillet and bring to a boil over high heat, scraping in any browned bits clinging to the bottom and sides of the pan. Boil for 2 or 3 minutes until the sauce is reduced to about ⅓ cup. Pour it over the chicken and serve at once.

ALTERNATIVE: If you like, you may cook the artichoke hearts with the chicken. In that case, omit the 2 tablespoons of butter and the lemon juice from the recipe. Add the artichoke hearts to the chicken after it has cooked with the shallots for 15 minutes and baste them well with the pan juices. Cover and cook, basting every 7 or 8 minutes, for 15 minutes longer, or until the chicken is done and the artichoke hearts are tender.

Sautéed Chicken with Mushrooms
Poulet Sauté à la Crème

To serve 4

A 2½- to 3-pound frying chicken, cut up
5 tablespoons butter
2 tablespoons vegetable oil
Salt

Freshly ground black pepper
1 cup sliced fresh mushrooms
¼ cup dry white wine
¾ cup heavy cream
2 tablespoons finely chopped fresh parsley

Following the directions in the recipe for sautéed chicken with artichoke hearts *(page 187)*, brown the chicken in 4 tablespoons of the butter and the oil in a heavy 8- to 10-inch skillet or sauté pan. Pour off all but a thin film of fat, return the chicken to the skillet and season it. Cover the skillet tightly and cook over high heat until the fat splutters. Immediately reduce the heat and cook the chicken slowly, basting it with pan juices every 7 or 8 minutes. After 30 minutes, or when the chicken is tender, remove it from the skillet and arrange the pieces attractively on a heated serving platter.

Add the mushrooms to the skillet and toss for 2 minutes, then pour in the wine and boil over high heat, stirring in any browned bits that cling to the pan. When the wine has almost cooked away, stir in the cream and cook it briskly for at least 3 or 4 minutes until it has reduced and thickened slightly. Taste and correct seasoning. Remove from heat and stir in the parsley, add the remaining 1 tablespoon of butter and tip the pan back and forth to blend it into the sauce. Pour the sauce and mushrooms over the chicken and serve at once.

Chicken in Lemon Sauce
Poulet Sauté au Citron

To serve 6 to 8

Two 3½-pound pullets, disjointed	¼ cup dry white wine
2 teaspoons salt	3 shallots, chopped
½ teaspoon pepper	1 tablespoon chopped parsley
2 tablespoons olive oil	2 tablespoons lemon juice
6 tablespoons butter	Lemon wedges

Wash and dry the chicken pieces; season with the salt and pepper.

Heat the oil and 3 tablespoons of the butter in a large skillet. Place the chicken pieces in it in a single layer and brown on all sides. Cover and cook over low heat until tender, about 45 minutes. Arrange the chicken on a hot serving platter and keep warm.

To the pan juices, add the wine, shallots and parsley. Bring to a boil, scraping the browned particles in the skillet into the liquid. Remove from the heat and stir in the remaining butter. When it has melted, add the lemon juice. Pour the liquid over the chicken and garnish with the lemon wedges.

Austrian Fried Chicken
Wiener Backhendl

To serve 4

	½ cup flour
A 3-pound frying chicken, cut into 4,	1 egg, lightly beaten
6 or 8 serving pieces and skinned	1½ cups bread crumbs
¼ cup fresh lemon juice	½ pound lard
1 tablespoon salt	Lemon wedges

In a glass, stainless-steel or enameled baking dish, toss the chicken with the lemon juice until all the pieces are thoroughly moistened. Marinate about 1½ hours, turning the pieces occasionally. Before frying, pat the pieces dry with paper towels, then salt them generously, dip them in the flour and shake off the excess. Then dip them in the egg. Roll each piece of chicken in the bread crumbs to coat it thoroughly.

If the chicken is cut into 8 pieces, no cooking after frying is necessary. If it is cut into 4 (in the Austrian tradition) or 6 pieces, preheat the oven to 250° and set a large baking dish on the middle shelf.

In a heavy 12-inch skillet, heat the lard until a light haze forms over it. (The melted fat should be about ¼ inch deep and should be kept at that depth.) Using tongs, add about half the chicken pieces. When these are a deep golden brown on one side, turn them with the tongs. If the chicken is cut into small pieces, transfer each to paper towels to drain before serving. If the pieces are larger, put each browned piece into the baking dish in the oven. In either case replace the cooked piece with an uncooked one as you fry it. Chicken cut into 6 pieces should be baked 5 to 10 minutes. One cut into 4 pieces should be baked 10 to 15 minutes.

Fry all the chicken in the same way, allowing more time for the dark meat than for the wings and breasts. The frying should take about ½ hour. Serve the chicken garnished with lemon wedges.

Kiev-style Fried Chicken
Poulet à la Kiev

To serve 4

2 chicken breasts, split in half	Pepper
⅛ pound sweet butter	About ½ cup flour
1 clove garlic, crushed	1 egg, beaten
2 teaspoons finely chopped chives or marjoram	About ½ cup bread crumbs
	Oil for deep-fat frying
Salt	Watercress

Skin the chicken breasts and remove the bones. Place each chicken breast between 2 pieces of waxed paper, skin-side down. Pound them with a wooden mallet until they are about ¼ inch thick. Remove the paper. In the middle of each breast place a small piece of firm cold butter, a bit of garlic, ½ teaspoon chopped chives or marjoram, salt and pepper. Roll up the meat, tuck in each end and secure with a skewer. Dust lightly with flour, brush with the beaten egg and roll in bread crumbs. Fry in deep, hot fat (350°) for 3 to 4 minutes until golden brown. Drain on paper towels and remove skewers. Serve on a hot platter and garnished with watercress.

Southern Fried Chicken with Gravy

To serve 4

A 2½-pound frying chicken, cut into
serving pieces
Salt

1 cup flour
1 cup lard, or ½ cup vegetable
shortening combined with
½ cup lard

Wash the chicken pieces under cold running water and pat them thoroughly dry with paper towels. Sprinkle the pieces with salt on all sides. Put the cup of flour in a sturdy paper bag. Drop the chicken into the bag a few pieces at a time and shake the bag until each piece is thoroughly coated with flour. Remove the chicken pieces from the bag and vigorously shake them free of all excess flour. Lay them side by side on a sheet of wax paper. Preheat the oven to 200° and in the middle of the oven place a shallow baking dish.

Over high heat melt the lard or combined lard and shortening in a 10- or 12-inch heavy skillet. The fat should be ¼ inch deep. If it is not, add a little more. When a light haze forms above it, add the chicken pieces, starting them skin side down. It is preferable to begin frying the legs and thighs first, since they will take longer to cook than the breasts and wings. Cover the pan and fry the chicken over moderate heat for about 6 to 8 minutes, checking every now and then to make sure the chicken does not burn. When the pieces are deep brown on one side, turn them over and cover the pan again. Transfer the finished chicken to the baking dish in the oven and continue frying until all the pieces are cooked. Keep the chicken warm in the oven while you make the gravy.

CREAM GRAVY
2 tablespoons flour
¾ cup chicken stock, fresh or canned

½ to ¾ cup light cream
Salt
White pepper

Pour off all but 2 tablespoons of fat in the frying pan. Add 2 tablespoons of flour, and stir until the fat and flour are well combined. Pour in the chicken stock and ½ cup of the light cream, and cook over moderate heat, beating with a whisk until the gravy is smooth and thick. If it is too thick for your taste, stir in the remaining cream to thin it. Strain it through a fine sieve if you wish. Taste for seasoning, then pour into a heated gravy boat and serve with the fried chicken arranged attractively on a heated serving platter.

Eight-Pieces Chicken
Cha-pa-kwai

To serve 2 to 4

A 2½-pound frying chicken
2 tablespoons soy sauce
1 tablespoon Chinese rice wine, or
   pale dry sherry
1 teaspoon salt
½ teaspoon sugar
1 scallion, including the green top,
   cut into 2-inch pieces and split in
   half

A ½ inch cube peeled fresh ginger
   root, crushed with a cleaver or
   kitchen mallet
3 cups peanut oil, or flavorless
   vegetable oil
½ cup flour
Salt
Freshly ground black
   pepper

PREPARE AHEAD: 1. On a chopping board, cut off the wings, legs and thighs of the chicken with a cleaver or large, sharp knife. Cut the body in half by cutting down through the breastbone and backbone. Then, one at a time, chop the 8 pieces of chicken across the bones into 2-inch pieces. Spread the chicken on a double thickness of paper towels and pat each piece thoroughly dry.

2. In a large bowl, combine the soy sauce, wine, salt, sugar, scallions and ginger, stirring until the salt and sugar dissolve. Add the chicken and toss the pieces about to coat them thoroughly with the mixture. Marinate at room temperature for 1 to 2 hours.

3. Have the chicken, flour and oil within easy reach.

TO COOK: Pour 3 cups of oil into a 12-inch wok or deep-fryer and heat the oil until a haze forms above it or it registers 375° on a deep-frying thermometer. Drain the chicken and discard the marinade. With paper towels, wipe the chicken pieces dry. Dip them in the flour, then vigorously shake off all but a light dusting of the flour. Drop the chicken into the hot oil and fry, turning the pieces frequently for 5 minutes, or until the pieces are golden brown on both sides. Remove them from the oil with a bamboo strainer or slotted spoon and drain them on a double thickness of paper towels. Season with salt and pepper to taste and serve on a heated platter.

Broiled Marinated Chicken

Kababe Morgh

To serve 4

1 cup finely grated onion
½ cup fresh lemon juice
2 teaspoons salt
2 two-pound chickens, each cut into
   8 serving pieces

4 tablespoons melted butter
⅛ teaspoon ground saffron (or ⅛
   teaspoon saffron threads
   pulverized with a mortar and pestle
   or the back of a spoon) dissolved
   in 1 tablespoon warm water

In a stainless-steel, enameled or glass bowl combine the onion, lemon juice and salt, stirring until they are thoroughly blended. Add the chicken and turn the pieces about with a spoon to coat them well. Marinate at room temperature for at least 2 hours or in the refrigerator for 4 hours, turning the pieces over occasionally.

Light a layer of coals in a charcoal broiler and let them burn until a white ash appears on the surface or preheat the stove broiler to its highest point.

Remove the chicken from the marinade and string the pieces tightly on 4 long skewers, pressing them together firmly. If you are broiling the chicken in an oven, suspend the skewers side by side across the length of a large roasting pan deep enough to allow about 1 inch of space under the meat.

Stir the melted butter and dissolved saffron into the marinade and brush the chicken evenly on all sides with 2 or 3 tablespoons of the mixture. Broil about 3 inches from the heat for 10 to 15 minutes turning the skewers occasionally and basting the chicken frequently with the remaining marinade. The chicken is done if the juices that trickle out are yellow rather than pink when a thigh is pierced with the point of a small, sharp knife.

Broiled Spiced Chicken

To serve 8

Two 2½-pound broilers, quartered
2 cups yoghurt
2 teaspoons salt
2 teaspoons black pepper
2 teaspoons ground cumin seed

1½ teaspoons cinnamon
1 teaspoon dried mint
½ teaspoon ginger
3 tablespoons lemon juice
Oil

Wash and dry the chickens, then marinate them in a mixture of all the remaining ingredients for three hours at room temperature. Be sure the chicken quarters are well covered with the yoghurt mixture, spreading it on with a knife if necessary.

Arrange the chicken on an oiled broiling pan, and broil on the lowest rack for 30 minutes on each side.

Chicken with Saffron Rice and Peas
Arroz con Pollo

To serve 4

A 2½- to 3-pound chicken, cut into
   6 to 8 serving pieces
Salt
Freshly ground black pepper
1 tablespoon lard
¼ pound salt pork, finely diced
1 cup finely chopped onions
1 teaspoon finely chopped garlic
1 tablespoon paprika

1 cup finely chopped tomatoes
1½ cups raw medium or long-grain
   regular-milled rice or imported
   short-grain rice
1 cup fresh or frozen peas
3 cups boiling water
⅛ teaspoon ground saffron or saffron
   threads crushed with a mortar and
   pestle or with the back of a spoon
2 tablespoons finely chopped parsley

Pat the chicken pieces completely dry with paper towels and sprinkle them liberally with salt and a few grindings of pepper. In a heavy 4-quart casserole, melt the lard over moderate heat. Add the salt pork dice and, stirring frequently, cook until they have rendered all their fat and become crisp and golden brown; then, with a slotted spoon, transfer them to paper towels to drain. Add the chicken to the fat in the casserole and brown it, turning the pieces with tongs and regulating the heat so that they color quickly and evenly without burning. Set the chicken aside on a platter.

Pour off all but a thin film of fat from the casserole. Stir in the onions and garlic and cook for about 5 minutes, or until the onions are soft and transparent but not brown. Stir in the paprika, then the tomatoes and bring to a boil, stirring frequently. Cook briskly, uncovered, for about 5 minutes, or until most of the liquid in the pan evaporates and the mixture is thick enough to hold its shape lightly in a spoon.

Return the chicken and pork dice to the casserole, and add the rice, peas, boiling water, saffron and 1 teaspoon of salt. Stir together gently but thoroughly. Bring to a boil over high heat, then reduce the heat to low, cover tightly and simmer for 20 to 30 minutes, or until the chicken is tender and the rice has absorbed all the liquid. Stir in the parsley, and taste for seasoning. Cover and let stand off the heat for 5 minutes before serving directly from the casserole.

Chicken Simmered in Red Wine
Coq au Vin à la Bourguignonne

To serve 4

THE ONIONS

½ pound lean salt pork, cut into
lardons, 1¼-inch strips ¼ inch
in diameter

1 tablespoon butter

12 to 16 peeled white onions, about
1 inch in diameter

Preheat the oven to 350°. Blanch the pork by simmering it in water for 5 minutes; drain on paper towels and pat dry. In a heavy 8- to 10-inch skillet, melt 1 tablespoon of butter over moderate heat, and in it brown the pork strips, stirring them or shaking the pan frequently, until they are crisp and golden. Remove them with a slotted spoon and set aside to drain on paper towels. Brown the onions in the rendered fat over moderately high heat, shaking the skillet occasionally to roll them around and color them as evenly as possible. Transfer the onions to a shallow baking dish large enough to hold them in one layer, and sprinkle them with a tablespoon or 2 of pork fat. Bake the onions uncovered, turning them once or twice, for 30 minutes, or until they are barely tender when pierced with the tip of a sharp knife. Remove from the oven, drain off fat, and set aside.

THE MUSHROOMS

2 tablespoons butter

2 tablespoons finely chopped shallots

or scallions

½ pound fresh mushrooms, whole if
small, quartered or sliced if large

Melt the butter over moderate heat in another skillet. When the foam subsides, cook the shallots, stirring constantly with a wooden spoon, for 30 seconds. Add the mushrooms and cook them with the shallots, stirring and turning them frequently, for 2 or 3 minutes. Add to the onions and set aside.

THE CHICKEN

A 2½- to 3-pound frying chicken, cut
up

¼ cup Cognac

Bouquet garni made of 4 parsley
sprigs and 1 bay leaf, tied together

½ teaspoon dried thyme, crumbled

1 large garlic clove, finely chopped

2 cups red Burgundy or other dry red
wine

2 tablespoons flour

½ cup beef or chicken stock, fresh or
canned

2 tablespoons finely chopped fresh
parsley

Wash the chicken in cold water and dry the pieces thoroughly. Reheat the pork fat remaining in the first skillet, adding a few tablespoons of vegetable oil, if needed, to make a film of fat ⅛-inch deep. Brown the chicken, a few pieces at a time. Then pour off almost all of the fat from the skillet, add the Cognac and set it alight with a match; or warm the Cognac first in a small saucepan over low heat, ignite it with a match and pour it flaming over the chicken a little at a time, shaking the skillet back and forth until the flame dies. Transfer the chicken to a heavy 3- to 4-quart casserole, and add the browned pork, *bouquet garni*, thyme and garlic.

Boil the wine briskly in a 1- to 1½-quart enameled or stainless-steel saucepan to reduce it to 1½ cups. With a wooden spoon, stir the flour into the glaze remaining in the skillet in which the chicken browned, scraping in any browned bits clinging to the bottom and sides of the pan. Pour the reduced wine into the skillet and stir in the stock. Over high heat, bring this sauce to a boil, stirring constantly, and cook it until thick and smooth. Strain through a fine sieve over the chicken.

Bring the casserole to a boil over high heat, cover tightly, and place on the middle shelf of the oven. After 30 minutes, gently stir in the onions and mushrooms, and moisten them well with the sauce. Continue baking for another 10 to 15 minutes, or until the chicken is tender. Discard the *bouquet garni*. Taste and correct the seasoning of the sauce. Sprinkle with chopped parsley and serve.

French Chicken Fricassee
Fricassée de Poulet à l'Ancienne

To serve 4

A 2½- to 3-pound frying chicken, cut up
8 tablespoons butter (1 quarter-pound stick)
Salt
White pepper
¼ cup flour
3 cups hot chicken stock, fresh or canned
Bouquet garni made of 4 parsley

sprigs and 1 bay leaf, tied together
¼ teaspoon dried thyme, crumbled
⅔ cup chicken stock, fresh or canned
16 to 24 peeled white onions, about 1 inch in diameter
¾ pound fresh mushrooms, whole if small, sliced or quartered if large
1 teaspoon lemon juice
2 egg yolks
½ cup heavy cream
2 tablespoons finely chopped fresh parsley

Wash the chicken quickly under cold running water and dry the pieces thoroughly with paper towels. In a heavy 2- to 3-quart flameproof casserole, melt 6 tablespoons of the butter over moderate heat. Using tongs, lay a few pieces of chicken at a time in the butter and cook them, turning them once or twice, for about 5 minutes, or until they stiffen slightly and are no longer pink. Do not let them brown. Remove to a plate and season with salt and white pepper.

With a wooden spoon, stir the flour into the butter remaining in the casserole and cook over low heat, stirring constantly, for 1 or 2 minutes without letting it brown. Remove from heat. Slowly pour in the hot chicken stock, beating vigorously to blend *roux* and liquid. Return to heat, whisking constantly until the sauce thickens and comes to a boil. Then reduce the heat and let the sauce simmer slowly for 1 minute.

Return the chicken to the casserole together with the juices that have collected on the plate, and add the *bouquet garni* and thyme. The sauce should almost cover the chicken; add more stock if it doesn't. Bring to a boil, cover, reduce heat and simmer for 30 minutes.

Meanwhile, combine ⅔ cup stock, the remaining 2 tablespoons butter and the onions in an 8- to 10-inch enameled or stainless-steel skillet. Bring to a boil, cover, and simmer over low heat for 15 to 20 minutes, or until the onions are tender when pierced with the tip of a sharp knife. With a slotted spoon, transfer the onions to a bowl. Stir the mushrooms and lemon juice into the stock remaining in the skillet. Bring to a boil, cover and simmer for 5 minutes. Add the mushrooms to the onions. Boil the liquid remaining in the skillet until it has reduced to 2 or 3 tablespoons, and pour it into the simmering casserole of chicken.

To test the chicken for doneness, pierce a thigh with the tip of a sharp knife; the juices should run pale yellow. With tongs, transfer the chicken to a plate and discard the *bouquet garni*. Skim the fat from the surface of the sauce, which by now should be as thick as heavy cream; if it isn't, boil the sauce rapidly uncovered until it reaches the desired consistency. With a wire whisk, blend the egg yolks and cream together in a bowl. Whisk in the hot sauce, 2 tablespoons at a time, until ½ cup has been added; then reverse the process and whisk the egg-yolk-and-cream mixture back into the remaining hot sauce. Bring it to a boil, stirring constantly, then boil slowly for 30 seconds. Taste and correct the seasoning with salt, white pepper and a few drops of lemon juice. Strain through a fine sieve into a large bowl.

Wash the casserole, arrange the chicken pieces, onions and mushrooms attractively in it, and pour the sauce over them. Do not use any juices that have accumulated under the chicken unless the sauce needs thinning. Before serving, cover the casserole and simmer it over moderate heat for 5 to 10 minutes, or until the chicken is hot. Do not let the sauce come to a boil again. Serve the chicken from the casserole or arranged on a heated platter, masked with sauce and sprinkled with parsley.

Chicken Curry

Murg Masalam

To serve 8

Two 3½-pound chickens, disjointed
1½ teaspoons turmeric
1½ teaspoons cumin seeds
1 teaspoon cinnamon
6 cloves
¼ teaspoon dried ground chili peppers

1 tablespoon minced ginger root
2 cloves garlic, minced
1½ cups chopped onions
½ teaspoon ground cardamom
2 pounds tomatoes, peeled and diced
2 teaspoons salt
Water
6 tablespoons butter

Wash the chicken pieces in cold water and place them in a Dutch oven with the turmeric, cumin, cinnamon, cloves, chili peppers, ginger, garlic, onions, cardamom, tomatoes and salt. Add enough water to reach just below the top of the ingredients. Dot top with butter. Bring to a boil, then cover and cook over low heat 1 hour or until the chicken is tender. Remove the cover and cook over high heat until liquid is evaporated and the chicken browned.

Chicken Paprika

Paprikás Csirke

To serve 4 to 5

A 3-pound frying chicken, cut up
Salt
2 tablespoons lard
1 cup finely chopped onions

½ teaspoon finely chopped garlic
1½ tablespoons sweet Hungarian paprika
1 cup chicken stock, fresh or canned
2 tablespoons flour
1½ cup sour cream

Pat the chicken pieces dry with paper towels and salt them generously.

In a 10-inch skillet, heat the lard over high heat until a light haze forms over it. Add as many chicken pieces, skin side down, as will fit in one layer. After 2 or 3 minutes, or when the pieces are a golden brown on the bottom side, turn them with tongs and brown the other side. Remove pieces as they brown and replace them with uncooked ones.

Pour off the fat, leaving only a thin film. Add the onions and garlic and cook them over medium heat 8 to 10 minutes, or until lightly colored. Off the heat, stir in the paprika; stir until the onions are well coated. Return the skillet to the heat and add the chicken stock. Bring to a boil, stirring in the brown bits from the bottom and sides of the pan.

Return the chicken to the skillet. Bring the liquid to a boil again, then turn the heat to its lowest point and cover the pan tightly. Simmer the chicken for 20 to 30 minutes, or until the juice from a thigh runs yellow when it is pierced with the point of a small sharp knife. When the chicken is tender, remove it to a platter. Skim the surface fat from the skillet. In a mixing bowl, stir the flour into the sour cream with a wire whisk, then stir the mixture into the simmering juices. Simmer 6 to 8 minutes longer, or until the sauce is thick and smooth, then return the chicken and any juices that have collected around it to the skillet. Baste with the sauce, simmer 3 or 4 minutes to heat the pieces through, and serve.

Chicken and Ham in Green Paradise
Yu-lang-chi

To serve 4 to 6

A 4-pound roasting chicken, preferably freshly killed	1 scallion, including the green top, cut into 2-inch pieces
3 slices cooked Smithfield ham, ⅛ inch thick, cut into 2-by-1-inch pieces	4 slices peeled fresh ginger root, about 1 inch in diameter and ⅛ inch thick
A 2-pound bunch broccoli	¼ teaspoon salt
2 quarts chicken stock, fresh or canned, or 2 quarts cold water, or a combination of both	1 teaspoon cornstarch dissolved in 1 tablespoon cold water

PREPARE AHEAD: 1. Wash the chicken inside and out under cold running water. Dry the chicken thoroughly with paper towels.

2. Cut off the broccoli flowerettes. Peel the stalks by cutting ⅛ inch deep into the skin and stripping it as if you were peeling an onion. Slice the stalks diagonally into 1-inch pieces, discarding the woody ends.

3. Have the chicken, ham, broccoli, chicken stock (or water), scallion, ginger and cornstarch mixture within easy reach.

TO COOK: In a heavy flameproof casserole or pot just large enough to hold the chicken snugly, bring the stock or water to a boil. Add the scallions and ginger, and place the chicken in the pot. The liquid should cover the chicken; add more boiling stock or water if it doesn't. Bring to a boil again, cover the pan, reduce the heat to low and simmer for 15 minutes. Then turn off the heat and let the chicken cool in the covered pot for 2 hours. The residual heat in the pot will cook the chicken through.

Transfer the chicken to a chopping board. (Reserve stock.) With a cleaver or knife, cut off wings and legs, and split the chicken in half lengthwise cutting through the breast and back bones. Cut the meat from the bones, leaving the skin in place. Then cut the meat into pieces about 2 inches long, 1 inch wide and ½ inch thick. Arrange the chicken and ham in alternating overlapped layers on a heated platter and cover with foil.

Pour 2 cups of the reserved stock into a 3-quart saucepan. Bring to a boil and drop in the broccoli. Return to a boil, turn off the heat, let it rest uncovered for 3 minutes, then remove the broccoli and arrange it around the chicken and ham. Or garnish the meat with only the flowerettes and serve the stems separately.

In a small saucepan, combine ½ cup of the stock with salt and bring to a boil. Give the cornstarch mixture a stir to recombine it and add it to the stock. When the stock thickens slightly and becomes clear, pour it over the chicken and ham. Serve at once.

Cornmeal-coated Chicken with Tomatoes
Pollo Rebozado

To serve 4

2 eggs
½ cup milk
2 tablespoons yellow cornmeal
1 teaspoon salt
¼ teaspoon freshly ground black
   pepper
A 3- to 3½-pound chicken, cut into
   6 to 8 serving pieces
½ cup vegetable oil
½ cup coarsely chopped onions

6 medium tomatoes, peeled, seeded
   and coarsely chopped, or substitute
   2 cups chopped, drained, canned
   Italian plum tomatoes
½ cup dry white wine
Bouquet of 3 parsley sprigs, 1 bay
   leaf, ½ teaspoon dried marjoram
   tied together in cheesecloth
1 teaspoon salt
Freshly ground black pepper

In a large mixing bowl, beat the eggs with a whisk or rotary beater for a minute or two only, then beat in the milk, the cornmeal, 1 teaspoon of salt and ¼ teaspoon of black pepper. Pat the chicken pieces completely dry with paper towels, then one at a time dip them into the egg and cornmeal batter, and when they are lightly coated lay them side by side on a long sheet of wax paper. Heat ¼ cup of the oil at high heat in a 10- to 12-inch skillet. Add the chicken and regulate the heat so that the pieces brown quickly without burning. Turn the chicken frequently with tongs or a slotted spoon. Transfer the chicken to paper towels to drain.

In a heavy 4-quart flameproof casserole, heat the remaining ¼ cup of oil over moderate heat until a light haze forms above it. Add the onions and cook, stirring, for 4 or 5 minutes, or until they are soft and transparent but not brown. Stir in the tomatoes, wine, bouquet, 1 teaspoon of salt and a few grindings of pepper. Cook, stirring frequently, for 5 minutes. Add the browned chicken to the casserole, basting the pieces well with the tomato sauce. Cover and simmer over low heat for 30 to 40 minutes, or until the chicken is tender but not falling apart. Taste for seasoning and serve directly from the casserole.

Chicken and Sauerkraut

Podvarak

To serve 4 to 5

1½ pounds sauerkraut
A 3-pound frying chicken, cut up
Salt
7 tablespoons bacon fat or lard

½ cup finely chopped onions
¼ teaspoon finely chopped garlic
1 tablespoon finely chopped hot chili
  peppers
Freshly ground black pepper
½ cup chicken stock

Wash the sauerkraut under cold running water, then soak it in cold water 10 to 20 minutes to reduce its sourness. Squeeze it dry by the handful.

Wash the chicken pieces quickly under cold running water, pat them dry with paper towels and salt generously. Over high heat, in a heavy 10-inch skillet, heat 4 tablespoons of the fat until a light haze forms over it. Brown the chicken pieces a few at a time, starting with the skin sides down and turning them with tongs. As each browns, remove to a platter and add a fresh piece to the pan until all the chicken is done. Set aside.

Heat the rest of the fat in the skillet until a light haze forms over it and add the onions and garlic. Cook them for 2 or 3 minutes, or until the onions are slightly translucent. Add the sauerkraut, chili peppers and a few grindings of black pepper. Cook uncovered for 10 minutes over medium heat. Using the tongs, lay the chicken pieces on top of the sauerkraut and pour the stock over the chicken. Bring the liquid to a boil, then reduce the heat to low and cook, covered, for 30 minutes, or until the chicken is tender. Serve the sauerkraut on a platter with the chicken, either surrounding it or as a bed for it.

Spiced Chicken and Rice

To serve 8

4 whole chicken breasts
3 teaspoons salt
½ teaspoon black pepper
½ teaspoon ginger
1 clove garlic, minced
1 pound raw rice
1 teaspoon cinnamon
6 tablespoons butter

2 cardamom pods
2 cloves
2 tablespoons yoghurt
½ teaspoon cumin
½ teaspoon saffron
10 almonds
10 raisins
¼ cup sliced onions

Cut the chicken breasts in half through the breastbones, wash and dry. Rub the breasts with a mixture of 1½ teaspoons of salt, the pepper, ginger and garlic. Let stand at room temperature 30 minutes.

Half-cook the rice with the cinnamon and remaining salt. Drain.

Heat 4 tablespoons of the butter in a skillet. Break the cardamom pods and add the seeds and the cloves to the butter. Add the chicken, brown on both sides, and then add the yoghurt.

Spread half the rice in a greased casserole or deep skillet. Arrange the chicken over it and cover with the remaining rice. Pour the skillet liquid from the chicken on the rice and sprinkle with the cumin and saffron. Place over medium heat for 5 minutes, then over low heat for 15 minutes.

Sauté the almonds, raisins and onions in the remaining butter until golden in color. Sprinkle on top of the rice and chicken before serving.

Cold Pickled Chicken
Escabeche de Gallina

To serve 4 to 6

1/3 cup olive oil

A 3- to 3½-pound chicken, cut into
 6 to 8 serving pieces

1 cup dry white wine

1 cup distilled white vinegar

1 cup hot water

2 medium onions, peeled, halved and
 cut in wedges ⅛ inch thick

3 carrots, scraped and cut diagonally
 into slices ⅛ inch thick

1 small leek, including 1 inch of the
 green, washed thoroughly and cut
 into rounds ⅛ inch thick

1 tablespoon salt

A bouquet of 1 celery top, 2 parsley
 sprigs, 2 bay leaves, 2 whole
 cloves and ¼ teaspoon thyme,
 wrapped together in cheesecloth

1 lemon, cut lengthwise into halves
 and then crosswise into ⅛-inch
 slices

In a heavy flameproof 4- to 5-quart casserole, heat the olive oil, tipping the casserole to coat the bottom evenly and turning the heat down to moderate if the oil begins to smoke. Pat the chicken dry with paper towels and brown it in the oil, a few pieces at a time. Start the pieces skin side down and turn them with tongs. Add the wine, vinegar, water, onions, carrots, leek, salt and bouquet, and bring to a boil over high heat. Reduce the heat to low, cover the casserole, and simmer undisturbed for 30 minutes, or until the chicken is tender but not falling apart. Remove the bouquet, and arrange the chicken pieces in a deep serving dish just large enough to hold them snugly in one layer. Pour the cooking liquid with the vegetables over the chicken. Decorate the top with the lemon slices, and cool to room temperature. Cover the dish and refrigerate for at least 6 hours, or until the cooking liquids have jelled. Serve on chilled plates, as the first or the main course.

Chicken Tetrazzini

To serve 4 to 6

A 4-pound chicken
1 medium-sized onion, sliced
1 carrot, sliced
1 stalk celery, sliced
Salt
Pepper
Cayenne pepper

1 bay leaf
½ pound mushrooms
6 tablespoons butter
3 tablespoons flour
½ cup cream
1 egg yolk
2 tablespoons sherry
½ pound thin spaghetti
1 cup grated Parmesan cheese

Tie up the chicken and place in a heavy saucepan with the sliced onion, carrot and celery; season with salt, pepper, cayenne and a bay leaf. Just cover the chicken with cold water and bring slowly to a boil. Simmer covered for 1 to 1¼ hours, until tender. Remove the chicken, reserving the stock, take the meat off the bones and cut the meat into thin strips.

Slice ½ pound mushrooms and cook in 2 tablespoons of butter 10 minutes over a moderate fire, until lightly browned.

In another pan melt 3 tablespoons of butter. Off the fire blend in 3 tablespoons of flour, salt and a pinch of cayenne pepper. Add 1½ cups of the reserved chicken stock and stir over the fire until the sauce comes to a boil.

In a separate bowl beat ½ cup cream and 1 egg yolk lightly with a fork and then add this mixture to the sauce. Stir until the sauce is hot but do not let it boil again. Add 2 tablespoons sherry, the chicken and mushrooms.

Meanwhile boil ½ pound thin spaghetti, in 3 to 4 quarts of boiling salted water, until tender, following the manufacturer's directions for cooking time. Drain in a colander and rinse quickly with cold water. Make a ring of spaghetti in a buttered casserole that can be used for serving. Place the chicken mixture in the center. Sprinkle with 1 cup grated Parmesan cheese and dot with 1 tablespoon of butter. Bake in a moderate oven at 350° for 20 to 30 minutes. If the top isn't nicely browned, finish with a few seconds under the broiler and serve immediately.

NOTE: This casserole may be prepared hours ahead of time and stored in the refrigerator. To reheat, let it stand at room temperature for ½ hour, then bake it at least 30 to 40 minutes.

Spanish Chicken Pie
Empanada Gallega

To serve 4 to 6

BREAD DOUGH

1 package or cake of active dry or
   compressed yeast
½ teaspoon sugar
½ cup lukewarm water (110° to 115°)

2½ to 3 cups all-purpose flour
1½ teaspoons salt
½ cup lukewarm milk (110° to 115°)
1 tablespoon olive oil
1 egg, lightly beaten

In a small bowl, sprinkle the yeast and sugar over ¼ cup of the lukewarm water. Let it stand for 2 or 3 minutes, then stir to dissolve the yeast completely. Set the bowl in a warm, draft-free place, such as an unlighted oven, for 8 to 10 minutes, or until the mixture doubles in volume.

Combine 2 cups of the flour and the salt in a deep mixing bowl, make a well in the center, and pour in the yeast, milk and remaining ¼ cup of lukewarm water. Slowly stir together, adding up to 1 cup more flour, a few tablespoons at a time, until the mixture becomes a medium-firm dough that can be lifted up in a moist, solid mass.

Place the dough on a lightly floured surface and knead it by pressing down, pushing it forward several times with the heel of your hand. Fold it back on itself and knead for at least 10 minutes, or until the dough is smooth and elastic. Sprinkle a little flour over and under the dough when necessary to prevent it from sticking to the board.

Gather the dough into a ball and place it in a large, lightly buttered bowl. Dust the top with flour, drape a towel over it, and set in the warm place for 1½ hours or until the dough doubles in bulk. Punch it down with one blow of your fist, cover with a towel and let it rise again for 45 minutes.

FILLING

A 2- to 2½-pound chicken, cut into
   6 to 8 serving pieces
1 large onion, quartered
3 tablespoons olive oil
½ cup finely chopped onions
½ teaspoon finely chopped garlic
1 medium-sized sweet red or green
   pepper, deribbed, seeded and cut
   into ¼-inch squares

½ cup finely chopped *serrano* ham
   or substitute prosciutto or other
   lean smoked ham
3 medium-sized tomatoes peeled,
   seeded and finely chopped, or
   substitute 1 cup chopped, drained,
   canned tomatoes
½ teaspoon salt
¼ teaspoon freshly ground black
   pepper

To prepare the filling: Place the chicken and quartered onion in a 3- to 4-quart saucepan and add enough water to cover them by 1 inch. Bring to a boil over high heat, meanwhile skimming off the foam and scum as they rise to the surface. Reduce the heat to low, cover and cook the chicken for 30 minutes or until tender but not falling apart. Transfer the chicken to a plate.

When the chicken is cool enough to handle, remove the skin with a small knife or your fingers. Cut or pull the meat away from the bones. Discard the skin and bones, and cut the chicken meat into ½-inch cubes. Set aside.

In a 10- to 12-inch skillet, heat the oil over moderate heat until a light haze forms above it. Add the onions, garlic and red or green pepper and, stirring frequently, cook for 8 to 10 minutes, or until the vegetables are soft but not brown. Stir in the ham, then add the tomatoes, raise the heat and cook briskly until most of the liquid in the pan evaporates and the mixture is thick enough to hold its shape lightly in a spoon. Add the chicken, salt and pepper, taste for seasoning and cool to room temperature.

Preheat the oven to 375°. With a pastry brush, coat a large baking sheet with 1 tablespoon of olive oil.

To assemble the pie, divide the dough into halves. On a lightly floured surface, roll each half into a circle about 12 inches in diameter and ¼-inch thick. Place one of the circles on the baking sheet and spoon the filling on top, spreading it to within about 1 inch of the outside edges. Place the second circle of dough over the filling, pressing it down firmly around the edges. Then fold up the entire rim of the pie by about ½ inch and press all around the outer edges with your fingertips or the tines of a fork to seal them securely. Let the pie rise in the warm place for about 20 minutes.

Brush the pie with the beaten egg and bake in the middle of the oven for 45 minutes, or until the top is golden. Serve hot, or at room temperature.

Chicken in Cornhusks
Tamales

To make 24 tamales

24 dried cornhusks, or substitute 24 sheets of baking parchment paper, 4 by 9 inches	1½ teaspoons salt
	1½ cups lukewarm beef or chicken stock, fresh or canned
⅓ cup lard	THE FILLING
2 cups instant *masa harina* (corn flour)	1½ cups *pollo en adobo (below)*,
2 teaspoons double-acting baking powder	cut in ¼-inch dice and moistened with its sauce

In a large bowl or pot, cover the cornhusks (if you are using them) with hot water and let them soak for 30 minutes. Then drain and pat the husks dry with paper towels.

Meanwhile, cream the lard with an electric beater at medium speed for 10 minutes, or beat and mash it against the sides of a bowl with a spoon for about 20 minutes, or until light and fluffy. In another bowl, mix the *masa harina*, baking powder and salt together, then beat it about ¼ cup at a time into the creamed lard, continuing to beat until the ingredients are thoroughly combined. Slowly pour in the lukewarm stock, stirring constantly; beat for 4 or 5 minutes until a soft, moist dough is formed.

Assemble the tamales one at a time in the following fashion: Place about a tablespoon of dough in the center of a cornhusk or sheet of paper and, with a knife or metal spatula, spread it into a rectangle about 3 inches by nearly 4 inches to reach almost to the long sides of the husk or paper. Drop a heaping tablespoon of filling in the center of the dough. Then fold one side of the wrapper a little more than halfway across the filling and bring the opposite side over the first fold. Turn the ends up to cover the seam, overlapping them across the top. Lay the tamales, seam side down, in a large colander in as many layers as necessary.

Place the colander in a deep pot about 1 inch larger in diameter than the colander, and pour enough water into the pot to come to an inch below the bottom of the colander. Bring the water to a vigorous boil over high heat, cover the pot securely and reduce the heat to low. Steam the tamales for an hour, keeping the water at a slow boil and replenishing it with boiling water as it evaporates. When the tamales are done, remove them from the colander with tongs, arrange them on a heated platter and serve at once. The tamales may be cooked ahead if you like and reheated by steaming them again for half an hour.

POLLO EN ADOBO

6 dried *ancho* chilies
1 cup boiling chicken stock, fresh or canned
1 cup coarsely chopped onions
3 medium tomatoes, peeled, seeded and coarsely chopped, or substitute 1 cup drained, canned Italian plum tomatoes
1 teaspoon finely chopped garlic
1 tablespoon white vinegar
1 teaspoon sugar
½ teaspoon ground coriander seeds
¼ teaspoon ground cinnamon
¼ teaspoon ground cloves
1½ teaspoons salt
¼ teaspoon freshly ground black pepper
4 tablespoons lard
A 3- to 3½-pound chicken, cut into 6 or 8 serving pieces

NOTE: Wear rubber gloves when handling the hot chilies.

Under cold running water, pull the stems off the chilies, break them in half, and brush out the seeds. With a small, sharp knife, cut away any large ribs. Tear the chilies into small pieces, pour 1 cup of boiling stock over them and let them soak for 30 minutes.

Pour the chilies and the stock into the jar of a blender and purée at high speed for about 15 seconds. Add the onions, tomatoes, garlic, vinegar, sugar, coriander, cinnamon, cloves, salt and black pepper, and blend for 30 seconds, or until the mixture is reduced to a thick purée.

In a heavy 8-inch skillet, heat 1 tablespoon of the lard over moderate heat. Add the purée and cook, uncovered, stirring occasionally, for 5 minutes. Remove from the heat; cover the skillet to keep the sauce warm.

Preheat the oven to 350°. Pat the chicken pieces dry with paper towels (they will not brown well if they are damp). In a heavy 10- to 12-inch skillet melt the remaining 3 tablespoons of lard over moderate heat until a light haze forms above it. Brown the chicken a few pieces at a time, starting them skin side down and turning them with tongs. As the pieces turn a rich golden brown, place them in a 3-quart heatproof casserole. Pour the chili sauce into the casserole and turn the chicken about in it until the pieces are thoroughly coated with the sauce. Cover the casserole tightly and bake, undisturbed, in the middle of the oven for 45 minutes. Then remove the cover and bake 15 minutes longer, basting the chicken every now and then with its sauce.

Chicken in Puff Pastry
Vol au vent à la Reine

To serve 6

PUFF PASTE	¾ cup ice water
2 cups flour	½ pound butter
1 teaspoon salt	1 egg

PUFF PASTE: Put 2 cups of flour on a marble slab or wooden board. Make a well in the center and in it put the salt. Work the flour into a paste with the water, adding just a little at one time to the well.

Roll into a square the size of a handkerchief. Put the butter in the center and wrap the sides and ends around the butter, completely covering it. Place in the refrigerator for ½ hour. Remove and roll into a long narrow strip. Fold in three. Turn the dough around so that the folded edge is facing you and roll out again, then fold in three. Place in the refrigerator for ½ hour. Remove and repeat the two rolling-out and folding processes. Chill and roll out once more. All this should be done 24 hours before baking.

The next day preheat the oven to 400°. Roll and fold the dough again. Then roll it out about ¼ inch thick and cut 2 rounds, 8 inches in diameter. With a round cutter, cut a round about 3 inches in diameter out of the center of one large round. Make diagonal cuts with a sharp knife on the small round. Brush a cookie sheet with cold water and place the whole round on it. Brush the edge of the round with cold water and place the second round on top of the first. Make diamond-shaped cuts on top of the second round and straight shallow cuts down the side. Place the small round in the center. Brush the small round and the top of the second round with beaten egg. Bake for about 20 minutes, or until golden brown.

CHICKEN FILLING
2 tablespoons butter
3 tablespoons flour
Salt
Cayenne pepper
1¼ cups chicken stock
¼ cup light cream

2 egg yolks
½ cup heavy cream
2 cups diced cooked chicken
½ pound mushrooms, sliced and
  sautéed
Parsley

CHICKEN FILLING: Melt the butter. Remove from the heat and blend in the flour, salt and cayenne pepper. Add the chicken stock and stir over the fire until the mixture comes to a boil. Add the light cream. Beat the egg yolks lightly with the heavy cream and add to the mixture. Cook until the sauce has thickened, but do not let it boil again. Add the chicken and the sautéed mushrooms and heat for 5 minutes.

Fill the puff pastry with the creamed chicken and serve immediately on a hot platter, garnished with parsley.

Duck & Other Poultry

Broiled Long Island Duckling

To serve 4

One 5- to 6-pound Long Island
   duckling, cut into quarters

MARINADE
¾ cup vegetable oil
½ cup red-wine vinegar
1 teaspoon salt
Freshly ground black pepper

1 cup thinly sliced onion
3 large garlic cloves, thinly sliced
2 large bay leaves, coarsely crumbled
Salt, preferably the coarse (kosher)
   variety

Wash the duck under cold running water and pat thoroughly dry. With poultry shears or a sharp knife, trim the quarters, cutting away all exposed fat. In a shallow glass, porcelain or stainless-steel pan large enough to hold the duck quarters in one layer, mix the oil, vinegar, salt and a few grindings of pepper. Add the onion, garlic and bay leaves. Lay the duck in this marinade, baste thoroughly and marinate at room temperature at least 3 hours, turning the pieces every half hour.

When you are ready to broil the duck, remove it from the marinade. Strain the marinade through a fine sieve and discard the vegetables. Preheat the broiler to its highest point. Arrange the duck, skin side down, on the broiler rack, sprinkle lightly with salt and broil 4 inches from the heat for about 35 minutes, regulating the heat or lowering the rack so the duck browns slowly without burning. Baste every 10 minutes or so with the marinade. Turn the pieces over with tongs, sprinkle with salt and broil 10 to 15 minutes longer, basting 2 or 3 times with the marinade. When the duck is tender and a deep golden brown, arrange it on a heated serving platter. Serve at once.

Broiled Duck

To serve 4

A 5- to 5½-pound duck
2 teaspoons lemon juice

1 teaspoon salt
½ teaspoon ground ginger
1 tablespoon melted butter

Have the butcher quarter the duck and remove the backbone and wing tips. Cut off all excess fat. Sprinkle the duck with the lemon juice, salt and ginger. Let it stand about half an hour to absorb the seasoning. Place it on a preheated broiler pan, skin side down, and put the pan 4 to 5 inches from the broiler heat. Broil for 20 to 25 minutes on one side, then turn the duck and cook it for another 20 to 25 minutes. Place the duck on a hot serving dish, brush it with melted butter and serve.

Duck with Apple and Bread Stuffing
Ente mit Äpfeln und Brot Füllung

To serve 4

A 4½- to 5-pound duck
Salt
Freshly ground black pepper
¾ pound lean ground beef,
   preferably chuck

¾ pound lean ground pork
1 egg, lightly beaten
½ cup dried bread crumbs
½ teaspoon dried marjoram
2 medium-sized cooking apples,
   peeled, cored and cut into
   ½-inch cubes

Preheat the oven to 425°. Wash the duck under cold running water and pat dry inside and out with paper towels. Rub the inside of the duck liberally with salt and pepper. For crisper skin, prick the surface around the thighs, the back, and the lower part of the breast with the tip of a sharp knife.

In a large bowl, combine the beef, pork, egg, crumbs, marjoram, 1 teaspoon of salt and a few grindings of pepper. Knead vigorously with both hands until the ingredients are well blended and the mixture is smooth. Then stir in the apples and spoon the stuffing loosely into the cavity. Close the opening by lacing it with skewers or sewing it with heavy thread. Fasten the neck skin to the back of the duck with a skewer and truss the bird securely.

Roast the duck, breast side up on a rack set in a large shallow pan, for 20 minutes, until it browns lightly. Pour off the fat from the roasting pan or draw it off with a bulb baster. Then reduce the heat to 350°, and roast for about 1 hour longer, removing the accumulated fat from the pan occasionally with a bulb baster. To test for doneness, pierce the thigh of the bird with the tip of a small, sharp knife. The juice should spurt out a clear yellow; if it is slightly pink, roast the bird for another 5 to 10 minutes. Transfer the duck to a heated platter and let it rest for 10 minutes before carving.

Roast Duck with Portuguese Rice

Arroz de Pato de Braga

To serve 4

A 5- to 6-pound oven-ready duck
1 large garlic clove, peeled and
   bruised with the side of a cleaver
Salt
Freshly ground black pepper
2 lemons
1 cup raw medium or long-grain
   regular-milled rice, or imported
   short-grain rice
¼ pound Portuguese *linguiça,* or
   substitute *chorizo* or any other

garlic-seasoned smoked pork
   sausage
2 tablespoons lard
1 medium-sized carrot, scraped and
   finely chopped
1 medium-sized onion, finely chopped
¼ pound *presunto* ham, or substitute
   serrano, prosciutto or other lean
   smoked ham, sliced ⅛ inch thick
   and cut into 1-inch pieces
2 tablespoons fresh lemon juice
8 tablespoons finely chopped parsley

Preheat the oven to 450°. Pat the duck completely dry with paper towels. Rub the bird inside and out with the crushed garlic clove, then sprinkle the cavity liberally with salt and a few grindings of pepper.

With a small, sharp knife or a vegetable peeler with a rotating blade, remove the peel from one of the lemons without cutting through to the bitter white pith beneath it. Place the peel inside the cavity of the duck, then close the opening securely by lacing it with skewers, or by sewing it with heavy white thread.

Fasten the neck skin to the back of the duck with a skewer and truss the bird securely. Slice the peeled lemon in half crosswise and rub its cut surface over the skin of the duck.

Place the duck breast side up on a rack set in a shallow open pan. Roast undisturbed in the middle of the oven about 20 minutes, or until the duck has begun to brown. Then reduce the heat to 350° and roast about 1½ hours longer. Basting is unnecessary.

To test for doneness, pierce the thigh of the duck with the tip of a small, sharp knife. The juices should run out a pale yellow; if tinged with pink, roast another 5 to 10 minutes.

While the duck is roasting, bring 2 quarts of water to a boil over high heat in a heavy 3- to 4-quart saucepan. Pour in the rice in a thin, slow stream so that the water keeps boiling. Reduce the heat to moderate and let the rice boil uncovered for 15 minutes, or until the grains are tender but still slightly firm to the bite. Drain the rice in a colander.

Place the sausages in an 8- to 10-inch skillet and prick them in two or three places with the point of a small, sharp knife. Add enough cold water to cover them completely and bring to a boil over high heat. Then reduce the heat to low and simmer uncovered for 5 minutes. Drain on paper towels, and slice the sausage into ⅛-inch-thick rounds.

In a heavy 12-inch skillet, melt the lard over high heat until it splutters. Drop in the sausage and cook, stirring frequently, for 3 or 4 minutes. Reduce the heat to low, add the carrot and onion and, stirring frequently, cook for about 5 minutes, or until the vegetables are soft but not brown. Add the ham and cook for 2 or 3 minutes longer. With a fork stir in the rice, lemon juice, and 6 tablespoons of parsley. Taste for seasoning and set aside, covered to keep warm.

Transfer the duck to a platter and, with a large spoon, skim as much of the fat as possible from the juices remaining in the roasting pan. Pour in ½ cup of water and bring it to a boil over high heat, meanwhile scraping in any brown particles clinging to the bottom and sides of the pan. Boil briskly, stirring, until the liquid thickens slightly and is reduced to ¼ cup.

To assemble, spread the rice mixture evenly on the bottom of a large, shallow casserole or in a deep heated platter. Carve the duck into serving pieces and arrange the pieces attractively, skin side up, on the rice. Spoon the reduced cooking liquid over the duck, sprinkle with the remaining 2 tablespoons of parsley, and garnish the casserole with the remaining lemon cut lengthwise into 8 wedges.

Duck with Orange
Caneton à l'Orange

To serve 4

A 4½-pound duck	½ teaspoon meat extract
1 tablespoon butter	3 teaspoons potato flour
4 tablespoons Marsala or brandy	1½ cups stock
2 finely chopped mushrooms	The juice of 2 oranges
1 orange rind, finely shredded	¼ cup red wine
Salt	1 tablespoon red currant jelly
Pepper	1 bay leaf
1 teaspoon tomato paste	2 oranges, sectioned and skinned
	4 chicken livers, sautéed and sliced

Truss the duck carefully and brown it all over very quickly in hot butter. Remove some of the fat from the pan. Pour the Marsala or brandy over the duck and remove it from the pan. Add the mushrooms, orange rind, salt and pepper, and cook slowly for 6 minutes. Remove from the heat and add the tomato paste, meat extract and flour. Stir until it is smooth, then add the stock. Stir over the heat until the mixture comes to a boil. Add the orange juice, wine and jelly. Taste for seasoning. Cut the duck up in pieces and put it back in the pan. Add the bay leaf, cover and cook very slowly for about 1 hour, or until the duck is tender. Arrange the duck on a hot serving dish. If the gravy is too thin, boil it until it has thickened. Add the orange sections and chicken livers, and serve in a sauceboat.

Braised Duck with Coriander Peas
Arroz con Pato

To serve 4

¼ cup fresh lemon juice
½ teaspoon ground cumin seeds
1 teaspoon salt
¼ teaspoon freshly ground black
   pepper
A 4- to 5-pound duck, cut into 6 to
   8 serving pieces and trimmed of
   all fat

¼ cup olive oil
2 twelve-ounce bottles light beer
1 cup bock beer (if not available,
   use 1 cup additional light beer)
2 cups raw long-grain rice
1 cup finely chopped fresh coriander
1 cup cooked fresh green peas or
   thoroughly defrosted frozen peas

In a small bowl combine the lemon juice, cumin seeds, ½ teaspoon salt and ⅛ teaspoon pepper. With your fingers brush the pieces of duck on all sides with the mixture. Place the duck on a plate, cover with foil, and let it rest at room temperature for 3 hours, or refrigerated for 6 hours.

In a heavy 4- to 5-quart flameproof casserole or saucepan, heat the oil over high heat until a light haze forms above it. Add the duck and brown it well on all sides, turning it frequently. Drain off and discard all but 2 tablespoons of fat from the casserole. Add the beer, bring to a boil over high heat, meanwhile scraping into it any brown bits from the bottom and sides of the pan. Reduce the heat to low, cover the casserole and cook the duck for 45 minutes, or until a leg shows no resistance when pierced with the tip of a knife. Transfer the duck to a heated plate and cover it with foil to keep it warm.

Pour off the cooking liquid from the casserole, strain, measure and return 3½ cups of it, and discard the rest. Bring to a boil over high heat, then stir in the rice and return to a boil. Reduce the heat to low, cover the casserole and simmer undisturbed for 20 minutes, or until the rice has absorbed all the cooking liquid. Stir in the coriander, peas, ½ teaspoon salt and ⅛ teaspoon pepper. Arrange the duck on the rice; cover the casserole and return it to low heat for a few minutes to heat the duck through. Serve from the casserole, or mound the rice and peas in the center of a serving platter and arrange the pieces of duck on top.

Roast Goose with Apple, Raisin and Nut Stuffing
Gänsebraten mit Äpfeln, Rosinen und Nüssen

To serve 6 to 8

An 8- to 10-pound young goose
   and its giblets
1 cup seedless raisins
3 tablespoons butter
1 cup finely chopped onions
4 cups soft white bread crumbs,
   made from fresh, homemade-type
   white bread pulverized in a blender
   or shredded with a fork

3 medium-sized cooking apples,
   peeled, cored and coarsely
   chopped
½ cup coarsely chopped blanched
   hazelnuts or almonds
¼ cup finely chopped parsley
1 teaspoon dried marjoram
1 teaspoon salt
Freshly ground black pepper

In a small saucepan, combine the goose gizzard and heart with enough water to cover them completely. Bring to a boil over high heat, reduce the heat to low and simmer uncovered for 40 minutes, or until they show no resistance when pierced with the tip of a small, sharp knife. Meanwhile, place the raisins in a bowl and pour 2 cups of boiling water over them. Let them soak for 20 minutes, or until plump. Drain the gizzard and heart, chop them fine and place them in a large mixing bowl. Add the drained raisins.

Preheat the oven to 325°. In a heavy 8- to 10-inch skillet, melt the butter over moderate heat. When the foam has almost subsided, add the onions and cook, stirring frequently, for 5 minutes, or until they are soft and transparent but not brown. Chop the goose liver into fine dice, add it to the onions, and cook, stirring constantly, for 2 or 3 minutes, or until the liver is light brown. With a rubber spatula, scrape the entire contents of the skillet into the mixing bowl. Add the bread crumbs, apples, chopped nuts, parsley, marjoram, salt and a few grindings of pepper, and toss the mixture together with a spoon until the ingredients are well combined. Taste for seasoning.

Wash the goose under cold, running water and pat it thoroughly dry inside and out with paper towels. Lightly salt and pepper the cavity and fill it loosely with the stuffing. Close the opening by lacing it with skewers or sewing it with a large needle and heavy white thread. Fasten the neck skin to the back of the goose with a skewer and truss the bird securely. For a crisper skin, prick the surface around the thighs, the back, and the lower part of the breast with the tip of a small, sharp knife.

Place the goose breast side up on a rack set in a large, shallow roasting pan, and roast in the middle of the oven for 3 to 3½ hours, or about 20 minutes to the pound. As the fat accumulates in the pan, draw it off with a bulb baster or large kitchen spoon and, if you like, save it for another use. Basting the goose is unnecessary. To test for doneness, pierce the thigh of the bird with the tip of a small, sharp knife. The juice that runs out should be pale yellow; if it is tinged with pink, roast the goose another 5 to 10 minutes. Let the goose rest in the turned-off oven with the door ajar for about 15 minutes for easier carving.

Rock Cornish Game Hens with Pine-Nut Stuffing

To serve 4

STUFFING
5 tablespoons butter
1 cup long-grain rice
2 cups chicken stock, fresh or canned
1 teaspoon salt
1 cup finely chopped onion
½ cup pine nuts

6 tablespoons finely chopped fresh
    parsley

4 Rock Cornish game hens, about 1
    pound each
2 teaspoons salt
4 tablespoons melted butter
Watercress

For the stuffing, melt 3 tablespoons of the butter in a 2-quart heavy casserole or saucepan over moderate heat. Add the rice and stir constantly for 2 to 3 minutes, or until most of the rice has turned milky and opaque. Do not let it brown. Then pour in the chicken stock, add the salt and bring the stock to a boil, stirring occasionally. Cover the pan tightly, reduce the heat to its lowest point and simmer for 18 to 20 minutes, or until the rice has absorbed all the liquid. Meanwhile, in a small skillet melt the remaining 2 tablespoons of butter and when the foam subsides add the onion. Cook over moderate heat for 8 to 10 minutes, then add the pine nuts. Cook 2 or 3 minutes longer, stirring, until the nuts are lightly browned. In a small mixing bowl combine the cooked rice, the onion, pine nuts and the parsley. Mix gently but thoroughly. Taste for seasoning.

Preheat the oven to 400°. Wash the birds under cold running water, then dry them inside and out with paper towels. Sprinkle the inside of each bird with ½ teaspoon of salt, then pack the cavities loosely with the stuffing; they should be no more than ¾ full. Skewer or sew the openings with thread, truss the birds securely and brush them with the melted butter. Place them on their sides on a rack set in a shallow roasting pan just large enough to hold them. Roast them in the middle of the oven for 15 minutes, then turn them on the other side and brush them with butter again. Roast for another 15 minutes. Turn them breast side up, brush with the remaining butter and salt each bird lightly. Roast, basting occasionally with the drippings in the bottom of the pan, for 15 to 20 minutes longer, or until the birds are golden brown all over and tender. Test for doneness by piercing the fleshy part of the thigh with the point of a sharp knife. The juice that spurts out should be yellow. If it is pink, roast a few minutes longer. Transfer the birds to a warm serving platter, pour the pan juices over them and serve, garnished with watercress.

216

Squab with Paprika Sauce
Paprikahühnchen

To serve 8

8 one-pound squabs
2 teaspoons salt
½ teaspoon pepper
8 slices bacon

1½ cups minced onions
2 tablespoons sweet Hungarian
  paprika
2 cups chicken stock
2 cups sour cream

Wash and clean the squabs, dry them thoroughly, then rub them with the salt and pepper. Chop, mash and reserve the livers. Cover the bacon with water, bring to a boil and cook for 3 minutes. Drain, dice, and put in a Dutch oven, skillet or casserole large enough to hold the birds. Cook the bacon until the fat runs out, then mix in the onions and paprika. Add the squabs and cook until they are browned, turning them frequently with two spoons. Do not prick the birds. Add the stock, cover, and cook over low heat for 30 minutes, turning the squabs occasionally. Mix in the livers, cover, and cook for 10 minutes longer, or until the squabs are tender. Remove to a heated platter and sprinkle with paprika. Blend the sour cream into the pan juices, taste for seasoning, and heat. Serve in a sauceboat.

Broiled Squab with Lemon-Soy Butter

To serve 4

4 squabs, about ¾ pound each
1 cup melted butter (½ pound)
2 tablespoons soy sauce

1 teaspoon lemon juice
Salt
Freshly ground black pepper
Watercress

Prepare the squabs for broiling by cutting them down the back from the neck to the tail with a large knife or poultry shears. Then spread the squabs out skin side up and, with a sharp blow of a meat cleaver or wooden mallet, break the curved rib bones so that the birds lie flat. Twist the wing tips under the shoulders.

Preheat the broiler to its highest point. Combine the butter, soy sauce and lemon juice in a large, shallow baking dish. Dip the squabs, one at a time, in the butter mixture to saturate them thoroughly. Arrange them, skin side down, on the broiler rack and sprinkle them generously with salt and a few grindings of black pepper. Slide the rack about 3 inches below the heat and broil the squabs for about 6 minutes undisturbed. Then brush them with the butter and turn them over with tongs. Brush the squabs with more of the butter mixture, sprinkle generously with salt and a few grindings of black pepper and broil about 6 minutes longer.

217

Watch them carefully for any sign of burning and regulate the broiler heat accordingly. The squabs should be crisp and golden brown when they are done. To serve, arrange them on a heated platter and pour the broiler pan juices over them. Garnish with crisp watercress.

Roast Turkey with Chestnut Stuffing

To serve 10 to 12

A 14- to 15-pound turkey
2 quarts chestnuts
1 cup oil
6 cups chicken stock or water
3 slices white bread
½ cup milk
1 pound sausage meat
1 large yellow onion, finely chopped
1 teaspoon chopped parsley
1 teaspoon chopped chives

½ teaspoon dried thyme
Salt
Pepper
2 tablespoons butter, softened
½ pound salt pork, thinly sliced
4 cups cold water
1 small onion, sliced
1 carrot, peeled and sliced
1 celery stalk with leaves, cut up
1 cup port wine
4 tablespoons flour

Wash the turkey under cold running water and pat it dry with paper towels. Reserve the giblets.

Preheat the oven to 400°. With a sharp knife, make a slit in the shell of each chestnut on the flat side. Put them into a shallow pan with the oil and cook in the oven for 5 minutes. Turn off the oven and remove the chestnuts. When they are cool enough to handle take off the shells and inner skin. Then simmer them in the chicken stock or water for 20 to 30 minutes, or until they are soft.

Put the bread in a large mixing bowl and pour the milk over it. In a frying pan, cook the sausage meat until it is browned, then remove it with a slotted spoon and add it to the bread. Reserve the sausage fat. Sauté the onion. Drain the chestnuts, put them through a strainer and add them to the sausage. Mix in the onion, sausage fat, parsley, chives, thyme, salt and pepper.

Preheat the oven to 350°. Put the stuffing into the turkey and secure the opening with small skewers and string. Spread the softened butter all over the turkey. Place the bird breast side up on a rack in a roasting pan and cover the breast and legs with slices of salt pork. Cover loosely with aluminum foil. Roast the turkey for about 3½ hours, or 15 minutes a pound.

In the meantime, prepare the giblets for the gravy. Place them in a saucepan with 4 cups of cold water. Bring to a boil over high heat, skimming off any scum that rises to the surface. Add the onion, carrot and celery, partially cover, and simmer slowly for 1 hour. Allow the giblets to cool in the stock, then remove and chop them fine. Strain the stock through a fine sieve, pressing down hard on the vegetables before discarding them. Skim any fat from
218

the surface of the stock, and reserve it for the gravy.

An hour before the turkey is due to be done, remove the aluminum foil and pour the port wine into the pan. Baste the turkey every 15 minutes with the pan juices. A turkey is done if the juices come out clear with no pink tinge when a fork pierces the leg. If you are using a meat thermometer it should be inserted in the leg, and the turkey is done when the thermometer registers 190°.

When the turkey is done remove it from the pan and let it stand for 10 to 15 minutes before carving. Meanwhile make the gravy. Blend the flour into the pan juices. Add the chopped giblets and 2 cups of stock and stir over the heat until the gravy comes to a boil. Taste for seasoning and serve in a sauceboat.

South American Stuffed Turkey
Pavo Relleno

To serve 10 to 12

A 12-pound turkey	1½ cups chopped onions
4½ teaspoons salt	¾ cup chopped green peppers
1½ teaspoons black pepper	½ pound ground pork
¾ cup grated onions	½ teaspoon thyme
2 garlic cloves, minced	3 cups ground almonds
3 cups dry red wine	3 tablespoons minced parsley
2 cups fresh bread crumbs	1 cup seedless raisins
¾ cup milk	1 cup sliced green olives
¼ pound bacon	3 hard-cooked eggs, diced

Clean and wash the turkey. Rub it with 3 teaspoons of the salt, 1 teaspoon of the pepper, the grated onions and garlic. Pour the wine over it and let it marinate in the refrigerator overnight, turning and basting it a few times.

When ready to prepare the stuffing, soak the bread crumbs in the milk. Fry the bacon until it is crisp, drain it on paper towels, then crumble it. Pour off all but 3 tablespoons of the bacon fat. Add the onions and peppers, and sauté them for 5 minutes. Add the pork, thyme and remaining salt and pepper. Cook, stirring frequently, until no pink remains in the pork. Mix in the almonds, bacon, parsley, raisins, olives, eggs and soaked bread crumbs. Taste for seasoning and cool.

Preheat the oven to 325°. Drain the turkey and stuff the cavity, closing the openings with skewers or by sewing. Place the turkey in a roasting pan and roast for about 3½ hours, or until it is tender and browned.

Fish & Shellfish

Sea Bass Fillets with Ginger
Ch'ao-yü-pien

To serve 2 to 4

1 pound boneless skinned sea bass
   or yellow pike fillets (or substitute
   any other firm white fish fillets)
2 teaspoons cornstarch
1 egg white
1 tablespoon Chinese rice wine, or
   pale dry sherry
2 teaspoons salt

4 tablespoons peanut oil, or flavorless
   vegetable oil
1 teaspoon finely chopped, peeled
   fresh ginger root
1 scallion, including the green top,
   finely chopped

PREPARE AHEAD: 1. Wash the fish fillets under cold running water and pat them dry with paper towels. With a cleaver or sharp knife, cut the fillets into 1½-inch squares about ½ inch thick.

2. Place the 2 teaspoons of cornstarch in a small bowl, add the fish pieces and toss them about until each piece is lightly coated. Add the egg white, wine and salt, and stir until thoroughly mixed.

3. Have the fish, and the oil, ginger slices and scallions within easy reach.

TO COOK: Set a 12-inch wok or 10-inch skillet over high heat for about 30 seconds. Pour in the 4 tablespoons of oil, swirl it about in the pan and heat for another 30 seconds, turning the heat down to moderate if the oil begins to smoke. Immediately add the ginger and scallions, and cook for a few seconds, but make sure they don't burn. Add the coated fish pieces and stir-fry gently for about 1 minute, or until the fish is firm and white. Transfer the entire contents of the pan to a heated platter and serve at once.

Baked Stuffed Striped Bass

To serve 4

STUFFING
2 tablespoons butter
2 tablespoons finely chopped
   scallions, including part of the
   green stem

2 tablespoons finely chopped green
   pepper
1 medium tomato, peeled, seeded and
   coarsely chopped
1 tablespoon finely chopped parsley
Salt
Freshly ground black pepper

For the stuffing, melt the 2 tablespoons of butter in a small skillet over moderate heat. When the foam subsides, add the chopped scallions and green pepper and cook, stirring constantly, for 2 to 3 minutes until the vegetables are wilted but not brown. Scrape into a small mixing bowl. Add the chopped tomato, parsley, salt and a few grindings of black pepper. Mix thoroughly.

A 2½- to 3-pound striped bass,
   eviscerated but head and tail left
   on (or other firm white-meat fish
   such as red snapper, pompano,
   haddock, cod, pollack, rockfish,
   whitefish or lake trout)
4 tablespoons melted butter
1 medium onion, peeled and thinly
   sliced

1 small green pepper, seeded and
   thinly sliced
6 sprigs fresh dill
½ cup dry vermouth
1 tablespoon lemon juice
Salt
Freshly ground black pepper

Preheat the oven to 375°. Wash the fish inside and out under cold running water, and dry it thoroughly with paper towels. Fill the fish with the stuffing, sew the opening with thread or close it with small skewers and crisscross kitchen string around the skewers to secure them. Brush 2 tablespoons of the melted butter on the bottom of a shallow, flameproof baking dish attractive enough to serve from, and place the fish in it, surrounding it with the sliced onion, the green pepper and sprigs of fresh dill.

Combine the vermouth with the lemon juice and the rest of the melted butter, pour it over the fish and vegetables and bring it to a boil on top of the stove. Sprinkle the fish with salt and a few grindings of black pepper, and immediately transfer the baking dish to the middle of the oven. Bake uncovered for about 30 minutes, basting the fish every 8 minutes or so with the pan juices. The fish is done when it flakes easily when prodded gently with a fork. Serve directly from the baking dish.

Poached Striped Bass
Bar Poché au Beurre Blanc

To serve 6

COURT BOUILLON
2 quarts water
2 cups dry white wine
¼ cup wine vinegar
3 onions, thickly sliced
2 carrots, cut in 1-inch chunks
4 celery stalks with leaves, cut in

1-inch chunks
4 parsley sprigs
2 bay leaves
1 teaspoon finely cut fresh tarragon
   or ½ teaspoon dried tarragon
1 teaspoon finely cut fresh thyme or
   ½ teaspoon dried thyme
2 tablespoons salt
10 peppercorns

In a 6- to 8-quart enameled or stainless-steel pot or soup kettle, bring all the ingredients for the court bouillon to a boil over high heat. Partially cover the pot, reduce the heat and simmer for 30 minutes. Strain through a large, fine sieve into a fish poacher or a large, deep roasting pan which has a cover, and set aside to cool.

FISH
A 3- to 3½-pound whole striped bass,
   cleaned and scaled, but with head
   and tail left on (or substitute such

firm, white-meat fish as red snapper,
   haddock, cod, pollack, rockfish,
   whitefish or lake trout)
Fresh parsley sprigs

When the court bouillon is lukewarm, wash the fish inside and out under cold running water. Without drying it, wrap the fish in a long, double-thick piece of damp, washed cheesecloth, leaving at least 6 inches of cloth at each end to serve as handles for lifting the fish in and out of the pan. Twist the ends of the cloth and tie them with string, then place the fish on the rack of the poacher or roasting pan and lower the rack into the court bouillon. The court bouillon should cover the fish by 1½ to 2 inches; add water if necessary.

Cover, and bring to a slow simmer over moderate heat; immediately reduce the heat and cook barely at a simmer for 15 minutes. Remove the pan from the heat and leave the fish in it for another 15 minutes. Then, using the ends of cheesecloth as handles, lift the fish from the pan and lay it on a large cutting board or platter. Open the cheesecloth and skin the fish with a small, sharp knife by making a cut in the skin at the base of the tail and gently pulling off the skin in strips from tail to gill. Holding both ends of the cheesecloth, carefully lift the fish and turn it over onto a heated serving platter. Peel off the skin on the upturned side. Garnish the fish with sprigs of fresh parsley and cover the platter loosely to keep the fish warm.

BEURRE BLANC
1/3 cup white-wine vinegar
1/3 cup dry white wine
2 tablespoons finely chopped shallots
    or scallions

1/2 teaspoon salt
1/8 teaspoon white pepper
1/2 pound butter, cut into 16
    tablespoon-sized pieces and
    thoroughly chilled

BEURRE BLANC: In a 1½- to 2-quart enameled saucepan, bring the vinegar, wine, shallots, salt and pepper to a boil over high heat and cook uncovered, stirring occasionally, until the liquid is reduced to about 1 tablespoon—it should be just a film on the bottom of the pan. Remove the pan from the heat and with a wire whisk immediately stir in 3 tablespoon-sized pieces of chilled butter, beating constantly until the butter is completely absorbed into the liquid.

Return the pan to the lowest possible heat and add the rest of the chilled butter 1 piece at a time, whisking constantly; and making sure that each piece is absorbed before adding the next. The finished sauce will be a thick, ivory-colored cream. Serve it at once in a warm, not hot, sauceboat.

To de-bone the fish for serving, divide the top layer into individual portions with a fish server without cutting through the spine. Leave the head and tail intact. Lift the portions with the fish server and a fork and arrange them attractively on another plate or platter. Then gently lift out the backbone in one piece, discard it and divide the bottom layer of fish into individual portions.

ALTERNATIVE: To serve poached bass cold, cook and skin it as described above. Cover the fish with plastic wrap or with aluminum foil and refrigerate it until it is thoroughly chilled. Serve the fish with mayonnaise, and garnish it with watercress, cucumber and lemon slices and cherry tomatoes.

Fresh Cod Steaks with Egg Sauce
Torsk med Eggesaus

To serve 4 to 6

1/2 cup salt

6 fresh codfish steaks, sliced 3/4 inch
    thick

If you don't have a long, narrow fish poacher, an enamel roasting pan 5 inches deep will do just as well. Fill the pan with water to a depth of 4 inches and add ½ cup of salt. Bring to a boil (over 2 burners, if necessary), reduce the heat slightly and gently slide the cod slices into the water with a spatula. Lower the heat until the water is bubbling slightly and simmer the fish for about 5 minutes. Be careful not to overcook or the fish will disintegrate. Remove the slices with a slotted spatula and drain them on a linen napkin or dish towel. Arrange the cod attractively on a heated platter and serve with egg sauce or alternate garnish (*below*).

223

EGG SAUCE

¼ pound butter

¼ cup hot fish stock *(from above)*

2 hard-cooked eggs, finely chopped

1 medium tomato, peeled, seeded and chopped

1 tablespoon finely chopped fresh parsley

1 tablespoon finely chopped chives

Salt

Freshly ground black pepper

ALTERNATE GARNISH

8 tablespoons (1 quarter-pound stick) butter, melted

1 lemon, thinly sliced

Parsley sprigs

EGG SAUCE: Melt the butter in a 1- to 1½-quart enameled or stainless-steel saucepan. Remove from the heat, beat in ¼ cup of the stock in which you poached the fish and stir in the chopped egg, tomato, parsley and chives. Add salt and pepper to taste. Heat almost to the boiling point, pour into a sauceboat, and serve with the cod. If you prefer, you can simply pour melted butter over the cod and garnish it with lemon slices and parsley.

In Norway, this dish is often accompanied by raw diced carrots, sprinkled with lemon juice, and boiled new potatoes.

Sliced Raw Fish
Sashimi

The most important factor in the preparation of "sashimi" is the absolute freshness of the fish. Frozen fish cannot be used. It is best to avoid fresh-water fish since they can carry parasites. Keep the fish refrigerated, wrapped in cheesecloth until ready to use. Handle the fish as little as possible; the warmth of your hands can spoil its freshness.

To serve 4 to 6

1 pound fresh filleted flounder, porgy, sea bass, striped bass, red snapper, squid, abalone or tuna, in one piece

DIPPING SAUCE

4 to 6 tablespoons Japanese soy sauce, or soy-based sauce *(below)*

GARNISH

A 2-inch section of *daikon* (Japanese white radish) or large icicle radish or white turnip, peeled, shredded and soaked in cold water until ready to use

1 carrot, peeled, shredded and soaked in cold water until ready to use

1 stalk celery, cut in half lengthwise, shredded and soaked in cold water until ready to use

CUTTING THE FISH: There are four basic fish-cutting methods for *sashimi* and a very sharp, heavy knife is indispensable to them all.

1. *Hira giri* (flat cut): This is the most popular shape, suitable for any filleted fish. Holding the fish firmly, cut straight down in slices about ¼ to ½ inch thick and 1 inch wide, depending on the size of the fillet.

2. *Kaku giri* (cubic cut): This style of cutting is more often used for tuna. Cut the tuna as above (flat cut), then cut the slices into ½-inch cubes.

3. *Ito zukuri* (thread shape): Although this technique may be used with any small fish, it is especially suitable for squid. Cut the squid straight down into ¼-inch slices, then cut lengthwise into ¼-inch-wide strips.

4. *Usu zukuri* (paper-thin slices): Place a fillet of bass or porgy on a flat surface and, holding the fish firmly with one hand, slice it on an angle into almost transparent sheets.

TO SERVE: *Sashimi* may be composed of one fish or a variety of fish. To serve as part of a meal, arrange the fish attractively on individual serving plates and decorate with strips of *daikon*, carrot and/or celery. Cover with plastic wrap and refrigerate for no more than 1 hour before serving.

Pour the dipping sauce of your choice into tiny individual dishes and accompany each serving of *sashimi* with its own dipping sauce.

SOY-BASED SAUCE

¼ cup Japanese all-purpose soy
  sauce
1 tablespoon *sake* (rice wine)
2 tablespoons preflaked *katsuobushi*
  (dried bonito)
MSG

GARNISH
1 tablespoon *wasabi* (green
  horseradish) powder, mixed with
  just enough cold water to make a
  thick paste and set aside to rest
  for 15 minutes

Combine the soy sauce, *sake, katsuobushi* and a sprinkle of MSG in a small saucepan and bring to a boil uncovered, stirring constantly. Strain through a fine sieve set over a small bowl and cool to room temperature.

Divide the dipping sauce among 6 tiny individual dishes, and serve it with *sashimi* of any kind.

Garnish each plate of *sashimi* with about ½ teaspoon of *wasabi,* this to be mixed into the dipping sauce to individual taste.

Baked Fish in Horseradish Sauce
Katerfisch

To serve 4

4 tablespoons butter
2 pounds gray, lemon or petrale
 sole fillets or 2 pounds flounder
 fillets, cut into serving pieces
2 tablespoons fresh lemon juice
½ teaspoon salt
2 medium-sized onions, peeled, thinly
 sliced and separated into rings

3 tablespoons tomato purée
1 tablespoon white wine vinegar or
 cider vinegar
½ teaspoon grated fresh horseradish
 or 1 teaspoon bottled horseradish,
 thoroughly drained and squeezed
 dry in a towel
2 medium-sized dill pickles, cut
 lengthwise into thin wedges

Preheat the oven to 375°. With 1 tablespoon of the butter, coat the bottom and sides of a shallow baking dish or casserole large enough to hold the fish in a single layer. Set the dish aside. Spread the fillets on wax paper, sprinkle them with lemon juice and salt, and let the fillets marinate for 10 minutes. In a heavy 8- to 10-inch skillet, melt 2 tablespoons of butter over moderate heat. When the foam subsides, drop in the onion rings and cook them, turning them frequently, for 5 minutes, or until the rings are soft and transparent but not brown.

Arrange the fish fillets side by side in the prepared baking dish. Beat the tomato purée, vinegar and horseradish together in a bowl, and spread the mixture evenly over the fillets. Scatter the onion rings and pickle wedges over the fish. Cut the remaining 1 tablespoon of butter into small pieces and dot the fish with them. Bake in the middle of the oven for about 15 minutes, or until the fillets are opaque and firm to the touch. Do not overcook. Serve at once, directly from the baking dish.

Fish Fillets with Wine Sauce
Filets de Soles à la Parisienne, Gratinés

To serve 6 to 8

Butter
2 tablespoons finely chopped
 shallots or scallions
3 pounds gray, lemon, or petrale

sole or flounder fillets, skinned and
 cut into serving pieces
Salt
Freshly ground black pepper
¾ cup dry white wine
Water

Preheat the oven to 350°. Butter the bottom of a shallow, flameproof baking-and-serving dish large enough to hold the fillets in one layer. Sprinkle the shallots over the bottom of the dish, lay the fillets over them, side by side, folding them in half if the fillets are less than ¼ inch thick. Season with salt and pepper. Pour in the wine and enough water to come almost to the top of the fish (about ½ to ¾ cup). Bring to a slow simmer on top of the stove, cover the dish with a sheet of buttered wax paper, and then poach on the middle shelf of the oven for 8 to 10 minutes, or until the fillets are just firm when pressed lightly with a finger. Remove the baking dish from the oven and set aside the wax paper. Increase the oven temperature to 425°. With a bulb baster, draw up all the liquid from the baking dish and strain into a 1½- to 2-quart enameled or stainless-steel saucepan. Re-cover the baking dish with the wax paper and set aside. Boil the poaching liquid over high heat until it has reduced to 1 cup.

SAUCE PARISIENNE
4 tablespoons butter
5 tablespoons flour
¾ cup milk
2 egg yolks
¼ to ½ cup heavy cream

A few drops of lemon juice
1 teaspoon salt
White pepper
2 to 3 tablespoons grated, imported
    Swiss cheese
2 teaspoons butter, cut in tiny pieces

SAUCE PARISIENNE: In a 2- to 3-quart enameled or stainless-steel saucepan, melt 4 tablespoons of butter over moderate heat. When the foam subsides, lift the pan from the heat and stir in the flour. Return to low heat and cook, stirring constantly, for a minute or two. Do not let this *roux* brown. Remove the pan from the heat and slowly pour in the reduced poaching liquid and the milk, whisking constantly. Then return to high heat and cook, stirring the sauce with a whisk. When it thickens and comes to a boil, reduce the heat and let it simmer slowly for 1 minute. Mix the egg yolks and ¼ cup cream together in a small bowl, and stir into it 2 tablespoons of the hot sauce. Add 2 more tablespoons of sauce, then whisk the now-heated egg-yolk-and-cream mixture back into the remaining sauce in the pan. Over moderate heat, bring the sauce to a boil, stirring constantly, and boil for 30 seconds. Remove it from the heat and season it with lemon juice, salt and a little white pepper. The sauce should be thick enough to coat the whisk lightly; if it is too thick, thin it with some or all of the remaining cream.

With a bulb baster, draw off any juices that have accumulated in the baking dish. Spread sauce under the fillets, lifting them gently with a spatula, then mask the tops of the fillets with the remaining sauce. Sprinkle on the grated cheese and dot the top with 2 teaspoons of butter. Bake in the top third of the oven for 10 to 15 minutes, or until the sauce bubbles, then slide under the broiler for 30 seconds, until it is browned. Serve at once.

Flounder with Shrimp or Parsley Sauce
Stegt Rødspaette

To serve 4

4 fillets of flounder, ½ pound each
Salt
Flour
½ cup dried bread crumbs
2 eggs

2 tablespoons water
8 tablespoons (1 quarter-pound stick)
  butter
2 tablespoons vegetable oil
½ pound small cooked shrimp,
  peeled and deveined
Lemon wedges

Rinse the fish in cold water and dry with paper towels. Salt lightly, dip in flour and shake off any excess. Spread the bread crumbs on wax paper. In a mixing bowl, beat the eggs together with the 2 tablespoons of water, then dip each fillet into the egg mixture and coat each side thoroughly with the bread crumbs. Let them rest for at least 10 minutes before cooking. Heat 2 tablespoons of butter and 2 tablespoons of oil in a heavy 10- to 12-inch skillet over moderate heat. When the foam subsides, sauté the fillets for 3 to 4 minutes on each side, turning them with a spatula. When golden brown, transfer the fillets to a heated platter. In a separate pan, melt 2 table-spoons of butter over moderate heat. Add the shrimp and toss them in the butter for 2 to 3 minutes until well coated. Place a line of the shrimp down the center of each fillet. Melt the remaining butter over low heat until it turns a rich, nutty brown, pour over the fish fillets, and garnish with lemon wedges. If you prefer, serve with a parsley sauce *(below)* in place of the shrimp and brown butter.

PARSLEY SAUCE
To make about 1½ cups

2 tablespoons unsalted butter
2 tablespoons flour
1 cup chicken stock,

freshly made or canned
Salt
2 tablespoons finely chopped parsley
2 teaspoons lemon juice

In a small, heavy saucepan, melt the butter over moderate heat. When the foam subsides, remove from the heat and stir in the flour with a wooden spoon. Pour in the stock all at once, beating vigorously with a wire whisk until the butter and flour *roux* and the liquid are well-blended. Return to low heat and cook, whisking constantly, until the sauce comes to a boil and is smooth and thick. Reduce the heat and simmer slowly for 2 to 3 minutes. Add salt to taste, stir in the parsley and lemon juice, and pour over the fish.

Fish and Chips

To serve 4

BATTER
1 cup flour
1 egg yolk
2 tablespoons beer

¼ teaspoon salt
3 tablespoons milk combined with
   3 tablespoons cold water
1 egg white

To prepare the batter, pour the flour into a large mixing bowl, make a well in the center and add the egg yolk, beer and salt. Stir the ingredients together until they are well mixed, then gradually pour in the combined milk and water, and continue to stir until the batter is smooth.

For a light texture, let the batter rest at room temperature for at least 30 minutes, although if necessary it may be used at once. In either case, beat the egg white until it forms unwavering peaks on the beater when it is lifted from the bowl. Then gently but thoroughly fold it into the batter.

CHIPS
Vegetable oil or shortening for
  deep-fat frying

2 pounds baking potatoes, sliced
  lengthwise into strips ½ inch
  thick and ½ inch wide

To cook the chips and fish, heat 4 to 5 inches of oil or shortening in a deep-fat fryer to a temperature of 375° on a deep-fat-frying thermometer. Preheat the oven to 250°, and line a large shallow roasting pan with paper towels.

Dry the potatoes thoroughly and deep-fry them in 3 or 4 batches until they are crisp and light brown. Transfer them to the lined pan to drain and place them in the oven to keep warm.

FISH
2 pounds fresh, firm white fish fillets
  such as haddock, sole, flounder
  or cod, skinned and cut into 3-by-

5-inch serving pieces
Malt vinegar
Salt

Wash the pieces of fish under cold running water and pat them completely dry with paper towels. Drop 2 or 3 pieces of fish at a time into the batter and, when they are well coated, plunge them into the hot fat. Fry for 4 or 5 minutes, or until golden brown, turning the pieces occasionally with a spoon to prevent them from sticking together or to the pan.

To serve, heap the fish in the center of a large heated platter and arrange the chips around them. Traditionally, fish and chips are served sprinkled with malt vinegar and salt.

Haddock with Potatoes and Tomato Sauce
Merluza a la Gallega

To serve 4

12 small firm boiling-type potatoes, each about 1½ inches in diameter, peeled
1 small onion, peeled and cut in half
1 small bay leaf
1½ pounds of haddock, hake or cod fillets
6 tablespoons olive oil

6 medium-sized garlic cloves, peeled and gently bruised with the flat of a knife
3 medium-sized tomatoes, peeled, seeded and coarsely chopped
½ teaspoon salt
1 tablespoon paprika
1 teaspoon red wine vinegar

In a heavy 12-inch skillet at least 2 inches deep, bring 2 quarts of water to a boil over high heat. Drop in the potatoes, onion, and bay leaf. There should be enough water to cover them completely; if necessary, add more. Boil briskly uncovered until the potatoes are tender but not falling apart. With a slotted spoon, transfer the potatoes to a plate. Add the fish fillets to the liquid remaining in the pan and reduce the heat to low. Cover the skillet tightly and simmer for 8 to 10 minutes, or until the fish flakes easily when prodded gently with a fork.

Meanwhile, heat the oil in a heavy 8- to 10-inch skillet over moderate heat until a light haze forms above it. Add the garlic cloves and, stirring frequently, cook them for about 5 minutes, or until light brown. With a slotted spoon, remove and discard them, then add the tomatoes and salt. Cook briskly, stirring and mashing the tomatoes with a large spoon, until the mixture is thick enough to hold its shape almost solidly in the spoon. Stir in the paprika and set aside.

Pour off all but 1 cup of liquid from the fish, discard the onion and bay leaf and return the potatoes to the skillet. With the back of a spoon, force the tomato mixture through a fine sieve, directly over the fish. Simmer over low heat for 5 minutes, basting the fish and potatoes frequently with the sauce. Sprinkle with the vinegar and serve at once, directly from the skillet or from a deep heated platter.

Finnan Haddie

To serve 4

1 small onion, cut into ⅛-inch slices and separated into rings
1 teaspoon whole black peppercorns

2 pounds smoked haddock, cut into 4 pieces
3 cups milk
Mustard sauce *(below)*

Strew the onion rings and peppercorns over the bottom of a heavy 10-inch skillet, and arrange the pieces of smoked haddock on top. Pour in the milk. The milk should just cover the fish; add more if necessary. Bring to a boil over high heat, then reduce the heat to low. Cover and simmer undisturbed for about 10 minutes, or until the fish flakes easily when prodded with a fork. Do not overcook.

With a slotted spatula, transfer the fish to a heated serving platter and discard the milk, onions and peppercorns. Serve the Finnan haddie at once, accompanied by a bowl of mustard sauce.

MUSTARD SAUCE

2 tablespoons butter	1 teaspoon Dijon-style prepared
2 tablespoons flour	mustard
1 cup milk	1 teaspoon dry hot English mustard
4 tablespoons heavy cream	½ teaspoon salt
1 teaspoon distilled white vinegar	Freshly ground black pepper

In a heavy 6- to 8-inch skillet, melt the butter over moderate heat. When the foam subsides, stir in the flour and mix together thoroughly. Pour in the milk and, stirring constantly with a whisk, cook over high heat until the sauce thickens heavily and comes to a boil. Reduce the heat to low and simmer for about 3 minutes, then beat in the cream, vinegar, prepared mustard, dry mustard, salt and a few grindings of pepper. Taste for seasoning and serve at once.

Halibut with Cream and Cheese
Heilbutt unterm Sahneberg

To serve 4

¼ cup dry white wine	4 tablespoons butter, softened
¾ cup water	2 pounds halibut fillets, cut into
½ cup coarsely chopped onions	serving pieces, or substitute 2
4 parsley sprigs	pounds fillets of any other firm,
1 small bay leaf	white fish
6 whole black peppercorns	½ teaspoon salt
6 or 8 strips of lean bacon, about	1 tablespoon flour
8 inches long	1 teaspoon fresh lemon juice
2 tablespoons finely chopped onions	⅛ teaspoon paprika
	½ cup heavy cream
	¼ cup freshly grated Parmesan cheese

In a heavy 1- to 1½-quart enameled or stainless-steel saucepan, bring the wine, water, ½ cup coarsely chopped onions, parsley, bay leaf and peppercorns to a boil over high heat. Reduce the heat to low and simmer, partially uncovered, for 20 minutes. Remove from the heat and set aside.

In a heavy 10- to 12-inch skillet, cook the bacon over moderate heat until it is lightly browned but still limp. With kitchen tongs, transfer the bacon to a double thickness of paper towels to drain. Pour off all but a tablespoon of fat from the skillet, add 2 tablespoons of finely chopped onions and cook over moderate heat, stirring frequently, for 5 minutes, or until the onions are soft and transparent but not brown.

Preheat the oven to 325°. Coat the bottom and sides of a shallow oven-proof serving dish large enough to hold the fish fillets in one layer with 2 tablespoons of the soft butter. Lay the fillets side by side in the bottom of the dish, and sprinkle them with ½ teaspoon of salt. Sprinkle the sautéed onions over the fish and lay the bacon strips on top. Strain the wine mixture over the fish, pressing down hard on the onions and herbs with the back of a spoon before discarding them. Bake the halibut in the middle of the oven for 12 to 15 minutes, or until the fish is firm and opaque. Discard the bacon and pour the cooking liquid through a fine sieve into a bowl. Cover the fish and set it aside in the baking dish.

To make the sauce, measure the strained cooking liquid and pour it into a small saucepan. If there is more than ½ cup, boil it briskly over high heat until it is reduced to that amount; if there is less, add more wine.

Bring the liquid to a boil over moderate heat. In a small bowl, make a paste of the remaining 2 tablespoons of butter and the flour, and when the mixture is smooth add it bit by bit to the poaching liquid. Reduce the heat and simmer, stirring constantly, for 5 minutes, or until the sauce thickens slightly. Remove the pan from the heat, and stir in the lemon juice and paprika. Taste for seasoning.

With a whisk or a rotary or electric beater, whip the cream in a chilled bowl until it forms firm peaks on the beater when it is lifted out of the bowl. Fold the cream gently into the sauce. Then, working quickly, pour the sauce over the fish and sprinkle the top with grated cheese. Slide the casserole under the broiler about 4 inches from the heat and broil for 1 or 2 minutes, or until the cheese melts and the sauce browns lightly. Serve at once, directly from the casserole.

Halibut Steaks with Herb Butter

To serve 6

HERB BUTTER
¼ pound softened butter

2 tablespoons minced chives
2 tablespoons minced parsley
2 tablespoons lemon juice

Cream the butter, then blend in the chives and parsley, adding the lemon juice a little at a time. Shape into a roll, wrap tightly in foil or waxed paper and chill until firm.

FISH	Salt
3 or 6 halibut steaks, cut 1¼ inches thick	Pepper
	2 tablespoons butter

Buy 3 or 6 halibut steaks, depending on the size of the fish. Rinse and dry the fish. Season with salt and pepper and arrange in a shallow buttered baking pan. Put small lumps of the butter on each steak. Bake in a preheated 350° oven 30 minutes, or until the fish flakes easily when tested with a fork and is delicately browned. Place a slice of the cold herb butter on each fish steak and serve immediately.

Baked Spiced Herring

1 tablespoon butter	
3 carrots, chopped	Sprig of thyme
3 onions, chopped	6 peppercorns
1 clove garlic, chopped	Pinch of allspice
4 sprigs of parsley, chopped	2 cloves
Salt	12 small herring
Pepper	Rings of sliced onion
White wine	Thin slices of carrot
1 bay leaf	¼ cup wine vinegar

Butter a large baking dish or casserole and cover the bottom with the chopped carrots, onions, garlic and parsley. Salt and pepper to taste. Add white wine to cover, and a bay leaf, the sprig of thyme, the peppercorns, allspice and cloves. Bring them to a boil and simmer for 20 minutes, or until the vegetables are tender.

Clean the fish and place them on top of the vegetables. Cover with the onion rings and carrot slices, add the wine vinegar and more wine—enough to cover. Bake at 350° for 20 minutes. Let the fish cool in the liquid, and serve chilled as a main course for luncheon, or as a first course for dinner.

Grilled Marinated Mackerel
Stekt Marinert Makrell

To serve 2

2 tablespoons olive oil
1 tablespoon lemon juice
½ teaspoon salt

Freshly ground black pepper
2 teaspoons finely chopped onion
2 mackerel, 1 pound each
3 tablespoons combined melted butter
   and vegetable oil

Have the fish dealer remove the backbones of the mackerel without cutting them in half. Preheat the broiler. In a shallow baking dish large enough to hold the fish laid out flat in one layer, combine the oil, lemon juice, salt, a few grindings of black pepper and the chopped onion. Place the mackerel in this marinade, flesh side down, for 15 minutes, then turn them over for another 15 minutes. Brush the broiler grill with 1 tablespoon of the melted butter and oil and place the mackerel on it, skin side down. Grill on only one side, about 3 inches from the heat, basting them from time to time with the remaining butter and oil. In 10 to 12 minutes they should have turned a light golden color and their flesh should flake easily when prodded with a fork. Serve at once, accompanied by tomato butter.

TOMATO BUTTER
8 tablespoons (1 quarter-pound stick)
   unsalted butter

2 tablespoons tomato paste
½ teaspoon salt
¼ teaspoon sugar

Cream the butter with an electric mixer set at medium speed or by beating it against the side of a bowl with a wooden spoon. When it is light and fluffy, beat in the tomato paste, salt and sugar. Transfer to a serving bowl and chill until ready to serve. Serve cold, with the hot grilled mackerel.

Baked Red Snapper and Potatoes
Besugo al Horno

To serve 4 to 6

2 two-pound red snappers, cleaned
   but with heads and tails left on,
   or substitute any firm white fish
1½ teaspoons salt
1 lemon, cut into 6 wedges
2 small black olives
¾ cup soft crumbs made from
   French or Italian bread, pulverized

in a blender or with a fork
1 teaspoon finely chopped garlic
1 tablespoon finely chopped parsley
2 tablespoons paprika
3 medium-sized boiling potatoes,
   peeled and cut into ¼-inch rounds
Freshly ground black pepper
1 cup water
½ cup olive oil

Preheat the oven to 350°. Wash the fish under cold running water and pat them dry, inside and out, with paper towels. Sprinkle the fish with 1 teaspoon of the salt, then place them side by side on a board or plate.

With a small, sharp knife, score each fish, by making three crosswise parallel cuts about ¼ inch deep, 2 inches long and 1½ inches apart. Insert a wedge of lemon skin side up in each cut. Insert a black olive in the exposed eye socket of each fish.

In a small bowl, combine the bread crumbs, garlic, parsley and paprika. Spread the potato slices evenly on the bottom of a 16-by-10-by-2-inch baking-serving dish. Sprinkle them with the remaining ½ teaspoon of salt and a few grindings of pepper and place the fish side by side on top. Pour the water down the side of the baking dish and pour the olive oil over the fish. Sprinkle them evenly with the bread-crumb mixture.

Bake in the middle of the oven for 30 minutes, or until the fish feels firm when pressed lightly with a finger and the potatoes beneath them are done. Serve at once, directly from the baking dish.

Red Snapper with Pimiento Sauce
Pescado Yucateco
To serve 8

3 tablespoons olive oil
½ cup coarsely chopped onions
⅔ cup pimiento-stuffed olives,
    quartered lengthwise
½ cup coarsely chopped sweet fresh
    red pepper or canned pimiento
2 tablespoons coarsely chopped fresh
    coriander
1 teaspoon annatto seeds,
    pulverized with a mortar and pestle

½ cup fresh orange juice
¼ cup fresh lemon juice
½ teaspoon salt
Freshly ground black pepper
1 tablespoon soft butter
A 4- to 5-pound red snapper, cleaned
    but with head and tail on, or any
    firm white whole fish
2 finely chopped hard-cooked eggs,
    or 2 cups shredded lettuce
    combined with 3 or 4 sliced radishes

Preheat the oven to 400°. In a heavy 8- to 10-inch skillet, heat the olive oil until a light haze forms above it. Add the onions and cook over moderate heat, stirring frequently, for 5 minutes, or until the onions are soft and transparent but not brown. Stir in the olives, fresh red pepper or pimiento, fresh coriander and ground annatto seeds, and cook, stirring occasionally, for 3 minutes longer. Then add the orange juice, lemon juice, salt and a few grindings of black pepper.

With a tablespoon of soft butter, grease the bottom and sides of a shallow heatproof casserole large enough to hold the fish comfortably. Place the fish in the casserole and pour the sauce over it. Bake, uncovered, in the middle of the oven for 30 minutes, basting the fish with its sauce every 10 minutes. The fish is done if its flesh feels firm when pressed with a finger. Be careful not to overcook.

Serve the baked fish directly from the casserole, sprinkled with the chopped egg, or—with one or two spatulas—transfer the fish carefully to a large heated platter, pour the sauce over and around it and garnish with the chopped egg or with the shredded lettuce and radishes.

Salmon with Béarnaise Sauce
Saumon Grillé Sauce Béarnaise

To serve 8

FISH
8 small salmon steaks

1½ teaspoons salt
½ teaspoon black pepper
½ cup melted butter

Sprinkle both sides of the salmon steaks with salt and pepper and let them stand for 20 minutes.

Heat a broiling pan brushed heavily with melted butter. Arrange the steaks on the pan and brush them well with melted butter. Broil about 2 inches from the source of heat for 7 minutes, or until delicately browned. Turn the steaks over and pour the remaining butter over them. Broil 7 minutes longer, or until the fish flakes easily when tested. Arrange on a hot serving dish and garnish with parsley and lemon wedges. Pass the sauce separately.

SAUCE
2 teaspoons chopped fresh, or ½ teaspoon dried, tarragon
3 teaspoons chopped shallots or onions
2 teaspoons chopped fresh, or ½ teaspoon dried, chervil
2 peppercorns

⅛ teaspoon salt
¼ cup tarragon vinegar
5 egg yolks
¾ cup melted butter
Dash cayenne pepper
1 teaspoon chopped fresh tarragon, chervil, chives or parsley (optional)

Combine the tarragon, shallots, chervil, peppercorns, salt and vinegar in a saucepan. Cook over a low heat until only about 1 tablespoon of the vinegar remains. Cool.

Beat the egg yolks with a whisk in a saucepan; strain the vinegar mixture into it. Place over very low heat, and gradually beat in the butter. Beat with the whisk until thickened, but do not let the sauce boil. Mix in the cayenne pepper and, if fresh herbs are available, the tarragon, chervil, chives or parsley, a teaspoon of any or a mixture.

Broiled Shad

To serve 4 to 6

6 tablespoons butter, cut into small
  pieces
2½ pounds shad, filleted but with
skin left on
Salt
Freshly ground black pepper
Lemon wedges

Preheat the broiler to its highest point. Choose a shallow, flameproof baking dish just large enough to hold the shad fillets comfortably. In it, over moderate heat, melt the butter on top of the stove. Wash the shad quickly in cold water, pat thoroughly dry with paper towels and dip in the butter. Turn over 2 or 3 times so that the fish is thoroughly coated with butter on both sides. Broil the fish, skin side down, about 4 inches from the heat, for 6 to 8 minutes, regulating the heat, if necessary, to prevent the fish from burning. Baste occasionally with the butter in the pan. Do not turn the shad over. The shad is done when its flesh is opaque and flakes easily when gently prodded with a fork. Before serving, preferably in its baking dish, sprinkle the shad lightly with salt and a few grindings of black pepper, and surround with the lemon wedges.

Fried Smelts with Herb Butter

To serve 4 to 6

8 tablespoons softened butter
  (1 quarter-pound stick)
½ teaspoon salt
Freshly ground black pepper
1 tablespoon finely chopped parsley
1 tablespoon finely chopped chives
1 tablespoon fresh lime juice
⅛ teaspoon Tabasco
18 smelts, with the backbone
  removed but the heads and tails
  left on
Salt
Flour
1½ to 2 cups vegetable shortening

Cream the butter by beating it with a wooden spoon against the sides of a mixing bowl until it is smooth and fluffy. Beat in the ½ teaspoon of salt, a few grindings of black pepper, the parsley, chives, lime juice and Tabasco.

Place the herb butter on a sheet of wax paper about 3 feet long; fold the wax paper over it, and pat and shape the enclosed butter into a long, ½-inch-thick cylinder. Refrigerate it for at least an hour, or until the butter is firm.

Wash the smelts under cold running water and pat them thoroughly dry, inside and out, with paper towels. If the fish dealer has not removed the backbone, sever it from the head, and with the tip of a sharp knife gently lift it out, cutting it off at the base of the tail.

Sprinkle the fish generously with salt and a few grindings of pepper, dip it in flour on both sides and shake off the excess. Heat the shortening (it should be at least ½ inch deep in the pan) over high heat in a 10-inch heavy skillet until a light haze forms over it. Add as many of the fish, spread open, as the pan will hold comfortably, and cook them over moderate heat on both sides for 3 to 4 minutes each until they are crisp and brown. Remove them to a double thickness of paper towels to drain, and brown the remaining fish in the same fashion, adding more shortening to the pan if necessary.

Place the fish, spread open and skin side down, on a heated serving platter. Quickly, cut the chilled herb butter into approximately 1- to 2-inch lengths depending upon the size of the fish, and place a small cylinder, lengthwise, in the center of each fish. Serve at once.

Barbecued Swordfish

To serve 4 to 6

MARINADE
2 tablespoons lemon juice
4 tablespoons orange juice
4 tablespoons soy sauce
2 tablespoons tomato paste
1 teaspoon minced garlic
1 teaspoon oregano

2 tablespoons finely chopped
 fresh parsley
½ teaspoon salt
Freshly ground black pepper

2 pounds swordfish, cut about 1 inch
 thick
1 tablespoon soft butter

Combine the lemon and orange juice, soy sauce, tomato paste, garlic, oregano, parsley, salt and a few grindings of black pepper in a large, shallow baking dish. Stir until all the ingredients are well combined. Place the swordfish in the dish, baste thoroughly and marinate for about 2 hours at room temperature, turning the fish over after the first hour.

Preheat the broiler to its highest point for at least 10 minutes. Then, with a pastry brush, grease the broiler rack with the tablespoon of soft butter. Lay the swordfish on the rack, brush heavily with the marinade and broil the fish 3 inches from the heat for about 5 minutes, brushing it once or twice with the marinade. When the surface of the fish is lightly browned, turn it over with a large spatula and broil on the other side for 5 minutes, brushing on the remaining marinade once or twice more to keep the surface of the fish well moistened. When the swordfish is done it should be a golden brown and firm to the touch. Be careful not to overcook. Transfer the fish to a heated platter, pour the broiling pan juices over it and serve at once, cut into appropriate portions.

238

Fried Brook Trout

To serve 4

8 strips of fat bacon
4 brook trout, about ¾ to 1 pound
  each, eviscerated but with heads
  and tails left on
Salt
Freshly ground black pepper
1½ to 2 cups white or yellow
  cornmeal

In a large, heavy skillet, cook the bacon over moderate heat until it is brown and crisp. Transfer the bacon to paper towels to drain.

Wash the fish under cold running water and dry them thoroughly with paper towels. Sprinkle them inside and out with salt and a few gridings of black pepper, then dip them in the cornmeal, shaking them gently to remove any excess. Heat the bacon fat in the skillet over high heat until a light haze forms over it. Add the fish and cook them for about 5 minutes on each side, turning them over carefully with tongs. Regulate the heat so that the trout will brown evenly without burning. Remove them to a heated platter, add the bacon strips and serve.

Trout Sautéed in Butter
Truites à la Meunière

To serve 4

11 tablespoons butter (1 quarter-
  pound stick plus 3 tablespoons)
4 whole fresh ½-pound trout or
  defrosted frozen trout, cleaned but
  with both the heads and tails left on
Salt
Flour
1 tablespoon oil
2 tablespoons lemon juice
4 tablespoons finely chopped fresh
  parsley

In a 1½- to 2-quart saucepan, clarify 8 tablespoons of the butter by melting it slowly, skimming off the surface foam. Spoon the clear butter on top into a heavy 6- to 8-inch skillet and discard the milky solids at the bottom of the pan. Set aside.

Wash the trout under cold running water and dry them completely with paper towels. Season them inside and out with salt; dip them in flour and then shake them to remove all but a light dusting of the flour. In a heavy 10- to 12-inch skillet, melt the remaining 3 tablespoons of butter with the oil over moderately high heat. When the foam subsides, add the trout and sauté them over high heat, turning them with kitchen tongs, for 5 or 6 minutes on each side, or until they are a golden color and just firm when pressed lightly with a finger. Transfer them to a heated platter and cover lightly to keep warm. Cook the clarified butter over low heat until it browns lightly. Do not let it burn. Sprinkle the trout with lemon juice and parsley, pour the hot butter over them and serve immediately.

Baked Trout with Mushrooms
Trotelle alla Savoia

To serve 4

4 cleaned, whole trout,
  1/2 to 3/4 pound each, with heads
  and tails left on, or substitute
  thoroughly defrosted frozen trout
Salt
Freshly ground black pepper
Flour
6 tablespoons butter

2 tablespoons olive oil
1/2 pound fresh mushrooms, thinly
  sliced
1 teaspoon lemon juice
3/4 cup thinly sliced scallions (white
  part plus 2 to 3 inches of green)
1/4 cup fresh white bread crumbs (made
  from about 1 slice French or Italian
  bread)

Preheat the oven to 425°. Wash the trout, inside and out, under cold running water and pat them dry with paper towels. Season the trout lightly with salt and pepper, then roll them in flour and brush or shake off the excess. In a heavy 10- to 12-inch skillet, melt 2 tablespoons of butter with the oil over high heat. When the foam subsides, add the trout and cook them for 4 to 5 minutes on each side, or until they are golden brown. Carefully transfer the trout to a plate. In a stainless-steel or enameled skillet, melt another 2 tablespoons of butter over moderate heat. Add the sliced mushrooms, sprinkle them with lemon juice, and shaking the skillet almost constantly, cook for about 3 minutes, or until they glisten with butter and are slightly softened. With a slotted spoon, remove the mushrooms from the skillet and spread them over the bottom of a buttered ovenproof baking dish just large enough to hold the 4 trout in one layer. Melt 1 tablespoon of butter in the skillet, add the scallions and cook them for 1 minute. Then with a slotted spoon transfer them to a bowl. In the remaining tablespoon of butter, and in the same skillet, lightly brown the bread crumbs.

Arrange the browned trout (adding any juices that have accumulated on the platter) on top of the mushrooms in the baking dish. Sprinkle them with the crisped bread crumbs and spread the scallions on top. Bake on the middle shelf of the oven for 10 minutes, or until the crumbs and scallions are brown. Serve directly from the baking dish.

Clams in White Wine with Onions and Tomatoes

Almejas a la Marinera

To serve 2

3 tablespoons olive oil
½ cup finely chopped onions
1 teaspoon finely chopped garlic
2 tablespoons coarsely crumbled
    white bread, trimmed of crusts
½ cup peeled, seeded and finely
    chopped tomatoes

1 hard-cooked egg, the yolk sieved
    and the white finely chopped
2 dozen small hard-shell clams,
    washed and thoroughly scrubbed
1 cup dry white wine
Salt
Freshly ground black pepper
2 tablespoons finely chopped parsley
1 lemon, cut into 6 or 8 wedges

To make the *sofrito*, heat the oil in a heavy 8- to 10-inch skillet, until a light haze forms above it. Add the onions and garlic. Stirring frequently, cook for 5 minutes or until the onions are soft and transparent but not brown.

Stir in the bread, tomatoes and sieved egg yolk. Cook for about 5 minutes, mashing and stirring with a spoon until most of the liquid in the pan evaporates and the mixture becomes a thick, smooth purée. Set aside.

Place the clams hinged side down in a heavy 10- to 12-inch skillet, pour in the wine and bring to a boil over high heat. Cover tightly, reduce the heat to low, and steam for 8 to 10 minutes or until the clams open. With tongs or a slotted spoon, remove the clams from the skillet and place them on a deep heated platter. Discard any clams that remain closed.

Strain the liquid in the skillet through a sieve directly into the *sofrito*. Bring to a boil, stirring; taste and season with salt and pepper.

Pour the sauce over the clams, sprinkle the top with the egg white and parsley and garnish the platter with the lemon wedges. Serve at once.

Clams with Sausage, Ham and Tomatoes

Amêijoas na Cataplana

To serve 4

½ pound *linguiça* sausage or substitute *chorizo* or other garlic-seasoned smoked pork sausage
½ cup olive oil
4 medium-sized onions, thinly sliced
1 teaspoon paprika
¼ teaspoon crushed hot dried red pepper
Freshly ground black pepper
¼ pound *presunto* ham, finely chopped, or substitute prosciutto or other lean smoked ham
2 medium-sized tomatoes, peeled, seeded and coarsely chopped
½ cup finely chopped parsley
½ cup dry white wine
1 tablespoon finely chopped garlic
2 small bay leaves, crumbled
36 small hard-shelled clams, washed and thoroughly scrubbed

With a small, sharp knife, remove the casings of the sausages. Crumble the meat coarsely and drop it into a sieve. Plunge the sieve into a pan of boiling water and boil briskly for 1 minute. Then spread the sausage meat out on a double thickness of paper towels to drain.

In a heavy 12-inch skillet or similar-sized casserole, heat the olive oil over moderate heat until a light haze forms above it. Add the onions and, stirring frequently, cook for 5 minutes, or until they are soft and transparent but not brown. Add the paprika, red pepper and a liberal grinding of black pepper and cook for a minute or two. Then add the sausage meat, ham, tomatoes, parsley, wine, garlic and bay leaves, raise the heat and bring to a boil. Stirring constantly, cook briskly until most of the liquid in the pan evaporates.

Arrange the clams hinged side down over the meat and tomato mixture, cover the skillet tightly and cook over moderate heat for about 10 minutes, or until all the clams open. Discard any that remain closed. To serve, transfer the clams to heated soup plates and ladle the sauce over them.

Curried Steamed Clams

Teesryo
To serve 6

¼ cup vegetable oil
1 tablespoon scraped, finely chopped fresh ginger root
2 large onions, peeled, cut lengthwise in half, then sliced lengthwise into paper-thin slivers
1 teaspoon salt
2 tablespoons ground coriander
1½ teaspoons turmeric
4 dozen small hard-shelled clams, washed and thoroughly scrubbed
1 fresh coconut, shelled, peeled and coarsely grated
1 tablespoon fresh lemon juice
1 tablespoon finely chopped fresh coriander
½ teaspoon ground hot red pepper

In a heavy 10- to 12-inch skillet, heat the vegetable oil over moderate heat until a light haze forms above it. Add the ginger and stir for a minute, then drop in the onions. Stirring constantly, fry for 7 or 8 minutes, until they are soft and golden brown. Watch carefully for any signs of burning and regulate the heat accordingly.

Stir in the salt and ground coriander, cook for a minute or so, then stir in the turmeric. When the mixture is well blended, add the clams, turning them about with a spoon to coat them evenly.

Cover the skillet tightly, reduce the heat to low, and steam for 8 to 10 minutes, or until the clams open.

Immediately transfer the entire contents of the skillet to a deep heated platter. Scatter the coconut over the clams and sprinkle them with lemon juice, fresh coriander and red pepper. Serve at once.

Sautéed Crab with Almonds

To serve 4

7 tablespoons butter	Salt
1 pound crabmeat	Pepper
2/3 cup almonds, blanched and split in half	1/3 cup heavy cream
	3 tablespoons chopped parsley

Melt 4 tablespoons of the butter in a medium skillet, add the crabmeat and toss lightly until it is delicately browned. While this is cooking, sauté the almonds in 3 tablespoons of butter over a rather brisk flame until they brown lightly. Salt and pepper them to taste and add them to the crabmeat. Finally, add the cream and the chopped parsley and let it cook up and boil for 2 minutes. Serve on rice or rounds of fried toast.

Lobster with Wine, Tomatoes and Herbs
Homard à l'Américaine

To serve 4 to 6

8 tablespoons butter (1 quarter-pound
   stick)
¼ cup finely chopped carrots
½ cup finely chopped onions
2 tablespoons finely chopped fresh
   parsley
1 teaspoon dried thyme
1 bay leaf
2 live lobsters, each 2 to 2½ pounds,
   cut into serving pieces
2 teaspoons salt
6 tablespoons olive or vegetable oil
⅓ cup cognac

5 large tomatoes, peeled, seeded and
   coarsely chopped (about 3 cups)
¼ cup finely chopped shallots or
   scallions
1 cup dry white wine
1 cup chicken stock, fresh or canned
1 tablespoon tomato paste
1 teaspoon bottled meat extract
1 tablespoon flour
½ teaspoon lemon juice
1 tablespoon finely cut fresh tarragon
   or 1 teaspoon dried tarragon,
   crumbled
Salt
Freshly ground black pepper

In a heavy 3- to 4-quart flameproof casserole, melt 4 tablespoons of the butter over moderate heat. When the foam subsides, stir in the carrots and onions, and cook, stirring, for 5 to 8 minutes, or until they are soft but not brown. Remove from the heat, stir in 1 tablespoon of the parsley, the thyme and bay leaf.

Remove and discard the gelatinous sac near the head of each lobster, if the fish dealer did not. Scoop out the greenish-brown tomalley (or liver) and set aside. If there is black roe (or coral) save it. Sprinkle the lobster with 2 teaspoons salt. Then heat the oil almost to the smoking point in a heavy 10- to 12-inch skillet, and sauté the lobster over high heat, turning frequently, for 4 or 5 minutes, or until the shells are red.

Remove all but a film of oil from the skillet and, off the heat, flame the lobster with cognac. Warm the cognac in a small saucepan over low heat, ignite it with a match, and pour it flaming over the lobster a little at a time. Shake the skillet gently until the flame dies. Using tongs, transfer the lobster pieces to the casserole. Pour the juices from the skillet over them, and stir in the tomatoes and shallots.

In the same skillet, combine the wine, stock, tomato paste and meat extract. Bring this sauce to a boil, stirring constantly; boil for 2 minutes, then pour it over the lobster. Stir the contents of the casserole together until all the lobster pieces are coated with the sauce. Bring to a boil over high heat; immediately reduce the heat, cover the casserole tightly, and simmer for 30 minutes, basting 2 or 3 times with the juices.

Meanwhile cream the remaining 4 tablespoons of butter by beating it vigorously against the sides of a small bowl with a wooden spoon until it is fluffy. Beat in the coral, tomalley, flour, lemon juice, tarragon, 1 tablespoon of parsley and a little salt and pepper. Press through a sieve and set aside. When the lobster is done, arrange the pieces on a large, heated platter and cover loosely to keep the lobster warm, or set the platter in a 250° oven.

Strain the entire contents of the casserole through a fine sieve into a 2- to 3-quart saucepan, pressing down on the vegetables with a spoon before discarding them. Boil the juices over high heat until reduced by about ½. Turn the heat to low and beat in the creamed butter mixture, 1 tablespoon at a time. Cook the sauce over low heat for 5 minutes; do not let it boil. Taste for seasoning. To serve, pour the sauce over the lobster.

Lobster on Skewers
Shishti Bosphorus

To serve 12

12 lobsters or 24 lobster tails	¼ cup grated onion
3 cups dry white wine	1 tablespoon salt
½ cup lemon juice	1½ teaspoons white pepper
½ cup vegetable oil	Mushroom caps
	½ cup brandy, heated

Remove the meat of the raw lobsters and cut it into 2-inch pieces. In a glass or pottery bowl, mix together the wine, lemon juice, oil, onion, salt and pepper. Marinate the lobster pieces in the mixture overnight in the refrigerator, basting and turning a few times. Drain.

Put the mushroom caps in the marinade, and let them stand for 10 minutes. Using 12 oiled skewers, alternately thread the lobster pieces and mushroom caps, starting and ending with lobster. Arrange the skewers on a broiling pan, and broil in a hot broiler for 10 minutes, turning the skewers to cook all sides. Arrange the skewers on a serving dish. Pour the warm brandy over them, set aflame and serve flaming.

Baked Oysters
Ostriche all' Italiana

To serve 4 to 6

2 tablespoons butter

1 cup fresh, white bread crumbs (made from about 3 slices of French or Italian bread)

1 teaspoon finely chopped garlic

2 tablespoons finely chopped fresh parsley, preferably the flat-leaf Italian type

2 dozen fresh oysters, shucked, or defrosted frozen oysters

3 tablespoons freshly grated imported Parmesan cheese

2 tablespoons butter, cut in tiny pieces

Preheat the oven to 450°. Choose an ovenproof platter or a shallow baking-and-serving dish that is just large enough to hold the oysters in one layer (about 8 by 10 or 12 inches). Butter the dish generously.

In a heavy 6- to 8-inch skillet, melt 2 tablespoons of butter over moderate heat. When the foam subsides, add the fresh, white bread crumbs and the garlic, and toss them in the butter for 2 or 3 minutes, or until they are crisp and golden. Stir in the finely chopped parsley. Spread about ⅔ cup of the bread-crumb mixture in the bottom of the buttered baking dish, and arrange the oysters over it in one layer. Mix the rest of the bread-crumb mixture with the grated cheese and spread the combination on the oysters. Dot the top with the tiny bits of butter.

Bake the oysters in the top third of the oven for 12 to 15 minutes, or until the crumbs are golden and the juices in the dish are bubbling.

Scallops Rémoulade

To serve 4 to 6

1½ to 2 pounds fresh bay scallops

Only very fresh, tiny bay scallops can be served raw successfully. (Frozen and defrosted ones will not do.) Wash the scallops quickly under cold running water and dry them thoroughly with paper towels. Chill until ready to serve.

RÉMOULADE SAUCE

1 cup mayonnaise, freshly made, or a good unsweetened commercial variety

1 teaspoon dry mustard

1 teaspoon lemon juice

¼ to ½ teaspoon garlic, finely chopped

1 tablespoon capers, drained, washed and finely chopped

1 tablespoon fresh tarragon, finely chopped, or 2 teaspoons finely crumbled dried tarragon

1 tablespoon finely chopped fresh parsley

1 hard-cooked egg, finely chopped

Salt

Cayenne or Tabasco

246

For the rémoulade sauce, combine the mayonnaise, dry mustard and lemon juice in a small mixing bowl. Stir in the chopped garlic, capers, tarragon, parsley and hard-cooked egg. Mix together gently but thoroughly, and season to taste with salt and a few grains of cayenne pepper or drops of Tabasco. Arrange the scallops, pierced with decorative picks, on a chilled serving plate and pass the rémoulade sauce separately.

Scallops with Mushrooms in White Wine Sauce
Coquilles Saint-Jacques à la Parisienne

To serve 6

1½ cups thoroughly degreased fresh or canned chicken stock, or water
1½ cups dry white wine
3 sliced shallots or scallions
3 celery tops with leaves, cut in

2-inch pieces
4 parsley sprigs
1 bay leaf
10 whole peppercorns
2 pounds whole bay scallops, or sea scallops cut into ½-inch slices
¾ pound fresh mushrooms, sliced

Preheat the oven to 375°. In a heavy 3- to 4-quart saucepan, bring the stock, wine, shallots, celery, parsley, bay leaf and peppercorns to a boil over high heat. Reduce the heat, and simmer uncovered for 20 minutes. Strain this court bouillon through a sieve into a 10- to 12-inch enameled or stainless-steel skillet. Add the scallops and mushrooms, cover and simmer for 5 minutes. Transfer the scallops and mushrooms to a large mixing bowl. Quickly boil the remaining court bouillon down to 1 cup.

SAUCE PARISIENNE
4 tablespoons butter
5 tablespoons flour
¾ cup milk
2 egg yolks

¼ to ½ cup heavy cream
A few drops of lemon juice
1 teaspoon salt
White pepper
¼ cup grated imported Swiss cheese

SAUCE PARISIENNE: In a 2- to 3-quart enameled or stainless-steel saucepan, melt 4 tablespoons of butter over moderate heat. When the foam subsides, lift the pan from the heat and stir in the flour. Return to low heat and cook, stirring constantly, for a minute or two. Do not let this *roux* brown. Remove the pan from the heat and slowly pour in the reduced poaching liquid and the milk, whisking constantly. Then return to high heat and cook, stirring the sauce with a whisk. When it thickens and comes to a boil, reduce the heat and let it simmer slowly for 1 minute. Mix the egg yolks and ¼ cup cream together in a small bowl, and stir into it 2 tablespoons of the hot sauce. Add 2 more tablespoons of sauce, then whisk the now-heated egg-yolk-and-cream mixture back into the remaining sauce in the pan. Over moderate heat bring the sauce to a boil, stirring constantly, and boil for 30 seconds. Remove from heat and season with lemon juice, salt and pepper. The sauce should coat a spoon fairly thickly; if it is too thick, thin it with more cream.

With a bulb baster, draw up and discard any juices that may have accumulated under the scallops and mushrooms. Then pour in about ⅔ of the *sauce parisienne* and stir together gently. Butter 6 scallop shells set on a baking sheet or in a broiler pan, or 6 shallow 4-inch baking dishes, and spoon the scallop mixture into them. Mask with the remaining sauce and sprinkle with cheese. Bake the scallops in the top third of the oven for 10 to 15 minutes or until the sauce begins to bubble, then slide them under a hot broiler for 30 seconds to brown the tops if desired. Serve at once.

Sautéed Scallops with Garlic Butter
Coquilles Saint-Jacques à la Provençale

To serve 4

	White pepper
2 pounds whole bay scallops, or sea	Flour
scallops cut into ¼-inch slices	2 tablespoons butter
Salt	3 tablespoons vegetable oil

Wash the scallops in cold water and dry them with paper towels. Season them with salt and pepper; then dip them in flour and shake them in a sieve or colander to remove all but a light dusting of flour. In a 10- to 12-inch enameled or stainless-steel skillet, melt 2 tablespoons of butter with the oil over moderate heat. When the foam subsides, sauté the scallops in two batches so they are not crowded in the pan, shaking the skillet and stirring the scallops until they are lightly browned. With a slotted spoon or spatula, transfer the scallops to a heated platter.

GARLIC BUTTER

8 tablespoons unsalted	2 tablespoons finely chopped fresh
butter (1 quarter-pound stick)	parsley
1 teaspoon finely chopped garlic	1 lemon, quartered

GARLIC BUTTER: In a 1½- to 2-quart saucepan, clarify 8 tablespoons of butter by melting it slowly, skimming off the foam. Spoon the clear butter on top into a 6- to 8-inch skillet and discard the milky solids at the bottom of the pan. Heat the butter until it sizzles, but do not let it brown. Remove it from the heat and quickly stir in the garlic. Pour the garlic butter over the scallops and serve at once, garnished with chopped parsley and lemon.

Shrimp Broiled in Garlic Sauce

Scampi alla Griglia

To serve 6

2 pounds large fresh shrimp in their shells or defrosted frozen shrimp	1 tablespoon finely chopped garlic
8 tablespoons (1 quarter-pound stick) of butter	1 teaspoon salt
½ cup olive oil	Freshly ground black pepper
1 tablespoon lemon juice	4 tablespoons finely chopped fresh parsley, preferably the flat-leaf Italian type
¼ cup finely chopped shallots or scallions	Lemon quarters

Shell the shrimp, but be careful not to remove the last small segment of shell or the tail. With a small sharp knife, slit each shrimp down the back and lift out the black or white intestinal vein. Wash the shrimp quickly under cold running water and pat them thoroughly dry with paper towels.

Preheat the broiler to its highest temperature. In a shallow flameproof baking dish or pan just large enough to hold the shrimp in one layer, melt the butter over low heat, and be careful not to let it brown. Stir in the ½ cup of olive oil, lemon juice, shallots, garlic, salt and a few grindings of pepper, add the shrimp and turn them in the butter and oil until they glisten on all sides. Broil them 3 to 4 inches from the heat for 5 minutes, then turn the shrimp over and broil them for 5 to 10 minutes longer, or until they are lightly browned and firm to the touch. Be careful not to overcook them. With tongs, transfer the shrimp to a heated serving platter, pour the sauce from the pan over them, and sprinkle with chopped parsley. Garnish with lemon quarters, and serve.

Shrimp Sauté in Cream

To serve 4 to 6

2 pounds shrimp	Pepper
Flour	1 tablespoon minced onion
3 tablespoons butter	1 tablespoon minced parsley
3 tablespoons olive oil	1 tablespoon minced tarragon
Salt	1½ cups heavy cream

Shell and devein the shrimp. Dredge them with flour. Melt the butter, add the oil, and sauté the shrimp for 3 or 4 minutes, or until they are lightly browned and cooked through. Salt and pepper to taste. Add the onion, parsley and tarragon, and toss with the shrimp. Gradually pour in the cream, stirring carefully, and continue stirring until the sauce is thickened and thoroughly blended.

Shrimp with Peas
Ch'ao-hsia-jen

To serve 2 to 4

1 pound raw shrimp in their shells (about 26 to 30 to the pound)	1 teaspoon salt
1 pound fresh peas, shelled, or 1 cup thoroughly defrosted frozen peas	2 tablespoons peanut oil, or flavorless vegetable oil
2 teaspoons cornstarch	1 scallion, including the green top, cut into 2-inch lengths
1 egg white	3 slices peeled fresh ginger root, about 1 inch in diameter and ⅛ inch thick
2 teaspoons Chinese rice wine, or pale dry sherry	

PREPARE AHEAD: 1. Shell the shrimp and, with a small, sharp knife, devein them by making a shallow incision down the back and lifting out the black or white intestinal vein with the point of the knife. Wash the shrimp under cold running water and pat them thoroughly dry with paper towels. Split each shrimp in half lengthwise, then cut each of the halves in two, crosswise.

2. Blanch the freshly shelled peas by dropping them into a quart of rapidly boiling water and letting them boil uncovered for 5 to 7 minutes, or until just tender when tasted. Then drain the peas into a large sieve or colander, and run cold water over them for a few seconds to stop their cooking and set their color. The frozen peas need only be thoroughly defrosted.

3. In a large mixing bowl, combine the shrimp and cornstarch, and

250

toss them together with a spoon until each shrimp piece is lightly coated with cornstarch. Add the egg white, wine and salt, and stir them with the shrimp until they are thoroughly mixed together.

4. Have the shrimp, peas, oil, scallions and ginger within easy reach.

TO COOK: Set a 12-inch wok or 10-inch skillet over high heat for 30 seconds. Pour in the 2 tablespoons of oil, swirl it about in the pan and heat for another 30 seconds, turning the heat down to moderate if the oil begins to smoke. Add the scallions and ginger, and stir-fry for 30 seconds to flavor the oil, then remove them with a slotted spoon and discard. Immediately drop the shrimp into the pan and stir-fry them for 2 minutes, or until they turn pink. Do not let the shrimp overcook. Then drop in the peas and stir-fry for about 1 minute to heat the peas through. Transfer the entire contents of the pan to a heated platter and serve at once.

Shellfish Stew

Zarzuela de Mariscos

To serve 6

A 1½ pound live lobster
12 large raw shrimp, in their shells
¼ cup olive oil
1 cup finely chopped onions
1 tablespoon finely chopped garlic
2 small sweet red or green peppers, deribbed, seeded and finely chopped
2 tablespoons finely chopped *serrano* ham, or substitute prosciutto or other lean smoked ham
6 medium-sized tomatoes, peeled, seeded and finely chopped
½ cup blanched almonds, pulverized
in a blender or with a nut grinder or mortar and pestle
1 large bay leaf, crumbled
⅛ teaspoon ground saffron or saffron threads crushed with a mortar and pestle or with the back of a spoon
1 teaspoon salt
Freshly ground black pepper
3 cups water
½ cup dry white wine
1 tablespoon fresh lemon juice
12 mussels, washed, scrubbed and with black tufts removed
12 small clams, washed and thoroughly scrubbed
½ pound sea scallops, cut in half

With a cleaver or large, heavy knife, chop off the tail section of the lobster at the point where it joins the body. Then cut the tail crosswise into 1-inch-thick slices. Twist or cut off the large claws, and cut the body of the lobster in half lengthwise. Remove and discard the gelatinous sac (stomach) in the head and the long white intestinal vein which is attached to it, but leave the greenish brown tomalley (liver) and the black coral (roe) if there is any.

Shell the shrimp but leave the tail shell attached. With a small, sharp knife, devein them by making a shallow incision down their backs and lifting out the intestinal vein with the point of the knife. Set the lobster and shrimp aside.

In a heavy 6- to 8-quart casserole, heat the olive oil over moderate heat until a light haze forms above it. Add the onions, garlic, and red or green peppers and, stirring frequently, cook for 5 minutes, or until the vegetables are soft but not brown.

Stir in the ham and cook for a minute or two. Then add the tomatoes, pulverized almonds, bay leaf, saffron, salt and a few grindings of pepper, raise the heat and bring to a boil. Cook briskly for about 5 minutes, or until most of the liquid in the pan evaporates and the mixture is thick enough to hold its shape lightly in a spoon.

Add the water, wine and lemon juice and bring to a boil. Stir thoroughly, then drop in the lobster, mussels and clams. Cover the casserole tightly, reduce the heat to moderate and cook for 10 minutes. Add the shrimp and scallops, cover, and cook 5 minutes longer. Discard any clams or mussels that have not opened.

Frogs' Legs Provencal

To serve 4

8 frogs' legs	tarragon
Flour	2 tablespoons finely chopped fresh
5 tablespoons butter	chives
2 to 3 teaspoons crushed garlic	2 tablespoons finely chopped fresh
Salt	parsley
Pepper	1 tablespoon brandy
2 tablespoons finely chopped fresh	2 tablespoons dry white wine

Wash the frogs' legs well in lemon juice and water. Dry them and dust lightly with flour. Put the butter in a pan, heat it to foaming, and add the crushed garlic. Cook for 1 minute, then put in the frogs' legs and shake the pan until they are golden on each side. Add the salt, pepper, tarragon, chives and parsley, and cook for another minute. Heat the brandy and wine, set them alight, and pour over the frogs' legs. Serve at once in a hot dish.

Snails

Escargots à la Bourguignonne

Fresh snails
Salt
White wine

1 cup butter, creamed
½ cup minced parsley
3 or 4 cloves garlic, minced

Soak the snails in warm water just long enough to break the membrane that covers the shell. Any snails that do not emerge should be discarded. Bring the snails to a boil in salted water, then remove them from their shells and rinse them with the wine or a little cold water. Wash the shells, dry them and butter the insides lightly.

Cream together the butter, parsley and garlic, adding salt to taste. Insert a snail into each shell and cover the entrance with the seasoned butter. Arrange on snail platters or on a large baking sheet and let them stand for several hours before you cook them, if you have the time.

Preheat the oven to 450°. Place the snails in the oven for about 10 minutes, or until they are thoroughly heated. Serve immediately.

NOTE: If you use canned snails, rinse them with ½ cup of white wine before proceeding as directed above.

Deep-fried Small Squid

Kalamarakia Tighanita

To serve 6 to 8 as an appetizer

Vegetable oil or shortening for deep-
   fat frying
4 pounds small squid, cleaned and cut
   crosswise into ½-inch-thick rings

Salt
Freshly ground black pepper
1 cup flour
3 lemons, cut lengthwise into wedges

Preheat the oven to 200° and line a baking pan with paper towels.

In a heavy 10- to 12-inch skillet, heat 1 to 2 inches of oil until hot but not smoking, or until it reaches a temperature of 375° on a deep-frying thermometer. Wash the squid under cold running water and pat them completely dry with paper towels. Sprinkle the squid liberally with salt and generous grindings of pepper. Pour the flour into a shallow bowl.

A dozen or so at a time, drop the squid into the flour and toss them about to coat them evenly. Then shake the squid in a sieve to remove the excess flour. Drop the squid into the hot oil and fry them for about 5 minutes, or until golden brown on all sides. As they brown, transfer them with a slotted spoon to the lined pan to drain, and keep them warm in the oven while you flour and fry the remaining batches.

Mound the squid on a heated platter and garnish with lemon wedges.

Mussels Stuffed with Rice and Pine Nuts

Midya Dolmasi

To serve 10 to 12 as a first course

1 cup olive oil
3 cups finely chopped onions
½ cup pine nuts (pignolia)
1½ cups uncooked long- or
  medium-grain rice

¼ cup dried currants
½ teaspoon ground cinnamon
¼ teaspoon ground allspice
1 teaspoon salt
4 cups water
6 dozen mussels in their shells

In a heavy 10- to 12-inch skillet, heat the oil over moderate heat until a light haze forms above it. Add the onions and, stirring frequently, cook for 8 to 10 minutes, or until they are soft and lightly browned. Stir in the pine nuts, cook for 2 or 3 minutes, then add the rice, currants, cinnamon, allspice and salt. Pour in 2 cups of the water and bring to a boil over high heat, stirring constantly. Reduce the heat to low, cover tightly and simmer for 20 minutes, or until all the liquid has been absorbed by the rice. Set aside off the heat.

Meanwhile, scrub the mussels with a stiff brush or stainless-steel mesh scouring pad under cold running water. With a small, sharp knife, open them one at a time in the following fashion: Holding the mussel firmly in one hand, cut along the joint between the two shells, starting at the broadest end and leaving them hinged together at the narrow end. Carefully pry the mussel open and cut and pull off the black ropelike tufts from the shell.

Place about 1 tablespoon of the stuffing mixture in each mussel, close the shells and hold them firmly together by looping a short length of string around the center two or three times, then tying it tightly in place.

Arrange the mussels in two layers in a large, heavy casserole, pour in the remaining 2 cups of water and bring to a boil over high heat. Reduce the heat to low, cover tightly and steam for 20 minutes. Remove the cover and let the mussels cool to room temperature in the casserole.

Then remove the mussels from the casserole with a slotted spoon and cut off the strings. Discard the cooking liquid. Arrange the mussels on a large platter or individual serving plates and serve chilled or at room temperature.

Jambalaya

To serve 4 to 6

¼ pound sliced bacon, cut in 1-inch pieces
½ cup finely chopped onion
2 medium-sized green peppers, seeded and cut in 1-inch strips
1 cup raw rice
1 teaspoon finely chopped garlic
A 1-pound 3-ounce can whole-pack tomatoes, drained and coarsely chopped

½ teaspoon thyme
1 teaspoon salt
Freshly ground black pepper
1½ to 2 cups chicken stock, fresh or canned
½-pound cooked smoked ham, cut in 2-inch by ½-inch strips
1 pound medium-sized raw shrimp, shelled and deveined
1 tablespoon finely chopped fresh parsley

Preheat the oven to 350°. In a heavy 3- or 4-quart casserole, fry the bacon over moderate heat until it has rendered its fat and is brown but not crisp. Drain on paper towels and reserve. Add the onions to the fat in the pan and cook them for 8 to 10 minutes, stirring occasionally until they are transparent but not brown. Mix in the green peppers. They will wilt slightly in about 3 minutes, at which point the rice should be stirred in. Turn the rice about in the hot fat and vegetables over moderate heat until the grains become somewhat opaque and milky. Then add the garlic, tomatoes, the bacon, thyme, salt and a few grindings of black pepper, stirring them together thoroughly. Pour in 1½ cups of chicken stock and bring it to a boil. Add the ham and stir again. Cover the casserole tightly and place it in the lower third of the oven. After 10 minutes add the shrimp, pushing them down beneath the rice, and continue to cook tightly covered for about 10 minutes longer, or until all of the stock is absorbed and the rice is tender. If at any point during this time the rice appears dry, add a few tablespoons more of the hot stock to it. Serve directly from the casserole if you wish, or mound the jambalaya on a large, heated platter. Garnish with fresh chopped parsley.

Shrimp Curry

Jhinga Kari

To serve 4 to 6

1 pound jumbo shrimp (10 to 15 to the pound)
1 tablespoon distilled white or cider vinegar
2 teaspoons salt
1 cup peeled, coarsely chopped fresh coconut
¼ cup coriander seeds
1¼ cups warm water
5 tablespoons vegetable oil

1 tablespoon scraped, finely chopped fresh ginger root
1 tablespoon finely chopped garlic
½ cup finely chopped onions
1 teaspoon turmeric
½ teaspoon ground cumin
¼ teaspoon ground hot red pepper
¼ teaspoon freshly ground black pepper
3 tablespoons finely chopped fresh coriander

Carefully shell the shrimp, leaving the last segment of the shell and the tail attached to each shrimp. With a small, sharp knife, devein the shrimp by making a shallow incision down the backs and lifting out the black or white intestinal vein with the point of the knife. Wash the shrimp under cold running water and pat them dry with paper towels. In a small bowl combine the shrimp with the vinegar and salt, and toss thoroughly. Turning occasionally, marinate the shrimp at room temperature for 15 to 20 minutes.

Combine the coconut, coriander seeds and water in the jar of an electric blender and blend at high speed for 1 minute. Turn off the machine, scrape down the sides of the jar with a rubber spatula and continue blending until the mixture is reduced to a purée.

Pour the purée into a fine sieve lined with a double thickness of dampened cheesecloth and set over a deep bowl. With a large spoon, press down hard on the coconut mixture to extract as much liquid as possible. Then gather the ends of the cheesecloth together and wring it vigorously to squeeze out any remaining liquid. Discard the pulp and set the coconut milk aside. (There should be about 1½ cups of the milk.)

In a heavy 8- to 10-inch skillet, heat 3 tablespoons of the vegetable oil over moderate heat until a drop of water flicked into it splutters instantly. Drain the shrimp and reserve the marinade. Drop the shrimp into the skillet, cover tightly, and cook for 30 seconds, then turn the shrimp over, cover again, and cook for 30 seconds, or until the shrimp are pink and firm but not brown. With a slotted spoon, return the shrimp to the marinade.

Pour the remaining 2 tablespoons of oil into the skillet, heat it, and add the ginger root. Stirring constantly, fry for 30 seconds, add the garlic, and continue stirring and frying for 1 minute. Still stirring, add the onions and fry for 7 to 8 minutes, until they are soft and golden brown. Add the turmeric, cumin, red pepper and black pepper, and stir for 1 minute. Then pour the shrimp marinade into the skillet and bring it to a boil immediately, scraping in any brown particles clinging to the bottom and sides of the pan.

Return the shrimp to the skillet, turning them about to coat them evenly. Pour in the reserved coconut milk and, stirring constantly, bring to a boil over high heat. Reduce the heat to moderate, sprinkle the top with 2 tablespoons of coriander, cover, and cook for 3 minutes. Taste for seasoning.

To serve, transfer the shrimp to a serving dish and pour the sauce remaining in the pan over them. Sprinkle the shrimp with the remaining tablespoon of coriander and serve at once with boiled rice and a chutney.

Shrimp curry, as it is made in India, contains such exotic ingredients as fresh coriander, ginger root and coconut—all obtainable in the United States.

Fresh Tuna and Potato Stew
Marmita-kua

To serve 4

¼ cup olive oil
1 cup finely chopped onions
1 teaspoon finely chopped
  garlic
3 medium-sized tomatoes,
  peeled and finely chopped,
  or substitute 1 cup chopped,
  drained, canned tomatoes
3 medium-sized firm boiling-type
  potatoes, peeled and sliced into

¼-inch-thick rounds
¼ teaspoon paprika
2 teaspoons salt
¼ teaspoon freshly ground black
  pepper
2 cups boiling water
1 pound fresh tuna or halibut, sliced
  1 inch thick and cut into pieces
  1 inch wide and 2 inches long
1 cup coarsely crumbled French or
  Italian bread

In a heavy 3- to 4-quart casserole, heat the olive oil over moderate heat until a light haze forms above it. Add the onions and garlic and cook, stirring occasionally, for 5 to 8 minutes or until the onions are lightly colored. Add the tomatoes, raise the heat and cook briskly, stirring frequently, until most of the liquid in the pan evaporates and the mixture is thick.

Add the potatoes, and turn them about with a spoon until they are evenly coated with the tomato mixture. Sprinkle with the paprika, salt, pepper and pour in the boiling water. The liquid should completely cover the potatoes; add more water if necessary. Bring to a boil over high heat, cover tightly, reduce the heat to low and simmer for about 15 minutes, or until the potatoes are barely tender. Stir in the fish, cover again and cook for 5 minutes, or until the potatoes are tender and the fish flakes easily. Do not overcook. Taste for seasoning, then sprinkle the bread over the top. Cover and cook over the lowest possible heat for 3 or 4 minutes. Serve at once.

Eggs

Swedish Hash with Eggs
Pytt i Panna

To serve 4 to 6

5 to 6 medium potatoes, peeled and
    diced into ¼-inch pieces (4 cups)
1 pound roast or boiled beef or lamb,
    diced into ¼-inch pieces (2 cups)
½ pound smoked or boiled ham,
    diced into ¼-inch pieces (1 cup)

2 tablespoons butter
2 tablespoons oil
2 medium yellow onions, finely
    chopped (about 1 cup)
1 tablespoon finely chopped parsley
Salt
Freshly ground black pepper
4 to 6 fried eggs or 4 to 6 raw egg yolks

The ingredients in *pytt i panna,* unlike those in most hashes, are cooked separately to retain their individual character. To present this dish in its most attractive and traditional form, it is essential that the potatoes and meat be diced into small pieces as neatly and uniformly as possible. Peel the potatoes and cut them in half lengthwise. Place them flat side down and cut them lengthwise into ¼-inch strips. Then cut these strips crosswise into ¼-inch strips. Drop the resulting dice into cold water to prevent them from discoloring. When ready to use, drain them in a colander, spread them out in a single layer on paper towels, and pat them thoroughly dry with more towels. Similarly cut the meats into ¼-inch dice.

Melt the butter and oil in a heavy 10- to 12-inch skillet over high heat. When the foam subsides, add the potatoes. Lower the heat to moderate and fry the potatoes for about 15 to 20 minutes, turning them about in the pan with a spoon until they are crisp and golden. Remove them from the pan and set them aside to drain on a double thickness of paper towels. Add a little more butter and oil to the pan if necessary, and in it, cook the onions until they are soft and transparent but not brown. Add the diced meats, raise the heat slightly, and fry with the onions about another 10 minutes. Shake the pan often so that the meat cubes brown lightly on all sides. Stir the fried potatoes into the meat and onions and cook briefly to heat the potatoes thoroughly. Then sprinkle the hash with parsley. Add salt and freshly ground black pepper to taste.

Arrange individual servings of the hash on warm plates. Make a depression in each serving with the back of a large spoon and top with a fried egg. Or you may wish to serve the hash in the traditional Swedish way: to do this, place a raw egg yolk in half of an eggshell and nestle the eggshell into each serving. The diners themselves mix the raw yolk into the hot hash.

Eggs Benedict

To serve 2 to 4

4 eggs
6 cups water
1 tablespoon white vinegar
4 three-inch rounds of white bread,

½ inch thick, or 2 English muffins
4 teaspoons soft butter
Four ¼-inch-thick slices cooked ham, cut into rounds 3 inches in diameter

To poach eggs successfully they must be very fresh or the whites will come away from their yolks during the poaching process. Pour 6 cups of water into a 10-inch enameled or stainless-steel skillet. Add 1 tablespoon of white vinegar and, over high heat, bring the water to a boil. Reduce the heat to low and, when the water is barely simmering, gently drop the eggs in one at a time, carefully turning the whites over the yolks with a wooden spoon. Let the eggs poach undisturbed for 3 to 4 minutes, or until the whites are set and the yolks still fluid. Remove them with a slotted spoon and keep them warm in a bowl of warm water.

Preheat the oven to 250°. Toast the rounds of bread or the split English muffins, spread each half with about a teaspoon of soft butter and top with a slice of hot or cold ham. Arrange them on a heatproof serving platter or individual plates and keep them warm in the oven while you make the hollandaise sauce.

BLENDER HOLLANDAISE
¼-pound stick of butter, cut into
  ½-inch pieces
3 egg yolks

1 teaspoon lemon juice
¼ teaspoon salt
Pinch of white pepper

BLENDER HOLLANDAISE: Melt the butter without browning it and keep it warm over very low heat. Combine the egg yolks, lemon juice, salt and pepper in the container of an electric blender. Cover the jar and blend at high speed for about 2 seconds. Then remove the cover and, still blending at high speed, slowly pour in the hot butter. For a finer sauce do not pour in the whey or milky solids on the bottom of the pan, although it will not be disastrous if you do. Taste for seasoning.

Working quickly, remove the poached eggs from the bowl of water and drain them on a kitchen towel. Place an egg atop each slice of ham, pour hollandaise sauce over each of them and serve at once.

French Omelet

To serve 1 to 2

3 eggs
Salt

Freshly ground black pepper
1 tablespoon butter
½ teaspoon soft butter

Break the eggs into a small mixing bowl, season with salt and pepper, and stir briskly with a table fork 20 to 30 seconds or until the whites and yolks are blended together. Heat an ungreased 7- to 8-inch omelet pan until it is very hot, drop in the tablespoon of butter and swirl it in the pan so that it melts quickly and coats the bottom and sides. When the foam begins to subside but before the butter browns, pour in the eggs.

Working quickly, stir the eggs with the flat of the fork, at the same time shaking the pan back and forth vigorously to prevent the eggs from sticking. In a few seconds, the eggs will form a film on the bottom of the pan and the top will thicken to a light, curded custard. Still shaking the pan with one hand, gently stir through the top custard with the other hand to spread the still-liquid eggs into the firmer areas; try not to pierce the bottom film. Then lift the edge closest to you with the fork and roll the omelet up lightly over to the far side of the pan. Let it rest for a moment on the lip of the pan, then tilt the pan and roll the omelet out onto a heated plate. Brush the top with soft butter and serve at once.

NOTE: To make a filled omelet, sprinkle a few tablespoons of grated cheese, finely chopped herbs or sautéed mushrooms over the eggs before rolling the omelet up. Do not stir in the filling. To serve more than 1 or 2, make several individual omelets. Large omelets are rarely successful.

Herb Omelet
Omelette aux Fines Herbes

To serve 1 or 2

3 eggs
1 teaspoon cold water
Salt
Pepper

½ cup finely chopped fresh parsley,
    chives, tarragon and thyme
¼ cup finely chopped onion
1 clove garlic, finely chopped
1 teaspoon butter

In a mixing bowl beat the eggs with the cold water. Season with salt and pepper, add the fresh parsley, chives, tarragon, thyme, onion and garlic. Stir briskly for half a minute until the ingredients are well mixed. Melt the butter in an omelet pan, add the egg-herb mixture and cook according to the directions given above.

Omelet with Peppers, Tomatoes and Ham
Pipérade

To serve 4

¼ cup olive oil
½ cup finely chopped onions
  or scallions
1 small garlic clove, finely chopped
2 small green peppers, seeded and cut
  in 1- by ½-inch strips (about ¾ cup)
1 pound firm, ripe tomatoes, peeled,
  seeded and coarsely chopped (about
  1½ cups)

2 teaspoons finely chopped fresh basil
  or 1 teaspoon dried basil, crumbled
⅛ teaspoon Tabasco
1 tablespoon olive oil
1 tablespoon butter
¼ pound smoked cooked ham cut in 1- by
  ½-inch julienne strips (about 1 cup)
6 to 8 eggs, lightly beaten
Salt
Freshly ground black pepper
1 tablespoon finely chopped fresh parsley

In a heavy 8- to 10-inch skillet, heat ¼ cup of oil. When the oil is very hot, stir in the onions and garlic, and cook over moderate heat, stirring frequently, for 5 minutes, or until they are soft but not browned. Stir in the green-pepper strips and cook, stirring occasionally, for 8 to 10 minutes, or until the peppers are barely tender. Drain the tomatoes and stir them into the skillet along with the basil and Tabasco. Increase the heat and cook, stirring constantly, for 2 or 3 minutes or until most of the liquid has evaporated. Cover the skillet lightly to keep the *pipérade* mixture warm and set aside.

In an 8-inch serving skillet or a shallow, flameproof serving dish, heat 1 tablespoon each of oil and butter. When the foam subsides, stir in the ham and cook over moderate heat for a few minutes to warm it through. Remove the ham with a slotted spoon and drain it on paper towels. Remove the skillet from the heat and let the fat cool to lukewarm. In a small bowl, beat the eggs with a fork or whisk until they are well blended, then season with salt and pepper. Return the skillet to low heat and pour in the eggs. Stirring with the flat of a table fork or a rubber spatula, cook the eggs until they begin to form soft, creamy curds. Gently spread the warm *pipérade* mixture over them, mixing some of the vegetables into the eggs. Scatter the ham on top, sprinkle with parsley, and serve at once.

Zucchini Omelet
Frittata alla Sardegnola

To serve 4

3 cups water
½ teaspoon salt
1 cup diced unpeeled fresh zucchini
2 tablespoons fresh white bread crumbs
3 tablespoons milk

4 tablespoons freshly grated imported Parmesan cheese
¼ teaspoon freshly grated lemon peel
¼ teaspoon salt
Pinch of sugar
4 eggs
2 tablespoons butter

Preheat the broiler to its highest setting. Bring the water and salt to a bubbling boil in a small saucepan. Drop in the diced zucchini and blanch it for 3 minutes, then drain thoroughly in a large sieve or colander. In a large mixing bowl, soak the bread crumbs in the milk for 5 minutes. Stir in the zucchini, grated cheese, lemon peel, salt and sugar. In another bowl, beat the eggs with a whisk or fork until they are just blended, then stir them gently into the bread-crumb-and-zucchini mixture. Melt the butter in a heavy 10-inch skillet. When the foam subsides, pour in the egg-and-zucchini mixture and cook over moderate heat for 2 or 3 minutes, or until the eggs are firm but still slightly moist. Slide under the broiler for 30 seconds to brown lightly. Slice into wedges and serve at once.

Shrimp Egg Foo Yung
Hsia-jen-ch'ao-tan

To serve 6

½ cup fresh or canned bean sprouts
½ pound raw shrimp in their shells
3 to 4 medium fresh mushrooms, cut into ¼-inch dice (about ½ cup)
3 eggs
¼ cup peanut oil, or flavorless

vegetable oil
FOO YUNG SAUCE
¾ cup chicken stock, fresh or canned
1 tablespoon soy sauce
½ teaspoon salt
1 tablespoon cornstarch dissolved in 2 tablespoons cold chicken stock, fresh or canned, or cold water

PREPARE AHEAD: 1. Rinse fresh bean sprouts in a pot of cold water and discard any husks that float to the surface. Drain and pat them dry. To crisp canned sprouts, rinse them under running water and refrigerate them in a bowl of cold water for 2 hours. Drain and pat them dry.

2. Shell the shrimp. With a small, sharp knife, make a shallow incision down their backs and lift out the intestinal vein. Wash the shrimp under cold water, pat them dry and cut them into ¼-inch dice.

3. Have the bean sprouts, shrimp, mushrooms, eggs and oil, and the stock, soy sauce, salt and cornstarch mixture within easy reach.

TO COOK: In a small saucepan, bring the stock to a boil. Add the soy sauce, salt and cornstarch mixture. Reduce the heat and cook for 2 minutes until the sauce is thick and clear. Keep warm over low heat.

Set a 12-inch wok or 8-inch skillet over high heat for 30 seconds. Pour in 1 tablespoon of oil, swirl it about in the pan and heat for another 30 seconds, turning the heat down if the oil begins to smoke. Add the shrimp and stir-fry for 1 minute, or until they are firm and light pink. Transfer them to a plate. Break the eggs into a bowl and beat them with a fork or whisk until they are well combined. Add the shrimp, bean sprouts and mushrooms. Set the pan again over high heat for 30 seconds. Add 1 tablespoon oil, swirl it about in the pan, reduce the heat to low, then pour in about ¼ cup of the egg mixture. Let it cook undisturbed for 1 minute, or until lightly browned. Turn the pancake over and cook for another minute. Transfer the pancake to a heatproof platter and cover with foil to keep warm. Following the same procedure, make 5 more pancakes with the remaining egg mixture. Add about 1 teaspoon of oil to the pan for each new pancake and stack them on the platter as you proceed. Serve with sauce poured over each pancake. Although not classic, some Chinese cooks garnish this dish with green peas.

ROAST PORK EGG FOO YUNG: Substitute ½ cup of diced roast pork for the cooked shrimp, but otherwise follow this recipe precisely.

Spanish Baked Eggs
Huevos a la Flamenca

To serve 6

SOFRITO

2 medium-sized tomatoes, or
    substitute ¾ cup chopped,
    drained, canned tomatoes
¼ cup olive oil
½ cup finely chopped onions
1 tablespoon finely chopped garlic
1 small sweet red or green pepper,
    peeled, seeded, deribbed and finely
    chopped
½ cup finely diced *serrano* ham, or
    substitute 2 ounces of prosciutto

or other lean smoked ham
1 *chorizo* sliced into ¼-inch-thick
    rounds, or substitute 3 ounces
    other garlic-seasoned smoked
    pork sausage
1 tablespoon finely chopped parsley
1 small bay leaf
1 teaspoon salt
¼ teaspoon freshly ground black
    pepper
⅓ cup water

SOFRITO: Drop the fresh tomatoes into a pan of boiling water and let

A tantalizing dish from Spain is made of eggs, asparagus, peas and pimiento, baked on a base of ham, sausage, tomatoes, onions, garlic and peppers.

them boil briskly for about 10 seconds. Run cold water over them, and with a small, sharp knife peel them. Cut out the stems, then slice the tomatoes in half crosswise. Squeeze the halves gently to remove the seeds and juices, and chop the tomatoes as fine as possible. (Canned tomatoes need only be thoroughly drained and chopped.)

In a heavy 10- to 12-inch skillet, heat the oil over moderate heat until a light haze forms above it. Add the onions, garlic and chopped pepper, and, stirring frequently, cook for 5 minutes, or until the vegetables are soft but not brown. Stir in the ham and sausage, then add the tomatoes, chopped parsley, bay leaf, salt, pepper and water, and bring to a boil. Cook briskly, uncovered, until most of the liquid in the pan has evaporated and the mixture is thick enough to hold its shape lightly in a spoon. Set aside.

EGGS

2 teaspoons olive oil
6 eggs
½ cup hot cooked fresh or frozen peas
6 hot cooked fresh or frozen
   asparagus tips, 3 to 4 inches long

6 to 8 strips of drained, canned
   pimiento, each about 3 inches long
   and ¼ inch wide
3 tablespoons pale dry sherry
Parsley sprigs

EGGS: Preheat the oven to 400°. Using a pastry brush, coat the bottom and sides of a 9-by-9-by-2-inch baking dish with the 2 teaspoons of oil. Discard the bay leaf and spread the *sofrito* evenly in the dish. One at a time, break the eggs into the dish, arranging them in a circle on top of the *sofrito*. Or break the eggs into a saucer and slide them gently into the dish.

Heap the peas in three or four mounds on the *sofrito* and arrange the asparagus in parallel rows, draping the pimiento strips decoratively over them. Sprinkle the eggs and vegetables with sherry, cover the dish, and bake in the middle of the oven for 20 minutes, or until an opaque film has formed over the egg yolks and the whites are firm. Serve at once, garnished with parsley.

HOW TO PEEL PEPPERS: Impale the pepper on the tines of a long-handled fork and turn it over a gas flame until the skin blisters and darkens. Or place it on a baking sheet and broil it 3 inches from the heat for about 5 minutes, turning it so all sides color evenly. Wrap the pepper in a damp towel, let it rest for a few minutes, then rub it with the towel until the skin slips off. Cut out the stem and white membranes or ribs, and discard the seeds.

French Cheese Soufflé
Soufflé au Fromage

To serve 4

1 tablespoon soft butter
1 tablespoon grated, imported Swiss
   cheese
3 tablespoons butter
3 tablespoons flour

1 cup hot milk
½ teaspoon salt
Pinch of white pepper
4 egg yolks
6 egg whites
1 cup grated, imported Swiss cheese
   or ½ cup each Swiss and freshly
   grated Parmesan cheese

Preheat the oven to 400°. Grease the bottom and sides of a 2-quart French soufflé dish or charlotte mold with 1 tablespoon of soft butter, then sprinkle in 1 tablespoon of grated imported Swiss cheese, tipping the dish to spread the cheese as evenly as possible on the bottom and on all sides. Set the dish aside.

In a 2- to 3-quart saucepan, melt 3 tablespoons butter over moderate heat. When the foam subsides, stir in the 3 tablespoons of flour with a wooden spoon and cook over low heat, stirring constantly for 1 or 2 minutes. Do not let the *roux* (the butter and flour mixture) brown. Remove the saucepan from the heat and pour in the hot milk, beating vigorously with a whisk until the *roux* and liquid are blended. Add the salt and pepper and return to low heat and cook, whisking constantly, until the sauce comes to a boil and is smooth and thick. Let it simmer a moment, then remove the pan from the heat and beat in the egg yolks, one at a time, whisking until each one is thoroughly blended before adding the next. Set aside.

With a large balloon whisk, beat the egg whites until they are so stiff that they form small points which stand straight up without wavering. (A rotary or electric beater may be used instead, but the whites will not mount as voluminously or have as fine a texture.) Stir a big spoonful of beaten egg white into the waiting sauce to lighten it; then stir in all but 1 tablespoon of the remaining grated cheese. With a spatula, lightly fold in the rest of the egg whites, using an over-under cutting motion.

Gently pour the soufflé mixture into the prepared dish; the dish should be about three quarters full. Lightly smooth the surface with a rubber spatula and sprinkle the remaining tablespoonful of cheese on top. For a decorative effect make a "cap" on the soufflé with a spatula by cutting a trench about 1 inch deep and 1 inch from the rim all around the dish. Place the soufflé on the middle shelf of the oven and immediately turn the heat down to 375°. Bake for 25 to 30 minutes, or until the soufflé puffs up about 2 inches above the rim of the dish and the top is lightly browned. Serve at once.

SOUFFLÉ AU FROMAGE ET AUX OEUFS MOLLETS (cheese soufflé with boiled eggs): Bring 2 quarts of water to a boil in a heavy 3- to 4-quart saucepan. Lower 4 eggs into the water and boil them slowly for 6 minutes (boil them for 7 minutes if they have been refrigerated). Drain immediately and run cold water into the pan. Tap the eggs gently on a hard surface to break their shells, and peel them under a stream of cold water. Preheat the oven to 400°. Prepare the soufflé mixture, following the directions in the previous recipe. Scoop half of it into a buttered and a cheese-lined 2-quart French soufflé dish or a charlotte mold. Arrange the eggs in a circle on top and cover each with a mound of the remaining soufflé mixture. Dot each mound with a teaspoon of grated cheese and place the soufflé on the middle shelf of the oven. Immediately turn the heat down to 375° and bake for 25 to 30 minutes. When you serve the soufflé, include an egg in each portion.

Dilled Salmon Soufflé

To serve 6

4 tablespoons butter
4 tablespoons finely chopped onion
4 tablespoons flour
1 cup milk
5 egg yolks
1 tablespoon tomato paste

1½ cups canned salmon, thoroughly
   drained and flaked (2 seven-ounce cans)
3 tablespoons finely cut fresh dill
1½ teaspoons lemon juice
1½ teaspoons salt
⅛ teaspoon cayenne
6 egg whites
Hollandaise sauce (optional)

Preheat the oven to 400°. Coat the bottom and sides of a 2-quart soufflé dish with a tablespoon of the butter and melt the remaining butter in a heavy saucepan. When the foam subsides add the onion and cook over moderate heat for about 3 minutes. Do not let the onions brown. Off the heat, mix in the flour and stir it to a smooth paste. Add the milk all at once and beat with a whisk to partially dissolve the flour. Then cook over moderate heat, whisking constantly, until the sauce is smooth and very thick. Remove the pan from the heat and beat into it, one at a time, the 5 egg yolks, then stir in the tomato paste, salmon, dill, lemon juice, salt and cayenne. Cool slightly. Meanwhile, with a large whisk or rotary beater, beat the egg whites, preferably in an unlined copper bowl, until they are stiff enough to form unwavering peaks on the beater when it is lifted out of the bowl. Stir a heaping tablespoon of the whites into the salmon mixture, then with a rubber spatula, fold in the remaining egg whites gently but thoroughly until no white streaks show; do not overfold. Pour the mixture into the soufflé dish, reduce the heat to 375° and bake undisturbed in the center of the oven for 35 to 40 minutes, or until it has puffed and is lightly brown. Serve, if you like, with hollandaise sauce.

Cheese

Pizza

To make 4 ten-inch pizzas

2 packages or cakes of dry or
  compressed yeast
Pinch of sugar
1¼ cups lukewarm water
3½ cups all-purpose or granulated
  flour

1 teaspoon salt
¾ cup olive oil
Corn meal
2 cups pizza sauce (*page 273*)
1 pound *mozzarella* cheese, coarsely
  grated or cut in ¼-inch dice
½ cup freshly grated imported
  Parmesan cheese

Sprinkle the yeast and a pinch of sugar into ¼ cup of lukewarm water. Be sure that the water is lukewarm (110° to 115°—neither hot nor cool to the touch). Let it stand for 2 or 3 minutes, then stir the yeast and sugar into the water until completely dissolved. Set the cup in a warm place (a turned-off oven would be best) for 3 to 5 minutes, or until the yeast bubbles up and the mixture almost doubles in volume. If the yeast does not bubble, start over again with fresh yeast.

    Into a large mixing bowl, sift the all-purpose flour and salt, or pour in the granulated flour and salt. Make a well in the center of the flour and pour into it the yeast mixture, 1 cup of lukewarm water and ¼ cup of the olive oil. Mix the dough with a fork or your fingers. When you can gather it into a rough ball, place the dough on a floured board and knead it for about 15 minutes, or until it is smooth, shiny and elastic. (If you have an electric mixer with a paddle and dough hook, all the ingredients can be placed in a bowl and, at medium speed, mixed with the paddle until they are combined. Then at high speed knead them with the dough hook for 6 to 8 minutes.) Dust the dough lightly with flour, place it in a large clean bowl and cover with a plate or pot lid. Set the bowl in a warm draft-free spot (again, an oven with the heat turned off is ideal) for about 1½ hours, or until the dough has doubled in bulk.

1 Mix flour, yeast, water, salt and olive oil for pizza dough.

2 Gather the dough into a large ball on a floured board.

3 Knead the dough by pushing with heel of one hand.

4 Now reverse the process, kneading with the other hand.

5 Place the dough in a bowl in a warm spot, and cover it.

6 When the dough has doubled in bulk take it out.

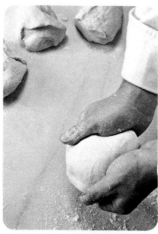

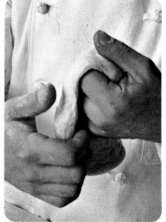

7 Divide the dough into quarters to make pies.

8 Press down with palm on a piece, flattening it.

9 Turn dough in your hands and stretch it out.

Now preheat the oven to 500°. Punch the dough down with your fists and break off about one fourth of it to make the first of the 4 pizzas. Knead the small piece on a floured board or pastry cloth for a minute or so, working in a little flour if the dough seems sticky. With the palm of your hand, flatten the ball into a circle about 1 inch thick. Hold the circle in your hands and stretch the dough by turning the circle and pulling your hands apart gently at the same time. When the circle is about 7 or 8 inches across, spread it out on the floured board again and pat it smooth, pressing together any tears in the dough. Then roll the dough with a rolling pin, from the center to the far edge, turning it clockwise after each roll, until you have a circle of pastry about 10 inches across and about ⅛ inch thick. With your thumbs, crimp or flute the edge of the circle until it forms a little rim. Dust a large baking sheet lightly with corn meal and gently place the pizza dough on top of it. Knead, stretch and roll the rest of the dough into 3 more pizzas. Pour ½ cup of the tomato sauce on each pie and swirl it around with a pastry brush or the back of a spoon. To make a cheese pizza, sprinkle the sauce with ½ cup of grated *mozzarella* and 2 tablespoons of grated Parmesan cheese. Dribble 2 tablespoons of the olive oil over the pizza and bake it on the lowest shelf or the floor of the oven for about 10 minutes, or until the crust is lightly browned and the filling bubbling hot.

ALTERNATIVE GARNISHES: You may top the pizza with almost any sort of seafood, meat or vegetable you like, using or omitting the *mozzarella* or Parmesan. Swirl the pie with ½ cup of pizza sauce first, as for a cheese pizza. Then top with such garnishes as shrimp, anchovies, sausage or *pepe-roni* slices, prosciutto slivers, tiny meatballs, garlic slices, strips of green pepper, capers, whole or sliced mushrooms. They may be used alone or in suitable combinations. Dribble 2 tablespoons of olive oil over the pizza after garnishing and before baking it.

10 Hold the dough and let its weight stretch it.

11 Use a rolling pin to work it into a circle.

12 Pour on the pizza sauce and top with your favorite garnishes.

To make about 3 cups

3 tablespoons olive oil
1 cup finely chopped onions
1 tablespoon finely chopped garlic
4 cups Italian plum or whole-pack
   tomatoes, coarsely chopped but
   not drained

1 six-ounce can tomato paste
1 tablespoon dried oregano, crumbled
1 tablespoon finely cut fresh basil or
   1 teaspoon dried basil, crumbled
1 bay leaf
2 teaspoons sugar
1 tablespoon salt
Freshly ground black pepper

In a 3- to 4-quart enameled or stainless-steel saucepan, heat the 3 table-spoons of olive oil and cook the finely chopped onions in it over moderate heat, stirring frequently, for 7 or 8 minutes. When the onions are soft and transparent but are not brown, add the tablespoon of finely chopped garlic and cook for another 1 or 2 minutes, stirring constantly. Then stir in the coarsely chopped tomatoes and their liquid, the tomato paste, oregano, basil, bay leaf, sugar, salt and a few grindings of black pepper. Bring the sauce to a boil, turn the heat very low and simmer uncovered, stirring occasionally, for about 1 hour.

When finished, the sauce should be thick and fairly smooth. Remove the bay leaf. Taste and season the sauce with salt and freshly ground black pepper. If you wish a smoother texture, purée the sauce through a food mill, or rub it through a sieve with the back of a large wooden spoon.

A cheese pizza is surrounded by possible garnishes: beef, cured sausage, prosciutto, mushrooms, sausage, capers, pepper, garlic, shrimp and anchovies.

Open-faced Cheese Tart
Quiche au Fromage

To make an 8- to 9-inch *quiche*

PÂTE BRISÉE (pastry dough or pie
   crust)
6 tablespoons chilled butter,
   cut in ¼-inch bits

2 tablespoons chilled vegetable
   shortening
1½ cups all-purpose flour
¼ teaspoon salt
3 to 5 tablespoons ice water

PÂTE BRISÉE: In a large, chilled mixing bowl, combine butter, vegetable shortening, flour and salt. Working quickly, use your fingertips to rub the flour and fat together until they blend and look like flakes of coarse meal. Pour 3 tablespoons of ice water over the mixture all at once, toss together lightly and gather the dough into a ball. If the dough seems crumbly, add up to 2 tablespoons more ice water by drops. Dust the pastry with a little flour and wrap it in wax paper or a plastic bag. Refrigerate it for at least 3 hours or until it is firm.

Remove the pastry from the refrigerator 5 minutes before rolling it. If it seems resistant and hard, tap it all over with a rolling pin. Place the ball on a floured board or table and, with the heel of one hand, press it into a flat circle about 1 inch thick. Dust a little flour over and under it and roll it out—from the center to within an inch of the far edge. Lift the dough and turn it clockwise, about the space of two hours on a clock; roll again from the center to the far edge. Repeat—lifting, turning, rolling—until the circle is about ⅛ inch thick and 11 or 12 inches across. If the pastry sticks to the board or table, lift it gently with a metal spatula and sprinkle a little flour under it.

Butter the bottom and sides of an 8- to 9-inch false-bottomed *quiche* or cake pan no more than 1¼ inches deep. Roll the pastry over the pin and unroll it over the pan, or drape the pastry over the rolling pin, lift it up and unfold it over the pan. Gently press the pastry into the bottom and around the sides of the pan, being careful not to stretch it. Roll the pin over the rim of the pan, pressing down hard to trim off the excess pastry. With a fork, prick the bottom of the pastry all over, trying not to pierce all the way through. Chill for 1 hour.

Preheat the oven to 400°. To keep the bottom of the pastry from puffing up, spread a sheet of buttered aluminum foil across the pan and press it gently into the edges to support the sides of the pastry as it bakes. Bake on the middle shelf of the oven for 10 minutes, then remove the foil. Prick the pastry again, then return it to the oven for 3 minutes or until it starts to shrink from the sides of the pan and begins to brown. Remove it from the oven and set it on a wire cake rack to cool.

CHEESE-CUSTARD FILLING

1 teaspoon butter

6 slices lean bacon, cut in ¼-inch
   pieces

2 eggs plus 2 extra egg yolks

1½ cups heavy cream

½ teaspoon salt

Pinch of white pepper

¾ cup grated imported Swiss cheese or
   Swiss and freshly grated Parmesan
   cheese combined

2 tablespoons butter, cut in tiny
   pieces

CHEESE-CUSTARD FILLING: Preheat the oven to 375°. In a heavy 8- to 10-inch skillet, melt the butter over moderate heat. When the foam subsides, cook the bacon until it is lightly browned and crisp. Remove from the skillet with a slotted spoon and drain on paper towels. With a wire whisk, rotary or electric beater, beat the eggs, extra egg yolks, cream and seasonings together in a large mixing bowl. Stir in the grated cheese. Place the cooled pastry shell on a baking sheet. Scatter the bacon over the bottom of the shell and gently ladle the egg-cheese custard into it, being sure the custard does not come within ⅛ inch of the rim of the shell. Sprinkle the top with dots of butter and bake in the upper third of the oven for 25 minutes or until the custard has puffed and browned and a knife inserted in the center comes out clean. To remove the *quiche* from the pan, set the pan on a large jar or coffee can and slip down the outside rim. Run a long metal spatula under the *quiche* to make sure it isn't stuck to the bottom of the pan, then slide the *quiche* onto a heated platter. Serve hot or warm.

Russian Cheese Dumplings

¼ pound pot cheese

½ pound cream cheese

Salt

Cayenne pepper

A pinch of chili pepper

1 tablespoon sour cream

¾ cup all-purpose flour

Butter

Paprika

Rub the pot cheese and cream cheese through a strainer and mix in salt, cayenne pepper, chili pepper and sour cream. Then carefully mix in the flour. Roll out in a long sausage on a floured board, cut in wedge-shaped pieces ¾ inch thick and drop into a pan of salted water that has been brought to a boil and just stopped. Poach gently for 15 to 20 minutes, until firm. Drain well and arrange on a long, flat platter. Pour a little hot butter over the dumplings, then sprinkle with paprika and bake in a moderate oven for 15 minutes.

Swiss Fondue

To serve 4

1 clove garlic, peeled

2 cups dry white wine, preferably
  Neuchâtel, Riesling or Chablis

1 teaspoon lemon juice

1 pound grated or shredded imported
  Swiss cheese, or half Gruyère and
  half Emmentaler combined (about
  4 cups)

3 tablespoons flour

Salt

Freshly ground black pepper

Ground nutmeg (optional)

2 tablespoons kirsch

1 large loaf Italian or French bread,
  cut into 1-inch cubes, with crust

Vigorously rub the inside of a fondue pan, flameproof casserole or heavy chafing dish with the peeled clove of garlic. Pour in the wine and lemon juice, and over moderate direct heat, bring it almost to a boil. Mix the grated or shredded cheese with the flour. Then, handful by handful, drop in the cheese, stirring constantly with a fork. Continue to stir until the cheese melts into a thick cream. Season to taste with salt, a few grindings of black pepper and a little nutmeg, if you like the flavor. Stir in the kirsch and set the pot over a table warmer such as a fondue warmer, an alcohol burner or an electric hot plate. If you are using a chafing dish, set the pan over hot water. Regulate the heat so that the fondue simmers gently but does not boil.

To eat the fondue, spear a bread cube with a long-handled fork (there are special fondue forks available for this purpose), dip the bread into the simmering cheese mixture and twirl the bread to coat it evenly with the fondue. If the fondue becomes too thick as it simmers, thin it with heated wine stirred in by the tablespoonful.

French-Style Cheese Fondue
Fondue de Fromage

To serve 6 to 8

2 cups dry white wine

2 garlic cloves, cut up

¾ pound imported Swiss cheese,
  freshly grated (about 3 cups)
  mixed with 1 tablespoon cornstarch

2 tablespoons butter

2 to 6 tablespoons heavy cream

Salt

Freshly ground black pepper

3 tablespoons kirsch

1 loaf French or Italian bread cut
  in 1-inch cubes

In a 1½- to 2-quart saucepan, boil the wine and garlic briskly until the wine has reduced to 1½ cups. Strain the reduced wine through a fine sieve into a fondue pot or the cooking pan of a chafing dish that has a lower pan to fill with water; discard the garlic. At the table or in the kitch-en, light the burner under the fondue pot or the chafing dish pan. Over direct heat, return the wine to a boil, then lower the heat at once and add the cheese-cornstarch mixture, stirring constantly with a table fork. Do not let this mixture boil; if it seems to be getting too hot, lift the pan off the heat for a few seconds to cool it. When all the cheese has melted and the fondue is smooth, stir in the butter and 2 tablespoons of cream. The fondue should be just thick enough to coat the fork heavily. If it seems too thick, add a little more cream, 1 tablespoon at a time. Season it with a little salt and pepper, stir in the kirsch, and serve at once, accompanied by a platter of bread cubes. If you are using a chafing dish, set the pan over hot water to keep the fondue warm.

To eat the fondue, spear a bread cube with a fork, dip the bread into the hot cheese and twirl the bread to coat it evenly with fondue. If the fon-due should thicken while you are eating it, heat a little cream and stir it in to thin it.

Welsh Rabbit

To serve 2 to 4

4 slices homemade-type white bread, trimmed of crusts and toasted
2 cups (½ pound) freshly grated sharp Cheddar cheese combined with 1 tablespoon flour

¼ cup beer
1 tablespoon butter
1 teaspoon Worcestershire sauce
¼ teaspoon dry English mustard
A pinch of cayenne pepper
1 egg yolk

Arrange the slices of toast in 2 to 4 shallow ovenproof dishes just large enough to hold them comfortably, and set aside.

In a heavy 2- to 3-quart saucepan, combine the cheese-and-flour mixture, beer, butter, Worcestershire sauce, mustard and cayenne pepper. Cook over moderate heat, without letting the mixture boil. Stir constantly with a fork until the cheese has melted completely and the mixture is smooth. In a small bowl break up the egg yolk with a fork. Off the heat, stir it into the cheese and, when it is thoroughly absorbed, taste for seasoning and pour the rabbit evenly over the toast. Place the dishes under the broiler for a min-ute or two to brown the cheese lightly, and serve at once.

NOTE: The traditional name for this dish is Welsh rabbit, presumably a jok-ing reference to the fact that cheese was often available when rabbits were not. In the late 18th Century, the dish came to be called Welsh rarebit, as it fre-quently still is, but rabbit is the correct designation.

Rice

Chinese Boiled Rice
Pai-fan

To serve 4

1 cup long-grain white rice   1¾ cups cold water

Rinse the rice by pouring it into a heavy 2-quart saucepan, adding enough cold water to cover it completely and giving the rice a thorough stir. Drain the rice, add the 1¾ cups of fresh cold water and bring the rice to a boil over high heat. If you have any reason to think the rice you are using is old—and, therefore, very dry—add another ¼ cup of water. Boil for 2 to 3 minutes, or until craterlike holes appear in the surface of the rice. Then cover the pan tightly, reduce the heat to low and cook for 20 minutes. Turn off the heat but do not uncover the pan. Let the rice rest for 10 minutes. Now remove the cover and fluff the rice with chopsticks or a fork. Serve the rice at once while it is still hot. If the rice must wait, keep it in a covered heatproof serving bowl in a preheated 250° oven. To reheat any leftover rice, place it in a colander and set the colander into 1 inch of water boiling in a large pot. Cover the pot and steam for 5 to 10 minutes—depending on how much rice you have.

Ham-and-Egg Fried Rice
Huo-t'ui-tan-chao-fan

To serve 3 to 4

½ cup shelled, fresh peas, or substitute thoroughly defrosted frozen peas
3 tablespoons peanut oil, or flavorless vegetable oil
2 eggs, lightly beaten
3 cups Chinese boiled rice, prepared according to the directions above
1 teaspoon salt
2 ounces boiled ham, sliced ¼ inch thick and cut into ¼-inch dice (about ½ cup)
1 scallion, including the green top, finely chopped

278

PREPARE AHEAD: 1. Blanch fresh peas by dropping them into 4 cups of boiling water and letting them boil uncovered for 5 to 10 minutes, or until tender. Then drain and run cold water over them to stop their cooking and set their color. Frozen peas need only be thoroughly defrosted.

2. Have the peas, oil, eggs, rice, salt, ham and scallions handy.

TO COOK: Set a 12-inch wok or 10-inch skillet over high heat for 30 seconds. Pour in 1 tablespoon of oil, swirl it about in the pan and immediately reduce the heat to moderate. Pour in the beaten eggs. They will form a film on the bottom of the pan almost at once. Immediately lift this film gently with a fork and push it to the back of the pan so that the still-liquid eggs can spread across the bottom of the pan to cook. As soon as the eggs are set, but before they become dry or begin to brown, transfer them to a small bowl and break them up with a fork. Pour the remaining 2 tablespoons of oil into the pan, swirl it around and heat it for 30 seconds. Add the rice and stir-fry for 2 to 3 minutes until all the grains are coated with oil. Add the salt, then the peas and ham, and stir-fry for 20 seconds. Return the eggs to the pan, add the scallions and cook only long enough to heat the eggs through. Serve at once.

Boiled Rice with Lemon
Riso al Limone

To serve 4

	2 tablespoons butter
6 quarts water	3 eggs
3 tablespoons salt	1 cup freshly grated imported
1 cup plain white raw rice, preferably	Parmesan cheese
imported Italian rice	4 teaspoons lemon juice

In a large soup pot or kettle, bring the water and salt to a bubbling boil over high heat. Pour in the rice in a slow stream so that the water never stops boiling. Stir once or twice, then reduce the heat to moderate and boil the rice uncovered and undisturbed for about 15 minutes, or until it is tender. Test it by tasting a few grains. As soon as the rice is done, drain it thoroughly in a large colander.

Over low heat, melt the butter in a 1-quart flameproof casserole and immediately add the hot drained rice. In a bowl, beat the eggs with a fork until they are well combined. Then beat in the cheese and lemon juice. Stir this mixture into the rice and cook over very low heat, stirring gently with a fork, for 3 or 4 minutes. Serve at once while the rice is still creamy.

Rice with Almonds and Sesame Seeds

Azerbaijan Pilaf

To serve 4 to 6

½ cup sliced blanched almonds
2 tablespoons butter
1 cup unconverted long-grain rice

2 cups chicken stock, fresh or canned
½ teaspoon white sesame seeds
¼ teaspoon ground ginger
¼ teaspoon salt
Freshly ground black pepper

Preheat the oven to 350°. Spread the almonds on a cookie sheet in a single layer and toast in the oven for about 5 minutes, watching for any sign of burning and regulate the heat accordingly. Set aside.

Melt the butter in a heavy 1½- to 2-quart casserole set over moderate heat. Add the rice and stir with a wooden spoon until the rice turns somewhat white and opaque. Stir in the sesame seeds, then pour in the chicken stock, ginger, salt and a few grindings of black pepper. Stirring constantly, bring to a boil, then cover the casserole tightly and bake in the center of the oven for 20 to 25 minutes, or until the liquid has all been absorbed and the rice is tender. Sprinkle the reserved almonds over the rice and serve at once.

Steamed Sautéed Rice

Pilav

To serve 4 to 6

2 tablespoons butter plus 4
  tablespoons melted butter
1 cup uncooked long- or medium-

grain white rice
2 cups chicken stock, fresh or canned
½ teaspoon salt
Freshly ground black pepper

In a heavy 2- to 3-quart saucepan, melt the 2 tablespoons of butter over moderate heat. When the foam begins to subside, add the rice and stir for 2 or 3 minutes until all the grains are evenly coated. Do not let the rice brown. Pour in the stock, add the salt and a few grindings of pepper, and bring to a boil, stirring constantly. Cover the pan and reduce the heat to its lowest point. Simmer for 20 minutes, or until all the liquid has been absorbed and the rice is tender but still slightly resistant to the bite.

Pour in the 4 tablespoons of melted butter and toss the rice with a fork until the grains glisten. Drape a towel over the rice and let it stand at room temperature for about 20 minutes before serving.

Braised Rice and Peas
Risi e Bisi

To serve 6

5 cups chicken stock, fresh or canned
4 tablespoons butter
½ cup finely chopped onions
2 cups fresh green peas (about 2
    pounds unshelled)

1½ cups plain white raw rice,
    preferably imported Italian rice
¼ pound cooked smoked ham, diced
    (about 1 cup)
2 tablespoons soft butter
½ cup freshly grated imported
    Parmesan cheese

Bring the chicken stock to a simmer in a 2- to 3-quart saucepan and keep it barely simmering over low heat. In a heavy 3-quart flameproof casserole, melt 4 tablespoons of butter over moderate heat. Add the onions and cook, stirring frequently until they are transparent but not browned. Add the peas, rice and diced ham. Cook for a minute or 2. When the rice grains are buttery and somewhat opaque, add 2 cups of the simmering stock and cook uncovered for about 5 minutes, stirring occasionally, until almost all of the liquid is absorbed. Add 1 more cup of stock and cook, stirring, until this stock is almost absorbed. Then add another cup of stock. After this is absorbed, the rice and peas should be tender. (If not, add more stock—½ cup at a time—and continue cooking and stirring.) Now gently stir in soft butter and grated cheese. Serve at once while the rice is creamy and hot.

Saffron Rice
Arroz con Azafrán

To serve 4 to 6

2 tablespoons olive oil
2 tablespoons finely chopped onions
1½ cups raw long-grain rice
3 cups boiling water

1½ teaspoons salt
⅛ teaspoon ground saffron, or
    saffron threads pulverized with a
    mortar and pestle or with the back
    of a spoon

In a heavy 10- to 12-inch skillet, heat the oil over moderate heat until a light haze forms above it. Add the onions and, stirring frequently, cook for 5 minutes, or until they are soft and transparent but not brown. Pour in the rice and stir for 2 or 3 minutes to coat the grains well with oil. Do not let the rice brown. Add the water, salt and saffron, and bring to a boil, still stirring. Cover the pan tightly and reduce the heat to its lowest point. Simmer undisturbed for 20 minutes, or until all the liquid has been absorbed by the rice and the grains are tender but not too soft.

    Fluff the rice with a fork before serving and taste for seasoning. If the rice must wait, drape the pan with a towel and keep it in a preheated 200° oven.

Braised Rice with Saffron
Risotto alla Milanese

To serve 6 to 8

7 cups chicken stock, fresh or canned
4 tablespoons butter
½ cup finely chopped onions
⅓ to ½ cup chopped uncooked beef
 marrow (optional)
2 cups plain white raw rice, preferably

imported Italian rice
½ cup dry white wine
⅛ teaspoon powdered saffron or
 saffron threads crushed to a powder
4 tablespoons soft butter
½ cup freshly grated imported
 Parmesan cheese

Bring the chicken stock to a simmer in a 2- to 3-quart saucepan and keep it barely simmering over low heat. In a heavy 3-quart flameproof casserole, melt 4 tablespoons of butter over moderate heat. Cook the onions in the butter, stirring frequently, for 7 or 8 minutes. Do not let them brown. Stir in the optional marrow, then add the rice and cook, stirring, for 1 or 2 minutes, or until the grains glisten with butter and are somewhat opaque. Pour in the wine and boil it until it is almost completely absorbed. Then add 2 cups of the simmering stock to the rice and cook uncovered, stirring occasionally, until almost all of the liquid is absorbed. Add 2 more cups of stock and cook, stirring occasionally. Meanwhile, stir the saffron into 2 cups of stock and let it steep for a few minutes. Then pour it over the rice. Cook until the stock is completely absorbed.

By now the rice should be tender. If it is still firm, add the remaining stock—½ cup at a time—and continue cooking and stirring until the rice is soft. Stir in 4 tablespoons of soft butter and the grated cheese with a fork, taking care not to mash the rice. Serve at once while the rice is creamy and piping hot.

Braised Rice with Shrimp

Risotto con Scampi

To serve 6 to 8

1 pound medium-sized fresh shrimp
   in their shells or thoroughly
   defrosted frozen shrimp
2 pounds fish heads and trimmings
2 quarts water
½ cup dry white wine
2 small onions, sliced
1 carrot, sliced

2 parsley sprigs
1 bay leaf
5 tablespoons butter
½ teaspoon finely chopped garlic
2 cups plain white raw rice, preferably
   imported Italian rice
4 tablespoons soft butter
½ cup freshly grated imported
   Parmesan cheese

Shell the shrimp carefully and save the shells. With a small sharp knife, slit each shrimp down the back and lift out the black or white intestinal vein. Wash the shrimp quickly under cold running water and dry them on paper towels.

In a 3- to 4-quart glass or enameled saucepan combine the shrimp shells, fish heads and trimmings, water and wine. Bring to a boil over high heat, removing the scum as it rises to the surface. Add the onions, carrot, parsley and bay leaf, reduce the heat and simmer partially covered, skimming the stock occasionally, for 30 minutes. Remove from the heat and strain the stock through a fine sieve into another saucepan, pressing down hard on the trimmings and vegetables with the back of a spoon to extract their juices before discarding them. Set the pan of strained stock over low heat and let it barely simmer.

In a heavy 8- to 10-inch skillet melt 1 tablespoon of butter over moderate heat. Toss in the shrimp and garlic and cook, stirring frequently, for 2 or 3 minutes, or until the shrimp are pink. Cover and set them aside.

Melt the remaining 4 tablespoons of butter over moderate heat in a heavy 3-quart flameproof casserole. Add the 2 cups of rice and cook, stirring constantly, for 2 or 3 minutes, or until the grains become somewhat opaque. Add 2 cups of the simmering stock and cook the rice uncovered over moderate heat, stirring occasionally, until almost all the liquid is absorbed. Add another 2 cups of stock and cook, stirring again, until it is absorbed. Then add 2 more cups of stock. When this is absorbed, the rice should be tender. If, however, the rice is still too firm, add more stock—½ cup at a time—and continue cooking and stirring until the rice is done.

With a fork, gently stir in the shrimp and garlic and the juice that will have accumulated in the skillet. Then stir in 4 tablespoons of soft butter and, finally, the freshly grated Parmesan cheese. Serve the *risotto con scampi* at once while it is creamy and hot.

Molded Rice with Chicken

Biram Ruzz

To serve 6 to 8

4 tablespoons softened butter, plus 2 tablespoons butter, cut into ¼-inch pieces	6 to 8 serving pieces
	Salt
3 cups uncooked medium- or long-grain white rice	Freshly ground black pepper
	1½ cups milk
A 2- to 2½-pound chicken cut into	1 cup heavy cream
	4 cups chicken stock, fresh or canned

NOTE: In Egypt, as in much of the Middle East, rice is eaten in enormous quantity. This mold, therefore, is mainly composed of rice (about 9 cups when cooked), and the chicken is more or less a flavorful accompaniment for the rice.

Preheat the oven to 400°. Using a pastry brush, heavily coat the bottom and sides of a round, deep 3-quart casserole or baking dish with the 4 tablespoons of softened butter.

Spread 1½ cups of the rice evenly in the dish, arrange the pieces of chicken skin side up on top and sprinkle them liberally with salt and pepper. In a small saucepan, bring the milk, cream and 2 cups of the stock to a boil over high heat and pour over the chicken. Spread the rest of the rice on top and dot evenly with the 2 tablespoons of the cut-up butter.

Bake uncovered on the lowest shelf of the oven for 15 minutes. Meanwhile, bring the remaining 2 cups of stock to a simmer in a small saucepan and keep it barely simmering over low heat. Pour 1 cup of the simmering stock into the casserole and bake for 15 minutes longer. Pour in the remaining stock and transfer the casserole to the upper third of the oven. Continue baking for another 30 minutes, then remove the casserole from the oven, cover tightly with a lid or foil and let it rest at room temperature for about 20 minutes.

To unmold and serve, run a sharp knife around the inside edges of the casserole to loosen the *biram ruzz* and let it rest for 10 minutes longer. Place a heated serving platter upside down over the top, and, grasping the casserole and platter together firmly, quickly invert them. The *biram ruzz* should slide out easily. Serve at once.

Saffron Rice with Seafood and Chicken
Paella

To serve 6

A 1½- to 2-pound live lobster
6 medium-sized raw shrimps in their
    shells
6 small hard-shelled clams
6 mussels
3 *chorizos*, or substitute ½ pound
    other garlic-seasoned smoked
    pork sausage
A 1½- to 2-pound chicken, cut into
    12 serving pieces
2 teaspoons salt
Freshly ground black pepper
½ cup olive oil
2 ounces lean boneless pork, cut
    into ¼-inch cubes
½ cup finely chopped onions
1 teaspoon finely chopped garlic

1 medium-sized sweet red or green
    pepper, seeded, deribbed and cut
    into strips 1½ inches long and ¼
    inch wide
1 large tomato, peeled, seeded and
    finely chopped
3 cups raw medium or long-grain
    regular-milled rice or imported
    short-grain rice
¼ teaspoon ground saffron or saffron
    threads pulverized with a mortar and
    pestle or with the back of a spoon
6 cups boiling water
½ cup fresh peas (½ pound) or
    substitute ½ cup thoroughly
    defrosted frozen peas
2 lemons, each cut lengthwise into
    6 wedges

NOTE: In Spain, a *paella* may be simple or elaborate. Vary the combination of chicken, meats and shellfish, if you like, to suit your taste.

With a cleaver or large, heavy knife, chop off the tail section of the lobster at the point where it joins the body and twist or cut off the large claws. Remove and discard the gelatinous sac (stomach) in the head and the long intestinal vein attached to it. Without removing the shell, cut the tail crosswise into 1-inch-thick slices and split the body of the lobster in half lengthwise, then crosswise into quarters. Set aside.

Shell the shrimp, leaving the tails intact. With a small, sharp knife, devein the shrimp by making a shallow incision down their backs and lifting out the intestinal vein with the point of the knife. Scrub the clams and mussels thoroughly with a stiff brush or soapless steel-mesh scouring pad under cold running water and remove the black, ropelike tufts from the mussels. Set the shrimp, clams and mussels aside on separate plates.

Place the sausages in an 8- to 10-inch skillet and prick them in two or three places with the point of a small, sharp knife. Add enough cold water to cover them completely and bring to a boil over high heat. Then reduce the heat to low and simmer uncovered for 5 minutes. Drain on paper towels and slice them into ¼-inch rounds.

Pat the chicken dry with paper towels and season it with 1 teaspoon of the salt and a few grindings of pepper. In a heavy 10- to 12-inch skillet, heat

¼ cup of the olive oil over high heat until a light haze forms above it. Add the chicken, skin side down, and brown it well, turning the pieces with tongs and regulating the heat so they color evenly without burning. As the pieces become a rich golden brown, remove them to a plate.

Add the lobster to the skillet. Turning the pieces frequently, cook over high heat for 2 or 3 minutes or until the shell begins to turn pink. Set the lobster aside on a separate plate and add the sausages to the pan. Brown the slices quickly on both sides, then spread them on paper towels to drain.

To make the *sofrito*, discard all the fat remaining in the skillet and in its place add the remaining ¼ cup of olive oil. Heat until a light haze forms above it, add the pork and brown it quickly on all sides over high heat. Add the onions, garlic, pepper strips and tomato. Stirring constantly, cook briskly until most of the liquid in the pan evaporates and the mixture is thick enough to hold its shape lightly in a spoon. Set the *sofrito* aside.

About a half hour before you plan to serve the *paella*, preheat the oven to 400°. In a 14-inch *paella* pan or a skillet or casserole at least 14 inches in diameter and 2- to 2½- inches deep, combine the *sofrito*, rice, the remaining 1 teaspoon of salt and the saffron. Pour in the boiling water and, stirring constantly, bring to a boil over high heat. Remove the pan from the heat immediately. (Taste the liquid for seasoning and add more salt if necessary.) Arrange the chicken, lobster, sausage, shrimp, clams and mussels on top of the rice and scatter the peas at random over the whole. Set the pan on the floor of the oven and bake uncovered for 25 to 30 minutes or until all the liquid has been absorbed by the rice and the grains are tender but not too soft. At no point should the *paella* be stirred after it goes in the oven.

When the *paella* is done, remove it from the oven and drape a kitchen towel loosely over the top. Let it rest for 5 to 8 minutes. Then garnish the *paella* with the lemons and serve at the table directly from the pan.

Steamed Rice with Carrots and Chicken

Shireen Polo

To serve 4 to 6

The peel of 2 oranges, cut into
strips 1 inch long and ⅛ inch wide

8 tablespoons (1 quarter-pound
stick) butter

3 medium-sized carrots, cut into
strips about 1 inch long and ⅛
inch wide

1 cup slivered blanched almonds

2 cups sugar

1 teaspoon ground saffron
dissolved in 1 tablespoon warm
water

¼ cup plus 2 tablespoons finely
chopped unsalted pistachios

2 cups imported Iranian rice or other
uncooked long-grain rice, soaked
and drained

¼ cup olive oil

A 2½- to 3-pound chicken, cut into
8 serving pieces

1 teaspoon salt

5 cups water

1 large onion, quartered

4 tablespoons melted butter
combined with 1 tablespoon water

Blanch the orange peel by dropping it into a small pan of cold water, bringing it to a boil, then draining it immediately and running cold water over it.

In a heavy 10- to 12-inch skillet, melt the butter over moderate heat. When the foam subsides, add the carrots and, stirring frequently, cook for 10 minutes, or until they are soft but not brown. Add the orange peel, almonds, sugar and saffron, and reduce the heat to low. Stir constantly until the sugar dissolves, then cover tightly and simmer for 30 minutes. Stir in the ¼ cup of pistachios and cook for 2 or 3 minutes longer. Set aside.

Meanwhile, bring 6 cups of water to a boil in a heavy 3- to 4-quart casserole with a tightly fitting lid. Pour in the rice in a slow, thin stream. Stir once or twice, boil briskly for 5 minutes, then drain in a sieve.

In a heavy 12-inch skillet, heat the olive oil until a light haze forms above it. Pat the chicken dry with paper towels and brown it in the oil, a few pieces at a time, turning it with tongs and regulating the heat so that they color richly and evenly without burning. As they brown, transfer the pieces to a plate. Pour off and discard the fat remaining in the skillet and replace the chicken in the pan. Sprinkle the pieces with the salt and scatter the onion quarters on top. Pour in the 5 cups of water, bring to a boil over high heat, cover and simmer over low heat for 30 minutes, or until the chicken is tender.

While the chicken is simmering, pour the melted butter and water mixture into the casserole and spread half of the rice evenly over it. Add 2 cups of the carrot mixture, smooth it to the edges, cover with the remaining rice and spread the rest of the carrot mixture on top. Cover tightly and steam for 20 minutes, or until the rice is tender.

To serve, remove the bones from the chicken breasts and thighs. Spread half the rice on a heated platter and arrange the chicken over it. Mound the rest of the rice on top and sprinkle it with the remaining pistachios.

Steamed Rice with Lamb, Dill and Lima Beans
Baghala Polo

To serve 6 to 8

2 tablespoons butter
1 medium-sized onion, peeled and
 cut into ¼-inch-thick slices
3 pounds lean boneless lamb
 shoulder, trimmed of excess fat
 and cut into 2-inch cubes
3 cups water
1 tablespoon salt
2 cups imported Iranian rice, or
 substitute other uncooked long-
 grain white rice, soaked and
 drained

4 cups finely cut fresh dill
1 pound shelled fresh baby lima
 beans or two 10-ounce packages
 frozen baby lima beans,
 thoroughly defrosted
8 tablespoons (1 quarter-pound
 stick) butter, melted
¼ teaspoon saffron threads,
 pulverized with a mortar and pestle
 or with the back of a spoon, and
 dissolved in 1 tablespoon warm
 water

In a heavy 3- to 4-quart casserole, with a tightly fitting lid, melt the 2 tablespoons of butter over moderate heat. When the foam begins to subside, add the onions and, stirring frequently, cook for about 10 minutes, or until the slices are richly browned. With a slotted spoon, transfer them to a plate.

A half-dozen pieces or so at a time, brown the lamb cubes in the fat remaining in the casserole, turning them with tongs or a spoon and regulating the heat so that they color deeply and evenly without burning. As they brown, transfer the cubes of lamb to the plate with the onions.

Pour the 3 cups of water into the casserole and bring to a boil over high heat, meanwhile scraping in the brown particles clinging to the bottom and sides of the pan. Return the lamb and onion to the casserole, add the salt, and reduce the heat to low. Cover tightly and simmer for about 1 hour and 15 minutes, or until the lamb is tender and shows no resistance when pierced with the point of a small, sharp knife. Transfer the lamb, onions and all the cooking liquid to a large bowl and set the casserole aside.

Preheat the oven to 350°. Bring 6 cups of water to a boil in a 5- to 6-quart saucepan. Pour in the rice in a slow, thin stream so the water does not stop boiling. Stir once or twice, boil briskly for 5 minutes, then remove the pan from the heat, stir in the dill and lima beans and drain in a fine sieve.

Grape Leaves with Rice, Pine Nuts and Currants

Yalantzi Dolmathes

To make 30

6 tablespoons olive oil	Freshly ground black pepper
1 cup finely chopped onions	2 tablespoons pine nuts (pignolia)
⅓ cup uncooked long- or medium-	2 tablespoons dried currants
grain white rice	40 preserved grape leaves
¾ cup water	2 tablespoons cold water
½ teaspoon salt	Lemon wedges

In a heavy 10- to 12-inch skillet, heat 3 tablespoons of the olive oil over moderate heat until a light haze forms above it. Add the onions and, stirring frequently, cook for 5 minutes, or until they are soft and transparent but not brown. Add the rice and stir constantly for 2 to 3 minutes, or until the grains are coated with oil. Do not let them brown. Pour in the water, add the salt and a few grindings of pepper and bring to a boil over high heat. Reduce the heat to low, cover tightly, and simmer for about 15 minutes, or until the rice is tender and has absorbed all the liquid. In a small skillet, heat 1 tablespoon of the remaining olive oil and in it cook the pine nuts until they are a delicate brown. Add them to the rice, then stir in the currants.

In a large pot, bring 2 quarts of water to a boil over high heat. Drop in the grape leaves and immediately turn off the heat. Let the leaves soak for 1 minute, then drain them in a sieve and plunge them into a bowl or pan of cold water to cool them quickly. Gently separate the leaves and spread them, dull sides up, on paper towels to drain.

Layer the bottom of a heavy 2- to 3-quart casserole with 10 of the leaves. Then stuff each of the remaining 30 leaves with about 1 tablespoon of the rice mixture. To stuff a grape leaf, spread the leaf, dull side up, flat on a plate, and place the tablespoonful of stuffing in the center of the leaf. Turn up the stem end of the leaf and then, one at a time, fold over each of the sides to enclose the stuffing completely. Starting again at the stem end, roll the grape leaf gently but firmly into a compact cylinder. The surfaces of the leaf will cling together sufficiently to hold the grape leaf dolma in shape.

Stack the stuffed leaves, side by side and seam sides down, in layers in the casserole and sprinkle them with the remaining 2 tablespoons of oil and the cold water. Place the casserole over high heat for 3 minutes, reduce the heat to low and simmer, tightly covered, for 50 minutes. Then uncover and cool to room temperature.

To serve, arrange the stuffed grape leaves attractively on a platter or individual plates and garnish with lemon wedges.

Grape Leaves with Rice and Meat
Dolmeh

To make 30

½ cup imported Iranian rice or other uncooked long-grain white rice, soaked and drained
6 tablespoons olive oil
½ cup finely chopped onions
½ pound lean ground lamb or beef
½ cup finely chopped scallions
½ cup finely chopped parsley, preferably flat-leaf parsley
¼ cup finely cut fresh dill, or substitute 2 tablespoons dried dill weed
2 teaspoons finely cut fresh mint, or 1 teaspoon dried mint
3 tablespoons fresh lemon juice
½ teaspoon turmeric
½ teaspoon oregano, crumbled
1 teaspoon salt
40 preserved grape leaves
2 tablespoons water
Lemon wedges

Over high heat, bring 1½ cups of water to a boil in a small saucepan. Pour in the rice in a slow, thin stream so the water does not stop boiling. Stir once or twice, boil briskly for 5 minutes, then drain in a sieve and set aside.

In a heavy 10- to 12-inch skillet, heat 4 tablespoons of the olive oil over moderate heat until a light haze forms above it. Add the onions and, stirring frequently, cook for 8 to 10 minutes, or until they are soft and golden brown. Stir in the ground meat and, mashing it with a fork to break up any lumps, cook until all traces of pink disappear. Tip the pan and drain off the excess fat. Then reduce the heat to low, add the rice, scallions, parsley, dill, mint, lemon juice, turmeric, oregano and salt and, stirring constantly, cook for 3 or 4 minutes. Set aside, off the heat.

Meanwhile, prepare the grape leaves according to the recipe above. Stuff and steam them in the same fashion, and serve garnished with lemon wedges.

Wild Rice

Riz Sauvage

To serve 8

2 cups wild rice	½ cup minced onions
4 teaspoons salt	1½ cups boiling beef stock
6 cups boiling water	1 teaspoon Worcestershire sauce
6 tablespoons butter	½ teaspoon black pepper

Preheat the oven to 350°. Wash the rice until the water runs clear. Add the salt to the boiling water, then add the rice. Cook over medium heat for 10 minutes, then drain the rice thoroughly. While the rice is cooking, melt the butter in a casserole and sauté the onions in it for 5 minutes. Add the drained rice and stir until it is well coated with the butter. Add the stock, Worcestershire sauce and pepper. Cover the casserole and bake for 25 minutes, or until the rice is tender and the liquid has been absorbed. Taste for seasoning and mix lightly with two forks before serving.

Wild Rice with Mushrooms

To serve 4 to 6

	1 teaspoon salt
4 tablespoons butter	2 cups chicken stock, fresh or canned
2 tablespoons finely diced scraped carrots	½ pound mushrooms, coarsely chopped
2 tablespoons finely diced celery	2 tablespoons finely chopped fresh parsley
2 tablespoons finely chopped onion	¼ cup finely chopped pecans
1 cup wild rice	

In a heavy enameled or stainless-steel 2-quart saucepan, melt 2 tablespoons of the butter over moderate heat, and, when the foam subsides, add the carrots, celery and onions, cover and cook for 10 to 15 minutes, stirring occasionally, until the vegetables are soft but not brown. Stir in the cup of rice and the salt and cook for 2 to 3 minutes uncovered, stirring to coat the rice thoroughly with the butter. In a small saucepan bring the stock to a boil and pour it over the rice. Bring to a boil again, cover tightly and reduce the heat to its lowest point. Cook undisturbed for 25 to 30 minutes, or until the rice is tender and has absorbed all the stock.

Meanwhile, over moderate heat melt the remaining 2 tablespoons of butter in an enameled or stainless-steel skillet. When the foam subsides, add the mushrooms and parsley; cook, stirring, for 5 minutes. Add the pecans and cook for 2 to 3 minutes more. With a fork, stir the contents of the skillet into the finished rice. Taste for seasoning and serve.

Dumplings & Noodles

Hungarian Potato Dumplings
Bramborové Knedlíky

To make 12 to 14 dumplings

5 medium-sized potatoes, boiled in
   their jackets, cooled, peeled and
   riced (about 2¾ cups riced)
⅓ cup flour

1 teaspoon salt
¼ cup farina or semolina
1 egg, lightly beaten
2 teaspoons milk

In a large saucepan, bring 5 quarts of water to a boil. In a mixing bowl, combine the riced potatoes, flour, salt, farina or semolina, egg and milk. Mix them together with a wooden spoon until they form a smooth paste. Dust your hands with flour and form the mixture into balls about 1 inch in diameter.

   Drop the dumplings into the boiling water and bring to a gentle boil again. Simmer the dumplings for about 10 minutes, or until they rise to the top.

Roman Dumplings
Gnocchi alla Romana

To serve 4 to 6

3 cups milk
1½ teaspoons salt
Pinch of ground nutmeg
Freshly ground black pepper

¾ cup semolina or farina
2 eggs
1 cup freshly grated imported
   Parmesan cheese
4 tablespoons butter, melted

Butter a large baking sheet and set it aside. In a heavy 2- to 3-quart saucepan, bring the milk, salt, nutmeg and a few grindings of pepper to a boil over moderate heat. Add the semolina or farina gradually, so the milk never stops boiling, stirring it constantly with a wooden spoon. Continue cooking and stirring until the semolina or farina is so thick that the
292

spoon will stand up unsupported in the middle of the pan. Remove the pan from the heat.

Beat the eggs lightly with a fork, add ¾ cup of freshly grated Parmesan cheese and stir the mixture into the semolina. When the ingredients are well blended, spoon the mixture onto the buttered baking sheet. Using a metal spatula or knife, which should be dipped in hot water from time to time to make the semolina easier to handle, smooth and spread the semolina into a sheet about ¼ inch thick. Refrigerate for at least an hour, or until the semolina is firm.

Preheat the oven to 400° and butter an 8- or 9-inch shallow baking-and-serving dish. With a 1½-inch biscuit cutter, cut the semolina into small circles. (Or use a sharp knife to cut it into triangles.) Transfer them to the baking dish, dribble in the melted butter, and sprinkle the top with the remaining ¼ cup of cheese. Bake the *gnocchi* on the middle shelf of the oven for 15 minutes, or until they are crisp and golden; if you want them browned, put them under a hot broiler for 30 seconds. Serve at once.

Spinach Dumplings
Gnocchi Verdi

To serve 4 to 6

4 tablespoons butter
2 ten-ounce packages frozen chopped
    spinach, thoroughly defrosted,
    squeezed completely dry, and
    chopped very fine (about 1½ cups),
    or 1½ pounds fresh spinach,
    cooked, squeezed and chopped
¾ cup *ricotta* cheese
2 eggs, lightly beaten

6 tablespoons flour
¾ cup freshly grated imported
    Parmesan cheese
½ teaspoon salt
½ teaspoon freshly ground black
    pepper
Pinch of ground nutmeg
6 to 8 quarts water
1 tablespoon salt
4 tablespoons melted butter

In an 8- to 10-inch enameled or stainless-steel skillet, melt 4 tablespoons of butter over moderate heat. Add the chopped fresh or frozen spinach and cook, stirring constantly, for 2 to 3 minutes, or until almost all of the moisture has boiled away and the spinach begins to stick lightly to the skillet. Now add the ¾ cup of *ricotta* cheese and cook, stirring, for 3 or 4 minutes longer.

With a rubber spatula, transfer the entire contents of the skillet to a large mixing bowl and mix in the 2 lightly beaten eggs, 6 tablespoons of flour, ¼ cup of the grated cheese, ½ teaspoon salt, pepper and nutmeg. Place in the refrigerator for 30 minutes to 1 hour, or until the *gnocchi* mixture is quite firm.

Preheat the broiler. Bring the 6 to 8 quarts of water and 1 tablespoon of salt to a simmer over moderate heat in a large soup pot or saucepan. Flour your hands lightly and pick up about 1 tablespoon of the chilled *gnocchi* mixture at a time. Shape the tablespoonfuls into small balls about 1½ inches in diameter. Gently drop the balls into the simmering water and cook them uncovered for 5 to 8 minutes, or until they puff slightly and are somewhat firm to the touch. With a slotted spoon, lift the *gnocchi* out of the water and set them aside on a towel to drain.

Now pour 2 tablespoons of the melted butter into a shallow 8-by-12-inch flameproof dish and swirl the butter around until the bottom of the dish glistens. Arrange the *gnocchi* in the dish in one layer about ¼-inch apart, dribble the remaining 2 tablespoons of melted butter over them, and sprinkle the *gnocchi* with the remaining ½ cup of grated cheese. Set under the broiler 3 inches from the heat for 3 minutes, or until the cheese melts.

Serve the *gnocchi* at once, directly from the baking dish. Serve additional grated cheese separately, if you wish.

Tiny Dumplings
Spätzle

To make about 4 cups

3 cups all-purpose flour	4 eggs
1 teaspoon salt	1 cup milk
¼ teaspoon ground nutmeg	1 cup fine dry bread crumbs
	(optional)
	¼ pound (1 stick) butter (optional)

In a large mixing bowl, combine the flour, ½ teaspoon of the salt and the nutmeg. Break up the eggs with a fork and beat them into the flour mixture. Pour in the milk in a thin stream, stirring constantly with a large spoon, and continue to stir until the dough is smooth.

Bring 2 quarts of water and the remaining ½ teaspoon of salt to a boil in a heavy 4- to 5-quart saucepan. Set a large colander, preferably one with large holes, over the saucepan and with a spoon press the dough a few tablespoons at a time through the colander directly into the boiling water. Stir the *Spätzle* gently to prevent them from sticking to each other, then boil briskly for 5 to 8 minutes, or until they are tender. Taste to make sure. Drain the *Spätzle* thoroughly in a sieve or colander. When *Spätzle* are served as a separate dish with roasted meats, such as *Sauerbraten*, they are traditionally presented sprinkled with toasted bread crumbs. To toast the crumbs, melt ¼ pound of butter in a heavy 6- to 8-inch skillet over moderate heat. When the foam almost subsides, drop in 1 cup of bread crumbs and cook, stirring constantly, until the crumbs are golden brown.

Italian Cornmeal Porridge
Polenta

To serve 6

1½ quarts water

2 teaspoons salt
1½ cups finely ground *polenta*
or yellow cornmeal

In a heavy 3- to 4-quart saucepan, bring the water and salt to a bubbling boil over high heat. Pour the uncooked *polenta* or cornmeal slowly into the boiling water, making sure that the boiling never stops, and stirring constantly to keep the mixture smooth. Reduce the heat and simmer the *polenta*, stirring frequently, for 20 to 30 minutes, or until it is so thick that the spoon will stand up unsupported in the middle of the pan.

The *polenta* can be served at once with gravy, butter and cheese, a meat stew or tomato sauce (*below*). Or, if you prefer, it can be spooned out while it is still hot onto a large buttered baking dish or sheet and with a metal spatula or knife, spread into a thin layer about 8 by 16 inches in size. It should then be refrigerated for about 2 hours. Once cool it can be fried in oil or butter, broiled or baked and served with a stew or sauce.

TOMATO SAUCE

To make about 1½ cups

2 tablespoons olive oil
½ cup finely chopped onions
2 cups Italian plum or whole-pack
tomatoes, coarsely chopped but
not drained

3 tablespoons tomato paste
1 tablespoon finely cut fresh basil
or 1 teaspoon dried basil
1 teaspoon sugar
½ teaspoon salt
Freshly ground black pepper

Using a 2- to 3-quart enameled or stainless-steel saucepan, heat the olive oil until a light haze forms over it. Add the onions and cook them over moderate heat for 7 to 8 minutes, or until they are soft but not browned. Add the tomatoes, tomato paste, basil, sugar, salt and a few grindings of pepper. Reduce the heat to very low and simmer, with the pan partially covered, for about 40 minutes. Stir occasionally.

Press the sauce through a fine sieve (or a food mill) into a bowl or pan. Taste for seasoning and serve hot.

Tortillas

To make 12

2¼ cups instant *masa harina* (corn flour)

1 teaspoon salt

1⅓ cups cold water

In a mixing bowl, combine the *masa harina* and salt, and gradually pour in 1 cup of water, stirring constantly. Knead the mixture with your hands, adding more water, a tablespoon at a time, until the dough becomes firm and no longer sticks to the fingers. If you have a tortilla press, break off small pieces of dough and shape them into balls the size of a walnut. Place one ball at a time between two 8-inch squares of wax paper, and press them into 5- to 6-inch circles. Or divide the dough into 3 or 4 batches and, with a rolling pin, roll each batch between long strips of wax paper until the dough is about ¹⁄₁₆ inch thick. With a plate or pot lid as a pattern, and a knife or pastry wheel, cut the dough into 5-inch rounds. Stack the rounds between pieces of wax paper.

Preheat the oven to 250°. Cook the tortillas one at a time. Heat an ungreased *comal,* a cast-iron griddle or a 7- to 8-inch cast-iron skillet over moderate heat. Unwrap the tortilla and cook it for 2 minutes on each side, turning it once with a spatula when the bottom becomes a delicate brown. Adjust the heat if it browns too fast. As you proceed, wrap the tortillas, 4 or 5 at a time, in foil, and keep them warm in the oven.

Tortillas may be cooked ahead and kept warm in the oven for 2 or 3 hours: Stack 10 together and wrap each batch with paper toweling, then with a damp cloth and finally in foil. To rewarm tortillas, brush both sides with water, and heat, one at a time, in a skillet for a few seconds.

Pork Tortillas

Enchiladas Rojas

To serve 6

THE SAUCE
6 dried *ancho* chilies
1 cup boiling water
5 fresh tomatoes, peeled, seeded and
  coarsely chopped, or substitute
  1²/₃ cups chopped, drained,
  canned Italian plum tomatoes
½ cup coarsely chopped onions
¼ teaspoon finely chopped garlic
½ teaspoon crumbled dried *epazote*,
  if available
Pinch of sugar

1 teaspoon salt
¼ teaspoon freshly ground black
  pepper
5 tablespoons lard
2 eggs
1 cup heavy cream

6 Spanish *chorizo* sausages, skinned
  and coarsely chopped, or substitute
  ¾ pound smoked, spiced pork
  sausage, skinned and chopped
²/₃ cup freshly grated Parmesan cheese
12 tortillas
½ cup coarsely chopped onions

NOTE: Wear rubber gloves when handling the hot chilies.

Under cold running water, pull the stems off the chilies. Cut or tear the chilies into halves, and brush out the seeds. With a small, sharp knife, cut away any large ribs; then tear them into small pieces. In a small bowl, soak the chilies in 1 cup of boiling water for 30 minutes.

Pour the chilies and their soaking water into the jar of an electric blender and blend at high speed for about 15 seconds. Add the tomatoes, ½ cup of the onions, the garlic, *epazote*, sugar, salt and black pepper, and blend for 30 seconds, or until the mixture is reduced to a smooth purée.

In an 8- to 10-inch skillet, melt 1 tablespoon of the lard over moderate heat until a haze forms above it. Pour in the chili and vegetable purée and, stirring frequently, cook it for 5 minutes. Remove the pan from the heat. In a small bowl, beat the eggs with a fork until they are well combined, then stir in the cream. Slowly pour the egg-cream mixture into the sauce in the skillet, stirring constantly to prevent the eggs from curdling. Cover the skillet and set it aside.

In another 8- to 10-inch skillet, melt 1 tablespoon more of the lard over moderate heat and add the chopped sausages. Fry for about 5 minutes, stirring constantly, until the sausages have rendered most of their fat and are lightly browned. With a slotted spoon, remove the sausages from the skillet and drain them on paper toweling. Discard the fat from the skillet. Place the sausages in a small bowl and stir in 3 tablespoons of the chili sauce and ⅓ cup of the grated cheese.

Preheat the oven to 350°. In the heavy skillet, melt the remaining 3 tablespoons of lard over moderate heat until a light haze forms above it. Fry and fill the tortillas, one at a time, in the following fashion: Dip a tor-

297

tilla in the tomato sauce, drop it into the hot lard, and fry it for a minute or so on each side, or until it becomes limp but not brown. Transfer the tortilla from the pan to a plate and place about ¼ cup of the sausage mixture in the center. Fold one side of the tortilla over the filling, then roll the tortilla completely into a thick cylinder. Place it seam side down in a shallow 8-by-12-inch baking dish. Fry and fill the remaining tortillas similarly, replenishing the lard in the frying pan when necessary. When the tortillas are all arranged in one layer in the baking dish, pour the remaining tomato sauce over them, and sprinkle the top with the ½ cup of the chopped onions and the remaining cheese. Bake in the middle of the oven for about 15 minutes, or until the cheese has melted and the enchiladas are lightly browned on top.

To serve, gently transfer the enchiladas with a spatula to heated individual plates and spoon some of the sauce over them.

Macaroni and Sausage Casserole

To serve 6

	Salt
1 pound pork sausage	Pepper
¼ cup olive oil	A pinch of oregano
1 large clove garlic, crushed	1 bay leaf
1 medium-sized yellow onion, sliced	2 cups water
1 pound mushrooms, sliced	1 pound macaroni
1 can tomato paste (6 ounces)	½ cup grated Parmesan cheese

Cut the sausages into 1-inch pieces and cook over a slow fire until well browned. In another pan heat ¼ cup of olive oil. Add a large clove of crushed garlic and cook 1 minute. Put the sliced onion and sliced mushrooms into the pan and cook until the onion is soft but not browned. Add the sausage, tomato paste, salt, pepper, oregano, bay leaf and water. Cover and simmer for about 1 hour.

In the meantime cook 1 pound of macaroni in plenty of boiling salted water. Drain and place in an ovenproof serving dish or casserole. Add the sausage mixture and blend lightly with 2 forks. Sprinkle with ½ cup of grated Parmesan cheese and bake in a moderate oven at 350° until heated through and lightly browned, about 20 minutes. Serve in the dish it was baked in.

Baked Noodles with Ham
Schinkenfleckerln

To serve 4

½ pound broad egg noodles

8 tablespoons (1 quarter-pound stick)
  butter

¼ cup finely chopped onions

½ cup sour cream

3 eggs, lightly beaten

1 cup diced cooked ham (about ¼
  pound)

Freshly ground black pepper

Salt

¼ cup bread crumbs

Preheat the oven to 350°. Drop the noodles into about 2 quarts of boiling salted water. Boil for 10 minutes, or until barely tender. Strain them through a colander or strainer, rinse them thoroughly with cold water, then drain. Spread the noodles out on a board and cut them into pieces as long as they are wide, making squares of about 1 inch.

Melt half the butter in an 8-inch skillet. When the foam subsides, add the onions. Cook them for 4 or 5 minutes, or until they are translucent. Add the noodle squares and the rest of the butter and toss them about until they are well coated. Cook over moderate heat for about 5 minutes.

With a wire whisk, beat the sour cream and eggs together in a large mixing bowl. Stir in the ham, a generous grinding of pepper, salt and the contents of the skillet. Butter a 2-quart casserole, scatter the bread crumbs over the butter, tip the casserole from side to side to spread them evenly, then fill the casserole with the noodle-and-ham mixture. Bake, uncovered, in the middle of the oven for 45 minutes, or until the mixture is firm.

To unmold, run a sharp thin knife around the inside of the casserole, place a warm platter over the top of it and, grasping the casserole and the platter together, turn them over. Serve with the bottom side up.

Egg Noodles with Butter and Cheese
Fettuccine al Burro

To serve 4

8 tablespoons (1 quarter-pound
   stick) butter, softened
¼ cup heavy cream
½ cup freshly grated imported
   Parmesan cheese

6 to 8 quarts water
1 tablespoon salt
1 pound *fettuccine*, commercial or
   homemade (*pages 308–310*)
1 canned white truffle, sliced very thin
   or finely chopped (optional)
Freshly grated imported Parmesan cheese

Cream the ¼ pound of softened butter by beating it vigorously against the sides of a heavy bowl with a wooden spoon until it is light and fluffy. Beat in the cream a little at a time, and then, a few tablespoonfuls at a time, beat in ½ cup of grated cheese. Cover the bowl and set it aside—in the refrigerator, if the sauce is not to be used at once. If you do refrigerate the sauce, be sure to bring to room temperature before tossing it with the *fettuccine*.

Set a large serving bowl or casserole in a 250° oven to heat while you cook the *fettuccine*. Bring the water and salt to a bubbling boil in a large soup pot or kettle. Drop in the *fettuccine* and stir gently with a wooden fork for a few moments to prevent the strands from sticking to one another or to the bottom of the pot. Boil over high heat, stirring occasionally, for 5 to 8 minutes, or until the pasta is tender. (Test it by tasting; it should be soft but *al dente*—that is, slightly resistant to the bite.) Immediately drain the *fettuccine* into a colander and lift the strands with 2 forks to make sure it is thoroughly drained. Transfer it at once to the hot serving bowl.

Add the creamed butter-and-cheese mixture and toss it with the *fettuccine* until every strand is well coated. Taste and season generously with salt and pepper. Stir in the optional truffle. Serve the *fettuccine* at once. Pass the extra grated cheese in a separate bowl.

Spaghetti with Egg and Bacon Sauce
Spaghetti alla Carbonara

To serve 4

4 tablespoons soft butter
2 whole eggs
2 egg yolks
1 cup freshly grated imported
   Parmesan cheese
6 to 8 quarts water
1 teaspoon salt

1 pound spaghetti, *spaghettini*
   or *linguine*
8 slices bacon, cut crosswise into
   ¼-inch strips
1 teaspoon dried red pepper flakes
   (optional)
½ cup heavy cream
Freshly ground black pepper

In a small bowl, cream the soft butter by beating it against the sides of the bowl with a wooden spoon until it is soft and fluffy. In another small bowl, beat the eggs and egg yolks with a fork or whisk until they are well blended, then stir in ½ cup of grated cheese. Set both bowls aside.

Heat a large ovenproof serving bowl or casserole in a 200° oven. At the same time, bring the water and salt to a bubbling boil in a large soup pot or kettle. Drop the spaghetti into the boiling water and stir it for a moment or two with a wooden spoon to be sure the strands do not stick to one another or to the bottom of the pot. Cook the spaghetti over high heat, stirring occasionally, for 7 to 12 minutes, or until it is tender. Meanwhile, fry the pieces of bacon in an 8- to 10-inch skillet over moderate heat until they are crisp. Pour off about half of the bacon fat and stir into the pan the optional red pepper and then the cream. Bring the cream to a simmer and keep it warm until the spaghetti is done.

When the spaghetti is cooked, drain it thoroughly in a large colander, lifting the strands with two forks to make certain all of the water runs off. Transfer the spaghetti to the heated serving bowl and stir in the creamed butter, tossing and turning the spaghetti with two forks to coat every strand. Then stir in the hot bacon-and-cream mixture and finally the beaten eggs and cheese, mixing everything together thoroughly. The heat of the pasta and other ingredients should cook the raw eggs on contact. Taste and season with salt and a few grindings of pepper. Serve the *carbonara* at once with the remaining ½ cup of grated cheese passed at the table.

Spaghetti with White Clam Sauce
Spaghetti con le Vongole

To serve 4 to 6

6 tablespoons olive oil	1 pound spaghetti, *spaghettini* or *linguine*
1 teaspoon finely chopped garlic	2 tablespoons soft butter
1 cup clam broth, fresh from the shucked clams (*below*) or bottled	3 dozen small hardshell clams, shucked
¼ cup dry white wine	2 tablespoons finely chopped fresh parsley, preferably the flat-leaf Italian type
6 to 8 quarts of water	Salt
1 tablespoon salt	White pepper

In a heavy 10- to 12-inch skillet, heat the olive oil until a light haze forms over it. Stir in the garlic and cook over moderate heat, stirring constantly, for about 30 seconds. Pour in the clam broth and wine and boil briskly over high heat until the foam disappears and the liquid has reduced to about ¾ cup. Remove from the heat and set aside.

In a large kettle or soup pot bring the water and the salt to a bubbling boil over high heat. Drop in the spaghetti and stir it gently with a wooden fork or spoon for a few moments to prevent the strands from sticking to one another or the bottom of the pot. Boil over high heat, stirring occasionally, for 7 to 12 minutes, or until the pasta is tender. Test it by tasting a strand; it should be soft but *al dente*—that is, slightly resistant to the bite. Immediately drain the spaghetti into a large colander, lifting the strands with a fork to be sure it is thoroughly drained. Transfer the spaghetti to a large heated serving bowl and toss it with the soft butter. Bring the sauce in the skillet to a boil over high heat and add the clams. Cook the clams, turning them constantly, for 1 or 2 minutes. Then pour the clams and sauce over the spaghetti, sprinkle with parsley, and toss together with two large forks until all the ingredients are well mixed. Taste and season with salt and white pepper. Serve at once.

Green Noodles with Red Clam Sauce

To serve 2 or 3

1 quart clams in shell	½ cup chopped parsley
1 medium-sized onion	1½ tablespoons chopped basil
1 stalk celery	Salt
1 carrot	Pepper
1 cup white wine or vermouth	½ cup tomato purée
½ cup olive oil	8 ounces green noodles
3 cloves garlic, finely chopped	Grated Gruyère cheese

Wash the clams well. Cut the onion, celery and carrot into fine strips, and put them in a large kettle. Add the wine and the clams. Cover tightly and steam until the clams open. Remove the clams from their shells and strain the broth. Heat the olive oil and the garlic, add the parsley, basil, and salt and pepper to taste. Reduce the clam broth by half, add it to the olive oil mixture and let it come to a boil. Add the tomato purée and cook until well blended. Thin with a dash of white wine or vermouth. Taste for seasoning. Add the clams, chopped.

Cook the noodles and drain. Pour the clam mixture over the noodles and top with grated cheese.

Baked Lasagne with Meat and Cream Sauces
Lasagne Pasticciate

To serve 6 to 8

LASAGNE

6 to 8 quarts water

1 tablespoon salt

½ pound *lasagne (pages 308-310)*

LASAGNE: Preheat the oven to 350°. Generously butter the bottom and sides of a 9-by-12-by-3-inch serving casserole or baking dish. In a large soup pot or kettle, bring the water and salt to a bubbling boil over high heat. Add the *lasagne*, stirring gently for a few moments with a wooden fork to be sure the strips do not stick to one another. Boil over high heat, stirring occasionally, until the *lasagne* is tender, but still *al dente*, or somewhat resistant to the bite—the time may vary between 10 and 25 minutes, depending on whether you use homemade or commercial *lasagne*. Set the pot under cold running water for a few moments to cool the pasta. Then lift out the strips and spread them side by side on paper towels to drain.

RAGÙ BOLOGNESE (MEAT SAUCE)

To make about 2½ cups

¼ pound smoked ham, coarsely chopped (about 1 cup)

1 cup coarsely chopped onions

¼ cup coarsely chopped carrots

½ cup coarsely chopped celery

4 tablespoons butter

2 tablespoons olive oil

¾ pound beef round, ground twice

¼ pound lean pork, ground twice

½ cup dry white wine

2 cups beef stock, fresh or canned

2 tablespoons tomato paste

½ pound chicken livers

Pinch of ground nutmeg

Salt

Freshly ground black pepper

Combine the chopped ham, onions, carrots and celery on a cutting board, and chop them together into very small pieces. (This mixture is called a *battuto*, which when cooked becomes a *soffritto*.) Melt 2 tablespoons of the butter over moderate heat in a heavy, 10- to 12-inch skillet. When the foam subsides, add the *battuto* and cook, stirring frequently, for about 10 minutes, or until it is lightly browned. With a rubber spatula, transfer the *soffritto* to a heavy 3- to 4-quart saucepan. Heat the 2 tablespoons of olive oil in the same skillet, and in it lightly brown the ground beef and the pork over moderate heat, stirring the meat constantly to break up any lumps. Then pour in the wine, increase the heat, and boil briskly, still stirring constantly, until almost all of the liquid in the skillet has cooked away. Add the meat to the *soffritto* in the saucepan, and stir in the stock and tomato paste. Bring to a boil over high heat, then reduce the heat and simmer, partially

303

covered, for 45 minutes, stirring occasionally. Meanwhile, over high heat melt 2 more tablespoons of butter in the original skillet, and when the foam subsides, add the chicken livers. Cook them for 3 or 4 minutes, or until they are firm and lightly browned. Chop the chicken livers into small dice, set them aside, and add them to the sauce 10 minutes before it is done. Taste the *ragù* and season it with nutmeg, salt and pepper.

BESCIAMELLA (CREAM SAUCE)

6 tablespoons butter	Pinch of ground nutmeg
6 tablespoons flour	1 teaspoon salt
2 cups milk	½ cup freshly grated imported
1 cup heavy cream	Parmesan cheese

BESCIAMELLA FOR LASAGNE: In a heavy 2- to 3-quart saucepan, melt the butter over moderate heat and stir in the flour. Remove the pan from the heat and pour in the milk and cream all at once, beating with a wire whisk until the flour is partially dissolved. Return the pan to high heat and cook, stirring constantly with the whisk. When the sauce comes to a boil and thickens into a smooth cream, reduce the heat and simmer, still stirring, for 2 or 3 minutes. Remove from the heat and season with nutmeg and salt.

Spread a layer of *ragù bolognese* about ¼ inch deep evenly over the bottom of the buttered casserole. Spread over it about 1 cup of *besciamella*. Lay one third of the *lasagne* on the *besciamella*, overlapping the strips slightly. Repeat the layers of *ragù*, *besciamella* and *lasagne* two more times, then top with the rest of the *ragù* and a masking of *besciamella*. Sprinkle with grated cheese. Bake 30 minutes, or until the sauce is bubbling hot.

Beef Rolls with Cream and Tomato Sauces
Cannelloni

To serve 6 to 8

PASTA	6 to 8 quarts water
Pasta dough (*pages 308–310*)	1 tablespoon salt

PASTA: On a floured board or cloth, roll out the pasta dough until it is paper thin, then cut it into about 36 rectangles of 2 by 3 inches. Bring the water and salt to a bubbling boil over high heat in a large soup pot or kettle. Drop in the pieces of pasta and stir gently with a wooden fork or spoon for a few moments to be sure they don't stick to one another or to the pot. Return the water to a boil and cook the pasta over high heat, stirring occasionally, for 5 minutes, or until the pasta is tender but not soft. Drain, cool slightly, then spread the pasta pieces side by side on paper towels to dry.

FILLING

2 tablespoons olive oil

¼ cup finely chopped onions

1 teaspoon finely chopped garlic

1 ten-ounce package frozen chopped spinach, defrosted, squeezed completely dry and chopped again (about ¾ cup) or ¾ pound fresh spinach, cooked, drained, squeezed and finely chopped

2 tablespoons butter

1 pound beef round steak, ground twice, or 1 cup finely chopped leftover beef

2 chicken livers

5 tablespoons freshly grated imported Parmesan cheese

2 tablespoons heavy cream

2 eggs, lightly beaten

½ teaspoon dried oregano, crumbled

Salt

Freshly ground black pepper

FILLING: Heat the olive oil in an 8- to 10-inch enameled or stainless-steel skillet. Add the onions and garlic, and cook over moderate heat, stirring frequently, for 7 or 8 minutes until they are soft but not brown. Stir in the spinach and cook, stirring constantly, for 3 or 4 minutes. When all of the moisture has boiled away and the spinach sticks lightly to the pan, transfer it to a large mixing bowl. Melt 1 tablespoon of butter in the same skillet and lightly brown the ground meat, stirring constantly to break up any lumps. Add the meat to the onion-spinach mixture. Then melt 1 more tablespoon of butter in the skillet and cook the livers, turning them frequently, for 3 or 4 minutes, until they are somewhat firm, lightly browned but still pink inside. Chop them coarsely. Then add them to the mixture in the bowl along with 5 tablespoons of grated Parmesan, 2 tablespoons of cream, the eggs and oregano. With a wooden spoon, mix the ingredients together, gently but thoroughly. Taste and season with salt and pepper.

BESCIAMELLA

4 tablespoons butter

4 tablespoons flour

1 cup milk

1 cup heavy cream

1 teaspoon salt

⅛ teaspoon white pepper

BESCIAMELLA FOR CANNELLONI: In a heavy 2- to 3-quart saucepan, melt the butter over moderate heat. Remove the pan from the heat and stir in the flour. Pour in the milk and cream all at once, whisking constantly until the flour is partially dissolved. Then return the pan to high heat and cook, stirring constantly with the whisk. When the sauce comes to a boil and is smooth, reduce the heat. Simmer, still stirring, for 2 or 3 minutes longer, or until the sauce is thick enough to coat the wires of the whisk heavily. Remove the sauce from the heat, and season with salt and white pepper.

TOPPING

3 cups tomato sauce

2 tablespoons freshly grated imported

Parmesan cheese

2 tablespoons butter, cut in tiny pieces

ASSEMBLING AND BAKING THE CANNELLONI: Preheat the oven to 375°. Place a tablespoon or so of the filling on the bottom third of each of the pasta rectangles and roll them up. Pour just a film of the tomato sauce into two 10-by-14-inch shallow baking-and-serving dishes. Lay the *cannelloni* side by side in one layer on the tomato sauce. Pour the *besciamella* over it and spoon the rest of the tomato sauce on top. Scatter in 4 tablespoons of grated cheese and dot with 2 tablespoons of butter. Bake the *cannelloni* uncovered in the middle of the oven for 20 minutes, or until the cheese is melted and the sauce bubbling. Slide the baking dishes under a hot broiler for 30 seconds to brown. Serve directly from the baking dish.

Meat Ravioli

To make about 45

Pasta dough (*pages 308–310*)

MEAT FILLING
3 tablespoons butter
4 tablespoons finely chopped onions
¾ pound finely ground raw veal
1 ten-ounce package frozen chopped spinach, defrosted, thoroughly squeezed and chopped again, or

¾ pound fresh spinach, cooked, squeezed and chopped
½ cup freshly grated imported Parmesan cheese
Pinch of ground nutmeg
3 eggs
Salt

MEAT-AND-SPINACH FILLING FOR RAVIOLI: Melt the 3 tablespoons of butter in a small skillet and cook the onions, stirring frequently for about 7 or 8 minutes, or until they are soft and transparent but not brown. Add the ¾ pound finely ground raw veal and cook, stirring constantly, until the veal loses its red color and any accumulating liquid in the pan cooks completely away. Transfer the entire contents of the skillet to a mixing bowl and stir in the chopped spinach, grated Parmesan cheese and a pinch of nutmeg. In a separate bowl, beat the eggs lightly and add them to the onion, veal and spinach mixture. Taste and season with salt.

1 Space little mounds of meat-and-spinach filling 2 inches apart on a sheet of pasta. Then with a brush dipped in water draw straight lines between the mounds.

Divide the pasta dough (prepared according to the recipe on page 308) into four pieces and roll out the first one quarter of the dough to make it as thin as possible. Cover the rolled pasta with a damp towel to prevent its drying out, and roll out the second quarter of dough to a similar size and shape. Using the first sheet of rolled-out pasta as a sort of checkerboard, place a mound of about 1 tablespoon of filling every 2 inches across and down the pasta. Dip a pastry brush or your finger into a bowl of water and make vertical and horizontal lines on the pasta, between the mounds of filling. Be sure to use enough water to wet the lines evenly (the water will act as a bond to hold the finished ravioli together). Carefully spread the second sheet of rolled-out pasta on top of the first one, pressing down firmly around the filling and along the wetted lines.

With a ravioli cutter, a pastry wheel or a small, sharp knife, cut the pasta into squares along the wetted lines. Separate the mounds of ravioli and set

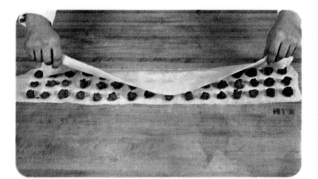

2 Now place a second sheet of pasta evenly over the first sheet. Work quickly; the sheets must remain damp and pliable or they will crack when pressed into shape.

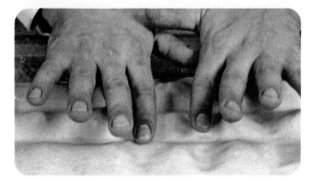

3 Press down between the mounds to form the ravioli envelopes. The wetted areas of the pasta sheet will act as a bond to seal the fillings into the envelopes.

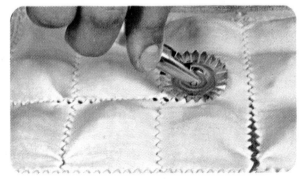

4 With a ravioli cutter (shown) or a knife separate the envelopes from each other. The ravioli is now ready to be cooked in salted boiling water.

them aside on wax paper. Roll out, fill and cut the 2 other portions of dough.

To cook, drop the ravioli into 6 to 8 quarts of rapidly boiling salted water and stir them gently with a wooden spoon, to keep them from sticking to one another or to the bottom of the pot. Boil the ravioli for about 8 minutes, or until they are tender, then drain them thoroughly in a large sieve or colander. Serve the ravioli with tomato sauce or add butter and Parmesan cheese, and gently stir them all together immediately before serving.

Homemade Egg Noodles
Pasta con Uova

This recipe explains how to make—by hand or with the aid of a pasta machine —the basic dough for egg noodles. Using this recipe, you can cut the dough into a variety of sizes and shapes to prepare cannelloni, ravioli, tagliarini, fettuccine, tagliatelle *and* lasagne.

To make about ¾ pound

1½ cups unsifted all-purpose flour
1 egg

1 egg white
1 tablespoon olive oil
1 teaspoon salt
Water

Pour the flour into a large mixing bowl or in a heap on a pastry board, make a well in the center of the flour and in it put the egg, egg white, oil and salt. Mix together with a fork or your fingers until the dough can be gathered into a rough ball. Moisten any remaining dry bits of flour with drops of water and press them into the ball.

1 Start homemade pasta by breaki an egg into the cuplike well you have formed in a mound of flour.

TO MAKE PASTA BY HAND: Knead the dough on a floured board, working in a little extra flour if the dough seems sticky. After about 10 minutes, the dough should be smooth, shiny and elastic. Wrap it in wax paper and let

2 Add egg white, oil and salt and fill up the well with flour pushed in from the edges of the mound.

3 Gather up the flour and begin to knead, adding drops of water if the crumbly mass proves too dry.

4 After 10 minutes of kneading, the dough becomes smooth, shiny and elastic. Divide it into two parts.

5 Complete the basic dough mixture by dusting each part with flour and rolling out into paper-thin sheets.

6 To make *fettuccine* from the dough, roll each of the thin sheets into a long, cylindrical jelly-roll shape.

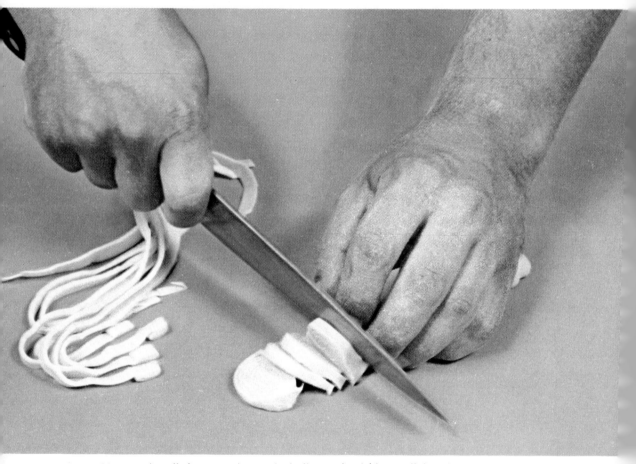

7 Now cut the rolled-up pasta into ¼-inch slices and quickly unroll them into *fettuccine* strips before the layers of pasta stick together.

the dough rest for at least 10 minutes before rolling it.

Divide the dough into 2 balls. Place 1 ball on a floured board or pastry cloth and flatten it with the palm of your hand into an oblong about 1 inch thick. Dust the top lightly with flour. Then, using a heavy rolling pin, start at one end of the oblong and roll it out lengthwise away from yourself to within an inch or so of the farthest edge. Turn the dough crosswise and roll across its width. Repeat, turning and rolling the dough, until it is paper thin. If at any time the dough begins to stick, lift it carefully and sprinkle more flour under it.

To make *cannelloni* and *ravioli,* follow the cutting directions in those recipes (*pages 304 and 306*). To make *tagliarini, fettuccine, tagliatelle* and *lasagne,* dust the rolled dough lightly with flour and let it rest for about 10 minutes. Then gently roll the dough into a jelly-roll shape. With a long sharp knife, slice the roll crosswise into even strips—⅛ inch wide for *tagliarini,* ¼ inch wide for *fettuccine* or *tagliatelle,* and 1½ to 2 inches wide for *lasagne.* Unroll the strips and set them aside on wax paper. In the same fashion, roll, shape and slice the second half of the dough.

A PASTA MACHINE will do both the kneading and rolling. Pull off about a third of the dough at a time, set the smooth rolls of the pasta machine as far apart as possible and feed the piece of dough through them. Reroll this strip 4 or 5 more times, folding under the ragged edges and dusting the dough lightly with flour if it feels sticky. When the dough is smooth, shiny and elastic, it has been kneaded enough. Now start to roll it out, setting the machine to the second notch and feeding the dough through with the rolls closer together. Then set the machine at the third notch and roll the dough thinner. Repeat, changing the notch after each rolling, until the dough is about 1/16 inch thick.

To make *tagliarini,* feed the dough through the narrow cutting blades of the pasta machine; to make *fettuccine* or *tagliatelle,* feed it through the wide blades. For *lasagne,* roll the dough into a jelly-roll shape and cut it by hand into 1½- to 2-inch-wide strips.

Homemade egg noodles may be cooked at once or covered tightly with plastic wrap and kept in the refrigerator for as long as 24 hours. Cook them in 6 to 8 quarts of rapidly boiling salted water for 5 to 10 minutes, or until just tender. To test, lift out a strand and taste it.

Vegetables

Boiled Artichokes
Artichauts au Naturel

To serve 6

6 twelve- to fourteen-ounce artichokes

1 lemon, cut

6 quarts water

3 tablespoons salt

Trim the bases of the artichokes flush and flat. Bend and snap off the small bottom leaves and any bruised outer leaves. Lay each artichoke on its side, grip it firmly, and slice about 1 inch off the top. With scissors, trim ¼ inch off the points of the rest of the leaves. Rub all the cut edges with lemon to prevent discoloring. To remove the chokes before cooking,

Artichokes are a treat simply boiled and served hot with melted butter, as shown above, or cold with an oil-and-vinegar dressing. How to prepare an artichoke for cooking is shown in the photographs on the opposite page.

312

To trim an artichoke before cooking, use a sharp knife to cut an inch or so off the top cone of leaves.

Then, using kitchen scissors, clip the sharp point off each of the artichoke's large outer leaves.

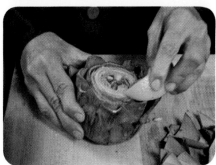

As you trim, rub all the cut edges of the leaves with lemon juice to prevent them from discoloring.

spread the top leaves apart and pull out the inner core of thistlelike yellow leaves. With a long-handled spoon, scrape out the hairy choke inside. Squeeze in a little lemon juice and press the artichoke back into shape.

In a large enameled kettle or soup pot, bring 6 quarts of water and 3 tablespoons of salt to a bubbling boil. Drop in the artichokes and return the water to a boil. Reduce the heat and boil briskly uncovered, turning the artichokes occasionally. It will take about 15 minutes to cook artichokes without their chokes, about 30 minutes with the chokes still in. They are done when their bases are tender when pierced with the tip of a sharp knife. Remove them from the kettle with tongs and drain them upside down in a colander. Serve the artichokes hot with melted butter or hollandaise sauce. Or chill the artichokes and serve cold with mayonnaise or oil-and-vinegar dressing.

Stuffed Artichoke Hearts
Fonds d'Artichauts Farcis

To serve 8

8 cooked or canned artichoke hearts	¼ cup minced onions
1½ teaspoons salt	¼ cup minced celery
½ teaspoon pepper	¼ cup minced carrots
6 tablespoons butter	1 cup chopped mushrooms

Scoop out the choke, or prickly center, of the artichoke hearts, then sprinkle the hearts with half the salt and pepper. Melt half the butter in a casserole. Add the artichokes and simmer them for 5 minutes, basting frequently.

Preheat the oven to 325°. Melt the remaining butter in a skillet and sauté the onions, celery, carrots and mushrooms for 8 minutes. Mix well, and season them with the remaining salt and pepper. Stuff the hearts with the sautéed vegetables. Return them to the casserole, cover with a piece of buttered wax paper, and bake for 20 minutes.

Buttered Green Beans
Haricots Verts au Naturel

To serve 6 to 8

	3 pounds green string beans, trimmed
	2 tablespoons butter
6 quarts water	Salt
3 tablespoons salt	Freshly ground black pepper

In a large kettle or soup pot, bring the water and 3 tablespoons of salt to a bubbling boil over high heat. Drop the beans in by the handful. Return the water to a boil, reduce the heat to moderate and boil the beans uncovered for 10 to 15 minutes, or until they are just tender. Do not overcook them. Immediately drain them in a large sieve or colander. If the beans are to be served at once, melt 2 tablespoons of butter in a 2- to 3-quart saucepan and toss the beans with the butter for a minute or two, season them with salt and pepper, then transfer them to a serving dish.

If the beans are to be served later, refresh them after they have drained by quickly plunging the sieve or colander into a large pot of cold water and letting it remain there for 2 or 3 minutes. Drain the beans thoroughly, place them in a bowl, cover and set aside—in the refrigerator if they are to wait for long. If you plan to serve them hot, reheat them in 2 tablespoons of hot butter, season them and let them warm through over moderate heat.

Green Beans in Tomato Sauce
Judías Verdes con Salsa de Tomate

To serve 4

1 teaspoon salt
1 pound fresh green string beans,
    trimmed and cut into 2-inch lengths
2 tablespoons olive oil
¼ cup finely chopped onions
1 teaspoon finely chopped garlic

4 medium-sized tomatoes, peeled,
    seeded and finely chopped, or
    substitute 1½ cups chopped,
    drained, canned tomatoes
1 tablespoon finely chopped parsley
2 teaspoons sugar
Freshly ground black pepper

In a heavy 3- to 4-quart saucepan, bring the salt and 2 quarts of water to a boil over high heat. Drop in the beans, a handful at a time. Bring to a boil again, reduce the heat to moderate and boil uncovered for 10 to 15 minutes until the beans are barely tender. Drain in a colander and set the beans aside.

Heat the olive oil in a heavy 10- to 12-inch skillet until a light haze forms above it. Add the onions and garlic and, stirring frequently, cook over moderate heat for 5 minutes, or until the onions are soft and transparent but not brown. Stir in the tomatoes, parsley, sugar and a few grindings of pepper, bring to a boil, and cook, uncovered, until most of the liquid evaporates and the mixture is thick enough to hold its shape lightly in a spoon.

Stir in the beans and simmer for a minute or two until they are heated through. Taste for seasoning and serve at once from a heated bowl.

String Beans with Water Chestnuts
Chao-ssŭ-chi-tou

To serve 4

1 pound fresh string beans
2 tablespoons peanut oil, or
    flavorless vegetable oil
1½ teaspoons salt
1 teaspoon sugar

10 water chestnuts, cut into ¼-inch
    slices
¼ cup chicken stock, fresh or canned
1 teaspoon cornstarch dissolved in 1
    tablespoon chicken stock, fresh or
    canned

PREPARE AHEAD: 1. Snap off and discard the ends of the beans, and, with a small knife, remove any strings. Cut the beans into 2-inch pieces.

2. Have the beans, oil, salt, sugar, water chestnuts, chicken stock and cornstarch mixture within easy reach.

TO COOK: Set a 12-inch wok or 10-inch skillet over high heat for 30 seconds. Pour in the 2 tablespoons of oil, swirl it about in the pan and heat for another 30 seconds, turning the heat down to moderate if the oil begins to smoke. Drop in the string beans and stir-fry for 3 minutes. Add

315

the salt, sugar and water chestnuts, and stir once or twice before pouring in the stock. Cover the pan and cook over moderate heat for 2 to 3 minutes until the beans are tender but still crisp. Now give the cornstarch mixture a stir to recombine it and add it to the pan. Cook, stirring, until the vegetables are coated with a light, clear glaze. Transfer the entire contents of the pan to a heated platter and serve at once.

Fava Beans with Sausage and Mint
Habas a la Catalana

To serve 4 to 6

1 pound *chorizos,* or other garlic-seasoned smoked pork sausage	1 tablespoon finely cut fresh mint
1 tablespoon lard	1 small bay leaf, crumbled
¼ pound salt pork, finely diced	½ teaspoon salt
½ cup finely chopped scallions	Freshly ground black pepper
1 teaspoon finely chopped garlic	4 cups cooked, fresh fava beans or substitute drained, canned favas or frozen baby lima beans
½ cup dry white wine	
½ cup water	2 tablespoons finely chopped parsley

Place the sausages in an 8- to 10-inch skillet and prick them in two or three places with the point of a small, sharp knife. Add enough cold water to cover them completely and bring to a boil over high heat. Reduce the heat to low and simmer uncovered for 5 minutes. Drain on paper towels, then slice the sausages into ¼-inch-thick rounds.

In a heavy 3- to 4-quart casserole, melt the lard over moderate heat. Add the salt pork and, stirring frequently, cook until the pieces have rendered all their fat and become crisp and golden brown. With a slotted spoon, transfer them to paper towels to drain.

Add the scallions and garlic to the fat in the pan and cook for about 5 minutes, or until the scallions are soft but not brown. Pour in the wine and water and add the sliced sausages, pork dice, mint, bay leaf, salt and a few grindings of pepper. Bring to a boil over high heat, reduce the heat to low and simmer partially covered for 20 minutes.

Add the beans and parsley and simmer uncovered, stirring frequently, for about 10 minutes longer, or until the beans are heated through.

Taste the *habas a la catalana* for seasoning and serve at once from a heated bowl or a deep heated platter.

White Beans with Tomatoes and Garlic

Fagioli all'Uccelletto

To serve 4 to 6

3 cups canned *cannellini* or other
    white beans (1½ one-pound
    cans); or 1½ cups dry white
    kidney, marrow, Great Northern or
    navy beans and 1½ quarts water
¼ cup olive oil

1 teaspoon finely chopped garlic
¼ teaspoon sage leaves, crumbled
2 large ripe tomatoes, peeled, seeded,
    gently squeezed of excess juice,
    and coarsely chopped
½ teaspoon salt
Freshly ground black pepper
1 tablespoon wine vinegar

If you are using dry beans, combine them with the water in a 3- to 4-quart saucepan and bring them to a boil over high heat. Boil briskly for 2 minutes, remove the pan from the heat and let the beans soak for 1 hour. Now bring the water to a boil again, turn the heat down to low, and simmer the beans for 1 to 1½ hours, or until they are tender; drain and set aside. If you are using canned beans, drain them in a large sieve or colander, wash them under cold running water, then set them aside in the sieve or colander.

In a heavy 8- to 10-inch skillet, heat the oil until a light haze forms over it. Add the garlic and sage and cook, stirring, for 30 seconds. Stir in the drained beans, tomatoes, salt and a few grindings of pepper. Cover and simmer over low heat for 10 minutes. Taste for seasoning, then stir in the vinegar. Serve in a heated bowl or on a deep platter.

Boston Baked Beans

To serve 6 to 8

4 cups dried pea or Great Northern
    beans
2 teaspoons salt
2 medium-sized whole onions, peeled
4 cloves

½ cup molasses
1 cup brown sugar
2 teaspoons dry mustard
1 teaspoon black pepper
2 cups water
½ pound salt pork, scored

Put the beans in a large saucepan and pour in enough cold water to cover them by at least 2 inches. Bring to a boil, let boil for 2 minutes, then let the beans soak in the water off the heat for about 1 hour. Bring them to a boil again, add 1 teaspoon of the salt, half cover the pan and simmer the beans as slowly as possible for about 30 minutes, or until they are partially done. Drain the beans and discard the bean water.

Preheat the oven to 250°. To bake the beans, choose a traditional 4-quart bean pot or a heavy casserole with a tight-fitting cover. Place 2 onions, each stuck with 2 cloves, in the bottom of the bean pot or casserole and cover with the beans. In a small mixing bowl, combine the molasses, ¾ cup of the brown sugar, mustard, and 1 teaspoon each of salt and black pepper. Slowly stirring with a large spoon, pour in the 2 cups of water.

Pour this mixture over the beans and push the salt pork slightly beneath the surface. Cover tightly and bake in the center of the oven for 4½ to 5 hours. Then remove the cover and sprinkle with the remaining ¼ cup of brown sugar. Bake the beans uncovered for another ½ hour and serve.

Refried Beans
Frijoles Refritos

To serve 4 to 6

2 cups dried pink beans or dried red
   kidney beans
6 cups cold water
1 cup coarsely chopped onions
2 medium tomatoes, peeled,
   seeded and coarsely
   chopped, or substitute ⅔
   cup chopped, drained, canned

Italian plum tomatoes
½ teaspoon finely chopped garlic
1 teaspoon crumbled and seeded dried
   pequín chili
¼ teaspoon crumbled *epazote*, if
   available
¼ teaspoon freshly ground black
   pepper
½ cup lard
1 teaspoon salt

NOTE: Wear rubber gloves when handling the hot chilies.

Place the beans in a colander or sieve and run cold water over them until the draining water runs clear. Pick out and discard any black or shriveled beans. In a 3-quart heavy pot, combine the water, ½ cup of the onions, ¼ cup of the tomatoes, ¼ teaspoon of the garlic, the chili, *epazote* (if used) and pepper, and drop in the beans. Bring the water to a boil over high heat, then half-cover the pan and reduce the heat to low. Simmer the beans for about 15 minutes and stir in 1 tablespoon of the lard. Simmer, half covered, for 1½ hours, add the teaspoon of salt, and over the lowest possible heat, simmer for another 30 minutes, or until the beans are very tender and have absorbed all their cooking liquid. During the last half hour of cooking, stir the beans gently now and then to prevent their sticking to the bottom of the pan. Remove the pan from the heat, and cover it to keep the beans warm.

In a heavy 12-inch skillet, melt 2 more tablespoons of the lard over moderate heat until a light haze forms above it. Add the remaining chopped onions and garlic, turn the heat down to moderate, and fry for about 5 minutes, or until the onions are transparent but not brown. Stir in the remaining tomatoes and simmer for 2 or 3 minutes. Fry the cooked beans in the following fashion: Add 3 tablespoons of the beans to the pan of simmering sauce, mash them with a fork, then stir in 1 tablespoon of the remaining lard. Continue adding and mashing the beans in similar amounts, following each addition with another tablespoon of lard until all the beans and lard have been used. Cook over low heat for 10 minutes, stirring frequently, until the beans are fairly dry.

To serve, transfer the beans to a serving bowl or individual dishes. *Frijoles refritos* are a traditional accompaniment to tortilla dishes.

Broccoli Braised in White Wine
Broccoli alla Romana

To serve 4 to 6

¼ cup olive oil	(about 2 pounds fresh broccoli with stems)
1 teaspoon finely chopped garlic	1½ cups dry white wine
5 to 6 cups fresh broccoli flowerets	½ teaspoon salt
	Freshly ground black pepper

In a heavy 10- to 12-inch skillet, heat the olive oil until a light haze forms over it. Remove the pan from the heat and stir the garlic in the hot oil for 30 seconds. Return to moderate heat and toss the broccoli flowerets in the oil until they glisten. Add the wine, salt and a few grindings of pepper and simmer uncovered, stirring occasionally, for 5 minutes. Then cover the skillet and simmer for another 15 minutes, or until the broccoli is tender. To serve, quickly transfer the flowerets with a slotted spoon to a heated bowl or deep platter. Briskly boil the liquid left in the skillet over high heat until it has reduced to about ½ cup and pour it over the broccoli.

Brussels Sprouts with Chestnuts

1 pound chestnuts	2 teaspoons potato flour
2 tablespoons butter	1 cup light stock
2 tablespoons sherry	1 bay leaf
1 teaspoon meat extract	1 pound Brussels sprouts
1 teaspoon tomato paste	Lemon juice

Cover the chestnuts with cold water, bring to a boil, and boil them for 2 to 3 minutes. Drain, shell and skin them. Heat the butter in a skillet and brown the chestnuts quickly. Pour the sherry over the nuts, then remove them from the pan. Add to the pan juices the meat extract, the tomato paste and the potato flour, then pour in the light stock. Stir over the heat until it is boiling, then return the nuts to the pan and add the bay leaf. Simmer gently until the chestnuts are just soft.

In the meantime, boil the Brussels sprouts in salted water with lemon juice added. Drain the sprouts when they are just tender, mix them with the chestnuts, and serve immediately in a heated casserole.

Cabbage in Sweet-and-Sour Sauce
Cavoli in Agrodolce

terrible

To serve 4 to 6

3 tablespoons olive oil
½ cup thinly sliced onions
1½ pounds cabbage, cut into ¼-inch
    strips (about 8 cups)

3 large tomatoes, peeled, seeded and
    coarsely chopped
2 tablespoons wine vinegar
2 teaspoons salt
Freshly ground black pepper
1 tablespoon sugar

Heat the olive oil in a heavy 10- to 12-inch skillet, add the onions and cook them over moderate heat, stirring constantly, for 2 or 3 minutes. When they are transparent but not brown, stir in the cabbage, tomatoes, vinegar, salt and a few grindings of pepper. Simmer uncovered, stirring frequently, for 20 minutes, or until the cabbage is tender. Then stir the sugar into the cabbage and cook a minute or 2 longer.

Braised Red Cabbage
Rødkaal

To serve 6

1 medium head red cabbage, 2 to
    2½ pounds
4 tablespoons butter, cut into small
    pieces

1 tablespoon sugar
1 teaspoon salt
⅓ cup water
⅓ cup white vinegar
¼ cup red currant jelly
2 tablespoons grated apple

Wash the head of cabbage under cold running water, remove the tough outer leaves, and cut the cabbage in half from top to bottom. Lay the flat sides down on the chopping board, cut away the core and slice the cabbage very finely. There should be approximately 9 cups of shredded cabbage when you finish.

Preheat the oven to 325°. Combine the butter, sugar, salt, water and vinegar in a heavy stainless-steel or enameled 4- to 5-quart casserole. When it comes to a boil and the butter has melted, add the shredded cabbage and toss thoroughly with two wooden spoons or forks. Bring to a boil again, cover tightly and place in the center of the oven to braise for 2 hours. There
320

is little danger that the cabbage will dry out during the cooking, but it is a good idea to check on the liquid level occasionally. Add a little water if it seems necessary.

About 10 minutes before the cabbage is finished, stir in the jelly and grated apple, replace the cover and complete the cooking.

The piquant taste of red cabbage will improve if, after it has cooled, it is allowed to rest for a day in the refrigerator and then reheated either on top of the stove or in a 325° oven.

Glazed Carrots
Carottes Glacées

To serve 4 to 6

	4 tablespoons butter
10 to 12 medium carrots, peeled and cut in 2-inch cylinders or olive shapes	2 tablespoons sugar
	½ teaspoon salt
	Freshly ground black pepper
1½ cups beef or chicken stock, fresh or canned	2 tablespoons finely chopped, fresh parsley

In a heavy 8- to 10-inch skillet, bring the carrots, stock, butter, sugar, salt and a few grindings of pepper to a boil over moderate heat. Then cover and simmer over low heat, shaking the skillet occasionally to roll the carrots about in the liquid. Check to see that the liquid is not cooking away too fast; if it is, add more stock. In 20 to 30 minutes the carrots should be tender when pierced with the tip of a sharp knife, and the braising liquid should be a brown, syrupy glaze. If the stock has not reduced enough, remove the carrots to a plate and boil the liquid down over high heat. Before serving, roll the carrots around in the pan to coat them with the glaze. Transfer the carrots to a heated vegetable dish, and sprinkle them with fresh parsley.

NOTE: This technique may also be used for parsnips and for white and yellow turnips.

Cauliflower with Garlic Sauce

Coliflor al Ajo Arriero

To serve 4 to 6

A 1- to 1½-pound head of
  cauliflower, trimmed and separated
  into florets
Salt
Vegetable oil or shortening for deep
  frying
White pepper
½ cup flour
2 eggs, lightly beaten
¾ cup soft fresh crumbs made from

French or Italian bread, trimmed
  of crusts and pulverized in a
  blender or pulled apart with a
  fork
6 tablespoons olive oil
2 garlic cloves, peeled and lightly
  bruised with the flat of a knife
1 tablespoon paprika
2 tablespoons white vinegar
3 tablespoons boiling water

Drop the cauliflower florets into enough lightly salted boiling water to cover them by at least 1 inch. Cook briskly uncovered for 8 to 10 minutes, or until the cauliflower shows only the slightest resistance when pierced with the point of a small, sharp knife. Drain on paper towels.

Heat 3 to 4 inches of vegetable oil or shortening in a deep-fat fryer or large, heavy saucepan until it reaches 350° on a deep-frying thermometer. Sprinkle the florets liberally with salt and a little white pepper, dip them in the flour and shake vigorously to remove the excess. Then dip them in the beaten eggs and into the crumbs. Turning them with tongs, deep-fry the florets (in two batches if necessary) for about 4 minutes, or until they are golden brown. Drain on paper towels. Then arrange them on a heated platter and drape with foil to keep them warm.

In a 6- to 8-inch skillet, heat the 6 tablespoons of olive oil over low heat until a light haze forms above it. Drop in the garlic cloves and, stirring constantly, cook for 2 or 3 minutes. Then remove them with a slotted spoon. Add the paprika, vinegar and water to the oil and, stirring constantly, cook for a minute or so. Then pour over the cauliflower, turn the florets about with a spoon to coat them evenly and serve at once.

Puréed Corn with Scallions and Peppers
Humitas

To serve 4 to 6

4 cups fresh corn kernels, cut from about 8 large ears of corn, or substitute 4 cups thoroughly defrosted frozen corn kernels
1/3 cup milk
2 eggs
2 teaspoons paprika
1/2 teaspoon salt
Freshly ground black pepper
1/4 cup butter
1/2 cup coarsely chopped scallions
1/4 cup coarsely chopped green pepper
1/3 cup freshly grated Parmesan cheese

Combine the corn and milk in the jar of a blender and blend at high speed for 30 seconds. Add the eggs, paprika, salt and a few grindings of black pepper and blend for 15 seconds longer, or until the mixture is thick and smooth.

(To make the corn mixture by hand, purée the corn through a food mill set over a bowl. Discard the pulp left in the mill. Add the milk, eggs, paprika, salt and pepper, and mix vigorously with a spoon or whisk until the mixture is thick and smooth.)

In a heavy 10-inch skillet, melt the butter over moderate heat. When the foam subsides, add the scallions and green pepper, and cook, stirring, for 4 or 5 minutes, or until the vegetables are soft but not brown. Pour in the corn mixture, reduce the heat, and simmer, uncovered, stirring frequently, for 5 to 7 minutes, or until the mixture thickens somewhat. Stir in the grated cheese and, as soon as it melts, remove the skillet from the heat. Serve as an accompaniment to meat dishes.

Cucumbers with Sour Cream and Dill
Schmorgurken mit saurem Rahm und Dill

To serve 6

6 medium-sized firm, fresh cucumbers (about 3 pounds)
2 teaspoons salt
2 tablespoons butter
1/2 cup finely chopped onions
2 tablespoons flour
2 cups milk
2 tablespoons sour cream
1 tablespoon finely chopped fresh parsley
1 tablespoon finely chopped fresh dill, or substitute 1 teaspoon dried dill weed

With a small, sharp knife, peel the cucumbers and cut them in half lengthwise. Seed them by running the tip of a small spoon down them, from end to end. Cut the cucumber halves crosswise into 1-inch pieces and place them in a large bowl. Sprinkle them with salt, tossing them about with a spoon to spread it evenly. Let the cucumbers stand at room temperature for 30 minutes, then drain off all the liquid and pat them dry with paper towels. In a heavy 10- to 12-inch skillet, melt the butter over moderate heat. When the foam subsides, add the onions and cook, stirring frequently, for 8 to 10 minutes, or until they color lightly. Add the flour and cook, stirring constantly, until the flour turns a golden brown. Watch for any sign of burning and regulate the heat accordingly. Pour in the milk and, stirring constantly, bring to a boil. Reduce the heat to low and simmer for 1 or 2 minutes, until the mixture thickens slightly. Add the cucumbers and simmer, uncovered, for 15 minutes. When the cucumbers are tender but not pulpy, add the sour cream, parsley and dill. Taste for seasoning. Serve in a heated bowl.

Stuffed Cucumbers
Gefüllte Gurken

To serve 6 to 8

2 cucumbers, 6 to 8 inches long	2 teaspoons finely chopped onions
½ teaspoon salt	2 tablespoons minced sour pickles
2 boneless sardines	1 teaspoon prepared French mustard
¼ pound boiled ham, diced	2 to 4 tablespoons mayonnaise,
2 hard-cooked eggs, coarsely	freshly made or a good commercial
chopped	brand

Cut ½ inch off the tip of each cucumber, then peel the cucumbers with a vegetable scraper or sharp knife. Cut out the seeds and center pulp with a long iced-tea spoon, leaving a shell about ¼ inch thick. Pour ¼ teaspoon of salt into each cucumber, rubbing it in evenly with your forefinger, let the shells stand about 15 minutes, then dry them inside with a piece of paper towel.

In a medium-sized mixing bowl, mash the sardines to a paste with a fork or wooden spoon. Add the ham, eggs, onions, pickles, mustard and 2 tablespoons of mayonnaise. Stir the ingredients together until the mixture holds its shape in a spoon. (If it seems too dry, add more mayonnaise.) Taste for seasoning. The amount of salt needed will depend on the saltiness of the sardines and ham.

Stuff the cucumbers by standing them on end and spooning the filling in, tamping it down with a spoon as you proceed. When they are all tightly packed, wrap them separately in wax paper or aluminum foil and refrigerate them for 2 hours, or until the filling is firm.

To serve, slice the cucumbers crosswise, on a slant, in slices about ½ inch thick.

Eggplant, Tomato and Chick-Pea Casserole
Musakka'a

To serve 6

1½ cups dried chick-peas,
  or substitute canned chick-peas
Olive oil
2 medium-sized eggplants, about 1
  pound each, washed but not
  peeled, and cut into 2-inch cubes
3 medium-sized onions, peeled and

cut into ¼-inch-thick slices
3 teaspoons salt
Freshly ground black pepper
12 medium-sized fresh, ripe
  tomatoes, peeled, seeded and
  finely chopped, or substitute 4 cups
  chopped, drained, canned
  tomatoes
1½ cups water

NOTE: Starting a day ahead, wash the dried chick-peas in a sieve under cold running water, then place them in a large bowl or pan and add enough cold water to cover them by 2 inches. Soak at room temperature for at least 12 hours. Drain the peas and place them in a heavy 2- to 3-quart saucepan.

Add enough fresh water to the chick-peas to cover them completely and bring to a boil over high heat. Reduce the heat to low and simmer partially covered for about 2 to 2½ hours until the peas are tender but still intact. Replenish with more boiling water from time to time if necessary. Drain the peas in a sieve or colander. (Canned chick-peas require no cooking and need only to be drained and rinsed thoroughly under cold running water.)

Preheat the oven to 400°. In a heavy 12-inch skillet, heat about 1 inch of oil over high heat almost to the smoking point. Drop in the eggplant cubes and, stirring frequently, cook for about 5 minutes, or until they are lightly browned on all sides. With a slotted spoon, transfer them to a 9-by-14-by-2½-inch baking-serving dish and spread them out evenly.

Add the onions to the oil remaining in the skillet and, stirring frequently, cook over moderate heat for 8 to 10 minutes, or until they are soft and delicately browned. Watch carefully for any signs of burning and regulate the heat accordingly.

Spread the onions and all of their cooking oil on top of the eggplant and pour over them an additional ½ cup of olive oil. Sprinkle the onions with 1 teaspoon of the salt and a few grindings of pepper. Scatter the chick-peas on top, and cover them with the tomatoes. Sprinkle with the remaining 2 teaspoons of salt and a few grindings of pepper and pour in the water.

Bring the *musakka'a* to a boil on top of the stove, then bake in the lower third of the oven for 40 minutes, or until the vegetables are very tender. Cool to room temperature and serve directly from the baking dish.

Eggplant with Cheese
Parmigiana di Melanzane

To serve 4

1½ pounds eggplant, peeled and cut in ½-inch slices
Salt
Flour

¼ to ½ cup olive oil
2 cups tomato sauce (*page 343*)
8 ounces *mozzarella* cheese, thinly sliced
½ cup freshly grated imported Parmesan cheese

Preheat the oven to 400°. Choose a shallow 1½- to 2-quart baking dish that is attractive enough to serve from and rub it with oil.

Sprinkle both sides of the eggplant slices with salt (to draw out their moisture) and spread them out in one layer on a platter or board. After 20 to 30 minutes, pat the eggplant dry with paper towels. Dip each slice in flour and shake or brush off the excess.

In a heavy 10- to 12-inch skillet, heat ¼ cup of olive oil until a light haze forms over it and brown the eggplant slices a few at a time, working quickly to prevent them from soaking up too much oil. If the oil cooks away, add more. As the eggplant browns, transfer the slices to fresh paper towels to drain.

Now pour ¼ inch of the tomato sauce into the oiled baking-and-serving dish. Spread the drained eggplant slices over the sauce, top them with a layer of *mozzarella* cheese, and sprinkle over it part of the grated Parmesan cheese. Repeat with 1 or 2 more layers (depending on the capacity of the baking dish), but be sure to finish up with layers of the tomato sauce, *mozzarella* and Parmesan. Cover the dish snugly with foil and bake in the middle of the oven for 20 minutes. Remove the foil and bake uncovered for 10 minutes longer.

Kale in Cream Sauce
Grønlangkaal

To serve 6 to 8

1 pound kale
2 teaspoons salt
4 tablespoons butter

4 tablespoons flour
1 cup milk
1 cup heavy cream
½ teaspoon freshly ground black pepper

Discard the tough outer stalks of the kale and wash the leaves carefully under cold running water, shaking to remove any sand. Shake the kale again to remove excess water, and tear it into large pieces. Place the kale in a 4- to 6-quart saucepan with ½ teaspoon of the salt and just enough cold water to barely cover it. Cook, tightly covered, over medium heat for about 15 minutes, or until the kale is very tender (test by tasting a leaf). Drain the kale through a sieve, pressing down on the vegetable with a large spoon to extract all of the moisture. Then chop very fine.

In a heavy 2- to 3-quart saucepan, prepare the following sauce. Melt the butter over medium heat; remove the pan from the heat and stir in the flour. Now add the milk and cream all at once, beating vigorously with a wire whisk. Return the pan to low heat and cook, whisking constantly, until the sauce comes to a boil and is smooth and thick. Add the remaining salt, pepper and the chopped kale, taste for seasoning if necessary and cook for another 1 or 2 minutes, or until the kale is heated through.

Mushrooms and Onions in Sour Cream

To serve 4 to 6

4 tablespoons butter
2 medium onions, thinly sliced
1 pound fresh mushrooms, 1 to 1½ inches in diameter

1 cup sour cream
1 teaspoon lemon juice
1 teaspoon salt
Freshly ground black pepper
2 teaspoons finely chopped fresh parsley

In a heavy 10-inch skillet, melt the butter over medium heat. When the foam subsides, add the onions and cook for 6 to 8 minutes until they are lightly colored. Stir in the mushrooms, cover the pan and cook, still over moderate heat, for about 7 minutes. Add the sour cream, lemon juice, salt and a few grindings of pepper; simmer, stirring, until the cream is heated through. Don't let it boil. Taste for seasoning and sprinkle with chopped parsley.

Mushrooms with Tomatoes and Bacon
Pilze mit Tomaten und Speck

To serve 4

1 pound fresh mushrooms
2 tablespoons butter
½ cup finely diced lean bacon
½ cup finely chopped onions

½ teaspoon salt
Freshly ground black pepper
3 medium-sized tomatoes, peeled, seeded and coarsely chopped
2 tablespoons finely chopped fresh parsley

Cut away any tough ends of the mushroom stems. Wipe the mushrooms with a damp paper towel, and cut them, stems and all, into ⅛-inch slices.

In a heavy 10- to 12-inch skillet, melt the butter over moderate heat.

When the foam subsides, add the bacon and cook, stirring frequently, until the bacon is crisp and light brown. Add the onions and cook, stirring frequently, for 5 minutes, or until the onions are soft and transparent but not brown. Then drop in the mushrooms and season with salt and a few grindings of pepper. Cook over high heat, turning the mushrooms frequently, for 3 or 4 minutes.

When the mushrooms are lightly colored, stir in the chopped tomatoes and simmer over low heat for about 10 minutes.

If there are more than 2 or 3 tablespoons of liquid left in the pan, increase the heat and boil briskly for a minute or so to reduce the excess. Then add the parsley and taste for seasoning. Serve at once from a heated bowl.

Peas Portuguese
Ervilhas Guisadas à Portuguésa

To serve 2 to 4

2 tablespoons butter	¼ cup finely chopped fresh coriander leaves
½ cup finely chopped onions	½ teaspoon sugar
¾ cup chicken stock, fresh or canned	Salt
3 cups cooked fresh green peas (about 3 pounds), or substitute 3 ten-ounce packages frozen peas, thoroughly defrosted but not cooked	Freshly ground black pepper
	4 ounces *linguiça* or *chorizo* (or substitute other garlic-seasoned smoked pork sausage), cut into ¼ inch slices
¼ cup finely chopped parsley	4 eggs

In a heavy 10-inch skillet or shallow flameproof casserole, melt the butter over moderate heat. When the foam has almost subsided, add the onions and, stirring frequently, cook for 8 to 10 minutes, or until they are lightly colored. Stir in the stock, freshly cooked or frozen peas, parsley, coriander, sugar, ¼ teaspoon of salt and a few grindings of pepper and overlap the sausage slices around the edge of the skillet. Bring to a boil over high heat, then reduce the heat to low, cover and simmer for 5 minutes.

Break 1 egg into a saucer and, holding the dish close to the pan, slide the egg on top of the peas. One at a time, slide the other eggs into the pan, keeping them well apart. Sprinkle them lightly with salt and pepper. Cover the skillet and cook for 3 or 4 minutes until the egg yolks are covered with an opaque film and the whites are set. Serve at once, directly from the skillet.

328

Braised Peas with Prosciutto
Piselli al Prosciutto

To serve 4

4 tablespoons butter
¼ cup finely chopped onions
2 cups fresh green peas (about 2
    pounds unshelled)

¼ cup chicken stock, fresh or canned
2 ounces prosciutto, cut in 1-by-¼-inch
    julienne strips (about ¼ cup)
Salt
Freshly ground black pepper

In a heavy 1- to 2-quart saucepan, melt the 2 tablespoons of butter over moderate heat and cook the finely chopped onions for 7 or 8 minutes, stirring frequently until they are soft but not brown. Stir in the green peas and chicken stock, cover, and cook for 15 to 20 minutes. When the peas are tender, add the strips of prosciutto and cook, uncovered, stirring frequently, for 2 minutes more, or until all the liquid is absorbed. Taste for seasoning. Serve the peas in a heated bowl.

Fresh Peas with Onions and Lettuce
Petits Pois Frais à la Française

To serve 4 to 6

1 firm 7- to 8-inch head Boston
    lettuce
3 cups fresh shelled green peas (about
    3 pounds)
12 peeled white onions, about ¾ inch
    in diameter

6 parsley sprigs, tied together
6 tablespoons butter, cut into ½-inch
    pieces
½ cup water
½ teaspoon salt
½ teaspoon sugar
2 tablespoons soft butter

Remove the wilted outer leaves of the lettuce and trim the stem. Rinse the lettuce in cold water, spreading the leaves apart gently, to remove all traces of sand. Cut the lettuce into 4 or 6 wedges, and bind each wedge with soft string to keep it in shape while cooking.

    In a heavy 3-quart saucepan, bring the peas, lettuce wedges, onions, parsley, 6 tablespoons butter, water, salt and sugar to a boil over moderate heat, toss lightly to mix flavors, then cover the pan tightly and cook for 30 minutes, stirring occasionally, until the peas and onions are tender and the liquid nearly cooked away. If the liquid hasn't evaporated, cook the peas uncovered, shaking the pan constantly, for a minute or two until it does. Remove the parsley and cut the strings off the lettuce. Gently stir in 2 tablespoons of soft butter; taste and season. Transfer to a heated vegetable dish and serve in small bowls.

Italian Stuffed Peppers

Peperoni Imbottiti

To serve 8

Olive oil
4 tablespoons butter
3 cups fresh white bread crumbs
    (preferably French or
    Italian bread)
2 teaspoons finely chopped garlic
1 two-ounce can flat anchovy fillets,
    rinsed in cold water, dried and
    finely chopped

6 tablespoons capers, rinsed in cold
    water and finely chopped
8 black olives (preferably
    Mediterranean style), stoned and
    finely chopped
4 tablespoons finely chopped parsley,
    preferably the flat-leaf Italian type
Salt
Freshly ground black pepper
4 large green peppers, cut in half
    lengthwise, piths and seeds removed

Preheat the oven to 400°. Pour 2 tablespoons of olive oil into a shallow baking dish large enough to hold the green pepper halves comfortably. Tip the dish back and forth to spread the oil evenly across the bottom.

In a heavy 8- to 10-inch skillet, melt the butter over moderate heat. When the foam subsides, add the bread crumbs and cook them, stirring constantly, until they are crisp and lightly browned. Remove the skillet from the heat and stir in the garlic. Then add the anchovies, capers, black olives and parsley and mix well. Taste and season with salt and pepper. If the stuffing mixture looks too dry and crumbly, moisten it with a little olive oil. Spoon the stuffing into the pepper halves and arrange them in the oiled baking dish. Dribble a few drops of oil over the top of each pepper. Bake in the middle of the oven for about 30 minutes, or until the peppers are tender but not limp and the stuffing is lightly browned on top. Serve hot or cold.

Sweet Peppers with Tomatoes and Onions

Peperonata

To serve 6

2 tablespoons butter
¼ cup olive oil
1 pound onions, sliced ⅛ inch thick
    (about 4 cups)
2 pounds green and red peppers,
    peeled by blanching first, seeded

and cut in 1-by-½-inch strips
    (about 6 cups)
2 pounds tomatoes, peeled, seeded
    and coarsely chopped (about
    3 cups)
1 teaspoon red wine vinegar
1 teaspoon salt
Freshly ground black pepper

In a heavy 12-inch skillet, melt the 2 tablespoons of butter with the ¼ cup of olive oil over moderate heat. Add the onions and cook them, turning them frequently, for 10 minutes, or until they are soft and lightly browned. Stir in the peppers, reduce the heat, cover the skillet and cook for 10 minutes. Add the tomatoes, vinegar, salt and a few grindings of black pepper; cover and cook for another 5 minutes. Then cook the vegetables uncovered over high heat, stirring gently, until almost all the liquid has boiled away.

Serve the *peperonata* as a hot vegetable dish, preceding or along with the main course, or refrigerate it and serve it cold as part of an *antipasto* or as an accompaniment to cold roast meats or fowl.

Butter-steamed New Potatoes
Smørdampete Nypoteter

To serve 4 to 6

	unsalted butter
20 to 24 tiny new potatoes	1 teaspoon salt
(about 1 inch in diameter)	⅛ teaspoon white pepper
8 tablespoons (1 quarter-pound stick)	3 tablespoons finely chopped fresh dill

Scrub the potatoes under cold running water; then pat them thoroughly dry with paper towels. Melt the ¼ pound of butter in a heavy, 6-quart casserole equipped with a cover. Add the potatoes and sprinkle them with salt and pepper. Then coat them thoroughly with the melted butter by rolling them about in the casserole. To ensure the success of this dish, the cover must fit the casserole tightly; if you have doubts, cover the casserole with a double thickness of aluminum foil, and pinch down the edges to seal it before putting on the lid. Cook over low heat (an asbestos pad under the pan ensures against scorching) for 30 to 45 minutes, depending on the size of the potatoes. Shake the casserole from time to time to prevent the potatoes from sticking. When the potatoes can be easily pierced with the tip of a sharp knife, they are done. Arrange them on a heated serving plate, sprinkle them with the chopped dill, and serve at once.

Roasted Potatoes
Hasselbackpotatis

To serve 6

6 baking potatoes, about 4 inches long and 2 inches wide	1 teaspoon salt
	2 tablespoons dry bread crumbs
1 tablespoon soft butter	2 tablespoons grated imported
3 tablespoons melted butter	Parmesan cheese (optional)

Preheat the oven to 425°. Peel the potatoes and drop them into a bowl of cold water to prevent them from discoloring. Place one potato at a time on a wooden spoon large enough to cradle it comfortably, and beginning at about ½ inch from the end, slice down at ⅛-inch intervals. (The deep, curved bowl of the wooden spoon will prevent the knife from slicing completely through the potato.) Drop each semisliced potato back into the cold water.

When you are ready to roast them, drain the potatoes and pat them dry with paper towels. With a pastry brush or paper towels, generously butter a baking dish large enough to hold the potatoes side by side in one layer and arrange them in it cut side up. Baste the potatoes with 1½ tablespoons of the melted butter, sprinkle them liberally with salt, and set them in the center of the oven. After 30 minutes sprinkle a few of the bread crumbs over the surface of each potato, baste with the remaining melted butter and the butter in the pan, and continue to roast another 15 minutes, or until the potatoes are golden brown and show no resistance when pierced with the tip of a sharp knife. If you wish to use the cheese, it should be strewn over the potatoes 5 minutes before they are done.

Roasted Potato Wedges
Brynt Potatis i Ugn

To serve 4 to 6

	4 tablespoons melted butter
4 medium-sized baking potatoes	Salt

Preheat the oven to 450°. Peel the potatoes and cut them in half lengthwise. Stand each half upright on a chopping board and slice it in thirds down its length, making 3 wedge-shaped pieces. Blanch the wedges by cooking them rapidly for 3 minutes in enough unsalted boiling water to cover them. Drain and pat them dry with paper towels.

With a pastry brush or paper towels, butter a baking dish large enough to hold the potatoes side by side in a single layer. Dribble melted butter over the tops and sprinkle them liberally with salt. Roast them in the center of the oven for 15 minutes, turn them, and roast another 15 minutes.

These crisp potato wedges make excellent accompaniments to roasted meats or poultry.

Sautéed Potato Balls
Pommes de Terre Noisette

To serve 6 to 8

	6 tablespoons butter
3 pounds potatoes	1 teaspoon salt
3 tablespoons oil	1 tablespoon minced parsley

Peel and wash the potatoes. With the small end of a melon ball cutter, scoop them into little balls. Heat the oil and half the butter in a skillet. When the foam subsides add the potato balls and cook them over medium heat until they are light gold in color, shaking the pan frequently. Add the salt, then cover and cook over low heat for 10 minutes, or until the potatoes are tender, shaking the pan a few times. Add the parsley and the remaining butter, shaking the pan until the butter melts. Serve at once.

Portuguese Fried Potatoes
Batatas à Portuguêsa

To serve 4

	and sliced into ¼-inch-thick rounds
3 tablespoons butter	½ teaspoon salt
3 tablespoons olive oil	Freshly ground black pepper
1½ pounds new potatoes, peeled	1 tablespoon finely chopped parsley

In a heavy 10- to 12-inch skillet, melt the butter in the olive oil over moderate heat. When the foam begins to subside, add the potatoes. Turning them frequently with a metal spatula, cook for 15 minutes or until they are tender and golden brown. Season with salt and a few grindings of pepper, then transfer the potatoes to a heated bowl or platter and serve at once, sprinkled with parsley if you like.

Deep-Fried Straw Potatoes

Kartoplia Solimkoi

To serve 4 to 6

4 medium-sized baking potatoes (about 2 pounds)

Vegetable oil for deep-frying
Salt

Peel the potatoes and cut them into straw-shaped strips, about 2½ inches long and ⅛ inch thick. Drop them into a bowl of ice water and set them aside until ready to fry. Drain the potatoes in a colander, spread them out on a double thickness of paper towels and pat them thoroughly dry.

Pour enough oil into a deep fryer to come 3 or 4 inches up the sides of the pan. For the first frying of the potatoes (there will be two in all), heat the oil until it reaches a temperature of 370° on a deep-frying thermometer. Drop the potatoes into the frying basket and immerse the basket in the hot oil, shaking it gently from time to time to prevent the potatoes from sticking together. Fry them for about 15 seconds, or until the potatoes are tender and a pale golden brown. Drain on a double thickness of paper towels, then fry and drain the remaining potatoes similarly. The potatoes may now rest for as long as an hour before refrying and serving.

Immediately before serving, reheat the oil until it reaches a temperature of 385° on a deep-frying thermometer. Drop all the potatoes into the basket and, shaking the basket occasionally, fry for 15 seconds, or until the potatoes are crisp and brown. Drain on paper towels and transfer to a large platter or bowl. Sprinkle lightly with salt, and serve at once.

Game Chips

To serve 4 to 6

4 cups vegetable oil or shortening
6 medium-sized baking potatoes

(about 2 pounds), peeled
2 teaspoons salt

Preheat the oven to 250°. Line a jelly-roll pan or large, shallow roasting pan with a double thickness of paper towels, and set it aside. In a deep-fat fryer or large, heavy saucepan, heat the oil to 360° on a deep-frying thermometer, or until a haze forms above it.

With a large knife or a vegetable slicer, cut the potatoes into slices 1/16 inch thick and drop them directly into cold water to remove the starch and prevent them from discoloring. When ready to use, drain them in a colander, spread them out in a single layer on paper towels, and pat them thoroughly dry with more towels.

Drop about ½ cup of the potatoes at a time into the hot fat and, turning the slices about with a slotted spoon, fry for 2 or 3 minutes, or until they are crisp and golden brown. Transfer the chips to the paper-lined pan and keep them warm in the oven while you proceed with the remaining batches.

To serve, heap the chips in a heated bowl and sprinkle them with the salt. Game chips are traditionally served with roasted birds, such as pheasant, in which case they may be arranged in a circle around the bird.

Potatoes with Apples
Himmel und Erde

To serve 8

1 tablespoon sugar
2 teaspoons salt
½ teaspoon freshly ground black
    pepper
2 cups cold water
9 medium-sized boiling potatoes
    (about 3 pounds), peeled and cut

into 1-inch cubes
1 pound tart cooking apples, peeled,
    cored and quartered
½ pound lean bacon, cut into ¼-
    inch dice
2 medium-sized onions, peeled and
    sliced ⅛-inch thick and separated
    into rings
1 teaspoon cider vinegar

In a heavy 12-inch skillet combine the sugar, 1 teaspoon of the salt and the black pepper in 2 cups of water. Then drop in the potatoes and apples and bring the water to a boil over high heat. Reduce the heat to moderate and cover the skillet tightly. Simmer, undisturbed, until the potatoes are tender but not falling apart.

Meanwhile, in an 8- to 10-inch skillet, cook the bacon over moderate heat until brown and crisp. With a slotted spoon, spread it out on a double thickness of paper towels to drain. Add the onions to the fat remaining in the skillet and cook over moderate heat, stirring frequently, for 8 to 10 minutes, or until the rings are soft and light brown.

Just before serving, stir the remaining teaspoon of salt and the teaspoon of vinegar into the potatoes and apples, and taste for seasoning. Then transfer the entire contents of the skillet to a heated bowl and serve topped with the onion rings and bacon.

Potato Paprika
Paprikás Burgonya

To serve 4 to 6

2 pounds boiling potatoes
3 tablespoons lard
2/3 cup finely chopped onions
1/4 teaspoon finely chopped garlic
1 tablespoon sweet Hungarian
   paprika
2 cups chicken or beef stock, fresh
   or canned, or 2 cups water

1/8 teaspoon caraway seeds
1 medium-sized tomato, peeled,
   seeded and chopped (about 1/4
   cup)
1 large green pepper with seeds and
   ribs removed, finely chopped
1 teaspoon salt
Freshly ground black pepper
1 pound Hungarian sausage
1/2 cup sour cream

Cook the potatoes in boiling water for 8 to 10 minutes, then peel and cut into 1/4-inch slices. In a 4-quart saucepan or casserole, heat the lard until a light haze forms over it, then add the onions and garlic. Cook for 8 to 10 minutes, or until lightly colored. Off the heat, stir in paprika. Stir until the onions are well coated. Return the pan to the heat, add stock or water, bring to a boil, and add caraway seeds, potatoes, tomato, green pepper, salt and a few grindings of pepper. Bring the liquid to a boil, stir, cover and simmer for 25 to 30 minutes until the potatoes are tender.

NOTE: The addition of Debreceni or another semisoft smoked sausage to potato paprika makes the dish a complete meal. Slice the sausage about 1/8 inch thick and add it when you add the potatoes.

Serve in a casserole as a vegetable or entrée for a luncheon dish. Top each portion with a tablespoon of sour cream.

Potatoes in Parsley Sauce
Patatas en Salsa Verde

To serve 4 to 6

5 tablespoons olive oil
6 small boiling potatoes (about 2
   pounds), peeled and sliced
   crosswise into 1/2-inch rounds
1/2 cup finely chopped onions

1 teaspoon finely chopped garlic
2 tablespoons finely chopped parsley
1 teaspoon salt
1/4 teaspoon freshly ground black
   pepper
1 1/2 cups boiling water

In a heavy 10- to 12-inch skillet, heat the olive oil over high heat until a light haze forms above it. Add the potatoes. Turning them frequently with a metal spatula, cook for 10 minutes, or until they are a light golden brown on all sides.

Scatter the onions, garlic, parsley, salt and pepper on top of the potatoes and pour in the boiling water. Do not stir. Instead, shake the pan back and forth for a minute or two to distribute the water evenly.

Cover the skillet tightly and simmer over low heat for about 20 minutes, or until the potatoes are tender but not falling apart. Shake the skillet back and forth occasionally to prevent the potatoes from sticking to the pan.

With a slotted spatula transfer the potatoes to a platter and pour a few teaspoonfuls of their cooking liquid over them. Serve the remaining liquid separately in a sauceboat.

Creamed Potatoes

To serve 8

3 pounds medium-sized potatoes
2 cups light cream
1 teaspoon salt

¼ teaspoon white pepper
⅛ teaspoon nutmeg
2 tablespoons butter
2 tablespoons minced parsley

Wash the unpeeled potatoes and cook them in boiling salted water for about 18 minutes, or until they are tender but still firm. Drain. When the potatoes are cool enough to handle, peel them and cut in ¼-inch slices.

Put the potato slices, cream, salt, pepper and nutmeg in a skillet and cook over high heat until the cream is reduced to half. Break the butter into small pieces and add it to the potatoes, swirling it in gently. Taste for seasoning, sprinkle with the parsley and serve.

Scalloped Potatoes with Cheese
Pommes de Terre Dauphinoises

To serve 6

1 garlic clove, peeled and bruised
  with the flat of a knife
2½ pounds firm boiling potatoes,
  old or new, peeled and cut into
  ⅛-inch slices (about 8 cups)

1½ cups grated, imported Swiss cheese
6 tablespoons butter, cut in ¼-inch
  bits
1 teaspoon salt
⅛ teaspoon coarsely ground black
  pepper
1¼ cups milk

Preheat the oven to 425°. Rub the bottom and sides of a flameproof baking-and-serving dish, 10 to 12 inches across and 2 inches deep, with the bruised garlic, and grease it lightly with butter. Dry the potato slices with a paper towel, then spread half of the slices in the bottom of the dish. Sprinkle them with half the cheese, butter bits, salt and pepper. Spread the rest of the slices in the dish and sprinkle the remaining cheese, butter, salt and pepper on top. Pour the milk into the side of the dish. Bring to a simmer over low heat and then bake in the upper third of the oven for 20 minutes, or until the potatoes are almost tender when pierced with the tip of a sharp knife. At this point remove any residual liquid with a bulb baster and bake for another 5 minutes, or until the potatoes are tender, the milk absorbed, and the top nicely browned. Serve at once.

Potato Pancakes with Applesauce

Kartoffelpuffer mit Apfelmus

To make about 8 pancakes

6 medium-sized potatoes (about 2
    pounds), preferably baking
    potatoes
2 eggs

¼ cup finely grated onion
⅓ cup flour
1 teaspoon salt
Bacon fat or lard
Applesauce or imported lingonberry
    (*Preiselbeeren*) preserves

Peel the potatoes and as you proceed drop them into cold water to prevent their discoloring. In a large mixing bowl, beat the eggs enough to break them up, add the onion and gradually beat in the flour and salt. One at a time, pat the potatoes dry and grate them coarsely into a sieve or colander. Press each potato down firmly into the sieve to squeeze out as much moisture as possible, then immediately stir it into the egg and onion batter.

Preheat the oven to 250°. In a heavy 8- to 10-inch skillet melt 8 tablespoons of bacon fat or lard over high heat until it splutters. Pour in ⅓ cup of the potato mixture and, with a large spatula, flatten it into a pancake about 5 inches in diameter. Fry it over moderate heat for about 2 minutes on each side. When the pancake is golden brown on both sides and crisp around the edges, transfer it to a heated, ovenproof plate and keep it warm in the oven. Continue making similar pancakes with the remaining batter, adding more fat to the pan when necessary to keep it at a depth of ¼ inch. Serve the pancakes as soon as possible with applesauce or lingonberry preserves.

Potato Pancakes with Chives
Rårakor med Gråslök

To serve 4

4 medium-sized baking potatoes
2 tablespoons chopped fresh chives

2 teaspoons salt
Freshly ground black pepper
2 tablespoons butter
2 tablespoons vegetable oil

Peel the potatoes and grate them coarsely, preferably into tiny slivers, into a large mixing bowl. Do not drain off the potato water that will accumulate in the bowl. Working quickly to prevent the potatoes from turning brown, mix into them the chopped chives, salt and a few grindings of pepper.

Heat the butter and oil in a 10- to 12-inch skillet over high heat until the foam subsides. The pan must be very hot, but not smoking. Using 2 tablespoons of potato mixture for each pancake, fry 3 or 4 at a time, flattening them out with a spatula to about 3 inches in diameter. Fry each batch of pancakes over medium-high heat for 2 or 3 minutes on each side, or until they are crisp and golden. Serve at once.

Spinach in Cheese Sauce

To serve 6

3 pounds fresh spinach
1 cup milk
2 tablespoons flour

2 tablespoons melted butter
Salt
Pepper
1 cup grated cheese

Preheat the oven to 350°. Soak the spinach in salted water for a few minutes to freshen it. Cut off the roots and wilted leaves. Wash thoroughly until no sand can be found in the bottom of the pan. Cook the spinach in a covered pan with only the water that drips from the leaves. When its crispness is gone drain the spinach and place it in a baking dish.

Meanwhile, heat the milk in the top of a double boiler. Blend together the flour and melted butter, then stir the mixture into the hot milk. Season to taste with salt and pepper. When the mixture begins to thicken, add the grated cheese. Stir until the cheese has melted and the sauce is smooth. Pour the sauce over the spinach and bake until it is browned.

Spiced Acorn Squash

To serve 8

4 medium-sized acorn squash
1/2 cup dark brown sugar
1 teaspoon cinnamon
1/2 teaspoon grated nutmeg
1/4 teaspoon ground cloves

1/2 teaspoon salt
8 tablespoons melted butter
(1 quarter-pound stick)
1/2 cup maple syrup
Eight 1/2-inch pieces of bacon
About 2 cups boiling water

Preheat the oven to 350°. Cut each squash in half and with a teaspoon scrape out the seeds and fibers. In a small bowl combine the brown sugar, cinnamon, nutmeg, cloves, salt and melted butter, and stir them together thoroughly.

Arrange the squash in a shallow ovenproof baking dish large enough to hold them all comfortably. Spoon an equal amount of the spiced butter mixture into the hollow of each squash and over that pour a teaspoon or so of maple syrup. Top with a piece of bacon. Now add boiling water to the baking dish—the water should be about 1 inch deep. Bake in the middle of the oven for 30 minutes, or until the squash can be easily pierced with the tip of a small, sharp knife. Serve at once.

Glazed Sweet Potatoes

To serve 6

6 sweet potatoes
1/2 cup brown sugar

1/2 teaspoon salt
4 tablespoons butter
1/4 cup water

Preheat the oven to 400°. Boil the sweet potatoes in salted water until they are tender. Peel the potatoes, cut them in half lengthwise, and place them in an oiled baking pan. Sprinkle them with the sugar and salt, and dot with the butter. Add the water to the pan. Bake, turning frequently, for about 20 minutes, or until the potatoes are brown.

Tomatoes Stuffed with Rice

Domates Yemistes me Rizi

To serve 6

1¼ cups water

½ cup uncooked long- or medium-
    grained rice

6 firm ripe tomatoes, each about 3
    inches in diameter

2 teaspoons salt

6 tablespoons olive oil

½ cup finely chopped onions

¾ cup canned tomato purée

½ cup finely chopped parsley,
    preferably flat-leaf parsley

2 tablespoons finely cut fresh mint,
    or substitute 1 tablespoon dried
    mint

2 teaspoons finely chopped garlic

¼ teaspoon oregano, crumbled

Freshly ground black pepper

In a small saucepan, bring 1 cup of water to a boil over high heat. Pour in the rice in a slow thin stream, stir once or twice, and cook briskly uncovered for 8 minutes, or until the rice is softened but still somewhat resistant to the bite. Drain the rice in a sieve and set aside.

Cut a ¼-inch slice off the stem ends of the tomatoes and set aside. With a spoon, hollow out the tomatoes, remove the inner pulp and discard the seeds. Chop the pulp and set it aside. Sprinkle the tomato cavities with 1 teaspoon of salt and turn them upside down on paper towels to drain.

Preheat the oven to 350°. Make the stuffing in the following fashion: In a heavy 10- to 12-inch skillet, heat the oil over moderate heat until a light haze forms above it. Add the onions and, stirring frequently, cook for 5 minutes, or until they are soft and transparent but not brown. Stir in the rice, tomato pulp, ½ cup of the tomato purée, the parsley, mint, garlic, oregano, the remaining teaspoon of salt and a few grindings of pepper. Stirring constantly, cook briskly until most of the liquid in the pan evaporates and the mixture is thick enough to hold its shape almost solidly in the spoon.

Arrange the tomatoes, cut side up, in a baking dish large enough to hold them side by side. Fill the tomatoes with the stuffing, packing it in firmly, and cover each tomato with its reserved top. Combine the remaining ¼ cup of tomato purée with the remaining ¼ cup of water and pour the mixture around the tomatoes. Bake uncovered in the middle of the oven for 20 minutes, basting the tomatoes once or twice with the cooking liquid. Cool to room temperature and serve the tomatoes directly from the baking dish.

Pennsylvania Dutch Tomatoes

To serve 4 to 6

4 to 5 large firm ripe tomatoes, 3 to
   4 inches in diameter, thickly sliced
2 teaspoons salt
Freshly ground black pepper
½ cup flour
4 to 6 tablespoons butter
2 tablespoons sieved brown sugar
1 cup heavy cream
1 tablespoon finely chopped fresh
   parsley

Sprinkle the tomatoes on both sides with salt and a few grindings of black pepper. Then dip the tomato slices in the flour, coating each side thoroughly and very gently shaking off any excess. In a 12-inch heavy skillet, preferably of the nonstick variety, melt the butter over moderate heat.

When the foam subsides, add the tomato slices and cook them for about 5 minutes, or until they are lightly browned. Sprinkle the tops with half the brown sugar, carefully turn the tomatoes over with a spatula and sprinkle with the rest of the brown sugar. Cook for 3 to 4 minutes, then transfer the slices to a heated serving platter.

Pour the cream into the pan, raise the heat to high and bring the cream to a boil, stirring constantly. Boil briskly for 2 to 3 minutes, or until the cream thickens. Taste for seasoning, then pour over the tomatoes. Sprinkle with the finely chopped parsley.

NOTE: Traditionally, this recipe is made with green tomatoes; however, they are not easily available. If you can find them, cook them somewhat more slowly and for a few minutes longer on each side.

Sherried Yams with Pecans

To serve 6

6 medium-sized yams or sweet
   potatoes
½ cup brown sugar
1 cup orange juice
1 tablespoon grated orange rind
⅓ cup sherry
1 cup pecans, coarsely chopped
2 tablespoons butter

Boil the yams or sweet potatoes in salted water until they are tender. Peel them and cut them in thick slices.

Preheat the oven to 350°. In a bowl, combine the sugar, orange juice, orange rind and sherry. Place a layer of yams in a baking dish, cover it with some of the sherry mixture, and sprinkle generously with pecans. Repeat layers of yams, liquid and pecans until the casserole is filled. Pour the remaining juice over the top, sprinkle with nuts, and dot with the butter. Cover and bake for 30 minutes, or until the juice has been absorbed by the yams and the top is browned.

Beef-stuffed Zucchini with Tomato Sauce

Zucchini Ripieni

To serve 4 to 6

1½ cups tomato sauce *(below)*
4 medium-sized zucchini, scrubbed
   but not peeled
¼ cup olive oil
½ cup finely chopped onions
½ teaspoon finely chopped garlic
½ pound ground beef chuck
1 egg, lightly beaten

2 ounces finely chopped prosciutto
   (about ¼ cup)
½ cup fresh white bread crumbs
   (from French or Italian bread)
6 tablespoons freshly grated imported
   Parmesan cheese
½ teaspoon dried oregano, crumbled
1 teaspoon salt
¼ teaspoon freshly ground black
   pepper

Prepare the tomato sauce *(below)*. Preheat the oven to 375°. Cut the zucchini in half lengthwise and spoon out most of the pulp, leaving hollow boat-like shells about ¼ inch thick. Set the shells aside and chop the pulp coarsely. Heat 3 tablespoons of olive oil in a heavy 8- to 10-inch skillet, add the onions and cook them over moderate heat for 8 to 10 minutes, or until they are soft and lightly colored. Add the zucchini pulp and the garlic and cook for about 5 minutes longer, stirring frequently. With a rubber spatula scrape the entire contents of the skillet into a large sieve set over a mixing bowl and let them drain.

Meanwhile heat a tablespoon of oil in the skillet, add the ground beef and brown it over moderate heat, stirring almost constantly with a large fork to break up any lumps. Scrape the beef into another sieve and let it drain.

Now in a large mixing bowl combine the drained vegetables and meat. Beat into them the lightly beaten egg, prosciutto, bread crumbs, 2 teaspoons of grated cheese, oregano, salt and pepper and taste for seasoning. Spoon this stuffing into the hollowed zucchini shells, mounding the top slightly. To bake the zucchini, use a 12-by-16-inch shallow baking dish into which 1½ cups of tomato sauce have been poured. Then carefully arrange the stuffed zucchini on the sauce. Sprinkle their tops with ¼ cup of cheese, dribble a few drops of olive oil over them and cover the dish tightly with aluminum foil. Bring the sauce to a simmer on top of the stove, then transfer the dish to the middle of the oven and bake the zucchini for 30 minutes, removing the foil after 20 minutes so that the tops of the zucchini can brown lightly. Serve directly from the baking dish.

TOMATO SAUCE
2 tablespoons olive oil
½ cup finely chopped onions
2 cups Italian plum or whole-pack
   tomatoes, coarsely chopped but
   not drained

3 tablespoons tomato paste
1 tablespoon finely cut fresh basil
   or 1 teaspoon dried basil
1 teaspoon sugar
½ teaspoon salt
Freshly ground black pepper

Using a 2- to 3-quart enameled or stainless-steel saucepan, heat the olive oil until a light haze forms over it. Add the onions and cook them over moderate heat for 7 to 8 minutes, or until they are soft but not browned. Add the tomatoes, tomato paste, basil, sugar, salt and a few grindings of pepper. Reduce the heat to very low and simmer, with the pan partially covered, for about 40 minutes. Stir occasionally.

Press the sauce through a fine sieve (or a food mill) into a bowl or pan. Taste for seasoning and serve hot.

Braised Zucchini
Courgettes Braisées
To serve 6 to 8

3 pounds zucchini
2 tablespoons salt
⅓ cup flour

3 tablespoons olive oil
3 tablespoons butter
½ cup broth
¼ teaspoon pepper

Scrub the zucchini well with a vegetable brush, then wash and dry it. Cut it in very thin slices, then place them in a bowl. Sprinkle the salt over the zucchini and let it stand for 30 minutes, stirring the slices a few times. Drain well, then dry the slices thoroughly with paper towels. Toss them in the flour.

Heat the oil and butter in a large skillet. Add the floured zucchini slices and cook until they are lightly browned. Add the broth and the pepper. Cover the skillet and simmer for 15 minutes, or until the zucchini is tender but still crisp.

Zucchini in Cheese Sauce

3 small zucchini
Salt
¼ cup milk

1 egg
⅔ cup grated cheese
4 tablespoons butter

Wash the zucchini and cut it crosswise into ½-inch slices. Cook them in a small amount of salted water until they are soft.

Preheat the oven to 400°. In a small bowl, beat the egg. Add the milk and grated cheese and mix well. Place the zucchini in a casserole and pour the cheese sauce over it. Dot the top with the butter. Bake, uncovered, until the cheese is melted and the top is nicely browned.

Salads

Iranian Mixed Salad

Salade Sabzi

To serve 8

2 cucumbers
1 head romaine lettuce
3 tomatoes, peeled and diced
1 cup thinly sliced radishes
½ cup thinly sliced green onions
¼ cup chopped dill

½ cup chopped parsley
¾ cup olive oil
⅓ cup lemon juice
1 clove garlic, minced
¾ teaspoon salt
½ teaspoon black pepper

Peel the cucumbers and cut them in thin slices. Wash and dry the lettuce and break it into bite-sized pieces. In a salad bowl, combine the cucumbers, lettuce, tomatoes, radishes, green onions, dill and parsley. Make a dressing of the oil, lemon juice, garlic, salt and pepper. Pour it over the salad, tossing it until the vegetables are well coated. Small pieces of *feta* or other goat's-milk cheese may be added.

Lettuce, Tomato and Avocado Salad

To serve 6

1 head lettuce
2 tomatoes
3 avocados

¾ cup olive oil
¼ cup lime or lemon juice
½ teaspoon salt
¼ teaspoon black pepper

Wash and dry the lettuce and tear it into serving-sized pieces. Peel the tomatoes and cut them into eights. Peel and slice the avocados. Arrange the prepared ingredients on individual salad plates. Make a dressing of the oil, fruit juice, salt and pepper, and pour it over the salads.

Caesar Salad

To serve 4 to 6

2 medium-sized heads romaine lettuce
10 to 12 croutons, preferably made
   from French or Italian-style bread
4 to 8 tablespoons vegetable oil
1 teaspoon finely chopped garlic
2 eggs

⅛ teaspoon salt
⅛ teaspoon freshly ground black
   pepper
½ cup olive oil
4 tablespoons lemon juice
1 cup freshly grated Parmesan cheese
6 to 8 flat anchovies (optional)

Separate the romaine lettuce and wash the leaves under cold running water. Dry each leaf thoroughly with paper towels. Then wrap the lettuce in a dry kitchen towel and chill while you assemble the other ingredients. Cut a loaf of bread into 1½-inch-thick slices. Trim the crusts and cut each slice into 1½-inch squares. In a heavy skillet, large enough to hold all the croutons in one layer, heat 4 tablespoons of the vegetable oil over high heat until a light haze forms above it. Add the croutons and brown them on all sides, turning them with tongs, and, if necessary, add up to another 4 tablespoons of oil. Remove the pan from the heat, then add the chopped garlic and toss the croutons about in the hot fat. Remove the croutons to paper towels to drain, cool and crisp.

Plunge the eggs into rapidly boiling water for 10 seconds, remove and set aside. Break the chilled romaine into serving-sized pieces and scatter them in the bottom of a large salad bowl, preferably glass or porcelain. Add the salt, pepper and olive oil, and toss the lettuce with two large spoons or, better still, with your hands. Then break the eggs on top of the salad, add the lemon juice and mix again until the lettuce is thoroughly coated with dressing. Add the cheese and anchovies, if you are using them, and mix again. Scatter the croutons on top and serve at once.

Endive Salad

To serve 8

2 pounds endive
¾ cup olive oil
¾ teaspoon salt

⅛ teaspoon pepper
⅛ teaspoon minced garlic
¼ cup wine vinegar

Wash the endive, remove any tough outer leaves and cut away the bottoms. Cut the endive in quarters, lengthwise. Soak it in ice water for 10 minutes. Drain the endive, wrap it in a towel and put it in the refrigerator to chill. Combine the olive oil, salt, pepper, garlic and vinegar in a jar, and shake vigorously. Arrange the endive in a salad bowl and pour the dressing over it.

Broad Bean Salad
Fool Midammis

To serve 4

1 cup dried *fool misri* (small fava or broad beans)
1 tablespoon *ads majroosh* (dried red lentils), or substitute other dried lentils
¼ cup olive oil

1 tablespoon fresh lemon juice
½ teaspoon salt
1 tablespoon finely chopped parsley, preferably flat-leaf parsley
8 pitted black olives, preferably the Mediterranean type

Wash the beans and lentils in a sieve or colander set under cold running water until the water runs clear. Then drain thoroughly.

In a heavy 3- to 4-quart saucepan, bring 1 quart of water to a boil over high heat. Add the beans and lentils, reduce the heat to low and partially cover the pan. Simmer for 3 to 4 hours, or until the beans are tender and show no resistance when pressed gently between your fingers. Check from time to time to make sure that the beans are moist. If they seem dry, add a few tablespoons of boiling water. When they are done, there should be almost no liquid left in the pan. Transfer the entire contents of the pan to a bowl and cool to room temperature.

With a whisk or fork, beat the oil, lemon juice and salt together in a deep bowl. Add the beans and lentils and, mashing them gently with a fork, stir until they absorb most of the dressing.

To serve, spread the bean mixture on a platter or individual plates, sprinkle the top with parsley, and garnish with olives.

Green Bean Salad
Bohnensalat

To serve 4

3 tablespoons red or white wine vinegar
3 tablespoons olive oil
½ cup chicken stock, fresh or canned
2 teaspoons salt

Freshly ground black pepper
1 teaspoon finely chopped fresh dill
1 teaspoon finely chopped parsley
1 pound fresh green beans
1 sprig fresh summer savory, or ¼ teaspoon dried summer savory

In a small bowl combine the vinegar, oil, chicken stock, 1 teaspoon of the salt and a few grindings of pepper, and beat them vigorously with a whisk to blend thoroughly. Stir in the dill and parsley, and taste for seasoning. Cover the bowl and set the dressing aside.

With a small, sharp knife, trim the ends off the beans, and cut them into 2-inch lengths. In a 3- to 4-quart saucepan bring 2 quarts of water, the remaining 1 teaspoon of salt and the summer savory to a bubbling boil over high heat. Drop the beans in by the handful. Return the water to a boil, reduce the heat to moderate, and boil the beans, uncovered, for 10 to 15 minutes, or until they are tender but still slightly firm. Do not overcook them. Immediately drain the beans in a colander and run cold water over them for a few seconds to set their color and keep them from cooking further. Spread them out on paper toweling and pat them dry.

Transfer the beans to a large mixing bowl and pour the dressing over them. Stir thoroughly to coat them well, taste for seasoning, and chill for at least 1 hour before serving.

Beet Salad
Rote Rübensalat

To serve 4

2 pounds fresh firm beets	½ teaspoon ground coriander seeds
2 teaspoons salt	6 whole black peppercorns
½ cup dry red wine	3 tablespoons olive oil
½ cup cider vinegar	1 teaspoon freshly grated
1 onion, peeled and thinly sliced	horseradish, or substitute
4 whole cloves	1 tablespoon bottled grated
	horseradish, thoroughly drained
	and squeezed dry in a towel

With a small, sharp knife cut the tops from the beets, leaving about 1 inch of stem on each. Scrub the beets under cold running water, then combine them in a 4- to 5-quart saucepan with enough cold water to cover them by 2 inches. Add 1 teaspoon of the salt and bring the water to a boil over high heat. Reduce the heat to low, cover the pan, and simmer until the beets show no resistance when pierced with the tip of a small, sharp knife. This may take anywhere from 30 minutes for young beets or as long as 2 hours for older ones. The beets should be kept constantly covered with water; add boiling water if necessary.

Drain the beets in a colander and, when they are cool enough to handle, slip off the skins. Cut the beets crosswise into ⅛-inch slices and place them in a deep glass or ceramic bowl.

In a 1½- to 2-quart enameled or stainless-steel saucepan, bring the red wine, vinegar, onion, cloves, coriander, peppercorns and the remaining 1 teaspoon of salt to a boil over high heat. Immediately pour the mixture over the beets. It should cover them completely; if it doesn't, add more wine. Cool to room temperature, cover the bowl tightly with aluminum foil or plastic wrap, and refrigerate for at least 24 hours.

Just before serving, discard the whole cloves and the peppercorns. Beat the olive oil and horseradish together in a small bowl and add it to the beets, turning the slices about with a spoon to coat them thoroughly with the dressing.

NOTE: If you prefer a somewhat thinner dressing, add up to ½ cup of cold water to the oil and horseradish. (Whole canned beets may be substituted for the cooked fresh beets. Slice them ⅛ inch thick and pour the hot marinade over them as described above. Use the canned beet juice in place of water if you wish to dilute the marinade.)

Cucumber Salad with Dill
Agurkesalat

To serve 4

2 large (8-inch) or 3 medium (6-inch) cucumbers
1 tablespoon salt

¾ cup white vinegar
1 tablespoon sugar
1 teaspoon salt
¼ teaspoon white pepper
2 tablespoons chopped fresh dill

Scrub the wax coating (if any) off the cucumbers and dry them. Score the cucumbers lengthwise with a fork and cut them in the thinnest possible slices; ideally, the slices should be almost translucent. Arrange them in a thin layer in a shallow china or glass dish and sprinkle with salt. Place 2 or 3 plates on top of the cucumbers (to press out excess water and bitterness) and let them rest at room temperature for a couple of hours.

Remove the plates, drain the cucumbers of all their liquid, and spread them out on paper towels. Gently pat the cucumbers dry with paper towels and return them to their dish. In a small bowl, beat together the vinegar, sugar, salt and pepper. Pour over the cucumbers and strew them with the chopped dill. Chill for 2 or 3 hours and just before serving, drain away nearly all of the liquid.

Finnish Cucumber Salad

5 small cucumbers
Salt
1 small bunch fresh dill
1 cup sour cream
1 clove garlic, crushed

Black pepper
Sugar
2 tablespoons fresh tomato pulp
2 tablespoons tarragon vinegar
¼ cup oil

Peel the cucumbers and cut them into very thin slices. Place them on a flat dish and sprinkle them well with salt. Leave them for ½ hour, then drain off the liquid and place them in a bowl. Chop the dill very fine and add it to the sour cream. Mix in the garlic, salt, pepper and a very little sugar. Stir in the tomato pulp, then add the vinegar and oil very slowly. Pour the dressing over the cucumbers, mix well, and chill thoroughly before serving.

Yoghurt with Cucumber and Tomato
Kheera ka Rayta

To serve 4

1 medium-sized cucumber
1 tablespoon finely chopped onions
1 tablespoon salt
1 small, firm ripe tomato, cut
   crosswise into ½-inch-thick
   rounds, sliced into ½-inch wide
   strips and then into ½-inch cubes

1 tablespoon finely chopped fresh
   coriander (*cilantro*)
1 cup unflavored yoghurt
1 teaspoon ground cumin, toasted
   in a small ungreased skillet over
   low heat for 30 seconds

With a small, sharp knife, peel the cucumber and slice it lengthwise into halves. Scoop out the seeds by running the tip of a teaspoon down the center of each half. Cut the cucumber lengthwise into ⅛-inch-thick slices, then crosswise into ½-inch pieces.

Combine the cucumber, onions and salt in a small bowl, and mix them together thoroughly with a spoon. Let the mixture rest at room temperature for 5 minutes or so, then squeeze the cucumbers gently between your fingers to remove the excess liquid.

Drop the cucumber pieces into a deep bowl, add the tomato and coriander, and toss together gently but thoroughly. Combine the yoghurt and cumin and pour it over the vegetables, turning them about with a spoon to coat them evenly. Taste for seasoning, cover tightly, and refrigerate for at least 1 hour, or until completely chilled, before serving.

Green Pepper Salad
Paprikasaláta

To serve 4

3 large green peppers
2 tablespoons white vinegar
1 teaspoon sugar

1 teaspoon salt
⅛ teaspoon freshly ground black
    pepper
½ cup mayonnaise, freshly made or
    a good commercial brand

Preheat the oven to 450°. Arrange the green peppers on a rack and heat them in the oven for 10 to 15 minutes, or until the skin begins to discolor and blister. Remove them, wrap them in a damp kitchen towel and let them rest for 10 minutes. Strip off the skins with a small knife, then remove the stems, seeds and ribs, and cut the peppers into strips ¼ inch wide and about 3 inches long.

    Combine the vinegar, sugar, salt and pepper in a mixing bowl. Add the strips of pepper, toss them with the mixture, cover and refrigerate from 2 to 12 hours. Drain them in a sieve or colander, transfer them to a mixing bowl and add the mayonnaise. Serve on lettuce as a salad or in small dishes as an accompaniment to cold meat.

Fresh Mushroom Salad
Sienisalaatti

To serve 4

½ pound fresh mushrooms, in ⅛-inch
    slices
1 cup water
1 tablespoon lemon juice
¼ cup heavy cream

1 tablespoon grated onion
Pinch of sugar
½ teaspoon salt
⅛ teaspoon white pepper
Lettuce leaves

In a 1-quart enamel, glass or stainless-steel saucepan, bring the water and lemon juice to a boil. Add the sliced mushrooms and cover the pan. Reduce the heat and simmer gently for 2 to 3 minutes. Then remove from the heat, drain the mushrooms in a sieve, and pat them dry with paper towels. In a 1-quart bowl, combine the heavy cream, grated onion, sugar, salt and pepper. Add the mushrooms and toss lightly in the dressing until they are well coated. Serve as a salad, on crisp, dry lettuce.

Raw Mushroom Salad

Insalata di Funghi Crudi

To serve 4

½ pound fresh mushrooms, thinly
sliced

2 teaspoons lemon juice

¼ cup thinly sliced scallion greens

3 tablespoons olive oil

½ teaspoon salt

In a serving bowl, toss the mushrooms with the lemon juice until the slices
are lightly moistened. Then add the scallion greens, oil and salt and toss
again. Chill the salad before serving it.

Potato Salad

Leichter Kartoffelsalat

To serve 4

6 medium-sized boiling potatoes
(about 2 pounds), scrubbed but
not peeled

1 cup finely chopped onions

⅔ cup chicken stock, fresh or
canned

⅓ cup olive oil

1 tablespoon white wine vinegar

2 teaspoons prepared Düsseldorf-
style mustard, or substitute 2
teaspoons other hot, prepared
mustard

2 teaspoons salt

1 teaspoon freshly ground black
pepper

1 tablespoon fresh lemon juice

Drop the unpeeled potatoes into enough lightly salted boiling water to
cover them completely. Boil them briskly until they show only the slightest
resistance when pierced with the point of a small, sharp knife. Be careful not
to let them overcook or they will fall apart when sliced. Drain the potatoes
in a colander, then peel and cut them into ¼-inch slices. Set the potatoes
aside in a bowl tightly covered with aluminum foil.

In a heavy 2- to 3-quart saucepan, combine the chopped onions, stock,
oil, vinegar, prepared mustard, salt and pepper. Bring to a boil over high
heat, stirring occasionally. Reduce the heat to low and simmer uncovered
for 5 minutes. Remove the pan from the heat and stir in the lemon juice.

Pour the sauce over the potato slices, turning them about with a spatula
to coat them evenly. Let the potatoes cool to room temperature, then taste
for seasoning and serve.

Radish and Onion Salad

Salat Znonit Beshamenet

To serve 4

1 tablespoon red wine vinegar
1 teaspoon sugar
1 teaspoon salt
Freshly ground black pepper
1 cup sour cream

24 medium-sized radishes, trimmed
    and cut crosswise into ⅛-inch-
    thick slices
1 small red onion, peeled, cut into
    ⅛-inch-thick slices and separated
    into rings

Combine the vinegar, sugar, salt and a few grindings of pepper in a salad or serving bowl and stir thoroughly. Beat in the cream a few tablespoons at a time, then fold in the radishes and onion rings. Taste for seasoning. Chill in the refrigerator for at least 1 hour before serving.

Spinach Salad

To serve 4 to 6

½ pound uncooked young spinach
1 large cucumber
1 teaspoon salt

4 medium-sized stalks celery
¼ cup coarsely chopped black olives
½ cup pine nuts

Wash the spinach under cold running water, drain and pat thoroughly dry with paper towels. Strip the leaves from the stems and discard the stems along with any tough or discolored leaves. Peel the cucumber and slice it in half lengthwise. Run the tip of a teaspoon down the center to scrape out the seeds. Cut the halves into strips ¼ inch wide and then crosswise into ¼-inch dice. To rid the cucumber of excess moisture, in a small bowl mix the diced cucumber with 1 teaspoon of salt. Let it rest for 15 minutes to ½ hour, then drain the liquid that will accumulate and pat the cucumber dice dry with paper towels.

Trim the leaves and stems of the celery; wash the stalks under cold water and dry them thoroughly with paper towels. Cut each stalk in ¼-inch strips and then cut into ¼-inch dice. Toss the spinach, cucumber and celery in a salad bowl, preferably of glass, add the olives and nuts and toss again. Chill until ready to serve.

DRESSING

2 tablespoons red wine vinegar
½ teaspoon salt
Freshly ground black pepper

½ teaspoon dry mustard
6 tablespoons vegetable oil

For the dressing, with a whisk beat the vinegar, salt, pepper and mustard together in a small bowl. Still whisking, gradually pour in the oil and beat until the dressing is smooth and thick. Pour over the salad, toss until all the ingredients are thoroughly coated with the dressing and serve at once on chilled salad plates.

Tomato Salad
Insalata di Pomodori
To serve 4 to 6

5 medium-sized firm ripe tomatoes,
  sliced ¼ inch thick
½ cup olive oil
2 tablespoons wine vinegar or lemon
  juice
1 tablespoon finely cut fresh basil or
  1 teaspoon dried basil

¼ teaspoon finely chopped garlic
1 teaspoon salt
Freshly ground black pepper
2 tablespoons thinly sliced scallions
1 tablespoon finely chopped fresh
  parsley, preferably the flat-leaf
  Italian type

Arrange the tomato slices in slightly overlapping concentric circles on a deep round plate or platter. For the dressing, thoroughly mix the oil, vinegar, basil, garlic, salt and a few grindings of pepper and spoon or pour this over the tomatoes. Combine the scallions and parsley and sprinkle on top.

Crabmeat and Cucumber Salad
Hsieh-jou-pan-huang-kua

To serve 4 to 6

2 medium-sized cucumbers
½ pound fresh crabmeat or one
  7½-ounce can crabmeat
2 tablespoons white vinegar

2 tablespoons soy sauce
1 teaspoon sugar
⅛ teaspoon ground white pepper
1 tablespoon sesame-seed oil

PREPARE AHEAD: 1. Pick over the crabmeat and discard all bits of shell and cartilage.

2. Peel the cucumbers and cut them lengthwise in two. With a small spoon, scrape the seeds out of each half, leaving hollow, boatlike shells. Shred the cucumbers, not too fine, with a cleaver or large, sharp knife.

TO ASSEMBLE: In a small glass or porcelain bowl, combine the vinegar, soy sauce, sugar, pepper and sesame-seed oil, and mix well. Add the cucumbers and crabmeat; toss to coat thoroughly with the dressing and chill slightly—no more than an hour—before serving.

Artichokes with Shrimp and Green Goddess Dressing

To serve 6

Six 10- to 12-ounce artichokes

6 quarts water
3 tablespoons salt

Trim the bases of the artichokes flush and flat so that they will stand upright without wobbling. Bend and snap off the small bottom leaves and any bruised outer leaves. Lay each artichoke on its side, grip it firmly and, with a large, sharp knife, slice about 1 inch off the top.

With scissors trim ¼ inch off the points of the rest of the leaves. Rub all the cut edges with lemon to prevent their discoloring. In an 8-quart enameled or stainless-steel pot (do not use aluminum; it will turn the artichokes gray), bring about 6 quarts of water and 3 tablespoons of salt to a boil. Drop in the artichokes and boil them briskly, uncovered, for about 30 minutes, turning occasionally. They are done when their bases show no resistance when pierced with the tip of a small, sharp knife. Drain them upside down in a colander. When they are cool enough to handle, spread their leaves apart gently, grasp the inner core of yellow, thistlelike leaves firmly and ease it out. Then, with a long-handled spoon, thoroughly scrape out and discard the fuzzy choke.

GREEN GODDESS DRESSING

3 cups mayonnaise, freshly made, or a good, unsweetened commercial variety
1 tablespoon tarragon wine vinegar
1 teaspoon lemon juice
1 tablespoon finely chopped anchovies (6 to 8 flat anchovies canned in olive oil)

1 tablespoon chopped fresh tarragon or 1 teaspoon dried crumbled tarragon
¼ cup finely chopped scallions, including part of the green stems
¼ teaspoon finely chopped garlic
¼ cup finely chopped parsley
⅛ teaspoon cayenne

GREEN GODDESS DRESSING: In a small mixing bowl, beat into the 3 cups of mayonnaise the vinegar, lemon juice, anchovies, tarragon, scallions, garlic, parsley and cayenne. Taste for seasoning and add a little salt if you think it needs it.

2 pounds shelled, cooked and chilled tiny shrimp, preferably the West Coast or Alaskan variety	6 rolled, caper-stuffed anchovies (optional) Lemon slices

In a large mixing bowl combine the shrimp and 1½ cups of the dressing, stirring them gently until the shrimp are well coated. Fill each artichoke cavity with the mixture, mounding it slightly on the top. Arrange the anchovy, if you are using it, in the center of each shrimp mound and chill the stuffed artichokes until ready to serve.

To serve, place the artichokes on chilled plates with the lemon slices. Pass the remaining Green Goddess dressing separately.

White Bean and Tuna Salad
Fagioli Toscanelli con Tonno

To serve 4 to 6

4 cups canned *cannellini* or other white beans (2 one-pound cans) or 2 cups dry white kidney, marrow, Great Northern or navy beans and 2 quarts water ¼ cup olive oil 1 tablespoon lemon juice	½ teaspoon salt Freshly ground black pepper ¼ cup finely chopped scallions 2 tablespoons finely chopped fresh parsley, preferably the flat-leaf Italian type 1 seven-ounce can tuna fish, preferably Italian tuna packed in olive oil

If you are using canned beans, drain them in a colander, wash them in cold water, then drain them again and spread on paper towels to dry before transferring them to a serving bowl. If you are using dry beans, combine them with water in a 3- to 4-quart saucepan and bring to a boil. Boil briskly for 2 minutes, remove from the heat and let the beans soak for 1 hour. Then cook them in the soaking water over low heat for 1 to 1½ hours, or until they are tender. Drain, transfer them to a serving bowl and cool.

To make the salad, combine the olive oil, lemon juice, salt and pepper and pour them over the beans. Add the scallions and parsley and gently mix them all together. Transfer the beans to a platter, break the tuna into chunks and arrange them on top.

Breads, Muffins & Pancakes

Braided Egg Bread
Challah

1 cake or package yeast
1 tablespoon sugar
½ cup lukewarm water
½ cup boiling water
A pinch of saffron
3 to 4½ cups sifted flour

1½ teaspoons salt
2 eggs
2 to 3 tablespoons vegetable oil
1 egg yolk, lightly beaten
2 tablespoons poppy seeds

Mix together the yeast, sugar and lukewarm water. Let stand 5 minutes.
Combine the boiling water and saffron, let stand until cool, then strain.
Sift 3 cups of the flour with the salt into a bowl. Make a well in the center and into it put the 2 eggs, oil, saffron water and the yeast mixture. Work in the sifted flour gradually, then add just enough of the remaining flour to make a soft dough. Knead on a floured surface until smooth and elastic. Place in an oiled bowl and brush the top with a little oil. Cover with a towel, set in a warm place and let rise 1 hour.
Punch down, cover again and let rise until the dough doubles in bulk. Divide the dough into 3 equal parts. With lightly floured hands, roll the dough into 3 strips of an even length. Braid them together and place in an oiled baking pan. Cover with a towel and let the loaf rise until double in bulk. Brush with the beaten egg yolk and sprinkle with the poppy seeds. Bake in a 350° oven 50 minutes or until browned. Cool on a cake rack.

American White Bread

To make one 9-inch loaf

1 package dry yeast
1 cup lukewarm milk
1½ tablespoons sugar
2½ to 3 cups all-purpose flour or
    bread flour

4 tablespoons soft butter
1 teaspoon salt

GLAZE
1 egg, lightly beaten with 1
    tablespoon milk

Sprinkle the yeast into a half cup of the lukewarm (110° to 115°) milk. Add 1 teaspoon of the sugar and stir until thoroughly dissolved. Place the mixture in a warm, draft-free place—such as an unlighted oven—for 5 to 8 minutes, or until the yeast has begun to bubble and almost doubled in volume.

Then pour it into a large mixing bowl, add the remaining ½ cup of milk and stir until the yeast is dissolved. With a large spoon, slowly beat into the mixture 1 cup of the flour and continue to beat vigorously until smooth. Still beating, add the butter, remaining sugar, salt and 1½ more cups of flour. Transfer the dough to a lightly floured surface and knead it by folding it end to end, then pressing it down, pushing it forward and folding it back for at least 10 minutes, sprinkling the dough every few minutes with small amounts of as much of the remaining flour as you need to prevent the dough from sticking to the board. When the dough is smooth and elastic, place it in a large, lightly buttered bowl. Dust it with a sprinkling of flour and cover the bowl loosely with a kitchen towel. Let the dough rise in a warm, draft-free place for 45 minutes to an hour, or until the dough doubles its bulk and springs back slowly when gently poked with a finger. Then punch the dough down again with one blow of your fist to reduce it to its original volume. Let it rise 30 to 40 minutes until it again doubles in bulk.

Preheat the oven to 375°. Lightly but thoroughly butter a 9-by-5-by-3-inch loaf pan. Shape the dough into a compact loaf, somewhat high and round in the center, and place it in the pan. Cover with a towel and let the dough rise in the same warm place (about 25 minutes) until it reaches the top of the pan. Thoroughly brush the top of the loaf with the egg and milk glaze. Bake in the lower third of the oven for 30 to 40 minutes, or until the loaf is golden brown and a toothpick inserted in its center comes out clean and dry. Cool before slicing.

Flat Armenian Bread with Sesame Seeds

Churek

To make 10 large rounds

1 package dry active yeast	6 cups all-purpose flour
1 tablespoon sugar	¼ pound unsalted butter, melted
2¼ cups lukewarm water (110° to 115°)	1 tablespoon salt
	2 tablespoons white sesame seeds

Sprinkle the yeast and 1 teaspoon of the sugar into ¼ cup of the lukewarm water in a small, shallow bowl. Let it stand 2 or 3 minutes, then stir to dissolve the yeast completely. Set the bowl aside in a warm, draft-free spot (such as an unlighted oven) for about 5 to 10 minutes, or until the mixture almost doubles in volume.

Pour the flour into a large mixing bowl and make a well in the center. Pour in the yeast mixture, remaining water, melted butter, remaining sugar and salt. With a large spoon, beat the flour into the liquid ingredients, continuing to beat for as long as 10 minutes, or until a soft, spongy dough is formed. Cover loosely with a kitchen towel and set aside in the warm, draft-free spot until the mixture doubles in volume.

Preheat the oven to 350°. Place the dough on a lightly floured surface and divide it into 10 equal parts. Roll out each part as thinly as possible into circles, then place 2 or 3 circles on a cookie sheet. Sprinkle lightly with cold water and a few sesame seeds and set the cookie sheet on the floor of the oven. Bake about 20 minutes, or until the bread is a pale golden brown. Transfer the breads with a wide spatula to a wire rack and bake the remaining rounds similarly. The bread will keep several days at room temperature if wrapped securely in foil.

French Bread

To make three 16-inch-long loaves

2¼ cups lukewarm water (110° to 115°)
1 package active dry yeast
1 teaspoon sugar
7 to 8 cups unsifted all-purpose flour

1 tablespoon salt plus ½ teaspoon salt dissolved in ½ cup water
1 tablespoon butter, softened, or substitute 1 tablespoon vegetable oil
½ cup white or yellow cornmeal

Pour ¼ cup of the lukewarm water into a small bowl and sprinkle in the yeast and sugar. Let the yeast and sugar rest for 2 or 3 minutes, then mix well. Set in a warm, draft-free place (such as an unlighted oven) for about 10 minutes, or until the yeast bubbles up and the mixture almost doubles in volume.

Place 7 cups of the flour and 1 tablespoon of salt in a deep mixing bowl and make a well in the center. Pour the yeast mixture and the remaining 2 cups of lukewarm water into the well and, with a large wooden spoon, gradually incorporate the dry ingredients into the water. Then stir with the spoon until the dough can be gathered into a medium-firm ball.

Place the ball on a lightly floured surface and knead, pushing the dough down with the heels of your hands, pressing it forward and folding it back on itself. As you knead, incorporate up to 1 cup more flour, adding it by the tablespoonful and using only enough to make a non-sticky dough. Continue to knead for 10 to 15 minutes, or until the dough is smooth and elastic.

With a pastry brush, spread the softened butter or vegetable oil over the inside of a large bowl. Set the dough in the bowl and turn it about in the grease to coat the entire surface. Drape the bowl with a kitchen towel and set it aside in the draft-free place for approximately 1½ hours, or until the dough doubles in volume.

Scatter the cornmeal on a large baking sheet and set the sheet aside. Then punch the dough down with a blow of your fist and divide it into three equal portions. On a lightly floured surface, roll and shape each portion into a slightly tapered loaf about 2 inches in diameter and 15 inches long. Place the loaves 2 inches apart on the cornmeal-coated baking sheet. With a very sharp knife make six diagonal slashes, each about 2 inches long and ½ inch deep, at 1½-inch intervals in the center part of the top of each loaf. Brush the three loaves with 2 tablespoons of the salt-and-water solution and set them aside in the warm, draft-free place for about 45 minutes longer, or until they double in volume.

Preheat the oven to 400° and place a large shallow pan half filled with boiling water on the oven floor or, if your oven is electric, directly on the bottom heating unit. Bake the bread on the lowest shelf of the oven for 15 minutes. Then reduce the oven temperature to 350°, brush the loaves with the salt-and-water solution and bake for 10 minutes. Brush again with the salt water and continue to bake the bread for about 20 minutes longer, or until the loaves are crisp and golden. Remove from the baking sheet and let the loaves cool on a wire rack before serving.

Portuguese Sweet Bread
Massa Sovada

To make two 9-inch round loaves

2 packages or cakes of active dry or compressed yeast	1 cup lukewarm milk (110° to 115°)
A pinch plus 1 cup sugar	3 eggs
¼ cup lukewarm water (110° to 115°)	¼ pound (1 stick) unsalted butter, cut into small bits
5 to 6 cups all-purpose flour	2 tablespoons softened butter
1 teaspoon salt	1 egg, lightly beaten

In a small bowl, sprinkle the yeast and a pinch of sugar over the lukewarm water. Let the mixture stand for 2 or 3 minutes, then stir to dissolve the yeast completely. Set the bowl in a warm, draft-free place, such as an unlighted oven, for 5 to 8 minutes, or until the mixture doubles in volume.

In a deep mixing bowl, combine the 1 cup of sugar, 4 cups of the flour and the salt. Make a well in the center, pour in the yeast and milk, and drop in the eggs. Gently stir together with a large spoon, then beat vigorously until all the ingredients are well combined. Beat in ¼ pound of butter, then add up to 2 cups more flour, beating it in ¼ cup at a time, and using as much as necessary to form a dough that can be gathered into a soft ball. If the dough becomes difficult to stir, work in the flour with your fingers.

Place the dough on a lightly floured surface, and knead it, pressing down and pushing it forward several times with the heel of your hand. Fold it back on itself and repeat for about 15 minutes until it is smooth and elastic.

Shape the dough into a ball and place it in a large, lightly buttered bowl. Dust the top with flour, drape with a towel and set aside in the warm, draft-free place for 45 minutes to an hour until the dough doubles in bulk.

With a pastry brush, coat the bottom and sides of two 9-inch pie plates with 2 tablespoons of softened butter. Punch the dough down with a single blow of your fist, then transfer it to a lightly floured surface and let it rest for 10 minutes. Divide the dough in two and pat the halves into flattened round loaves about 8 inches across. Place them in the pie plates and let them rise in a warm place for about 40 minutes.

Preheat the oven to 350°. With a pastry brush, coat the top of both loaves with beaten egg. Bake in the middle of the oven for about 1 hour, or until the loaves are golden brown and crusty. Cool on cake racks.

Honey Bread

Yemarina Yewotet Dabo

To make one 8½-inch round bread

1 package active dry yeast
¼ cup lukewarm water (110° to 115°)
1 egg
½ cup honey
1 tablespoon ground coriander
½ teaspoon ground cinnamon
¼ teaspoon ground cloves
1½ teaspoons salt
1 cup lukewarm milk (110° to 115°)
6 tablespoons melted unsalted butter
4 to 4½ cups all-purpose flour

In a small, shallow bowl, sprinkle the yeast over the lukewarm water. Let the mixture stand for 2 or 3 minutes, then stir it to dissolve the yeast completely. Set the bowl in a warm, draft-free place, such as an unlighted oven, for about 5 minutes, or until the yeast bubbles up and the mixture almost doubles in volume.

Combine the egg, honey, coriander, cinnamon, cloves and salt in a deep bowl, and mix them together with a wire whisk or spoon. Add the yeast mixture, milk and 4 tablespoons of the melted butter, and beat until the ingredients are well blended. Stir in the flour, ½ cup at a time, using only as much as necessary to make a dough that can be gathered into a soft ball. When the dough becomes too stiff to stir easily, blend in the additional flour with your fingers.

On a lightly floured surface, knead the dough by folding it end to end, then pressing it down and pushing it forward several times with the heel of your hand. Rub your hands with a little melted butter if the dough sticks to the board or your fingers, but do not use any extra flour lest the dough become stiff and hard. Repeat for about 5 minutes, or until the dough is smooth and elastic.

Shape the dough into a ball and place it in a large, lightly buttered bowl. Drape a kitchen towel over the bowl and set in a warm, draft-free spot for about 1 hour, or until the dough rises and doubles in bulk.

With a pastry brush, spread the remaining melted butter evenly over the bottom and sides of a 3-quart soufflé dish or other round 3-quart baking dish at least 3 inches deep. Punch the dough down with a single blow of your fist, then knead it again for 1 or 2 minutes. Shape the dough roughly into a round and place it in the buttered baking dish, pressing it down into the corners so that it covers the bottom of the dish completely. Return the dough to the warm, draft-free place for about 1 hour, or until it has doubled in bulk and risen at least as high as the top rim of the dish.

Preheat the oven to 300°. Bake the bread in the middle of the oven for 50 to 60 minutes, until the top is crusty and light golden brown. Turn the bread out of the pan onto a cake rack to cool. *Yemarina yewotet dabo* may be served while it is still somewhat warm, or may be allowed to cool completely. Traditionally, it is eaten spread with butter and honey.

Danish Christmas Fruit Loaf
Julekage

To make 1 large loaf

2 packages or cakes of active dry or
  compressed yeast
¼ cup sugar
½ cup lukewarm milk
¼ teaspoon salt
½ teaspoon vanilla
½ teaspoon grated lemon rind

2 eggs, lightly beaten
½ teaspoon ground cardamom
3 to 4 cups sifted flour
1 cup mixed candied fruits (lemon,
  orange, cherry, pineapple)
1 tablespoon flour
8 tablespoons (1 quarter-pound
  stick) unsalted butter, softened

Sprinkle the yeast and 1 tablespoon of the sugar over the lukewarm milk. Let the mixture stand in the cup for 2 or 3 minutes, then stir gently to dissolve them. Set in a warm place, perhaps in an unlighted oven. When the yeast begins to bubble in about 8 to 10 minutes, stir it gently, and with a rubber spatula, transfer it to a large mixing bowl. Stir in the salt, vanilla, lemon rind, eggs, cardamom and the remaining sugar. Then add 3 cups of flour, a little at a time, stirring at first and then kneading with your hands until the dough becomes firm enough to be formed into a ball.

Shake the candied fruits in a small paper bag with 1 tablespoon of flour. (The flour will prevent the fruits from sticking together and enable them to disperse evenly throughout the dough.) Now add the fruits and the softened butter to the dough and knead for about 10 minutes, adding more flour, if necessary, to make the dough medium-soft. The finished dough should be shiny and elastic, and its surface blistered. Shape into a ball and place in a large bowl. Dust the top lightly with flour, cover with a kitchen towel and set it in a warm, draft-free spot (again, an unlighted oven is ideal). In 45 minutes to 1 hour the dough should double in bulk and leave a deep depression when two fingers are pressed into the center.

After removing the dough, preheat the oven to 350°. Punch the dough down with your fists and knead again quickly. Shape it into a fat loaf and put it into a lightly buttered 1½-quart loaf pan. Cover again with the towel and let the dough rise in a warm spot for 15 to 20 minutes until it is almost double in bulk.

Bake the *julekage* in the center of the oven for 45 minutes. Remove the loaf from the pan and let it cool on a cake rack. It will keep well for 2 or 3 weeks if wrapped well in aluminum foil and refrigerated.

Finnish Bread

Suomalaisleipä

To make 1 loaf

4 packages or cakes of active dry or
    compressed yeast
3 teaspoons dark brown sugar
1¼ cups lukewarm water

1 tablespoon melted butter
1½ teaspoons salt
2 cups all-purpose flour
1½ cups rye flour
1 tablespoon soft butter

Sprinkle the yeast and 1 teaspoon of the brown sugar over ¼ cup of the lukewarm water. Be absolutely sure that the water is lukewarm—neither too hot nor too cool to the touch. Let the mixture stand for 2 or 3 minutes, then stir it to dissolve the yeast completely. Set the cup aside in a warm, draft-free spot (such as an unlighted oven) for 5 to 7 minutes, or until the mixture has begun to bubble and has almost doubled in volume.

Pour the yeast mixture into a large mixing bowl, add the remaining cup of lukewarm water, and, with a wooden spoon, mix in the remaining 2 teaspoons of brown sugar, the melted butter, salt, white flour and 1 cup of the rye flour. When the mixture forms a smooth dough, gather it into a ball, cover the bowl loosely with a kitchen towel and let it rest at room temperature for about 10 minutes.

Transfer the dough to a floured pastry cloth or board and knead it by pulling the dough into an oblong shape, folding it end to end, then pressing it down and pushing it forward several times with the heels of your hands. Turn the dough slightly toward you and repeat the process—pulling, folding, pushing and pressing. Continue to knead, using the extra rye flour to sprinkle over the dough and pastry cloth if it becomes sticky.

When the dough is elastic and smooth, gather it into a rough ball and place it in a large, lightly buttered bowl. Dust the top of the dough lightly with flour, cover it again with the kitchen towel and let it rest in the warm, draft-free spot (the oven, again) for about 45 minutes, until it has doubled in bulk and no longer springs back when it is poked with a finger.

On page 423, a portion of the directions for the Rice Pudding recipe are missing. They were printed in error with the Plum Pudding recipe on pages 420-422.

Here is the complete Rice Pudding recipe:

Rice Pudding
Arroz Doce

To serve 4 to 6

1½ cups milk
A 2-inch piece of vanilla bean
A 2-inch piece of stick cinnamon
6 pieces lemon peel, each about
    1½ inches long and ½ inch wide
⅛ teaspoon plus ¼ teaspoon salt

6 cups water
½ cup raw medium or long-grain
    regular-milled rice or imported
    short-grain rice
3 egg yolks
⅓ cup sugar
1 teaspoon ground cinnamon

In a 1- to 1¼-quart saucepan, bring the milk, vanilla bean, cinnamon stick, pieces of lemon peel and ⅛ teaspoon of the salt to a boil over moderate heat. Cover the pan tightly, remove it from the heat and let the seasonings steep for 20 to 30 minutes.

Meanwhile, bring 6 cups of water to a boil in a 2- to 3-quart saucepan. Pour in the rice in a slow stream, stirring constantly, so that the water continues to boil. Add the remaining ¼ teaspoon of salt, reduce the heat to moderate, and boil the rice uncovered 15 to 20 minutes, or until tender. Drain the rice in a colander, turning it about with a fork to separate the grains, then spread it out on a double thickness of paper towels.

In a large bowl, beat the egg yolks and sugar together with a whisk or a rotary or electric beater until light and lemon colored. Beating constantly, pour in the milk in a thin stream. Then return the mixture to the saucepan and cook over low heat, stirring constantly with a wooden spoon until the custard thickens enough to coat the spoon lightly. Do not let it come anywhere near the boil or it may curdle. Remove the vanilla bean and cinnamon stick, add the rice to the custard and cook over low heat for 2 minutes, stirring constantly with a fork. Pour the pudding into a deep platter or a baking dish about 12-by-8 inches and no more than ½ inch deep. Cool to room temperature and just before serving, sprinkle the top lightly with cinnamon.

On page 421, in the Plum Pudding recipe, please disregard paragraphs two and three, beginning: "Meanwhile, bring 6 cups of water to a boil . . ." and ending: ". . . sprinkle the top lightly with cinnamon."

(over)

The Caraway Rye Bread recipe on page 365 is incomplete. Here is the recipe printed in its entirety:

Caraway Rye Bread

To make two 13-inch loaves

½ cup lukewarm water (110° to 115°)
1 package active dry yeast
1 teaspoon sugar
2 to 2½ cups white all-purpose flour
2 to 2½ cups rye flour
1 tablespoon salt

1 cup lukewarm milk (110° to 115°)
¼ cup distilled white vinegar
1 tablespoon unsalted butter, softened
½ cup white or yellow cornmeal
1 egg white, beaten to a froth
3 tablespoons caraway seeds

Pour ¼ cup of the water into a small bowl and sprinkle in the yeast and sugar. Let it rest for 2 or 3 minutes, then stir. Set the bowl in a warm, draft-free place (such as an unlighted oven) for 5 to 8 minutes, or until the yeast bubbles and the mixture almost doubles in volume.

Place 2 cups of white flour, 2 cups of rye flour and the salt in a deep mixing bowl and make a well in the center. Pour in the yeast mixture, the remaining ¼ cup of lukewarm water, the milk and vinegar and, with a large wooden spoon, gradually incorporate the dry ingredients into the liquid. Stir until the mixture is smooth, then beat until the dough can be gathered into a ball. Place on a lightly floured surface and knead, pushing the dough down with the heels of your hands, pressing it forward and folding it back on itself. Sprinkle equal amounts of rye and white flour over the ball by the tablespoonful, adding up to ½ cup more of each if necessary to keep the dough from sticking to your hands. Knead for about 10 minutes, or until the dough is smooth and elastic.

With a pastry brush, spread the softened butter evenly over the inside of a large bowl. Place the dough in the bowl and turn it about to butter the entire surface. Drape the bowl with a kitchen towel and set it aside in the draft-free place for about 1½ hours, or until the dough doubles in volume. Punch the dough down with your fist and set it in the draft-free place to rise again for 45 minutes, or until it has doubled in volume.

Scatter the cornmeal on a large baking sheet and set aside. Cut the dough in half and shape each half into a tapering loaf about 12 inches long and 2½ inches wide in the center. Place the loaves 2 inches apart on the baking sheet and, with a large knife, make ½-inch-deep diagonal slashes at 2-inch intervals on the top of each loaf. Set the loaves in the draft-free place to rise for about 30 minutes.

Preheat the oven to 400°. Brush the egg white over the tops of the loaves. Sprinkle the loaves with the caraway seeds and place them in the center of the oven for 15 minutes. Reduce the oven temperature to 375° and bake for 30 to 35 minutes longer, until the loaves are golden brown. Transfer to wire racks and let them cool before serving.

Preheat the oven to 375°. With a pastry brush or paper towel, lightly spread a cookie sheet with the tablespoon of soft butter and sprinkle it with flour, tipping the sheet to coat it evenly. Turn it over and tap it on a hard surface to knock off any excess flour. Punch the dough down with your fist, and knead it again briefly on the pastry board. Shape it into a round, flat loaf about 9 or 10 inches in diameter, and set on the cookie sheet. Bake 1 hour, or until the bread has a dark-brown crust and a toothpick or skewer inserted in its center comes out dry and clean. Remove to a cake rack to cool, and serve, if possible, while still warm.

Caraway Rye Bread

To make two 13-inch loaves

½ cup lukewarm water (110° to 115°)

1 package active dry yeast

1 teaspoon sugar

2 to 2½ cups white all-purpose flour

2 to 2½ cups rye flour

1 tablespoon salt

1 cup lukewarm milk (110° to 115°)

¼ cup distilled white vinegar

1 tablespoon unsalted butter, softened

½ cup white or yellow cornmeal

1 egg white, beaten to a froth

3 tablespoons caraway seeds

Pour ¼ cup of the water into a small bowl and sprinkle in the yeast and sugar. Let it rest for 2 or 3 minutes, then stir. Set the bowl in a warm, draft-free place (such as an unlighted oven) for about 10 minutes, or until the yeast bubbles and the mixture almost doubles in volume.

Place 2 cups of white flour, 2 cups of rye flour and the salt in a deep mixing bowl and make a well in the center. Pour in the yeast mixture, the remaining ¼ cup of lukewarm water and the milk and vinegar and, with a large wooden spoon, gradually incorporate the dry ingredients into the liquid. Stir until the mixture is smooth, then beat until the dough can be gathered into a ball. Place the ball on a lightly floured surface and knead, pushing the dough down with the heels of your hands, pressing it forward and folding it back on itself. As you knead, sprinkle equal amounts of rye and white flour over the ball by the tablespoonful, adding up to ½ more of each if necessary to make a medium-firm dough. Knead until the dough is smooth and elastic.

Whole-Wheat Bread

To make one 9-by-5-by-3-inch loaf

½ cup lukewarm water (110° to 115°)
1 package active dry yeast
1 teaspoon sugar
¼ cup dark molasses
½ cup lukewarm milk (110° to 115°)
2 to 2½ cups whole-wheat flour

1 cup unsifted all-purpose flour
1 teaspoon salt
4 tablespoons butter, cut into ½-inch bits and softened, plus 2 tablespoons butter, softened
1 egg lightly beaten with 1 tablespoon milk

Pour the lukewarm water into a small bowl and sprinkle in the yeast and sugar. Let the yeast and sugar rest for 2 or 3 minutes, then mix well. Set the bowl in a warm, draft-free place (such as an unlighted oven) for about 10 minutes, or until the yeast bubbles up and the mixture almost doubles in volume.

Pour the molasses into the milk and stir until well blended. Then place 2 cups of whole-wheat flour, the cup of all-purpose flour and the salt in a deep mixing bowl and make a well in the center. Pour in the yeast and the molasses-and-milk mixtures and, with a large wooden spoon, gradually incorporate the dry ingredients into the liquid ones. Stir until the mixture is smooth, then beat in the 4 tablespoons of butter bits, a few teaspoonfuls at a time. Continue to beat until the dough can be gathered into a medium-soft ball.

Place the ball on a lightly floured surface and knead, pushing the dough down with the heels of your hands, pressing it forward and folding it back on itself. As you knead, sprinkle whole-wheat flour over the ball by the tablespoonful, adding up to ½ cup flour if necessary to make a firm dough. Knead for about 10 minutes longer, until the dough is smooth and elastic.

With a pastry brush, spread 1 tablespoon of the softened butter evenly over the inside of a large bowl. Set the dough in the bowl and turn it about to butter the entire surface. Drape the bowl with a kitchen towel and set it aside in the draft-free place for 1 to 1½ hours, or until the dough doubles in volume.

Brush the remaining tablespoon of softened butter over the bottom and sides of a 9-by-5-by-3-inch loaf pan. Punch the dough down with a blow of your fist and, on a lightly floured surface, shape it into a loaf about 8 inches long and 4 inches wide. Place the dough in the buttered pan and set it in the draft-free place to rise again for about 45 minutes.

Preheat the oven to 450°. (If you have used the oven to let the bread rise, gently transfer the loaf to another warm place to rest while the oven heats.) Brush the top of the whole-wheat bread with the egg-and-milk mixture, then bake in the middle of the oven for 35 to 40 minutes, or until the loaf is golden brown. To test for doneness, turn the loaf out on a flat surface and rap the bottom sharply with your knuckles. The loaf should sound hollow; if not, slide it back into the pan and bake for 5 to 10 minutes longer.

Place the finished whole-wheat bread on a wire rack and let it cool before serving.

Leola's Cornbread

To make one 9-inch loaf

1½ cups yellow cornmeal
1 cup all-purpose flour
⅓ cup sugar
1 teaspoon salt
1 tablespoon baking powder

2 eggs
6 tablespoons melted and cooled butter
8 tablespoons melted and cooled vegetable shortening
1½ cups milk

Preheat the oven to 400°. Sift into a mixing bowl the cornmeal, flour, sugar, salt and baking powder. Beat the eggs lightly, add the melted butter and shortening, and stir in the 1½ cups of milk. Pour into the bowl of dry ingredients and beat together for about a minute, or until smooth. Do not overbeat. Lightly butter an 8-by-12-inch shallow baking pan and pour in the batter. Bake in the center of the oven for about 30 minutes, or until the bread comes slightly away from the edge of the pan and is golden brown. Serve hot.

NOTE: If you wish you may bake the cornbread in a 9-by-5-by-3-inch loaf pan. Increase the baking time to 45 minutes.

Irish Soda Bread

To make one 8-inch round loaf

1 tablespoon butter, softened
4 cups all-purpose flour

1 teaspoon baking soda
1 teaspoon salt
1 to 1½ cups buttermilk

Preheat the oven to 425°. With a pastry brush coat a baking sheet evenly with the tablespoon of softened butter.

Sift the flour, soda and salt together into a deep mixing bowl. Gradually add 1 cup of the buttermilk, beating constantly with a large spoon until the dough is firm enough to be gathered into a ball. If the dough crumbles, beat more buttermilk into it by the tablespoon until the particles adhere.

Place the dough on a lightly floured board, and pat and shape it into a flat circular loaf about 8 inches in diameter and 1½ inches thick. Set the loaf on the baking sheet. Then with the tip of a small knife, cut a ½-inch-deep X into the dough, dividing the top of the loaf into quarters.

Bake the bread in the middle of the oven for about 45 minutes, or until the top is golden brown. Serve at once.

Banana Bread

To make one 9-by-5-by-3-inch loaf

9 tablespoons butter, softened
¾ cup unsalted shelled pecans
¼ cup seedless raisins
2 cups all-purpose flour
1 tablespoon double-acting baking
    powder

¼ teaspoon ground nutmeg,
    preferably freshly grated
½ teaspoon salt
2 large ripe bananas (about 1 pound)
1 teaspoon vanilla extract
½ cup sugar
1 egg

Preheat the oven to 350°. With a pastry brush, spread 1 tablespoon of softened butter evenly over the bottom and sides of a 9-by-5-by-3-inch loaf pan and set it aside.

Reserve ¼ cup of the most perfectly shaped pecan halves for the garnish. Chop the rest of the nuts coarsely and toss them with the raisins and 1 tablespoon of the flour. Sift the remaining flour with the baking powder, nutmeg and salt.

Peel the bananas, chop them coarsely, and put them into a small bowl. With the back of a table fork, mash the bananas to a smooth purée. Stir in the vanilla and set aside.

In a deep bowl, cream the remaining butter and the sugar together, beating and mashing them with a large spoon against the sides of the bowl until the mixture is light and fluffy.

Add the egg, and when it is well blended beat in the flour and the bananas alternately, adding about one third of each mixture at a time, and continue to beat until the batter is smooth. Gently but thoroughly stir in the chopped pecans and raisins.

Ladle the batter into the loaf pan and arrange the reserved pecan halves attractively on the top. Bake the bread in the middle of the oven for 50 to 60 minutes, or until a cake tester or toothpick inserted into the center of the loaf comes out clean. Remove the bread from the oven and let it cool in the pan for 5 minutes, then turn it out on a wire cake rack.

Serve the banana bread either warm or cool.

Apple Muffins

To make about 16 muffins

6 tablespoons butter, softened
2 cups unsifted flour
4 teaspoons double-acting baking
   powder
¼ teaspoon baking soda
½ teaspoon ground mace
½ teaspoon salt

¼ cup sugar
2 eggs
1 cup sour cream
3 medium-sized firm ripe cooking
   apples, 2 apples peeled, cored
   and finely chopped (about 1 cup)
   and 1 apple cored and cut
   lengthwise into ⅛-inch-thick
   slices

Preheat the oven to 425°. With a pastry brush, spread 2 tablespoons of softened butter evenly inside 16 muffin cups (each cup should be about 2½ inches across at the top). Combine the flour, baking powder, baking soda, mace and salt, and sift them together into a bowl. Set aside.

In a deep bowl, cream the remaining 4 tablespoons of butter and the sugar, beating and mashing them against the sides of the bowl with the back of a large spoon until the mixture is light and fluffy. Beat in the eggs, one at a time. Then add about 1 cup of the flour mixture and, when it is well incorporated, beat in ½ cup of the sour cream. Repeat, beating in the remaining flour and then the rest of the cream and stir until the batter is smooth. Stir in the chopped apples and spoon the batter into the muffin cups, filling each cup about halfway to the top. Insert a slice of apple, peel side up, partway into the top of each muffin.

Bake in the middle of the oven for 15 to 20 minutes, or until the muffins are brown and a cake tester or toothpick inserted in the centers comes out clean. Turn the muffins out of the tins and serve at once.

Cinnamon Muffins

Mantecadas de Astorga

To make about 20

½ pound (2 sticks) unsalted butter,
   softened
1 cup sugar

1½ cups all-purpose flour
6 eggs
1 tablespoon ground cinnamon

Preheat the oven to 350°. Line the cups of two 12-cup muffin tins with paper cupcake liners. The cups should measure about 2½ inches in diameter across the bottom.

With an electric mixer, beat the butter, sugar and 2 tablespoons of the flour together until the mixture is light and fluffy. Then beat in the eggs, one at a time. Combine the remaining flour and the cinnamon and sift them slowly over the mixture, beating all the while. Continue to beat until the batter is smooth. (To make the batter by hand, cream the butter, sugar and 2 tablespoons of the flour together by mashing and beating them against the side of the bowl with a large spoon until fluffy. Beat in the eggs, one at a time. Then combine the remaining flour and the cinnamon and gradually sift them into the batter, beating well after each addition.)

Ladle the batter into the paper-lined muffin cups, filling each one about half full. Bake in the middle of the oven for 15 minutes, or until the tops of the muffins are golden brown and firm to the touch. Carefully turn the muffins out of the tins and serve warm or at room temperature.

Baking-Powder Biscuits

To make about 10

2 teaspoons butter, softened plus 8
   tablespoons butter, cut into
   ¼-inch bits

2 cups all-purpose flour
2 teaspoons double-acting baking
   powder
1 teaspoon salt
⅔ cup milk

Preheat the oven to 400°. With a pastry brush, spread the 2 teaspoons of softened butter evenly over a baking sheet. Set aside.

Combine the flour, baking powder and salt and sift them into a deep bowl. Add the 8 tablespoons of butter bits and rub the flour and fat together with your fingertips until they resemble flakes of coarse meal. Pour in the milk all at once and mix briefly with a wooden spoon, stirring just long enough to form a smooth soft dough that can be gathered into a compact ball. Do not overbeat.

Place the dough on a lightly floured surface and roll or pat it into a rough circle about ½-inch thick. With a biscuit cutter or the rim of a glass, cut the dough into 2½-inch rounds. Gather the scraps into a ball, pat or roll it out as before and cut as many more biscuits as you can.

Arrange the biscuits side by side on the buttered baking sheet and bake in the middle of the oven for about 20 minutes, or until they are a delicate golden brown. Serve at once.

ADDITIONAL INGREDIENTS FOR	Parmesan cheese
CHEESE-AND-HERB BISCUITS	¼ cup finely cut fresh chives
¼ freshly grated imported	¼ cup finely chopped fresh parsley

CHEESE-AND-HERB BISCUITS: Following precisely the directions for baking-powder biscuits, prepare the dough and gather it into a ball. While the dough is still in the bowl, knead into it the grated cheese, chives and parsley. Place the dough on a lightly floured surface, then roll, cut and bake the biscuits as described above.

Popovers

To make 8	1 cup all-purpose flour
	¼ teaspoon salt
2 eggs	2 tablespoons melted vegetable
1 cup milk	shortening

Preheat the oven to 450°. In a large mixing bowl, beat the eggs with a rotary or electric beater for a few seconds until they froth. Still beating, pour in the milk, and then the flour, salt and a tablespoon of the melted shortening. Continue to beat until the mixture is smooth, but don't overbeat.

With a pastry brush, grease an 8-cup muffin tin or, preferably, heavy popover pans, with the remaining shortening. Pour enough batter into each cup to fill it about ⅔ of the way to the top. Bake in the center of the oven for 20 minutes. Then reduce the heat to 350° and bake 10 to 15 minutes longer, or until the popovers have puffed to their fullest height, and are golden brown and crusty. Serve at once.

Cottage-Cheese Pancakes

To make about 3 dozen 2-inch
   pancakes

1 cup creamed cottage cheese (8
   ounces)
5 eggs, lightly beaten
½ cup unsifted flour

16 tablespoons butter (½ pound),
   melted and cooled
1 teaspoon vanilla extract
A pinch of salt

Preheat the oven to its lowest setting. Meanwhile, line a large baking sheet with paper towels and place it in the middle of the oven.

With the back of a spoon, rub the cottage cheese through a fine sieve into a deep mixing bowl. Beating constantly, pour in the eggs gradually and, when they are well incorporated, add the flour by the tablespoonful. Stir in 8 tablespoons of the cooled melted butter, the vanilla and salt.

Warm a large heavy griddle over moderate heat until a drop of water flicked onto it splutters and evaporates instantly. Grease the griddle lightly with a pastry brush dipped into the remaining 8 tablespoons of butter. Cook 5 or 6 pancakes at a time. To form each cake, pour about a tablespoon of the batter on the griddle, leaving enough space between them so that they can spread into 2-inch rounds. Fry them for 2 minutes on each side, or until they are golden and crisp around the edges.

As they brown, transfer the cakes to the paper-lined baking sheet and keep them warm in the oven while you fry the rest. Repeat the procedure, brushing the griddle with melted butter when necessary, until all the cottage-cheese pancakes are fried. Serve at once with jelly or jam.

Griddlecakes

To make 18 to 20 pancakes

2 cups all-purpose flour
2 teaspoons baking powder
2 teaspoons sugar

1 teaspoon salt
3 eggs, lightly beaten
2 cups milk
¼ cup melted butter
¼ cup vegetable oil

Sift the flour, baking powder, sugar and salt together into a large mixing bowl. Make a well in the center of the flour and pour into it the eggs and milk. With a large spoon mix together only long enough to blend, then stir in the melted butter. Do not overmix; the pancakes will be lighter if the batter is not too smooth. Heat a griddle or heavy skillet over moderate heat until a drop of water flicked onto it evaporates instantly.

Grease the griddle or skillet very lightly with a pastry brush dipped in oil; continue to grease when necessary. Pour the batter from a pitcher or small ladle into the hot pan to form pancakes 4 inches in diameter. Cook 2 to 3 minutes until small, scattered bubbles have formed—but have not broken—on the surface . Immediately turn with a spatula and cook for a minute until the other side of the pancake is golden brown. Stack on a heated plate and serve with melted butter and maple syrup.

Sour-Cream Waffles
Fløtevafler

Makes 6 waffles

5 eggs
½ cup sugar
1 cup flour, sifted

1 teaspoon ground cardamom
   or ginger
1 cup sour cream
4 tablespoons unsalted butter, melted

Beat the eggs and sugar together for 5 to 10 minutes in an electric mixer or by hand with a wire whisk until it falls back into the bowl in a lazy ribbon when the beater is lifted out. Now, with a rubber spatula, alternately fold in half the flour, cardamom (or ginger), and sour cream, and then the remaining flour. Lightly stir in the melted butter and set the batter aside for 10 minutes. If you use a nonelectric Norwegian waffle iron, heat it, ungreased, until it is so hot that a drop of water sputters when flicked across its surface. Pour about ¾ cup of the batter in the center of the hot iron, close the top and cook over direct heat for 5 minutes on each side. Serve with lingonberry or another tart jam. This batter may be used in any regular American electric waffle iron.

Canning Directions

To ensure consistent results in home canning, use standard canning jars or jelly glasses with matching lids. An airtight seal is imperative. Examine each one carefully and discard those with covers that do not fit securely or those with edges that have cracks or chips.

Wash the jars, glasses, lids and rings in hot, soapy water and rinse them with scalding water. Place them in a large, deep pot and pour in sufficient hot water to submerge them completely. Bring to a boil over high heat. Then turn off the heat and let the pan stand while you finish cooking the food that you plan to can. The jars or glasses must be hot when the food is placed in them.

To be ready to seal the glasses, grate a 4-ounce bar of paraffin into the top of a double boiler (preferably one with a pouring spout), and melt it over hot water. Do not let the paraffin get so hot that it begins to smoke; it will catch fire easily.

When the food is ready for canning, remove the jars or glasses from the pot with tongs and stand them upright on a level surface. Leave the lids and rings in the pot until you are ready to use them. Fill and seal the jars one at a time, filling each jar to within ⅛ inch of the top and each glass to within ½ inch of the top. Each jar should be sealed quickly and tightly with its ring and lid.

The jelly glasses should also be sealed at once. Pour a single thin layer of hot paraffin over the surface of jelly, making sure it covers the jelly completely and touches all sides of the glass. If air bubbles appear on the paraffin prick them immediately with a fork or the tip of a knife. Let the glasses rest until the paraffin cools and hardens; then cover them with metal lids.

Relishes & Preserves

Apple Chutney

To make 3 pints

8 cups coarsely diced, peeled and
  cored green cooking apples (about
  3 pounds)
2 cups coarsely chopped onions
  (about 1 pound)
2 cups white seedless raisins
2 cups dark-brown sugar

1½ cups malt vinegar
1 tablespoon mustard seeds, crushed
  with a mortar and pestle or
  wrapped in a towel and crushed
  with a rolling pin
1½ teaspoons mixed pickling spice,
  tied in cheesecloth
½ teaspoon ground ginger
½ teaspoon cayenne pepper

In a heavy 4- to 5-quart pot, combine the apples, onions, raisins, brown
sugar, vinegar, mustard seeds, pickling spice, ginger and cayenne pepper.
Bring the mixture to a boil, stirring occasionally, then reduce the heat to
low and simmer uncovered for 2 hours, or until most of the liquid has
cooked away and the mixture is thick enough to hold its shape in a spoon.
Stir it frequently as it begins to thicken, to prevent the chutney from sticking to the bottom and sides of the pan.

  Remove the pot from the heat. With a large spoon, ladle the chutney immediately into hot sterilized jars, filling them to within ⅛ inch of the top
and following the directions for canning and sealing on page 374.

Beet Relish

To make 4 pints

2 cups chopped cooked beets
4 cups chopped cabbage
1 cup sugar

½ cup prepared horseradish
1 teaspoon salt
1 teaspoon pepper
Vinegar

In a large saucepan mix together the beets, cabbage, sugar, horseradish, salt and pepper. Cover the mixture with vinegar and cook for 20 to 30 minutes, or until the vinegar is absorbed. Turn into jars and seal while hot, following the directions on page 374.

Red Chili Paste
Ají Molido con Aceite

To make about 2 cups

1 cup tightly packed dried *hontaka* chilies
2 cups boiling water

6 tablespoons olive oil
½ teaspoon finely chopped garlic
¼ teaspoon salt
1 cup boiling beef or chicken stock, fresh or canned, or boiling water

NOTE: Wear rubber gloves when handling the hot chilies.

Break the dried chilies in half and brush out the seeds. Place the chilies in a bowl, pour 2 cups of boiling water over them, and let them soak for 2 hours. Drain the chilies and discard the soaking water. Combine the chilies, oil, garlic, salt and boiling stock or water in the jar of a blender and purée at high speed for 1 minute, or until the mixture is reduced to a smooth purée. Scrape into a bowl and cover with plastic wrap. Chili paste can be used as a substitute for fresh hot chilies in many South American dishes. It will keep for 2 to 3 weeks if it is tightly covered and refrigerated.

Cranberry-Orange Relish

To make 1 quart

½ cup water
½ cup orange juice

1 cup granulated sugar
1 pound whole cranberries
2 tablespoons grated orange rind

In a 3- or 4-quart saucepan, stir the water, orange juice and sugar together until the sugar is thoroughly dissolved. Add the cranberries, bring to a boil and cook for 3 to 5 minutes, stirring occasionally, until the skins of the berries begin to pop and the berries are tender but not mushy.

Remove the pan from the heat and stir in the orange rind. Transfer the mixture to a serving bowl, let cool, and then chill for at least an hour.

Cucumber Relish

To make 2 pints

4 cups small whole cucumbers
1 onion, sliced
1 red pepper, seeded and chopped
⅛ cup salt

½ cup brown sugar
A pinch of turmeric
1 teaspoon white mustard seed
1 teaspoon prepared horseradish
Vinegar

Mix together the cucumbers, onion and red pepper. Cover them with the salt and let the mixture stand overnight. In the morning drain it and wash off the salt. Put the vegetables in a saucepan and add the brown sugar, turmeric, mustard seed and horseradish. Cover with vinegar and heat to the boiling point. Turn into clean jars, following the directions on page 374.

Curried Relish

To make 3½ cups

4 pounds tomatoes, cubed
2½ cups chopped onions
1½ tablespoons salt
Cider vinegar

1 tablespoon flour
1 tablespoon dry mustard
2 tablespoons curry powder
1 tablespoon brown sugar
1½ teaspoons dried ground chili peppers

Put the tomatoes and onions in a bowl in layers, sprinkling each layer with salt. Let them stand overnight.

Drain off the accumulated liquid and turn the tomato-onion mixture into a heavy saucepan. Add enough vinegar to cover the mixture. Bring to a boil and cook over high heat for 5 minutes. Mix the flour, mustard, curry powder, brown sugar and chili peppers with a little vinegar, then stir the paste into the tomato mixture. Cook over low heat for 1 hour, stirring occasionally. Let the mixture cool, then turn it into glass jars, cover them, and put the relish in the refrigerator. It will keep indefinitely.

Serbian Vegetable Relish

Srpski Ajvar

To serve 2 to 4

1 large eggplant (about 1½ pounds)
3 large green peppers (about 1 pound)
1 teaspoon salt

Freshly ground black pepper
½ teaspoon finely chopped garlic
2 tablespoons lemon juice
6 tablespoons vegetable oil
2 tablespoons finely chopped parsley

Preheat the oven to 500°. Place the eggplant and green peppers on a rack set in a baking pan. Bake the green peppers for 25 minutes, then remove them. Bake the eggplant 15 to 20 minutes longer, or until it is tender. Wrap the eggplant in a damp towel and let it stand for about 10 minutes to loosen its skin. Peel the green peppers, remove and discard the seeds and ribs, then chop the peppers very finely and transfer them to a glass mixing bowl. Peel the eggplant, chop it very finely and squeeze it dry in a kitchen towel.

Add the eggplant, the salt and a few grindings of black pepper to the chopped green peppers in the mixing bowl. Then, with a wooden spoon, stir in the garlic, lemon juice and vegetable oil, mixing all the ingredients together thoroughly. Taste for seasoning. Chill and garnish with the parsley.

Bread and Butter Pickles

To make 4 to 5 pints

12 medium-sized cucumbers, cut into
    ¼-inch slices
1½ pounds onions, thinly sliced
½ cup salt
3 cups vinegar

3 cups sugar
½ teaspoon turmeric
¼ cup mustard seed
2 teaspoons celery seed
¼ teaspoon cayenne pepper

In a large glass or stainless-steel bowl, combine the sliced cucumbers, onions and salt. Let the mixture stand for 3 hours, then pour it into a colander to drain. Rinse with cold water, then drain again.

In an 8- to 10-quart saucepan, combine the vinegar, sugar, turmeric, mustard seed, celery seed and cayenne pepper. Bring to a boil and add the drained cucumber and onion slices. Reduce the heat to low, bring just to a simmer and simmer for 2 minutes. Avoid actual boiling to prevent the cucumber slices from softening too much. They should remain crisp.

Cool the pickles you want to serve immediately and pack the rest in hot, sterilized jars.

Bramble Jelly

To make about 4 cups

2 quarts fresh, ripe blackberries (about 3 pounds)	2 cups water 2½ cups sugar

Pick over the berries carefully, removing any stems and discarding fruit that is badly bruised or shows signs of mold. Do not discard any underripe berries; although tarter than ripe ones, they contain more pectin (the substance that jells the fruit), and a few will help ensure a firm jelly. Wash the berries in a colander under cold running water and drop them into an 8- to 10-quart pot. Add the 2 cups of water and bring to a boil over high heat. Reduce the heat to low and simmer uncovered for 1 hour, crushing the berries from time to time against the sides of the pot with a large spoon until the fruit becomes a coarse purée.

Line a colander or a sieve with protruding handles with 4 layers of dampened cheesecloth, and set it in another large pot. Pour in the berry purée. Allow the juice to drain through into the pot without disturbing it; squeezing the cheesecloth will make the final jelly cloudy.

When the juice has drained through completely, discard the berries and bring the juice to a boil over high heat. Boil the juice briskly, uncovered, until it is reduced to 3 cups, then add the sugar and cook, stirring until the sugar dissolves. Boil uncovered, without stirring, until the jelly reaches a temperature of 220° (or 8° above the boiling point of water in your locality) on a jelly, candy or deep-frying thermometer.

Remove the pot from the heat and carefully skim off all of the surface foam with a large spoon. Ladle the jelly immediately into hot sterilized jars or jelly glasses, filling them according to the directions on page 374.

Blueberry Jam

6 cups fresh blueberries
3 tablespoons lemon juice

7 cups sugar
1 bottle liquid pectin

Wash the blueberries and put them in a large, heavy kettle. Crush them and add the lemon juice and sugar. Bring to a full rolling boil, stirring constantly. Boil for 1 minute, then remove from the heat and stir in the pectin. Continue to stir for 5 minutes, skimming the froth from the top of the liquid. This will allow the jam to cool slightly and prevent the fruit from floating. Ladle the jam quickly into sterilized glasses and cover at once with paraffin, following the directions on page 374.

Grapefruit Marmalade

To make about 4 pints

3 large, ripe grapefruit
2½ to 3 quarts cold water

8 to 10 cups sugar, preferably
superfine

Wash the grapefruit and pat dry with paper towels. With a knife or rotary peeler remove the skins without cutting into the bitter white pith. Cut the peel into strips about 1 inch long and ⅛ inch wide. Cut away and discard the white outer pith. Slice the fruit in half crosswise, wrap the halves one at a time in a double thickness of damp cheesecloth, and twist the cloth to squeeze the juice into a bowl. Wrap the squeezed pulp in the cheesecloth and tie securely. Add enough cold water to the bowl to make 3½ quarts of liquid. Drop in the bag of pulp and strips of peel. Let the mixture stand at room temperature for at least 12 hours.

Pour the entire contents of the bowl into an 8- to 10-quart stainless-steel or enameled pot, and bring to a boil over high heat. Reduce the heat to low and, stirring occasionally, simmer uncovered for 2 hours. Discard the bag of pulp and measure the mixture. Add 1 cup of sugar for each cup of mixture, stir thoroughly, and bring to a boil over moderate heat. When the sugar has dissolved, increase the heat to high and, stirring occasionally, boil briskly for about 30 minutes, until the marmalade reaches a temperature of 220° (or 8° above the boiling point of water in your locality) on a jelly, candy or deep-frying thermometer. Remove from the heat. With a large spoon, skim off the surface foam. Ladle the marmalade into hot sterilized jars or jelly glasses (*directions, page 374*). To prevent the peel from floating to the top, gently shake the jars occasionally as they cool.

Pear Conserve

To make 5 quarts

8 pounds pears
4 lemons

8 pounds sugar
½ pound preserved ginger

Peel, core and quarter the pears. Put them through a food chopper, using the medium blade. Put the lemons through a food chopper, using the small blade. Mix the chopped pears and lemons with the sugar and ginger, cover, and let stand overnight. In the morning, preheat the oven to 350°. On top of the stove, bring the mixture to a boil. Then place it in the oven and cook it for 10 minutes. Reduce the heat to 300° and cook for about 1½ hours, or until the jam is thick and amber colored. Turn it into hot, sterile jars. Allow it to cool, then seal the jars.

Plum Jam

To make about 1 quart

4 pounds firm, ripe blue or red plums   4 pounds sugar (10 cups)

Wash the plums under cold running water and pat them dry with paper towels. Then cut them in half and pry out the pits. With a nutcracker or the tip of a knife, break open 12 of the pits and remove their kernels. Combine the plum halves and the 12 kernels in a 6- to 8-quart pot. Stir in the sugar.

Let the mixture rest at room temperature for 30 minutes, then set the pot over low heat and cook, stirring constantly with a wooden spoon, until the sugar dissolves. Bring to a boil over high heat, reduce the heat to moderate, and cook, stirring occasionally, for 45 minutes, or until the jam thickens and reaches a temperature of 221° (or 9° above the boiling point of water in your locality) on a jelly, candy or deep-frying thermometer. Remove from the heat. With a large spoon, carefully skim off the foam from the surface and ladle the jam into hot sterilized jars or jelly glasses, following the directions for canning and sealing on page 374.

Plum Preserves
Šljiva Slatko

To make 4 cups

4 cups sugar

2 pounds damson plums, sliced in
half and pitted

3 tablespoons lemon juice

Slatko is a Serbian specialty consisting of pieces of large fruit or whole small fruits, such as cherries or berries, that hold their shape during cooking. To avoid breaking up the fruit, do not stir it but shake the pan often to prevent sticking or burning. The most popular *slatko* is made from plums. To prepare it, combine the sugar and plums in a 2- to 3-quart saucepan, with the plums on the bottom. Cover tightly and cook on medium heat for 10 minutes, then shake the pan gently to distribute the sugar evenly. Replace the cover and cook over medium heat for 15 to 20 minutes longer, or until all the sugar is dissolved.

Add the lemon juice and boil for 8 to 10 minutes, or until the liquid thickens to a thin syrup that, if tested, registers 234° on a candy thermometer or forms a soft ball when a little is dipped into cold water.

Off the heat, skim off any foam on top of the fruit with a wooden spoon, then cover the pan and let the plums stand for 12 hours at room temperature before serving. If the *slatko* has become watery during this time, boil it again for a short time, and cool it again.

Because of the syrup in which it is cooked and kept, *slatko*, refrigerated in a covered glass container, will keep for as long as two years. It may be served as a simple dessert or as preserves.

Cakes

Layer Cake with Praline Topping
Frankfurter Kranz

To serve 10

THE CAKE
1 tablespoon butter, softened
2 tablespoons flour
¼ pound plus 4 tablespoons
   unsalted butter (1½ sticks),
   softened
1 cup sugar

1 cup all-purpose flour
1½ teaspoons finely grated lemon
   peel
6 eggs, at room temperature
¾ cup cornstarch
1 tablespoon double-acting baking
   powder
¾ cup rum

Preheat the oven to 325°. With a pastry brush or paper towel, coat the bottom, sides and tube of a 9-inch tube cake pan with 1 tablespoon of soft butter. Sprinkle the butter with 2 tablespoons of flour, tip it from side to side to spread the flour evenly, then invert the pan and rap the bottom sharply to remove the excess flour.

In a large bowl, cream ¼ pound plus 4 tablespoons of butter, 1 cup of sugar, 1 tablespoon of the flour and the lemon peel together by mashing and beating them against the sides of the bowl with a large spoon. Then beat in the eggs, one at a time, and continue to beat until smooth. Combine the remaining flour, cornstarch and baking powder, and sift them into the butter a little at a time, beating well after each addition.

Pour the batter into the cake pan and bake in the middle of the oven for 40 minutes, or until a cake tester inserted in the center comes out clean. Let the cake cool in the pan for 10 minutes. Then run a knife around the inside edges of the pan, place a wire cake rack on top and, grasping rack and pan firmly together, turn them over. The cake should slide easily out of the pan. When the cake has cooled completely, slice it crosswise with a large, sharp knife into three equal layers. (It is easiest to cut if baked a day in advance.) Spread the layers on a long strip of foil or wax paper and sprinkle each layer with ¼ cup of rum.

10 egg yolks, at room temperature

⅛ teaspoon cream of tartar

1 pound unsalted butter (4 sticks),
softened

⅔ cup water

½ cup rum

To make the butter-cream filling, beat the 10 egg yolks in a large bowl with a whisk or a rotary or electric beater until they are thick and lemon colored. Set the beaten yolks aside. Cream the pound of soft butter by mashing and beating it against the sides of a bowl with a large spoon until it is light and fluffy. Set it aside.

Bring 1⅓ cups of sugar, ⅛ teaspoon cream of tartar and ⅔ cup of water to a boil over moderate heat in a small saucepan, stirring only until the sugar dissolves. Increase the heat to high and boil the syrup briskly without stirring until it reaches a temperature of 236° on a candy thermometer, or until a drop spooned into cold water immediately forms a soft ball.

Pour the syrup in a thin stream into the reserved egg yolks, beating constantly with a whisk or a rotary or electric beater. Continue beating for 4 or 5 minutes longer, or until the mixture is thick and smooth. Gradually add ½ cup of rum, and continue to beat until the mixture has cooled to room temperature and is thick. Now beat in the reserved butter, a tablespoon or so at a time, and when it is completely absorbed, cover the bowl with wax paper or plastic wrap and refrigerate the butter cream for at least 30 minutes, or until it can be spread easily.

TOPPING

1 tablespoon butter

½ cup cold water

1 cup sugar

1 cup blanched almonds

Meanwhile prepare the praline topping in the following fashion: With a pastry brush or paper towel, coat a baking sheet with 1 tablespoon of butter and set it aside. In a small saucepan, bring 1 cup of sugar and ½ cup of water to a boil over moderate heat, stirring until the sugar dissolves. Increase the heat to high and boil briskly, undisturbed, until the syrup reaches a temperature of 236° on a candy thermometer, or a drop of syrup spooned into cold water immediately forms a soft ball. Stir in the nuts and cook until the syrup reaches a temperature of 310° on a candy thermometer, or until the syrup caramelizes and turns a rich golden brown.

Pour the syrup evenly onto the baking sheet. When it is cool and firm, break the praline into small pieces and pulverize it in a blender for a few seconds or crush it with a mortar and pestle. Spread it out on wax paper.

To assemble the cake, place the bottom layer in the center of a large cake plate and, with a spatula, spread it with about ½ inch of butter cream. Set the second layer on top and spread it with another ½-inch layer of butter cream. Finally set the top layer of cake in place and mask the top and sides with the remaining butter cream (if you like, reserve some butter cream to decorate the cake). Gently press the crushed praline over the sides of the cake and sprinkle the remainder over the top. Any extra butter cream may be piped on top of the cake through a pastry tube fitted with a decorative tip.

An elegant dessert for special occasions, this rum-flavored cake from Germany, called *Frankfurter Kranz*, has a butter-cream filling and a praline topping.

Almond Cake with Raspberry Filling
Mandeltorte

To serve 6 to 8

	2 whole eggs
CAKE	6 egg yolks
1 ½ cups blanched almonds	½ cup sugar
2 tablespoons butter, softened	⅓ cup flour
4 tablespoons fine dry bread crumbs	6 egg whites

Preheat the oven to 350°. Spread the almonds in a shallow roasting pan or jelly-roll pan and toast them in the oven, turning them occasionally, for about 5 minutes, or until they are golden brown. Pulverize the nuts in an electric blender or with a nut grinder or a mortar and pestle, and set them aside. With a pastry brush or paper towel, lightly coat the bottom and sides of two round 8-inch layer-cake pans with 1 tablespoon of soft butter each. Sprinkle 2 tablespoons of bread crumbs into each pan, tip the pans from side to side to spread the crumbs evenly, then invert the pans, and rap them gently on a table to remove the excess crumbs. Set the pans aside.

With an electric mixer, a whisk or rotary beater, beat the eggs, egg yolks and sugar together until the mixture is thick enough to fall back on itself in a slowly dissolving ribbon when the beater is lifted from the bowl. Then beat in the flour and ground almonds.

In a separate bowl, beat the egg whites with a whisk, rotary or electric beater until they form firm unwavering peaks on the beater when it is lifted from the bowl. With a rubber spatula, gently but thoroughly fold the egg whites into the egg yolk batter using an over-under cutting motion rather than a stirring motion. Pour the batter into the cake pans and spread it out evenly. Bake in the middle of the oven for 20 minutes, or until a cake tester inserted in the center comes out clean. Cool the cakes in the pans for 5 minutes, then run a sharp knife around the outside edges of the cakes, and turn them out on a rack. Cool completely.

GLAZE AND FILLING	2 tablespoons rum
2¼ cups sifted confectioners' sugar	1 tablespoon fresh lemon juice
1 egg white	½ cup raspberry or strawberry jam

Meanwhile, combine the confectioners' sugar, egg white, rum and lemon juice in a large bowl. Beat these ingredients together for about 5 minutes, or until they are smooth and as thick as heavy cream. If the glaze seems too thin, beat in additional confectioners' sugar, a teaspoonful at a time.

To assemble, place one of the layers in the center of a large serving platter. With a small metal spatula or a knife, spread raspberry or strawberry jam over the cake. Set the other layer on top, and coat it with the rum glaze.

Hazelnut Cake
Haselnusstorte

HAZELNUT CAKE

To make 1 ten-inch cake

6 eggs, separated
1 whole egg

¾ cup sugar
1 cup ground hazelnuts
⅓ cup bread crumbs
1 teaspoon flour

Preheat the oven to 275°. In a large bowl, beat the egg yolks and the whole egg together with a wire whisk, or rotary or electric beater, continuing to beat until the mixture is thick and light yellow in color. Gradually beat in ½ cup of the sugar, then the nuts and the bread crumbs. Continue to beat until the mixture forms a dense, moist mass.

In another bowl, beat the egg whites with the wire whisk or rotary or electric beater until they begin to foam, then add ¼ cup of the sugar, 1 tablespoon at a time. Continue to beat until the whites form stiff, unwavering peaks when the beater is lifted from the bowl. With a rubber spatula, mix about ¼ of the whites into the hazelnut mixture, then sprinkle the flour over it and gently fold in the rest of the whites. Continue to fold until no trace of the whites remains. Be careful not to overfold.

Butter and flour a 10-inch springform pan. Turn the pan over and strike it on the table to remove any excess flour. Pour the batter into the pan, smooth the top with a spatula and bake the cake in the middle of the oven for 35 to 45 minutes, or until it shrinks away slightly from the sides of the pan. Remove the upper part of the pan as soon as you take it from the oven and let the cake cool, then slice it into two equal layers, using a long, sharp, serrated knife.

THE FILLING AND TOPPING
1½ cups heavy cream

1 tablespoon sugar
1 teaspoon vanilla extract
⅓ cup ground hazelnuts

THE FILLING: Whip the chilled cream with a wire whisk or rotary or electric beater until it begins to thicken. Add the sugar and vanilla and continue to whip until the cream holds its shape firmly.

Reconstruct the cake by first placing the bottom layer on a sheet of wax paper at least 18 inches square. Spread whipped cream on top to a thickness of ½ inch and place the other layer over it. With a spatula, completely mask the cake with the rest of the whipped cream.

THE TOPPING: Scatter the ⅓ cup of ground hazelnuts on the wax paper around the cake. Then lift a small portion of the paper and toss the nuts on to the cake. Repeat until all the nuts are used. Serve at once.

Orange-Walnut Cake

To make one 8-inch cake

1 tablespoon butter, softened
½ cup dry bread crumbs
6 egg yolks
10 tablespoons sugar
¼ cup grated raw apple
Grated rind of 1 orange (about 2
tablespoons)
1 tablespoon lemon juice
1 tablespoon brandy
¼ teaspoon salt
1½ cups finely grated walnuts
6 egg whites
1 cup heavy cream, stiffly whipped

Preheat the oven to 325°. With a pastry brush, butter the bottom and sides of an 8-inch, 3-inch-deep springform cake pan. Toss in ¼ cup of the bread crumbs and tip the pan from side to side to coat it evenly. Rap the pan sharply to dislodge any excess crumbs. With a whisk or rotary or electric beater, beat the egg yolks for about a minute, then slowly pour in 8 tablespoons of the sugar. Continue beating until the mixture falls back upon itself in a ribbon when the beater is lifted out of the bowl. Beat in the apple, orange rind, lemon juice, brandy and salt, and with a spatula fold in the remaining bread crumbs and walnuts. In another bowl beat the whites until they froth, then add 2 tablespoons of the sugar, continuing to beat until the whites form firm, unwavering peaks on the beater when it is lifted out of the bowl. Gently but thoroughly fold the whites into the egg yolk mixture until no streaks of white show. Pour the batter into the springform pan and with the spatula spread the mixture out evenly. Bake the torte in the center of the oven for 30 minutes, or until it has puffed and has begun to come slightly away from the sides of the pan. Turn off the heat and let the cake rest for 15 minutes before removing it from the oven. Remove the sides of the pan and cool the torte on a cake rack. Spread the top of the cake with the whipped cream and serve.

Chocolate Cake with Sour-Cream Frosting

To make one 9-inch cake

Six 1-ounce squares of unsweetened
    chocolate
12 tablespoons unsalted butter
    (1½ quarter-pound sticks),
    softened
2¼ cups sugar
4 eggs
1 teaspoon vanilla
2 cups all-purpose flour
1½ level teaspoons baking powder
¼ teaspoon salt
1½ cups milk

Preheat the oven to 375°. Break the chocolate into small pieces, place in a small saucepan and melt over moderate heat, stirring constantly with a spoon. Do not let it boil. Cool to room temperature. In a large mixing bowl, cream the butter and sugar together by mashing and beating it with a large spoon until it is light and fluffy. Beat in the eggs, one at a time, then beat in the melted chocolate and vanilla. Sift the flour, baking powder and salt together into another bowl. Beat ¼ cup of the dry ingredients into the chocolate mixture, then beat in ¼ cup of milk. Continue adding the flour and milk alternately in similar amounts, beating until the batter is smooth.

Butter and flour three 9½-inch circular cake pans. Invert the pans and rap them on the edge of the table to knock out any excess flour. Divide the batter equally among the three pans and bake them in the center of the oven for 15 to 20 minutes, or until a knife inserted in the center of the cakes comes out dry and clean. Turn the cakes out on cake racks to cool.

Spread the top of each cake with about ¼ inch of the chocolate sour-cream frosting and place the layers one on top of another on a cake

plate. With a long metal spatula or knife, thoroughly coat the sides of the cakes with the remaining frosting, and add more frosting to the top of the cake if you wish. Decorate the top with the halved walnuts.

CHOCOLATE SOUR-CREAM FROSTING
Three 6-ounce packages semisweet
   chocolate bits

¼ teaspoon salt
1½ cups sour cream
12 to 15 shelled walnut halves

CHOCOLATE SOUR-CREAM FROSTING: In the top of a double boiler, melt the chocolate over boiling water. With a whisk or spoon, stir into it the salt and the sour cream. Ice the cake while the frosting is still warm.

Sacher Cake
Sachertorte

To make 1 nine-inch round cake

6½ ounces semisweet chocolate,
   broken or chopped in small chunks
8 egg yolks
8 tablespoons (¼-pound stick)
   unsalted butter, melted

1 teaspoon vanilla extract
10 egg whites
Pinch of salt
¾ cup sugar
1 cup sifted all-purpose flour
½ cup apricot jam, rubbed through
   a sieve

Preheat the oven to 350°. Line two 9-by-1½-inch round cake pans with circles of wax paper.

In the top of a double boiler, heat the chocolate until it melts, stirring occasionally with a wooden spoon. In a small mixing bowl, break up the egg yolks with a fork, then beat in the chocolate, melted butter and vanilla extract.

With a wire whisk or a rotary or electric beater, beat the egg whites and pinch of salt until they foam, then add the sugar, 1 tablespoon at a time, continuing to beat until the whites form stiff, unwavering peaks on the beater when it is lifted from the bowl.

Mix about ⅓ of the egg whites into the yolk-chocolate mixture, then reverse the process and pour the chocolate over the remaining egg whites. Sprinkle the flour over the top. With a rubber spatula, using an over-and-under cutting motion instead of a mixing motion, fold the whites and the chocolate mixture together until no trace of the whites remains. Do not overfold.

Pour the batter into the 2 lined pans, dividing it evenly between them. Bake in the middle of the oven until the layers are puffed and dry and a toothpick stuck in the center of a layer comes out clean.

Remove the pans from the oven and loosen the sides of the layers by run-

ning a sharp knife around them. Turn them out on a cake rack and remove the wax paper. Let the layers cool while you prepare the glaze.

THE GLAZE

3 ounces unsweetened chocolate,
   broken or chopped into small
   chunks
1 cup heavy cream

1 cup sugar
1 teaspoon corn syrup
1 egg
1 teaspoon vanilla extract

THE GLAZE: In a small heavy saucepan, combine the chocolate, cream, sugar and corn syrup. Stirring constantly with a wooden spoon, cook on low heat until the chocolate and sugar are melted, then raise the heat to medium and cook without stirring for about 5 minutes, or until a little of the mixture dropped into a glass of cold water forms a soft ball. In a small mixing bowl beat the egg lightly, then stir 3 tablespoons of the chocolate mixture into it. Pour this into the remaining chocolate in the saucepan and stir it briskly. Cook over low heat, stirring constantly, for 3 or 4 minutes, or until the glaze coats the spoon heavily. Remove the pan from the heat and add the vanilla. Cool the glaze to room temperature.

When the cake layers have completely cooled, spread one of them with apricot jam and put the other layer on top. Set the rack in a jelly-roll pan and, holding the saucepan about 2 inches away from the cake, pour the glaze over it evenly. Smooth the glaze with a metal spatula. Let the cake stand until the glaze stops dripping, then, using two metal spatulas, transfer it to a plate and refrigerate it for 3 hours to harden the glaze. Remove it from the refrigerator ½ hour before serving.

Black Forest Cherry Cake
Schwarzwälder Kirschtorte

To serve 8 to 10

CHOCOLATE CURLS
8 ounces semisweet bar chocolate

To make chocolate curls to garnish the cake, the bar or chunks of chocolate should be at room temperature but not soft. Hold the chocolate over wax paper or foil and shave the bar or square into thin curls with a sharp narrow-bladed vegetable peeler. Draw the peeler along the wide surface of the chocolate for large curls, and along the narrow side for small ones. Refrigerate or freeze the curls until you are ready to use them.

CAKE
1 tablespoon butter, softened	1 teaspoon vanilla extract
6 tablespoons flour	1 cup sugar
10 tablespoons sweet butter	1/2 cup sifted flour
6 eggs, at room temperature	1/2 cup unsweetened cocoa

Preheat the oven to 350°. With a pastry brush or paper towel, lightly coat the bottoms and sides of three 7-inch round cake pans with soft butter using about 1 tablespoon of butter in all. Sprinkle 2 tablespoons of flour into each pan, tip them from side to side to spread the flour evenly, then invert the pans and rap them sharply on a table to remove any excess flour. Set the pans aside.

Clarify 10 tablespoons of butter in a small saucepan by melting it slowly over low heat without letting it brown. Let it rest for a minute off the heat, then skim off the foam. Spoon the clear butter into a bowl and set aside. Discard the milky solids at the bottom of the pan.

In an electric mixer, beat the eggs, vanilla and 1 cup of sugar together at high speed for at least 10 minutes, or until the mixture is thick and fluffy. (By hand with a rotary beater, this may take as long as 20 minutes of uninterrupted beating.)

Combine the 1/2 cup of sifted flour and the unsweetened cocoa in a sifter. A little at a time sift the mixture over the eggs, folding it in gently with a rubber spatula. Finally, add the clarified butter 2 tablespoons at a time. Do not overmix. Gently pour the batter into the prepared cake pans dividing it evenly among the three of them.

Bake in the middle of the oven for 10 to 15 minutes, or until a cake tester inserted into the center of each cake comes out clean. Remove the cakes from the oven and let them cool in the pans for about 5 minutes. Then run a sharp knife around the edge of each cake and turn them out on racks to cool completely.

SYRUP
¾ cup sugar

1 cup cold water
⅓ cup kirsch

Meanwhile, prepare the kirsch syrup in the following fashion: Combine ¾ cup of sugar and 1 cup of cold water in a small saucepan and bring to a boil over moderate heat, stirring only until the sugar dissolves. Boil briskly, uncovered, for 5 minutes, then remove the pan from the heat and when the syrup has cooled to lukewarm stir in the kirsch.

Transfer the cakes to a long strip of wax paper and prick each layer lightly in several places with the tines of a long fork. Sprinkle the layers evenly with the syrup and let them rest for at least 5 minutes.

FILLING AND TOPPING
3 cups chilled heavy cream
½ cup confectioners' sugar
¼ cup kirsch
1 cup poached pitted fresh red

cherries or 1 cup drained and
rinsed canned sour red cherries
Fresh sweet red cherries with stems,
or substitute maraschino cherries
with stems, drained and rinsed

If you are using fresh cherries for the filling, poach them in the following fashion: Remove their stems and pits, then combine them with 2 cups of water and ¾ cup of sugar in a small saucepan. Bring to a boil over high heat, then reduce the heat to low, simmer for 5 minutes, or until the cherries are tender. Drain them in a colander, discarding the syrup, and pat the cherries completely dry with paper towels. Canned cherries need only be rinsed in cold water and patted completely dry with paper towels.

In a large chilled bowl, beat the cream with a whisk or a rotary or electric beater until it thickens lightly. Then sift ½ cup of confectioners' sugar over the cream and continue beating until the cream forms firm peaks on the beater when it is lifted out of the bowl. Pour in the ¼ cup kirsch in a thin stream, and beat only until the kirsch is absorbed.

To assemble the cake, place one of the three layers in the center of a serving plate. With a spatula, spread the top with a ½-inch-thick layer of whipped cream and strew the cup of fresh or canned cherries over it leaving about ½ inch of cream free of cherries around the perimeter. Gently set a second layer on top of the cherries and spread it with ½ inch of whipped cream. Then set the third layer in place. Spread the top and sides of the cake with the remaining cream.

With your fingers, gently press chocolate curls into the cream on the sides of the cake and arrange a few chocolate curls and fresh or maraschino cherries attractively on top.

An English Christmas fruitcake, in the background, is surrounded by such ingredients as candied fruit, raisins, eggs, flour, almonds and spirits

English Christmas Cake

To make one 12-inch round fruitcake

CAKE

½ pound (2 sticks) plus 4 tablespoons butter, softened

2 cups finely chopped mixed candied fruit peel

2 cups white raisins

1½ cups dried currants

1 cup seedless raisins

½ cup candied cherries, cut in half

½ cup finely chopped candied angelica

2 cups all-purpose flour

½ teaspoon double-acting baking powder

½ teaspoon salt

1 cup dark-brown sugar

1 cup shelled almonds, pulverized in a blender or with a nut grinder or mortar and pestle

4 eggs

¼ cup pale dry sherry, rum or brandy

¼ cup red currant jelly

The basic fruitcake becomes an attractive holiday greeting when decorated with
a white-icing snow scene, tiny trees and a minature Santa Claus.

Preheat the oven to 325°. Using a pastry brush, coat the bottom and sides of
a 12-by-3-inch springform cake pan with 2 tablespoons of the softened butter. Coat one side of a 20-inch strip of wax paper with 2 tablespoons of butter, and fit the paper, greased side up, inside the pan.

In a large bowl, combine the fruit peel, white raisins, currants, seedless raisins, cherries and angelica. Sprinkle the fruit with ½ cup of the flour, tossing
it about with a spoon to coat the pieces evenly. Set aside. Then sift the remaining 1½ cups of flour with the baking powder and salt. Set aside.

In another large bowl, cream the remaining ½ pound of butter with the
brown sugar by mashing and beating them against the sides of the bowl
until they are light and fluffy. Add the pulverized almonds, then beat in the
eggs one at a time. Add the flour-and-baking-powder mixture, a half cup or
so at a time, then beat the fruit mixture into the batter. Finally, add the sherry and pour the batter into the springform pan. It should come to no more
than an inch from the top. If necessary, remove and discard any excess.

Bake in the middle of the oven for 1 hour and 45 minutes, or until a cake tester inserted in the center of the cake comes out clean. Let the cake cool for 30 minutes before removing the sides of the springform, then slip it off the bottom of the pan onto a cake rack to cool completely. Then carefully peel off the paper.

Heat the currant jelly in a small saucepan over moderate heat until it reaches a temperature of 225° on a candy thermometer or is thick enough to coat a wooden spoon lightly. With a small metal spatula, spread the hot glaze evenly over the top and sides of the cake.

MARZIPAN

2 cups almond paste
1 teaspoon almond extract
½ teaspoon salt

1 cup light corn syrup
7 cups confectioners' sugar (2 pounds), sifted

To make the marzipan, use an electric mixer, preferably one equipped with a paddle. Crumble the almond paste in small pieces into the bowl, add the almond extract and ½ teaspoon of salt, and beat at medium speed until well blended. Gradually add the corn syrup in a thin stream, beating constantly until the mixture is smooth. Then beat in the 7 cups of confectioners' sugar, ½ cup at a time. As soon as the mixture becomes so stiff that it clogs the beater, knead in the remaining sugar with your hands. From time to time it will be necessary to soften the marzipan as you add the sugar by placing it on a surface and kneading it for a few minutes. Press the ball down, push it forward, and fold it back on itself, repeating the process as long as necessary to make it pliable.

On a clean surface, roll out half the marzipan into a circle about ½ inch thick. Using a 12-inch pan or plate as a pattern, cut a 12-inch disc out of the circle with a pastry wheel or small, sharp knife. Roll and cut the remaining marzipan into a 36-by-3-inch strip. Gently set the disc of marzipan on top of the cake and press it lightly into place. Wrap the strip of marzipan around the cake, pressing it gently to secure it. If the strip overlaps the top, fold the rim down lightly.

Wrap the cake in foil or plastic, and let it stand at room temperature for at least 48 hours before icing. The cake may be stored for longer periods; it improves with age, and can be kept for several months.

ICING

6 cups confectioners' sugar, sifted
4 egg whites

1 tablespoon strained fresh lemon juice
⅛ teaspoon salt

Just before serving, ice the cake. Combine the 6 cups of confectioners' sugar, egg whites, lemon juice and ⅛ teaspoon salt in a large mixing bowl.

Before it is frosted, the glazed fruitcake is fitted with a top of marzipan, its edges gently turned down to meet a similar strip wrapping the outside.

With a whisk or a rotary or electric beater, beat until the mixture is fluffy but firm enough to stand in soft peaks on the beater when it is lifted out of the bowl. With a small metal spatula, spread the icing evenly over the sides and top of the cake. Then decorate the cake to your taste with swirls of icing, holly and mistletoe, candied fruits, or even small china figurines.

A traditional Eastern European honey cake, rich with almonds, raisins, candied orange peel and spices, has a tradition-shattering ingredient—instant coffee.

Honey Cake
Ugat Dvash

To make one 9-inch loaf cake

1 teaspoon plus ¼ cup flavorless vegetable oil

4 tablespoons plus 2 cups all-purpose flour

¼ cup seedless raisins

¼ cup candied orange peel

3 egg yolks

¾ cup honey

⅓ cup sugar

2 teaspoons finely grated lemon peel

4½ teaspoons instant coffee

(preferably instant *espresso*) dissolved in 1 tablespoon boiling water

1 teaspoon double-acting baking powder

¼ teaspoon baking soda

¼ teaspoon ground cinnamon

¼ teaspoon ground allspice

A pinch of ground cloves

¼ teaspoon salt

3 egg whites

½ cup sliced blanched almonds

398

Preheat the oven to 325°. Using a pastry brush coat the bottom and sides of a 9-by-5-by-3-inch loaf pan with 1 teaspoon of the oil. Sprinkle the oiled pan with 2 tablespoons of the flour, tipping the pan from side to side to spread the flour evenly. Then invert the pan and rap the bottom sharply to remove the excess flour. Combine the raisins and orange peel in a bowl, add 2 tablespoons of the flour and turn the fruit about with a spoon until it is evenly and lightly coated. Set aside.

In a deep bowl, beat the egg yolks with a whisk or a rotary or electric beater until frothy. Then beat in the remaining ¼ cup of oil, the honey, sugar, lemon peel, and the instant coffee dissolved in water. Combine the remaining 2 cups of flour, the baking powder, soda, cinnamon, allspice, cloves and salt and, beating constantly, sift them into the egg-yolk batter, ¼ cup or so at a time. Stir in the raisins and orange peel.

Rinse off the whisk or beater, and in a separate bowl beat the egg whites until they form firm unwavering peaks on the beater when it is lifted from the bowl. With a rubber spatula, thoroughly fold the egg whites into the batter, using an over-under cutting motion rather than a stirring motion.

Pour the batter into the loaf pan and spread it out evenly. Decorate the top with the almonds, arranging the slices to make simple daisy shapes in the center of the cake and a stripe at each end. Bake in the middle of the oven for 1 hour and 15 minutes, or until a cake tester or toothpick inserted in the center comes out clean. Cool in the pan for 4 or 5 minutes, then run a sharp knife around the edges and place the cake on a rack to cool completely. Honey cake is often served with unsalted butter.

Sand Cake
Sandkage

To make one 8-inch round cake

2 teaspoons unsalted butter, softened	1 tablespoon brandy
1 tablespoon dry bread crumbs	1 teaspoon vanilla
16 tablespoons (2 quarter-pound sticks) unsalted butter	1 teaspoon grated lemon rind
1 cup sugar	2 cups all-purpose flour
4 eggs, at room temperature	1 tablespoon cornstarch
	¼ teaspoon salt
	2¼ teaspoons double-acting baking powder

Preheat the oven to 350°. With a pastry brush or a paper towel, lightly spread the bottom and sides of an 8-inch tube pan (including the inner cone of the pan) with the 2 teaspoons of soft butter. Sprinkle the bottom and sides of the pan with bread crumbs, and tap out any excess crumbs.

Cream the ½ pound of butter and sugar together with an electric mixer set at medium speed or by beating them against the sides of a bowl with a wooden spoon until very light and fluffy. Now beat in the 4 eggs, 1 at a time, making sure that each one is thoroughly incorporated before adding another. Then beat in the tablespoon of brandy, teaspoon of vanilla and teaspoon of grated lemon rind. Should the mixture appear to be curdling, beat it very hard until it becomes smooth again. Sift the flour, cornstarch, salt and baking powder together into a mixing bowl and add them to the butter-egg mixture. Beat vigorously until the ingredients are all absorbed.

Pour the batter into the prepared tube pan. Rap the pan once sharply on the table to eliminate any air pockets, and bake in the center of the oven for 50 to 60 minutes, or until the top is golden brown and springy when lightly touched. Run a knife around the edge of the cake to loosen it from the pan; then place the cake on a wire cake rack to cool.

Apricot Upside-down Cake

To serve 8

2 tablespoons butter	1 cup all-purpose flour
1 cup brown sugar	1 teaspoon baking powder
2½ cups drained apricot halves	½ cup hot water
3 egg yolks	3 egg whites
1 cup sugar	Maraschino cherries
A pinch of salt	Whipped cream

In a skillet melt the butter and add the brown sugar. Stir until the brown sugar has melted, and remove from the heat. Add the apricot halves cut side down; gently spoon the sugar syrup over them until they are evenly coated.

In a large mixing bowl beat the egg yolks lightly and add the sugar and salt. Beat vigorously until the mixture is creamy. Sift the flour and baking powder together and add this to the egg mixture a little at a time, moistening the mixture after each addition with the hot water.

In another mixing bowl beat the egg whites with a wire whisk until they form soft peaks. With a rubber spatula fold the egg whites into the batter until no trace of the whites remains.

Place the apricot halves, cut side down, to form one layer in a baking pan. Pour the sugar syrup and then the batter over the apricots and bake in a 350° oven for 30 to 40 minutes, or until the cake is golden brown and springy to the touch. Place a plate over the cake and turn out the cake so that the apricots are on top. Place a maraschino cherry in the center of each apricot and let the cake cool. Top with whipped cream before serving.

Marmalade Pudding

To serve 6 to 8

5 tablespoons butter, softened
1 cup all-purpose flour
1½ teaspoons baking powder
½ teaspoon ground cinnamon
¼ teaspoon salt
⅔ cup sugar

2 eggs, lightly beaten
¼ cup milk combined with ¼ cup
  water
1 teaspoon finely grated orange peel
1 teaspoon vanilla extract
1 cup orange marmalade, preferably
  imported Seville orange marmalade

Preheat the oven to 350°. Using a pastry brush, coat the bottom and sides of a 9-by-5-by-3-inch loaf pan with 1 tablespoon of the softened butter. Sift the flour, baking powder, cinnamon and salt into a small bowl, and set aside.

In a large mixing bowl, cream the remaining 4 tablespoons of butter and the sugar together, beating and mashing them against the sides of the bowl with a spoon until they are light and fluffy. Beat in the eggs. Then beat in the sifted flour mixture, ¼ cup at a time, moistening the mixture after each addition with a little of the combined milk and water. Continue beating until all the ingredients are combined and the batter is smooth. Then beat in the orange peel and vanilla.

Stirring constantly, melt the marmalade over low heat in a small pan; then pour it into the loaf pan. Pour in the batter, and bake in the middle of the oven for 40 to 50 minutes, or until a cake tester inserted in the center of the pudding comes out clean.

Cool the pudding in the pan for about 10 minutes. Then run a long, sharp knife around the inside edges of the pan. Place an inverted serving plate over the pan and, grasping the pan and plate firmly together, quickly turn them over. The pudding should slide out easily. Serve warm.

Indian Puffs
Indianerkrapfen

To make 12 puffs

THE BATTER
¼ cup all-purpose flour

¼ cup cornstarch
4 eggs, separated
½ teaspoon vanilla extract
¼ cup sugar

Preheat the oven to 400°. Sift the flour and cornstarch into a bowl.

Beat the egg yolks lightly with a fork and add the vanilla extract. With a wire whisk or a rotary or electric beater, beat the egg whites until they begin to foam, then, 1 tablespoon at a time, beat in the sugar. Continue beating until the whites form stiff, unwavering peaks.

Mix about ¼ of the egg whites into the yolks with a rubber spatula, then reverse the process and pour the yolk mixture over the rest of the whites. Sprinkle the flour and cornstarch on top of the yolks, then fold gently until no trace of flour remains.

Lightly butter and flour a 12-cup muffin tin. Turn the tin over and strike it on the table to remove any excess flour.

Pour the batter into the cups, filling each cup ⅔ full. Bake in the middle of the oven for 12 minutes, or until the cakes are lightly browned. Remove from the oven and run a knife around each cake to loosen it, then lift them from the tin and cool on a cake rack.

THE FILLING
1½ cups heavy cream, chilled

1 tablespoon sugar
1 teaspoon vanilla extract

THE FILLING: Whip the chilled cream until it begins to thicken, add the sugar and vanilla and continue to whip until the cream holds its shape firmly. Refrigerate.

With a sharp knife, slice around each cake almost to the bottom, leaving a ¼-inch rim around circumference. Pull out the insides of the cakes, leaving thin shells. Fill each cake shell, then refrigerate for 1 hour.

Another method: cut off a ¼-inch slice from the top and remove the insides. Replace the top after filling.

THE GLAZE
4 ounces unsweetened chocolate
⅔ cup chilled heavy cream
1 cup sugar

4 tablespoons water
2 tablespoons white corn syrup
1 egg, lightly beaten
1 tablespoon vanilla extract

THE GLAZE: Combine the chocolate, cream, sugar, water and corn syrup in the top part of a double boiler. Stir them together over low heat until the chocolate melts and the sugar dissolves. Raise the heat to medium and cook without stirring for about 5 minutes longer, or until a little of the mixture dropped into a glass of cold water forms a soft ball.

Remove the pan from the heat and stir 3 tablespoons of the hot mixture into the lightly beaten egg. Then beat the egg mixture briskly into the chocolate mixture and add the vanilla.

Transfer the cakes upside down to a cake rack set on a jelly-roll pan (or right side up if using alternate method) and pour over them the warm glaze from the saucepan. Refrigerate to chill the glaze, and serve.

Rum Cream Roll

Brazo de Gitano

To make one 15-inch roll	¼ cup sugar
	⅛ teaspoon salt
2 tablespoons butter, softened	4 egg whites
6 tablespoons flour	Rum cream filling *(page 404)*
4 egg yolks	Confectioners' sugar

Preheat the oven to 400°. With a pastry brush, coat the bottom and sides of a 10½-by-15½-inch jelly-roll pan with 1 tablespoon of butter. Line the pan with a 20-inch-long strip of wax paper and let the extra paper extend over the ends. Brush the remaining butter over the paper and sprinkle it with 2 tablespoons of flour, tipping the pan from side to side to spread it evenly. Turn the pan over and rap it sharply to remove the excess. Set aside.

With a whisk or a rotary or electric beater, beat the egg whites until they are stiff enough to form unwavering peaks on the beater when it is lifted from the bowl. In another bowl and with the same beater, beat the egg yolks, sugar and salt together until thick and lemon colored. Then sprinkle the remaining 4 tablespoons of flour on top of the egg whites, pour the yolks over them and, with a rubber spatula, fold together lightly but thoroughly, using an over-under cutting motion rather than a stirring motion.

Pour the batter into the pan, spread it into the corners with a spatula, and smooth the top. Bake in the middle of the oven for 8 minutes, or until the cake begins to come away from the sides of the pan. Remove the cake from the oven and carefully turn it out on a fresh sheet of wax paper. Gently peel off the layer of paper on top of the cake and, starting at one long edge, roll the cake into a loose cylinder. Set aside to cool to room temperature.

To assemble the cake, unroll it and spread the top evenly with rum cream filling. Roll up the cake and place it on a serving plate. Just before serving, sprinkle the top and sides of the cake liberally with confectioners' sugar.

RUM CREAM FILLING

2 cups milk	2 egg yolks
2 two-inch pieces stick cinnamon	¼ cup sugar
1 four-inch piece vanilla bean,	¼ cup flour
broken into ½-inch lengths	1 tablespoon dark rum

In a heavy 1- to 1½-quart saucepan, bring the milk, cinnamon stick and vanilla bean to a boil over moderate heat. Cover and set aside off the heat.

In a large mixing bowl, beat the egg yolks and sugar with a whisk or a rotary or electric beater until thick and lemon colored. Beat in the flour 1 tablespoon at a time. Discard the cinnamon stick and vanilla bean and slowly pour the milk into the egg yolk mixture, beating constantly. Return the mixture to the pan and cook over low heat, stirring constantly with a whisk, until the mixture comes to a boil and thickens heavily. Stir in the rum and set aside off the heat to cool to room temperature. Stir every now and then to prevent a crust from forming on the surface. The cream can be kept in the refrigerator for 2 or 3 days, before being used.

Cheesecake

To make one 9-inch cheesecake	2 tablespoons sugar
	½ teaspoon cinnamon
1 six-ounce box Graham crackers,	6 tablespoons unsalted butter, melted
finely crumbled (¾ cup)	2 tablespoons soft butter

In a mixing bowl, with a large spoon combine the finely crumbled Graham crackers, the sugar and cinnamon. Stir the melted butter into the cracker crumbs until they are well saturated. With a pastry brush, heavily butter a 9-inch, 3-inch-deep springform pan with the 2 tablespoons of soft butter. With your fingers, pat an even layer of the cracker-crumb mixture on the bottom and sides of the pan to form a shell. Refrigerate while you make the filling.

FILLING
3 eight-ounce packages cream
  cheese, softened
1¼ cups sugar
6 egg yolks
1 pint sour cream

3 tablespoons all-purpose flour
2 teaspoons vanilla
1 tablespoon lemon juice
1 tablespoon finely grated lemon rind
6 egg whites
2 tablespoons confectioners' sugar

Preheat the oven to 350°. Cream the softened cheese by beating it with a spoon in a mixing bowl until it is smooth. Then gradually beat in the sugar. Beat in the egg yolks one at a time, and continue to beat until all the ingredients are well combined. Stir in the sour cream, flour, vanilla, lemon juice and lemon rind.

With a large whisk or rotary beater, beat the egg whites, preferably in an unlined copper bowl, until they are stiff enough to form unwavering peaks on the beater when it is lifted out of the bowl. With a rubber spatula fold the egg whites gently but thoroughly into the cream cheese mixture until no streaks of white show, but be careful not to overfold.

Pour the filling into the pan, spreading it out evenly with a rubber spatula. Bake in the middle of the oven for 1 hour. Then turn off the oven, and with the oven door open, let the cake rest on the oven shelf for 15 minutes. Remove and let cool to room temperature. Before serving, remove the sides of the pan and sprinkle the cake with confectioners' sugar.

Pies & Pastries

Apple Pie

To make one 9-inch pie

2½ cups all-purpose flour
8 tablespoons chilled vegetable
    shortening or lard
4 tablespoons chilled butter, cut in

¼-inch pieces
¼ teaspoon salt
6 tablespoons ice water
1 tablespoon melted and cooled
    butter

In a large mixing bowl, combine the flour, vegetable shortening or lard, butter and salt. Working quickly, use your fingertips to rub the flour and fat together until they look like flakes of coarse meal. Pour the ice water over the mixture, toss together, and press and knead gently with your hands until the dough can be gathered into a compact ball. Dust very lightly with flour, wrap in wax paper and chill for at least ½ hour.

Lightly butter a 9-inch pie plate and divide the ball of dough in half. On a floured surface, roll out half of the ball into a circle about ⅛ inch thick and 13 to 14 inches in diameter. Lift it up on the rolling pin and unroll it over the pie plate. Be sure to leave enough slack in the middle of the pastry to enable you to line the plate without pulling or stretching the dough. Trim the excess pastry with a sharp knife, so that the pastry is even with the outer rim of the pie plate. Preheat the oven to 375°.

FILLING
¾ cup granulated sugar
1 teaspoon cinnamon
¼ teaspoon allspice
¼ teaspoon nutmeg
1 tablespoon flour

6 cups of peeled, cored and sliced
    Greening apples, about ⅛ inch
    thick (1¾ to 2 pounds)
1 tablespoon lemon juice
2 tablespoons butter, cut in small
    pieces

For the filling, combine the sugar, cinnamon, allspice, nutmeg and flour in a large mixing bowl. Add the apples and the lemon juice, and toss together gently but thoroughly. Fill the pie shell with the apple mix-

406

ture, mounding it somewhat higher in the center. Although the apple filling may appear quite high, it will shrink considerably during the baking. Dot the top of the filling with the 2 tablespoons of butter.

For the upper crust, roll out the remaining half of the dough into a circle the same size and thickness as the bottom crust. Lift it up on the rolling pin and drape it gently over the filling. With a scissors, trim the top crust to within ¼ inch of the pie plate. Tuck the overhanging ¼ inch under the edge of the bottom crust all around the rim and then press down with the tines of a fork to seal the two crusts securely. Brush the pastry evenly with the melted butter and cut two small gashes in the center of the top crust to allow the steam to escape. Bake the pie in the middle of the oven for 40 minutes, or until the crust is golden brown. Serve warm or at room temperature with vanilla ice cream or heavy cream.

Cheese Pie
Crostata di Ricotta

To make 1 nine-inch pie

PASTA FROLLA

2 cups unsifted all-purpose flour

12 tablespoons lard or butter,
    at room temperature

but not soft

4 egg yolks

¼ cup sugar

3 tablespoons dry Marsala

1 teaspoon freshly grated lemon peel

½ teaspoon salt

PASTA FROLLA (pastry crust): In a large mixing bowl, make a well in the center of 2 cups of flour. Drop into it the butter (or lard), egg yolks, sugar, Marsala, lemon peel and salt. With your fingertips, mix the ingredients together, incorporating as much flour as you can. With the heels of your hands, work in the rest of the flour until the dough is smooth and can be gathered into a ball. Do not, however, knead the dough or work it any more than necessary. (If you have an electric mixer with a paddle attachment, all of the ingredients can be placed in the bowl at once and mixed at low speed until they are just combined.) The dough can be rolled out at once, but if it seems at all oily, refrigerate it for about 1 hour, or until it is firm but not hard.

Break off about ¼ of the dough, dust lightly with flour and cover with wax paper or plastic wrap; set aside in the refrigerator. Reshape the rest of the dough into a ball and place on a lightly floured board or pastry cloth. With the heel of your hand, flatten the ball into a disk about 1 inch thick. Dust a little flour over both sides of the disk to prevent the dough from sticking, and begin rolling it out—starting from the center and rolling to within an inch of the far edge. Gently lift the dough, turn clockwise, and roll out again from the center to the far edge. Repeat lifting, turning and rolling until the disk is about ⅛ inch thick and at least 11 inches across.

If the dough sticks to the board or cloth while you are rolling it out, lift it gently with a wide metal spatula and sprinkle a little flour under it.

Lightly butter the bottom and sides of a 9-by-1½-inch spring-form or false-bottom cake pan. Then, starting at the nearest edge of the circle, lift the pastry and drape it over the rolling pin. Place the pin in the middle of the buttered pan, and unfold the pastry over it, leaving some slack in the center. Gently press the pastry into the bottom and around the sides of the pan, taking care not to stretch it. Roll the pin over the rim of the pan, pressing down hard to trim off the excess pastry around the top.

Unwrap the remaining pastry, place it on a lightly floured board or cloth, flatten it with the heel of your hand and roll it into a rectangle about 12 inches long. With a pastry wheel or sharp knife, cut the rectangle into long, even strips about ½ inch wide.

RICOTTA FILLING

5 cups *ricotta* cheese (2½ pounds), or whole-curd cottage cheese rubbed through a coarse sieve
½ cup sugar
1 tablespoon flour
½ teaspoon salt
1 teaspoon vanilla extract
1 teaspoon freshly grated orange peel
4 egg yolks

1 tablespoon white raisins, rinsed and drained
1 tablespoon diced candied orange peel
1 tablespoon diced candied citron
2 tablespoons slivered blanched almonds or pine nuts
1 egg white mixed with 1 tablespoon water

RICOTTA FILLING: Preheat the oven to 350°. Combine the *ricotta* cheese with ½ cup of sugar, 1 tablespoon flour, ½ teaspoon salt, the vanilla, grated orange peel and egg yolks, and beat until they are thoroughly mixed. Stir in the raisins and the candied orange peel and citron. Spoon this filling into the pastry shell, spreading it evenly with a rubber spatula. Sprinkle the top with slivered almonds or pine nuts, then weave or crisscross the pastry strips across the pie to make a lattice design. Brush the strips lightly with the egg-white-and-water mixture. Bake on the middle shelf of the oven for 1 to 1¼ hours, or until the crust is golden and the filling is firm.

Mince Pies

To make eight 2½-inch pies

8 teaspoons butter, softened

Short-crust pastry (*page 410*)
1½ cups mincemeat

Preheat the oven to 375°. With a pastry brush, coat the bottom and sides of eight 2½-inch tart tins with the softened butter, allowing 1 teaspoon of butter for each tin. (These mince pies are most successful baked in specialized tart tins, available in well-stocked housewares stores; check the size by measuring the diameter of the bottom, not the top.)

On a lightly floured surface, roll out the pastry into a circle about ⅛ inch thick. With a cookie cutter or the rim of a glass, cut sixteen 3½-inch rounds of pastry. Gently press 8 of the rounds, 1 at a time, into the tart tins. Then spoon about 3 tablespoons of mincemeat into each pastry shell. With a pastry brush dipped in cold water, lightly moisten the outside edges of the pastry shells and carefully fit the remaining 8 rounds over them. Crimp the edges of the pastry together with your fingers or press them with the tines of a fork. Trim the excess pastry from around the rims with a sharp knife, and cut two ½-inch long parallel slits about ¼ inch apart in the top of each of the pies.

Arrange the pies on a large baking sheet, and bake them in the middle of the oven for 10 minutes. Reduce the heat to 350° and bake for 20 minutes longer, or until the crust is golden brown. Run the blade of a knife around the inside edges of the pies to loosen them slightly, and set them aside to cool in the pans. Then turn out the pies with a narrow spatula and serve.

MINCEMEAT
To make about 3 quarts

½ pound fresh beef suet, chopped fine
4 cups seedless raisins
2 cups dried currants
1 cup coarsely chopped almonds
½ cup coarsely chopped candied citron
½ cup coarsely chopped dried figs
½ cup coarsely chopped candied orange peel
¼ cup coarsely chopped candied lemon peel
4 cups coarsely chopped, peeled and cored cooking apples
1¼ cups sugar
1 teaspoon ground nutmeg
1 teaspoon ground allspice
1 teaspoon ground cinnamon
½ teaspoon ground cloves
2½ cups brandy
1 cup pale dry sherry

Combine the suet, raisins, currants, almonds, citron, dried figs, candied orange peel, candied lemon peel, apples, sugar, nutmeg, allspice, cinnamon and cloves in a large mixing bowl and stir them together thoroughly. Pour in the brandy and sherry, and mix with a large wooden spoon until all the ingredients are well moistened. Cover the bowl and set the mincemeat aside in a cool place (not the refrigerator) for at least 3 weeks. Check the mincemeat once a week. As the liquid is absorbed by the fruit, replenish it with sherry and brandy, using about ¼ cup at a time. Mincemeat can be kept indefinitely in a covered container in a cool place, without refrigeration, but after a month or so you may refrigerate it if you like.

SHORT-CRUST PASTRY

6 tablespoons unsalted butter, chilled
  and cut into ¼-inch bits
2 tablespoons lard, chilled and cut
  into ¼-inch bits

1½ cups all-purpose flour
¼ teaspoon salt
1 tablespoon sugar
3 to 4 tablespoons ice water

In a large, chilled bowl, combine the butter, lard, flour, salt and sugar. With your fingertips rub the flour and fat together until they look like coarse meal. Do not let the mixture become oily. Pour 3 tablespoons of ice water over the mixture all at once, toss together lightly, and gather the dough into a ball. If the dough crumbles, add up to 1 tablespoon more ice water by drops until the particles adhere. Dust the pastry with a little flour and wrap it in wax paper. Refrigerate for at least 1 hour before using.

Deep-Dish Peach Pie with Cream-Cheese Filling

To serve 6

8 tablespoons butter (1 quarter-
  pound stick), softened
8 tablespoons cream cheese, softened

1¼ cups all-purpose flour
2 tablespoons sugar
¼ teaspoon salt
2 tablespoons heavy cream

In a large mixing bowl, cream the butter and cheese by beating them together with a large spoon until smooth and fluffy. Sift the combined flour, sugar and salt into the mixture, add the cream and, with your hands or a large spoon, mix thoroughly until the dough can be gathered into a compact ball. Dust lightly with flour, wrap in wax paper and refrigerate while you prepare the filling.

FILLING
1½ pounds fresh peaches (8 to 10
  medium-sized peaches)
1 tablespoon flour
2 tablespoons brown sugar

3 tablespoons melted butter
2 teaspoons vanilla
1 egg yolk, lightly beaten with 2
  teaspoons cold water
1 teaspoon sugar

Preheat the oven to 350°. To peel the peaches easily, drop them into a pan of boiling water. Scoop them out after about 30 seconds, and while they are still warm, remove their skins with a small, sharp knife. Cut the peaches in half, discard the pits and slice thinly.

Combine the peaches, flour, brown sugar, melted butter and vanilla in a large bowl, and with a large spoon mix them together gently but thoroughly. With a rubber spatula, scrape the entire contents of the bowl into an 8-inch-square baking dish about 2½ inches deep. Spread the peaches out evenly. On a lightly floured surface, roll the pastry into a 10- to 11-inch square. Lift it up on the rolling pin and gently drape it over the top of the dish. Crimp the edges of the pastry to secure it around the outside of the dish and brush the pastry evenly with the egg-yolk-water mixture, then sprinkle with the sugar. Cut 2 small slits in the top of the pie to allow steam to escape and bake in the middle of the oven for 35 to 40 minutes, or until the crust is golden brown. Serve directly from the dish.

Pecan Pie

To make one 9-inch pie

1 1/4 cups all-purpose flour

4 tablespoons chilled vegetable
   shortening or lard

2 tablespoons chilled butter, cut in
   1/4-inch pieces

1/8 teaspoon salt

3 tablespoons ice water

Preheat the oven to 400°. In a large mixing bowl, combine the flour, vegetable shortening or lard, butter and salt. Use your fingertips to rub the flour and fat together until they look like flakes of coarse meal. Pour the ice water over the mixture, toss together, and press and knead gently with your hands only until the dough can be gathered into a compact ball. Dust very lightly with flour, wrap in wax paper and chill for at least 1/2 hour. Lightly butter a 9-inch pie plate. On a floured surface, roll the dough out into a circle about 1/8 inch thick and 13 to 14 inches in diameter. Lift it up on the rolling pin and unroll it over the pie plate, leaving enough slack in the middle of the pastry to enable you to line the plate without pulling or stretching the dough. Trim the excess pastry to within 1/2 inch of the rim of the pie plate and fold the extra 1/2 inch under to make a double thickness all around the rim. With the tines of a fork or with your fingers, press the pastry down around the rim.

To prevent the unfilled pastry from buckling as it bakes, either set another pie plate lightly buttered on the underside into the pastry shell or line it with a sheet of lightly buttered foil. In either case do not prick the pastry, or the filling will run out when it is added later. Bake the shell in the middle of the oven for 8 minutes, then remove the pan or foil and let the shell cool while you make the filling.

FILLING

4 eggs

2 cups dark corn syrup

2 tablespoons melted butter

1 teaspoon vanilla

1 1/2 cups pecans

With a wire whisk or rotary beater, beat the eggs in a mixing bowl for about 30 seconds. Then slowly pour in the syrup and continue to beat

411

until they are well combined. Beat in the melted butter and vanilla, and stir in the pecans. Carefully pour the filling into the pie shell. Bake in the middle of the oven for 35 to 40 minutes, or until the filling is firm. Serve the pie warm or cooled to room temperature.

Strudel

To make 1 six-foot *Strudel* (cut into sections)

¾ cup lukewarm water
1 large egg, lightly beaten
¼ teaspoon white vinegar

2 tablespoons butter, melted
2½ cups bread flour (all-purpose flour will not do)
¾ teaspoon salt
Melted butter
Bread crumbs

Preheat the oven to 450°. In a small mixing bowl, combine the water, egg, vinegar and butter, all of which should be at room temperature, then add the mixture to the flour and salt in a large mixing bowl. Stir by hand for about 5 minutes or by using an electric mixer with a pastry arm for about 3 minutes, or until the mixture becomes a firm dough. .

Form the dough into a ball and transfer it to a floured surface to knead it. Traditionally, *Strudel* dough is kneaded by repeatedly lifting it up about 2 feet and throwing it against the table, continuing for about 10 minutes, or until the dough becomes smooth and elastic. However, the dough can be kneaded like other doughs—by pulling it into an oblong shape, pressing it down and pushing it forward several times with the heels of the hands, then turning it slightly and repeating the process until it is smooth and elastic. This usually takes about 10 minutes.

Form the dough into a ball again, place it on a floured surface, cover it with a warm (but not hot) inverted metal or earthenware bowl and let it rest for 30 minutes.

Meanwhile, cover a large table (about 6 by 4 feet) with a tablecloth, and sprinkle the cloth generously with flour. With a pastry brush, coat the top of the dough with melted butter. Roll it out to a thickness of about ⅛ inch, then begin stretching it over the backs of your hands. Working quickly, continue lifting the dough and stretching it by pulling your hands apart until it is almost paper-thin and drapes over all 4 sides of the table. With scissors, trim off the thick outer edges of the *Strudel* dough.

Brush the stretched dough generously with melted butter and then sprinkle it with bread crumbs. Place whatever filling you plan to use *(pages 413 and 414)* along the long edge nearest you, in a 3-inch strip, to within 2 inches of the ends, then lift the tablecloth on that side and use it to roll the dough around the filling, jelly-roll fashion. Brush the top of the roll with melted butter and sprinkle it with bread crumbs. With a sharp knife, cut it into sections that will fit comfortably on your baking sheets.

Lightly butter 1 or 2 large baking sheets, place the sections on it, seam sides down with the aid of a metal spatula. Bake in the middle of the oven for 10 minutes, then reduce the heat to 400°. Bake for 20 minutes longer, or until the *Strudel* is crisp and brown.

NOTE: Prepared *Strudel* dough (phyllo) is available in many areas. The usual package of prepared dough contains 4 sheets, designed to be made into 2 *Strudel* rolls, both of them together holding about as much filling as the one long roll made from the recipe above.

To prepare packaged *Strudel* dough, preheat the oven to 400°, then unroll one sheet on a large damp kitchen towel and, using a pastry brush, coat it with butter, then sprinkle it with bread crumbs. Unroll a second sheet over the first and similarly coat it with butter and sprinkle it with bread crumbs. Spread the filling along a 3-inch strip of the dough nearest you and use the towel to roll it up, jelly-roll fashion. Bake in the middle of the oven for 25 to 30 minutes, or until golden brown.

Apple Filling for Strudel
Äpfel Strudelfülle

To make filling for 1 six-foot *Strudel*

8 large green cooking apples (about 5 pounds) peeled, cored and cut into ½-inch slices	2 teaspoons cinnamon
	¾ cup seedless white raisins
¾ cup sugar	1 tablespoon grated lemon peel
	¾ cup ground almonds

In a large mixing bowl, combine the apples, sugar, cinnamon, raisins and lemon peel. Sprinkle the 3-inch strip of *Strudel* (*page 412*) nearest you with the ground almonds, then distribute the apple mixture evenly along the strip to within 2 inches of the ends, then lift the tablecloth on that side and use it to roll the dough around the filling, jelly-roll fashion. Brush the top of the roll with melted butter and sprinkle it with bread crumbs, then cut into sections that will fit comfortably on your baking sheets. Bake in the middle of a preheated 450° oven for 10 minutes, then reduce the heat to 400°. Bake for 20 minutes, or until the *Strudel* is crisp and brown. NOTE: Cut the quantities in half to make one phyllo *Strudel* roll.

Cherry Filling for Strudel
Kirschen Strudelfülle

To make filling for 1 six-foot *Strudel*

8 cups sour pitted cherries, fresh or
  canned (drained)

2 cups sugar
2 teaspoons grated lemon peel
¾ cup ground almonds

Combine the cherries, sugar and lemon peel in a bowl. Sprinkle the almonds onto the 3-inch strip of *Strudel* (*page 412*) nearest you.

Spread the cherries evenly along the strip to within 2 inches of the
ends, then lift the tablecloth on that side and use it to roll the dough
around the filling, jelly-roll fashion. Brush the top of the roll with melted
butter and sprinkle it with bread crumbs, then cut into sections that will
fit comfortably on your baking sheets. Bake in the middle of a preheated
450° oven for 10 minutes, then reduce the heat to 400°. Bake for 20 minutes or until the *Strudel* is crisp and brown.

Greek Pastry with Walnuts and Honey Syrup
Baklava

To make one 9- by 13-inch pastry

¾ pound butter (3 quarter-pound
  sticks), cut into ¼-inch bits
½ cup vegetable oil
40 sheets *filo* pastry, each about 16

inches long and 12 inches wide,
  thoroughly defrosted if frozen
4 cups shelled walnuts pulverized in
  a blender or with a nut grinder
  or mortar and pestle

Clarify the butter in a heavy saucepan or skillet in the following fashion:
Melt the butter slowly over low heat without letting it brown, skimming off
the foam as it rises to the surface. Remove the pan from the heat, let it rest
for 2 or 3 minutes, then spoon off the clear butter and discard the milky solids.

Preheat the oven to 350° and stir the vegetable oil into the clarified butter. Using a pastry brush coat the bottom and sides of a 13-by-9-by-2½-
inch baking dish with about 1 tablespoon of the mixture.

Fold a sheet of *filo* in half crosswise, lift it up gently and unfold it into the
prepared dish. Press the pastry flat, fold down the excess around the sides
and flatten it against the bottom. Brush the entire surface of the pastry lightly with the butter and oil mixture, and lay another sheet of *filo* on top, folding it down and buttering it in similar fashion. Sprinkle the pastry evenly
with about 3 tablespoons of walnuts.

Repeat the same procedure using two sheets of buttered *filo* and 3 tablespoons of the pulverized walnuts each time to make 19 layers in all.

Spread the 2 remaining sheets of *filo* on top and brush the *baklava* with all of the remaining butter and oil mixture.

With a small, sharp knife score the top of the pastry with parallel diagonal lines about ½ inch deep and 2 inches apart, then cross them diagonally to form diamond shapes. Bake in the middle of the oven for 30 minutes. Reduce the heat to 300° and bake for 45 minutes longer, or until the top is crisp and golden brown.

SYRUP

1½ cups sugar	1 tablespoon fresh lemon juice
¾ cup water	1 tablespoon honey

Meanwhile, make the syrup. Combine the sugar, water and lemon juice in a small saucepan and, stirring constantly, cook over moderate heat until the sugar dissolves. Increase the heat to high and, timing it from the moment the syrup boils, cook briskly, uncovered, for about 5 minutes, or until the syrup reaches a temperature of 220° on a candy thermometer. Remove the pan from the heat and stir in the honey. When the *baklava* is done, remove it from the oven and pour the syrup over it. Cool and serve.

Fritters with Honey Syrup
Loukoumades

To make about 3 dozen fritters

SYRUP

1 cup sugar	½ cup water
½ cup honey	1 tablespoon fresh lemon juice

To make the syrup, combine the sugar, honey, water and lemon juice in a small saucepan and cook, stirring constantly, until the sugar dissolves. Increase the heat to high and cook briskly, uncovered and undisturbed, until the syrup reaches a temperature of 220° on a candy thermometer, or until the syrup thickens sufficiently to coat a spoon lightly. Pour the syrup into a bowl or heatproof pitcher and set aside to cool.

FRITTERS

1 package active dry yeast	½ teaspoon salt
A pinch of sugar	½ cup lukewarm milk (110° to 115°)
1¼ to 1½ cups lukewarm water (110° to 115°)	1 egg
3 cups all-purpose flour	Vegetable oil or shortening for deep-fat frying

In a small, shallow bowl, sprinkle the yeast and a pinch of sugar over ¼ cup of the lukewarm water. Let stand for 2 or 3 minutes, then stir to dissolve the yeast completely. Set the bowl in a warm, draft-free place (such as an unlighted oven) for 8 to 10 minutes, or until the mixture doubles in volume.

Combine the flour and salt in a deep mixing bowl, make a well in the center and pour in the yeast, milk and 1 cup of lukewarm water. Drop in the egg and stir the center ingredients together with a spoon. Then slowly incorporate the flour and beat vigorously until the batter is smooth and just thick enough to hold its shape in a flexible ribbon when the spoon is lifted from the bowl. If the batter is too rigid, beat in up to ¼ cup more lukewarm water, a tablespoon at a time. Drape a kitchen towel loosely over the bowl and set aside in a warm, draft-free place for about 45 minutes until the batter doubles in bulk.

Preheat the oven to 200°, and line a large shallow roasting pan with a double thickness of paper towels.

In a deep-fat fryer with a frying thermometer or an electric deep fryer or saucepan, heat 3 to 4 inches of oil or shortening until it reaches a temperature of 375°. Dip a tablespoon in cold water, scoop up a level measure of the batter and with another spoon push it into the hot oil. Repeat until you have made 6 fritters, dipping the spoons into the cold water before scooping each measure of batter. Turning the fritters frequently with a slotted spoon to keep them apart, fry them for 2 or 3 minutes, or until golden brown. Transfer them to the lined pan to keep warm in the oven while you fry the remaining fritters.

To serve, mound the fritters on a large platter and pour the syrup evenly over them. Or, if you prefer, pass the syrup separately in a pitcher. *Loukoumades* are sometimes served sprinkled with ground cinnamon or chopped nuts.

Viennese Jam Pockets

Tascherln

To make 25 pockets

1¼ cups unsalted butter, softened
⅔ cup sugar
2 hard-cooked egg yolks
1 egg yolk, lightly beaten
1 teaspoon grated orange peel

2 teaspoons vanilla extract
½ teaspoon salt
3¼ cups sifted all-purpose flour
1½ cups thick jam or preserves
  (apricot is suggested)
1 tablespoon water
2 egg whites

Cream the butter and sugar together by beating them against the side of a bowl with a wooden spoon or by using an electric mixer at medium speed until the mixture is light and fluffy.

Rub the hard-cooked egg yolks through a sieve with a wooden spoon, then stir them, the egg yolk, orange peel, vanilla and salt into the butter-sugar mixture. Add the flour ½ cup at a time; stir until the mixture becomes a slightly stiff dough. Shape the dough into a ball, wrap it in wax paper or plastic wrap and refrigerate it for about an hour.

On a lightly floured surface, roll the dough out into a 15-inch square about ⅛ inch thick. With a pastry wheel or sharp knife, cut the large square into 3-inch squares. Drop a teaspoon of jam onto the center of each square. Then lift a corner of each square and fold it over the opposite corner, forming a triangle. Seal the edges by pressing them firmly with the tines of a fork, then refrigerate them for 30 minutes.

Preheat the oven to 350°. With a pastry brush or paper towel lightly butter two 14-by-17-inch baking sheets, sprinkle a handful of flour over the butter, and knock out the excess flour by striking the inverted sheet against the edge of a table. Arrange the chilled triangles on the baking sheets, leaving at least ½ inch of space between them. Gently prick the center of each triangle with a fork. Mix the water and the egg whites together by beating them lightly with a fork. Then, with a pastry brush, coat each triangle lightly with the egg white mixture.

Bake the triangles on the middle shelf of the oven for 10 or 15 minutes, or until they are lightly browned. Remove them from the baking sheets with a metal spatula and cool them on a cake rack before serving.

Dessert Specialties

Chilled Chocolate Loaf
Dolce Torinese

To serve 8

½ pound semisweet chocolate, cut in
  small pieces
¼ cup rum
16 tablespoons (½ pound) soft
  unsalted butter
2 tablespoons "superfine" sugar
2 eggs, separated

1½ cups grated blanched almonds
  (about 5 ounces)
Pinch of salt
12 butter biscuits (Petits Beurre or Social
  Tea), cut into 1-by-½-inch pieces
Confectioners' sugar
½ cup heavy cream, whipped
  (optional)

Lightly grease the bottom and sides of a 1½-quart loaf pan with vegetable oil and invert the pan over paper towels to drain. In a heavy 1- to 1½-quart saucepan, melt the chocolate over low heat, stirring constantly. When all the chocolate is dissolved, stir in the rum and remove the pan from the heat. Cool to room temperature.

Cream the soft butter by beating it vigorously against the sides of a large heavy mixing bowl until it is light and fluffy. Beat in the sugar and then the egg yolks, one at a time. Stir in the grated almonds and cooled chocolate. In a separate bowl, beat the egg whites and salt with a rotary beater or wire whisk until they are stiff enough to cling to the beater in soft peaks. With a rubber spatula, fold them into the chocolate mixture. When no streaks of white show, gently fold in the cut-up biscuits, discarding the biscuit crumbs. Spoon the mixture into the greased loaf pan and smooth the top with a spatula to spread it evenly. Cover tightly with plastic wrap and refrigerate for at least 4 hours, or until the loaf is very firm.

Unmold the loaf an hour or so before serving time. To do so, run a sharp knife around the sides of the pan and dip the bottom into hot water for a few seconds. Place a chilled serving platter upside down over the pan and, grasping both sides, quickly turn the plate and pan over. Rap the plate on the table; the loaf should slide out easily. If it does not, repeat the whole process. Smooth the top and sides of the unmolded loaf with a metal spatula, then return it to the refrigerator. Just before serving, sieve a little confectioners' sugar over the top. Cut the loaf into thin slices and serve it, if desired, with whipped cream.

Meringues with Chocolate Sauce
Hovdessert

Makes 18 to 20

MERINGUES
4 egg whites (at room temperature)
Pinch of salt

1 cup superfine sugar
1 tablespoon soft butter
2 tablespoons flour

MERINGUES: Preheat the oven to 250°. In a large bowl, beat the egg whites and salt with a wire balloon whisk or a rotary or electric beater until the mixture is foamy. Gradually beat in the sugar and continue beating for at least 5 minutes, or until the egg whites are very stiff and form solid, unwavering peaks when the whisk is lifted out of the bowl.

With a pastry brush or paper towels, grease a cookie sheet with the soft butter, sprinkle it with flour and shake the pan to coat it evenly. Now turn the pan over and tap it against a hard surface to knock off any excess flour.

Drop mounds of meringue (about 1 tablespoon) onto the cookie sheet. The mounds should be about 2 inches high and 1 inch wide; their shape and size will not alter in the baking process. Set the cookie sheet in the middle of the oven for 50 minutes. This is actually a drying rather than a true baking process and the meringues should remain as colorless as possible. If they seem to be taking on color, turn the oven down to 200°. They should be dry and crisp, but tender, when they are done. Serve with the following sauce.

CHOCOLATE SAUCE
1 cup sugar

¾ cup water
1 cup unsweetened cocoa

CHOCOLATE SAUCE: Bring the sugar and water to a rolling boil in a heavy saucepan and boil briskly for 2 minutes. Remove the pan from the heat and add all of the cocoa, beating rapidly with a wire whisk until the sauce is smooth and satiny. Spoon about 1 tablespoon over each meringue. (Two meringues per person is a customary serving.) This sauce may also be served hot or cold over ice cream, or used as a cold syrup to make chocolate milk or hot cocoa.

Apricot Pancakes
Palacsintak Barackízzel

To make about 14 to 24 pancakes

3 eggs
1 cup milk
⅓ cup club soda, freshly opened
⅞ cup sifted flour
3 tablespoons granulated sugar

¼ teaspoon salt
1 teaspoon vanilla extract
4 to 6 tablespoons butter
¾ cup apricot jam
1 cup ground walnuts or filberts
Confectioners' sugar

Beat the eggs lightly with the milk in a small bowl. Combine with the club soda in a large mixing bowl. With a wooden spoon stir in the flour and sugar, then add the salt and vanilla extract. Continue to stir until the batter is smooth.

Melt 1 teaspoon of butter in an 8-inch skillet, preferably a pancake skillet. When the foam subsides, ladle in enough batter to cover the bottom of the skillet thinly and tilt the skillet from side to side to spread it evenly. Cook for 2 to 3 minutes, or until lightly browned on one side, then turn and brown lightly on the other. When a pancake is done, spread 2 teaspoons of jam over it, roll it loosely into a cylinder, then put it in a baking dish in a 200° oven to keep warm until the pancakes are finished. Add butter to the skillet as needed. Serve warm as a dessert, sprinkled with the walnuts and confectioner's sugar.

Plum Pudding

To make 4 puddings

1½ cups dried currants
2 cups seedless raisins
2 cups white raisins
¾ cup finely chopped candied mixed fruit peel
¾ cup finely chopped candied cherries
1 cup blanched slivered almonds
1 medium-sized tart cooking apple, peeled, quartered, cored and coarsely chopped
1 small carrot, scraped and coarsely chopped
2 tablespoons finely grated orange peel

2 teaspoons finely grated lemon peel
½ pound finely chopped beef suet
2 cups all-purpose flour
4 cups fresh soft crumbs, made from homemade-type white bread, pulverized in a blender or shredded with a fork
1 cup dark-brown sugar
1 teaspoon ground allspice
1 teaspoon salt
6 eggs
1 cup brandy
⅓ cup fresh orange juice
¼ cup fresh lemon juice
½ cup brandy, for flaming (optional)

In a large, deep bowl, combine the currants, seedless raisins, white raisins, candied fruit peel, cherries, almonds, apple, carrot, orange and lemon peel, and beef suet, tossing them about with a spoon or your hands until well mixed. Stir in the flour, bread crumbs, brown sugar, allspice and salt.

Meanwhile, bring 6 cups of water to a boil in a 2- to 3-quart saucepan. Pour in the rice in a slow stream, stirring constantly, so that the water continues to boil. Add the remaining 1/4 teaspoon of salt, reduce the heat to moderate, and boil the rice uncovered 15 to 20 minutes, or until tender. Drain the rice in a colander, turning it about with a fork to separate the grains, then spread it out on a double thickness of paper towels.

In a large bowl, beat the egg yolks and sugar together with a whisk or a rotary or electric beater until light and lemon colored. Beating constantly, pour in the milk in a thin stream. Then return the mixture to the saucepan and cook over low heat, stirring constantly with a wooden spoon until the custard thickens enough to coat the spoon lightly. Do not let it come anywhere near the boil or it may curdle. Remove the vanilla bean and cinnamon stick, add the rice to the custard and cook over low heat for 2 minutes, stirring constantly with a fork. Pour the pudding into a deep platter or a baking dish about 12-by-8 inches and no more than 1/2 inch deep. Cool to room temperature and just before serving, sprinkle the top lightly with cinnamon.

In a separate bowl, beat the eggs until frothy. Stir in the 1 cup of brandy, the orange and lemon juice, and pour this mixture over the fruit mixture. Knead vigorously with both hands, then beat with a wooden spoon until all the ingredients are blended. Drape a dampened kitchen towel over the bowl and refrigerate for at least 12 hours.

Spoon the mixture into four 1-quart English pudding basins or plain molds, filling them to within 2 inches of their tops. Cover each mold with a strip of buttered foil, turning the edges down and pressing the foil tightly around the sides to secure it. Drape a dampened kitchen towel over each mold and tie it in place around the sides with a long piece of kitchen cord. Bring two opposite corners of the towel up to the top and knot them in the center of the mold; then bring up the remaining two corners and knot them similarly.

Place the molds in a large pot and pour in enough boiling water to come about three fourths of the way up their sides. Bring the water to a boil over high heat, cover the pot tightly, reduce the heat to its lowest point and steam the puddings for 8 hours. As the water in the steamer boils away, replenish it with additional boiling water.

When the puddings are done, remove them from the water and let them cool to room temperature. Then remove the towels and foil and re-cover the molds tightly with fresh foil. Refrigerate the puddings for at least 3 weeks before serving. Plum puddings may be kept up to a year in the refrigerator or other cool place; traditionally, they were often made a year in advance.

To serve, place the mold in a pot and pour in enough boiling water to come about three fourths of the way up the sides of the mold. Bring to a boil over high heat, cover the pot, reduce the heat to low and steam for 2 hours. Run a knife around the inside edges of the mold and place an inverted serving plate over it. Grasping the mold and plate firmly together, turn them over. The pudding should slide out easily.

Christmas pudding is traditionally accompanied by Cumberland rum butter or brandy butter.

If you would like to set the pudding aflame before you serve it, warm the ½ cup of brandy in a small saucepan over low heat, ignite it with a match and pour it flaming over the pudding.

CUMBERLAND RUM BUTTER

To make about ¾ cup

4 tablespoons unsalted butter, softened	through a sieve
	¼ cup light rum
½ cup light-brown sugar, rubbed	⅛ teaspoon ground nutmeg

Combine the butter, sugar, rum and nutmeg in a bowl, and beat with an electric beater until smooth and well blended. (By hand, cream the butter by beating and mashing it against the sides of a mixing bowl with a spoon until it is light and fluffy. Beat in the sugar, a few tablespoons at a time, and then the rum and nutmeg.) Refrigerate for at least 4 hours, or until firm.

BRANDY BUTTER

To make about ¾ cup

	½ cup superfine sugar
4 tablespoons unsalted butter, softened	3 tablespoons brandy
	½ teaspoon vanilla extract

Combine the butter, sugar, brandy and vanilla in a bowl, and beat with an electric beater until the mixture is smooth and well blended. (By hand, cream the butter by beating and mashing it against the sides of a mixing bowl with a spoon until it is light and fluffy. Beat in the sugar, a few tablespoons at a time, and continue beating until the mixture is very white and frothy. Beat in the brandy and vanilla.) Refrigerate at least 4 hours, or until firm.

Rice Pudding
Arroz Doce

To serve 4 to 6

1½ cups milk
A 2-inch piece of vanilla bean
A 2-inch piece of stick cinnamon
6 pieces lemon peel, each about
    1½ inches long and ½ inch wide
⅛ teaspoon plus ¼ teaspoon salt

6 cups water
½ cup raw medium or long-grain
    regular-milled rice or imported
    short-grain rice
3 egg yolks
⅓ cup sugar
1 teaspoon ground cinnamon

In a 1- to 1¼-quart saucepan, bring the milk, vanilla bean, cinnamon stick, pieces of lemon peel and ⅛ teaspoon of the salt to a boil over moderate heat. Cover the pan tightly, remove it from the heat and let the seasonings steep for 20 to 30 minutes.

Orange Liqueur Soufflé
Soufflé au Grand Marnier

To serve 4

2 tablespoons soft butter
3 tablespoons sugar
5 egg yolks
⅓ cup sugar
¼ cup Grand Marnier (1 two-ounce

bottle)
1 tablespoon freshly grated orange
    peel
7 egg whites
¼ teaspoon cream of tartar
Confectioners' (powdered) sugar

Preheat the oven to 425°. Grease the bottom and sides of a 1½-quart soufflé dish with 2 tablespoons of soft butter. Sprinkle in 3 tablespoons of sugar, tipping and shaking the dish to spread the sugar evenly. Then turn the dish over and knock out the excess sugar. Set aside.

In the top of a double boiler, beat the egg yolks with a whisk, rotary or electric beater until they are well blended. Slowly add the sugar and continue beating until the yolks become very thick and pale yellow. Set the pan over barely simmering (not boiling) water and heat the egg yolks, stirring gently and constantly with a wooden spoon or rubber spatula, until the mixture thickens and becomes almost too hot to touch. Stir in the Grand Marnier and grated orange peel and transfer to a large bowl. Set the bowl into a pan filled with crushed ice or ice cubes and cold water, and stir the mixture until it is quite cold. Remove it from the ice.

In a large mixing bowl, preferably of unlined copper, beat the egg whites and the cream of tartar with a clean whisk or rotary beater until they form stiff, unwavering peaks. Using a rubber spatula, stir a large spoonful of beaten egg white into the egg-yolk mixture to lighten it. Gently fold the remaining egg whites into the mixture. Spoon the soufflé into the buttered, sugared dish, filling it to within 2 inches of the top. Smooth the top of the soufflé with the spatula. For a decorative effect, make a cap on the soufflé by cutting a trench about 1 inch deep 1 inch from the edge all around the top.

Bake on the middle shelf of the oven for 2 minutes, then reduce the heat to 400°. Continue baking for another 20 to 30 minutes, or until the soufflé has risen about 2 inches above the top of the mold and the top is lightly browned. Sprinkle with confectioners' sugar and serve it at once.

Salzburg Soufflé
Salzburger Nockerl

To serve 6

2 egg yolks
1 teaspoon vanilla extract
½ teaspoon grated lemon peel

1 tablespoon flour
4 egg whites
Pinch of salt
2 tablespoons sugar
Confectioners' sugar

Preheat the oven to 350°. In a medium-sized mixing bowl, break the egg yolks up with a fork and stir in the vanilla and lemon peel. Sprinkle the flour over the yolk mixture. In another bowl, using a wire whisk or rotary or electric beater, beat the egg whites with a pinch of salt until they cling to the beater. Add the sugar and beat until the whites form stiff, unwavering peaks. With a rubber spatula, stir an overflowing tablespoon of the whites into the yolk-and-flour mixture, then reverse the process and fold the yolk mixture into the rest of the egg whites, using an over-under cutting motion instead of a mixing motion. Don't overfold.

Generously butter an oval or oblong 8-by-10-by-2-inch baking dish attractive enough to serve from. Using the rubber spatula, make 3 mounds of the mixture in the dish. Bake the *Nockerl* in the middle of the oven 10 to 12 minutes, or until it is lightly brown on the outside but still soft on the inside. Sprinkle with confectioners' sugar and serve immediately.

Strawberry Shortcake

To make 6 small shortcakes

4 cups all-purpose flour
6 tablespoons sugar
5 teaspoons baking powder
2 teaspoons salt
12 tablespoons butter (1½ quarter-pound sticks) chilled and cut into bits
1½ cups heavy cream
6 teaspoons melted and cooled butter
2 pints of fresh, ripe strawberries
1½ teaspoons sugar
1 pint heavy cream for topping

Preheat the oven to 450°. Sift the flour, sugar, baking powder and salt together into a large mixing bowl. Add the butter, and, with your fingertips, rub the dry ingredients and butter together until most of the lumps disappear and the mixture resembles coarse meal. Pour in the heavy cream and, with your hands or a large spoon, mix thoroughly until a soft dough is formed. Gather it into a compact ball and transfer it to a lightly floured board. Knead the dough for about a minute by folding it end to end and pressing it down and pushing it forward several times with the heel of your hand. Then roll the dough out into a circle about 1 inch thick. With a 3-inch cookie cutter, cut out 6 circles. Cut the remaining dough into six 2½-inch circles. (If there isn't enough dough, gather the scraps together, knead briefly and roll out again.) Arrange the 3-inch circles on a lightly buttered cookie sheet. Brush each with a teaspoon of melted butter, then top with the smaller circle. Bake in the middle of the oven for 12 to 15 minutes until firm to the touch and golden brown.

Meanwhile, chop half the strawberries coarsely, reserving the most attractive ones for the top. Separate the shortcakes. Spread a layer of chopped strawberries on the bottom circles, sprinkle with sugar and gently place the smaller circles on top. Garnish with the whole strawberries. Strawberry shortcake is traditionally served with heavy cream.

Ices & Custards

Italian Flavored Ices
Granite
To make about 1½ pints of each flavor

LEMON ICE
2 cups water
1 cup sugar
1 cup lemon juice

ORANGE ICE
2 cups water
¾ cup sugar
1 cup orange juice
Juice of 1 lemon

COFFEE ICE
1 cup water
½ cup sugar
2 cups strong *espresso* coffee

STRAWBERRY ICE
1 cup water
½ cup sugar
2 cups fresh ripe strawberries, puréed
    through sieve or food mill
2 tablespoons lemon juice

In a 1½- to 2-quart saucepan, bring the water and sugar to a boil over moderate heat, stirring only until the sugar dissolves. Timing from the moment the sugar and water begin to boil, let the mixture cook for exactly 5 minutes. Immediately remove the pan from the heat and let the syrup cool to room temperature.

Depending on which of the flavored ices you want to make, stir in the lemon juice, or the orange and lemon juices, or *espresso* coffee, or the puréed strawberries and lemon juice. Pour the mixture into an ice-cube tray from which the divider has been removed.

Freeze the *granita* for 3 to 4 hours, stirring it every 30 minutes and scraping into it the ice particles that form around the edges of the tray. The finished *granita* should have a fine, snowy texture. For a coarser texture that is actually more to the Italian taste, leave the ice-cube divider in the tray and freeze the *granita* solid. Then remove the cubes and crush them in an ice crusher.

NOTE: If you use frozen strawberries rather than fresh ones, make the syrup with only ¼ cup of sugar.

Lemon-Orange Ice

To make 1½ pints

¾ pound large sugar cubes
3 medium navel oranges

2 cups water
¼ cup fresh lemon juice
Fresh mint

Rub about 10 sugar cubes over the skins of the whole oranges to saturate them with the orange oil. Then squeeze the oranges. If they do not produce 1 cup of juice, use another orange. In a 1½ or 2-quart saucepan, bring the water and all of the sugar cubes to a boil over high heat, stirring until the sugar dissolves. Timing from the moment when it begins to boil, let the mixture boil briskly, without stirring, for 5 minutes. Immediately remove the pan from the heat and cool the syrup to room temperature. Stir in the orange juice and lemon juice, and pour into 2 ice-cube trays. Freeze for 3 to 4 hours at least, beating the ice after a half hour to break up the solid particles that will form on the bottom and sides of the tray. Continue to beat every half hour until the ice has a fine and snowy texture. Serve on chilled dessert plates or in sherbet glasses and garnish with the mint.

Tangerine Ice
Mandarine Délice

To serve 8

8 tangerines
¾ cup sugar

½ cup water
¼ cup Mandarine or other tangerine
    liqueur

Wash and dry the tangerines. Cut a circular piece about the size of a quarter from the stem end of each fruit. Put it aside. Carefully scoop out the pulp of the tangerines without breaking the shells. Discard the seeds and purée the pulp in a blender or force it through a heavy sieve or food mill.

Combine the sugar and water in a saucepan. Bring to a boil, stirring until the sugar melts, then simmer until the syrup has thickened. Let it cool slightly, then add it with the liqueur to the tangerine purée. Blend them thoroughly, fill the shells with this mixture, and replace the tops of the tangerines. Place the tangerines in the freezing compartment until the filling is frozen.

Assorted Ice Creams
Gelati

To make 1 to 1½ quarts of each flavor

VANILLA ICE CREAM

2 cups light cream	8 egg yolks
2-inch piece of vanilla bean or	½ cup sugar
1 teaspoon vanilla extract	1 cup heavy cream

VANILLA: In a 1½- or 2-quart enameled or stainless-steel saucepan, bring the light cream and the vanilla bean almost to a boil over low heat. (If you are using vanilla extract, do not add it now.) Meanwhile combine the egg yolks and sugar in a bowl. Beat them with a whisk, rotary or electric beater for 3 to 5 minutes, or until they are pale yellow and thick enough to fall from the whisk or beater in a lazy ribbon. Then discard the vanilla bean from the saucepan and pour the hot cream slowly into the beaten egg yolks, beating gently and constantly. Pour the mixture back into the saucepan and cook over moderately low heat, stirring constantly with a wooden spoon, until it thickens to a custard that lightly coats the spoon. Do not allow the mixture to boil or it will curdle. Stir in the heavy cream, and if you are using the vanilla extract instead of the vanilla bean, add it now. Strain the custard through a fine sieve into a mixing bowl and allow it to cool to room temperature.

Now pack a 2-quart ice cream freezer with layers of finely crushed or cracked ice and coarse rock salt in the proportions recommended by the freezer manufacturer. Add cold water if the manufacturer advises it. Then pour or ladle the cooled *gelato* into the ice cream can and cover it. If you have a hand ice cream maker, let it stand for 3 or 4 minutes before turning the handle. It may take 15 minutes or more for the ice cream to freeze, but do not stop turning at any time, or the *gelato* may be lumpy. When the handle can barely be moved, the ice cream should be firm. If you have an electric ice cream maker, turn it on and let it churn for about 15 minutes, or until the motor slows or actually stops.

To harden the *gelato*, scrape the ice cream from the sides down into the bottom of the can and cover it very securely. Drain off any water that is in the bucket and repack it with ice and salt. Let it stand for 2 or 3 hours.

PISTACHIO ICE CREAM

2 cups light cream	1 cup heavy cream
8 egg yolks	7 drops green food coloring
6 tablespoons sugar	5½ tablespoons chopped shelled
2½ tablespoons ground or crushed	pistachio nuts
shelled pistachio nuts	¼ cup ground blanched almonds

PISTACHIO: Heat the light cream and beat the egg yolks and sugar together. Add the ground pistachio nuts and make the custard as described in the vanilla recipe. Then stir in the heavy cream and vegetable coloring, and strain this mixture. Add the chopped pistachio nuts and ground almonds. Cool and freeze.

COFFEE ICE CREAM

2 cups light cream	6 tablespoons sugar
2-inch strip of fresh lemon peel	2 tablespoons *espresso* coffee
8 egg yolks	2 cups heavy cream

COFFEE: Heat the light cream with the lemon peel and beat the egg yolks and sugar together. Discard the peel and make the custard as described in the vanilla recipe. Add the *espresso* coffee (instant or freshly brewed) and heavy cream; strain, cool and freeze.

CHOCOLATE ICE CREAM

2 cups milk	2 cups heavy cream
4 egg yolks	4 ounces semisweet chocolate, melted
10 tablespoons sugar	½ teaspoon vanilla extract

CHOCOLATE: Heat the milk, beat the egg yolks and sugar together, and make the custard as described in the vanilla recipe. Then stir in the heavy cream, melted chocolate and vanilla extract. Strain, cool and freeze.

Old-fashioned Vanilla Ice Cream

To make about 1½ quarts

4 cups heavy cream	⅛ teaspoon salt
¾ cup sugar	1½-inch piece of vanilla bean

In a heavy 1½- or 2-quart enameled or stainless-steel saucepan, heat 1 cup of the cream, the sugar, salt and the vanilla bean over low heat, stirring until the sugar is dissolved and the mixture is hot but has not come to a boil. Remove from heat and lift out the vanilla bean. Split the bean in half lengthwise and, with the tip of a small knife, scrape the seeds into the cream mixture. When the mixture has cooled somewhat, stir in the remaining 3 cups of cream.

Pack a 2-quart ice-cream freezer with layers of finely crushed or cracked ice and coarse rock salt in the proportions recommended by the freezer manufacturer, adding cold water if the directions call for it. Then pour or ladle the cream mixture into the ice-cream container and cover it. Let it stand for 3 or 4 minutes. Then turn the handle, starting slowly at first, and crank continuously until the handle can barely be moved. Wipe the lid carefully, remove it and lift out the dasher. Scrape the ice cream off the dasher into the container and pack down with a spoon. Cover the container securely. Drain off any water in the bucket and repack it with ice and salt. Replace the container and let it stand 2 or 3 hours before serving.

Coffee Cream
Café Liégeois
To serve 4

4 egg yolks, well beaten
½ cup sugar

¼ cup water
3 tablespoons extra strong coffee
2 cups cream
Whipped cream

Put the beaten egg yolks in a bowl. Then put the sugar and water in a pan and cook until they form a light syrup. Cool the syrup and pour it gradually into the yolks, then beat the mixture in an electric mixer until it becomes stiff; add the coffee and cream. Chill in the refrigerator until the mixture is set, but not frozen. Serve in tall glasses and top with whipped cream.

Soft Custard
Natillas
To serve 6

3 cups milk
2 cinnamon sticks each 4 inches
   long
4 eggs

2 egg yolks
½ cup sugar
6 ladyfingers
Ground cinnamon

In a heavy 1- to 1½-quart saucepan, heat the milk with the cinnamon sticks until small bubbles begin to form around the edge of the pan. Remove from the heat.

With a whisk or a rotary or electric beater, beat the eggs, egg yolks and sugar in a mixing bowl for 3 or 4 minutes, or until pale yellow and slightly thickened. Beating constantly, slowly pour in the hot milk in a thin stream. Return the mixture to the saucepan. Stirring constantly, cook over low heat until the custard thickens enough to lightly coat the spoon. Do not let the custard come anywhere near a boil or it will curdle. Cool the custard to room temperature.

Just before serving, spoon the custard into six individual dessert dishes, place a ladyfinger in each dish, and sprinkle the custard lightly with ground cinnamon.

Burnt Custard

To serve 6 to 8

8 egg yolks	1 quart heavy cream
6 tablespoons sugar	1 tablespoon vanilla extract

Preheat the oven to 350°. With a whisk or a rotary or electric beater, beat the egg yolks and 2 tablespoons of the sugar together in a mixing bowl for 3 or 4 minutes, or until the yolks are thick and pale yellow.

Heat the cream in a heavy 1½- to 2-quart saucepan until small bubbles begin to form around the edges of the pan. Then, beating constantly, pour the cream in a slow stream into the beaten egg yolks. Add the vanilla extract and strain the mixture through a fine sieve into a 6-by-6-inch baking dish at least 2 inches deep.

Place the dish in a large shallow pan on the middle shelf of the oven and pour enough boiling water into the pan to come halfway up the sides of the dish. Bake for about 45 minutes, or until a knife inserted in the center comes out clean. Remove the dish from the water and cool to room temperature. Refrigerate for at least 4 hours, or until the cream is thoroughly chilled.

About 2 hours before serving, preheat the broiler to its highest point. Sprinkle the top of the cream with the remaining 4 tablespoons of sugar, coating the surface as evenly as possible. Slide the dish under the broiler about 3 inches from the heat, and cook for 4 or 5 minutes, or until the sugar forms a crust over the cream. Watch carefully for any signs of burning and regulate the heat accordingly. Cool the cream to room temperature, then refrigerate it again until ready to serve.

Caramel Custard
Crème Caramel

To serve 6

CARAMEL

½ cup sugar

¼ cup water

Pinch of cream of tartar

CUSTARD

2 cups milk

1 teaspoon vanilla extract

¼ cup sugar

3 eggs plus 2 extra egg yolks

To line a 1-quart metal or porcelain mold or six 4-ounce heatproof porcelain or glass individual molds with caramel, it is necessary to work quickly. Remember in handling the caramel that it will be over 300°, so be extremely careful with it. Place the mold (or molds) on a large strip of wax paper. Then, in a small, heavy saucepan or skillet, bring the sugar and water to a boil over high heat, stirring until the sugar dissolves. Stir in a pinch of cream of tartar and—gripping a pot holder in each hand—boil the syrup over moderate heat, gently tipping the pan back and forth almost constantly, until the syrup turns a rich, golden, tea-like brown. This may take 10 minutes or more. As soon as the syrup reaches the right color, remove the pan from the heat and carefully pour the caramel syrup in a thin stream into the mold (or the first of the individual molds). Still using the pot holders, tip and swirl the mold to coat the bottom and sides as evenly as possible. When the syrup stops moving, turn the mold upside down on the wax paper to cool somewhat and to let any excess syrup run out.

Preheat oven to 325°. In a 1- to 1½-quart saucepan, bring the milk almost to a boil over moderate heat. Remove the pan from the stove and add the vanilla extract. With a wire whisk, rotary or electric beater, beat the sugar, eggs and extra egg yolks until they are well mixed and thickened. Stirring gently and constantly, pour in the milk in a thin stream. Strain through a fine sieve into the caramel-lined mold and place the mold (or molds) in a large pan on the middle shelf of the oven. Pour enough boiling water into the pan to come halfway up the sides of the mold. Bake the custard—lowering the oven temperature if the water in the pan begins to simmer—for about 1 hour, or until a knife inserted in the center of the custard comes out clean. Remove the mold from the water and refrigerate the custard for at least 3 hours, or until it is thoroughly chilled.

To unmold and serve the large custard, run a sharp knife around the sides and dip the bottom of the mold briefly in hot water. Then wipe the outside of the mold dry, place a chilled serving plate upside down over the mold and, grasping both sides firmly, quickly turn the plate and mold over. Rap the plate on a table and the custard should slide easily out of the mold. Unmold the individual custards carefully, turning them out one at a time on individual serving plates. Pour any extra caramel remaining in the mold (or molds) over the custard. Serve cold.

Coconut Custard
Leche Flan

To serve 8 to 10

	¾ cup brown sugar
1 cup packaged shredded coconut	3 tablespoons water
1½ cups light cream	12 egg yolks
2 cups milk	1 cup sugar

Preheat the oven to 325°. Bring the coconut, cream and milk to a boil; remove from the heat and let the mixture stand for 30 minutes. Then force the mixture through a sieve set over a bowl, pressing down hard to extract all the juices from the coconut. Or purée the mixture in an electric blender.

Combine the brown sugar and water in a saucepan. Cook, stirring steadily, until the sugar dissolves and the mixture becomes a deep golden brown. Pour the syrup into a 1½-quart mold, turning it about quickly to coat the mold evenly.

Reheat the coconut milk. Beat the egg yolks and sugar together. Gradually add the hot coconut milk, stirring steadily to prevent curdling. Strain into the mold. Place the mold in another pan and pour enough hot water around the mold to reach halfway up the sides. Place on the bottom rack of the oven and bake for 50 minutes, or until a knife inserted in the center comes out clean. Let the mold cool, then put it into the refrigerator and chill. To unmold, run a spatula or knife around the edge of the mold, place a serving dish upside down over the mold, and quickly turn over.

Custard with Marsala

Zabaione

To serve 4

5 egg yolks plus 1 whole egg

2 tablespoons sugar
½ cup Marsala

Combine the 5 egg yolks, 1 whole egg and 2 tablespoons of sugar in the top of a double boiler above simmering water or in a medium-sized heat-proof glass bowl set in a shallow pan of barely simmering water. Beat the mixture with a wire whisk or a rotary beater until it is pale yellow and fluffy. Then gradually add the Marsala and continue beating until the *zabaione* becomes thick enough to hold its shape in a spoon. This process may take as long as 10 minutes.

Spoon the *zabaione* into individual dessert bowls, compote dishes or large stemmed glasses, and serve it while it is still hot.

Pineapple Custard

Quesillo de Piña

To serve 6 to 8

THE CARAMEL
1 cup sugar
½ cup water

THE CUSTARD
3 eggs
2 egg yolks
A 15-ounce can condensed milk
1½ cups pineapple juice
¼ cup sugar

To line a 6-cup metal or porcelain mold with caramel, it is necessary to work quickly. Remember in handling the caramel that its temperature will be over 300°, so be extremely careful with it. Place the mold on a large strip of wax paper. Then, in a small, heavy saucepan or skillet, bring the sugar and water to a boil over high heat, stirring until the sugar dissolves. Boil the syrup over moderate heat, gripping a pot holder in each hand and gently tipping the pan back and forth almost constantly, until the syrup turns a rich, golden, tea-like brown. This may take 10 minutes or more. As soon as the syrup reaches the right color, remove the pan from the heat and carefully pour the caramel syrup all at once into the mold. Still using the pot holders, tip and swirl the mold to coat the bottom and sides as evenly as possible. When the syrup stops moving, turn the mold upside down on the wax paper to drain and cool.

Preheat the oven to 325°. In a large mixing bowl, beat the eggs and egg yolks with a whisk or a rotary or electric beater until they thicken and turn a light yellow. Gradually pour in the condensed milk, pineapple

434

juice and sugar, and beat until all the ingredients are well combined. Strain through a fine sieve into the caramel-lined mold, and place the mold in a large pan on the middle shelf of the oven. Pour enough boiling water into the pan to come halfway up the sides of the mold. Bake the custard for about 1 hour, or until a knife inserted in the center of the custard comes out clean. Remove the mold from the water, let it cool to room temperature, then refrigerate the custard for at least 3 hours, or until it is thoroughly chilled.

To unmold and serve the large custard, run a sharp knife around the sides, and dip the bottom of the mold briefly in hot water. Then wipe the outside of the mold dry, place a chilled serving plate upside down over the mold and, grasping mold and plate together firmly, quickly turn them over. Rap the plate on a table and the custard should slide easily out of the mold. Pour any caramel remaining in the mold over the custard.

Chocolate Mousse
Mousse au Chocolat

To serve 6 to 8

Vegetable oil
4 egg yolks
¼ cup superfine sugar
2 tablespoons Cognac
6 ounces semisweet chocolate,

cut in small chunks
3 tablespoons strong coffee
8 tablespoons soft unsalted
   butter (1 quarter-pound stick),
   cut in ½-inch pieces
4 egg whites
½ cup chilled heavy cream

Brush the inside of a 1-quart charlotte (cylindrical) or ring mold with a film of vegetable oil. Invert the mold on paper towels to drain.

In a heatproof mixing bowl, beat the egg yolks and sugar with a whisk, rotary or electric beater for 2 or 3 minutes, or until they are pale yellow and thick enough to form a ribbon when the whisk is lifted from the bowl. Beat in the Cognac.

Set the mixing bowl over a pan of barely simmering (not boiling) water, and continue beating for 3 or 4 minutes, or until the mixture is foamy and hot. Then set the bowl over a pan of iced water and beat for 4 minutes longer, or until the mixture is cool and as thick and creamy as mayonnaise.

In a heavy 1- to 1½-quart saucepan set over low heat, or in the top of a double boiler over simmering water, melt the chocolate with the coffee, stirring constantly. When all the chocolate has dissolved, beat in the butter, one piece at a time, to make a smooth cream. Then beat the chocolate mixture into the egg yolks and sugar. In a separate bowl, with a clean whisk or beater, beat the egg whites until they are stiff enough to form stiff peaks on the wires of the whisk. Stir about one fourth of the egg whites into the chocolate mixture to lighten it, then very gently fold in the remaining egg whites. Spoon the mousse into the oiled mold or dessert cups, and refrigerate for at least 4 hours or until it has set.

To unmold and serve the *mousse au chocolat*, run a long, sharp knife around the sides of the mold and dip the bottom of it in hot water for a few seconds. Then wipe the outside of the mold dry, place a chilled serving plate upside down over the mold and, grasping both sides firmly, quickly turn the plate and mold over. Rap the plate on a table and the mousse should slide easily out of the mold. If the mousse doesn't unmold at once, repeat the whole process.

With a wire whisk, rotary or electric beater, whip the chilled cream in a large chilled bowl until it is firm enough to hold its shape softly. Garnish the mousse with the whipped cream.

Lemon-Cream Dessert
Zitronencreme

To serve 6

1 envelope unflavored gelatin
¼ cup cold water
3 egg yolks
½ cup plus 3 tablespoons sugar
¼ cup fresh lemon juice
2 teaspoons finely grated lemon peel

1 cup heavy cream
3 egg whites
1 lemon, cut lengthwise into halves
    and cut crosswise into paper-thin
    slices (optional)
½ cup heavy cream (optional)
1 teaspoon confectioners' sugar
    (optional)

In a heatproof measuring cup or small bowl, sprinkle the gelatin over ¼ cup of cold water. When the gelatin has softened for 2 or 3 minutes, set the cup in a small skillet of simmering water and stir until the gelatin dissolves completely. Remove the skillet from the heat, but leave the cup of gelatin in the skillet.

With a wire whisk or a rotary or electric beater, beat the egg yolks with ½ cup of the sugar until the yolks are pale yellow and thick enough to fall back in a ribbon when the beater is lifted from the bowl. Stir in the dissolved gelatin, the lemon juice and the lemon peel. With the same whisk or beater whip the cream in a large chilled bowl until it is firm enough to hold its shape softly. Then, with a rubber spatula, gently but thoroughly fold the cream into the egg and lemon mixture, using an over-under cutting motion rather than a stirring motion.

Wash and dry the whisk or beater; then, in a separate bowl, use it to beat the egg whites until they are frothy. Sprinkle in the remaining 3 tablespoons of sugar and continue beating until the egg whites are stiff enough to stand in unwavering peaks when the whisk is lifted from the bowl. Gently fold the egg whites into the lemon mixture and continue to fold until no trace of white can be seen in the mixture.

Spoon the lemon cream into six individual dessert dishes or into a large serving bowl. Cover it tightly and refrigerate it for at least 3 hours before serving.

If you like, you may garnish the dessert with lemon slices and whipped cream. Whip the cream with a wire whisk or a rotary or electric beater until it holds its shape softly, sprinkle it with confectioners' sugar, and beat until the cream is stiff enough to form firm, unwavering peaks. With a pastry bag fitted with a decorative tip, pipe rosettes or decorative swirls of whipped cream on top of the dessert.

Pumpkin Pudding

Pudim de Abóbora

To serve 6

1½ cups milk
½ cup firmly packed brown sugar
¼ teaspoon freshly grated orange peel
¼ teaspoon ground ginger

½ teaspoon ground cinnamon
½ teaspoon salt
3 eggs, lightly beaten
1 cup freshly cooked puréed pumpkin
  or winter squash, or canned puréed
  pumpkin

Preheat the oven to 350°. In a large mixing bowl, combine the milk, brown sugar, orange peel, ginger, cinnamon and salt. Stir thoroughly, then add the lightly beaten eggs and the puréed pumpkin. Beat vigorously with a spoon until the mixture is smooth, and pour it into a 1-quart shallow greased baking dish. Place the dish in a large pan in the middle of the oven and pour enough boiling water into the pan to come halfway up the sides of the baking dish. Bake the pudding for about 1¼ hours, or until a knife inserted in the center of the pudding comes out clean. Remove the dish from the water and either cool the pudding to room temperature before serving or refrigerate for at least 3 hours, or until thoroughly chilled. If you like, the pudding may be made in six 4-ounce porcelain or glass molds; in that case, bake it for about 40 minutes, until firm.

Fruit Sweets

Apple-Mint Crisp
Pastel de Manzana

To serve 6

1 tablespoon butter, softened
1 cup sugar
1 cup all-purpose flour
½ teaspoon double-acting baking
   powder
1 egg
1 tablespoon dried mint leaves

1 tablespoon ground cinnamon
4 medium-sized tart cooking apples
   (about 2 pounds), peeled,
   quartered, cored and cut
   lengthwise into ¼-inch slices
1 cup heavy cream, whipped
   (optional)

Preheat the oven to 350°. With a pastry brush, coat the bottom and sides of an 8-by-8-by-2-inch baking dish with softened butter. Set aside. Combine the sugar, flour and baking powder and sift them into a mixing bowl. Make a well in the center and drop in the egg. Mix together with two table knives until the flour has thoroughly absorbed the egg.

In a large mixing bowl, stir the mint leaves and cinnamon together. Add the apples and toss them about with a large spoon until the slices are evenly coated on all sides. Arrange the slices in the baking dish and scatter the flour mixture over them, spreading and pressing it gently into a smooth layer to cover the apples completely. Bake in the middle of the oven for 45 minutes, or until the topping is crusty. Remove the dish from the oven, cover it tightly with a lid or foil, and set aside to cool. Serve, at room temperature, accompanied if you like with a bowl of whipped cream.

Dutch Apple Pudding
Appelschoteltje

To serve 6 to 8

1 cup milk
¼ teaspoon grated lemon rind
Pinch of salt
12 tablespoons butter
½ cup flour
10 tablespoons sugar

8 sour apples, peeled and thinly
  sliced
3 egg yolks, beaten
3 egg whites, stiffly beaten
8 zwieback, finely crumbed
Whipped cream (optional)

In a saucepan bring the milk, lemon rind and salt to a boil. Knead 3 tablespoons of the butter with the flour and slowly stir into the hot milk, cooking and stirring until thickened. Stir half the sugar and 5 tablespoons of butter into the sauce.

Melt 2 tablespoons of butter in a skillet; add the apples and the remaining sugar. Simmer for 10 minutes.

Very gradually stir the hot sauce into the beaten egg yolks, then add the apples. Let this mixture cool, then fold in the egg whites.

In a buttered 1½-quart baking dish, make layers of the zwieback crumbs and apple mixture, starting and ending with the crumbs. Dot with the remaining butter. Bake in a preheated 325° oven 45 minutes. Serve warm with whipped cream, if desired.

First Frost Apples
Rauhreif

To serve 4 to 6

1 cup heavy cream, chilled
6 tablespoons sugar
¼ teaspoon vanilla extract

⅓ cup fresh orange juice
2 tablespoons fresh lemon juice
6 large eating apples (preferably
  Rome Beauty or red or yellow
  Delicious), about 2 ½ pounds

In a large chilled mixing bowl, beat the cream with a whisk or a rotary or electric beater until it begins to thicken. Sprinkle in 3 tablespoons of sugar and the vanilla extract; continue beating until the cream is firm enough to hold stiff unwavering peaks on the beater when it is lifted from the bowl.

Combine the orange juice, lemon juice and the remaining 3 tablespoons of sugar in another large bowl. Working with one apple at a time, quarter, peel, and core it and immediately grate it into the sugared juice with the coarse side of a grater. Stir the grated apples occasionally to keep them well moistened and to prevent them from discoloring. Chill the whipped cream and the apple mixture separately until you are ready to serve them. (Tightly covered, whipped cream can be kept for an hour or so.) At the last possible minute, fold the apple mixture into the whipped cream with a rubber spatula, blending them together lightly but thoroughly. Spoon the apple cream into chilled individual dessert bowls or parfait glasses and serve immediately.

Apples with Almond Topping
Fransk Äppelkaka

To serve 6

2 cups cold water	¼ pound unsalted butter, softened
¼ lemon	⅔ cup sugar
4 large tart cooking apples	3 egg yolks
½ cup sugar	½ cup ground blanched almonds
2 teaspoons unsalted butter, softened	2 teaspoons lemon juice
	3 egg whites
	Pinch of salt

In a 1½- to 2-quart saucepan, combine the cold water, the juice of the lemon quarter and the lemon quarter itself. Halve, peel and core each apple and, as you proceed, drop the halves into the lemon-water to prevent discoloration. Then stir the sugar into the water. Bring it quickly to the boil, stirring occasionally, lower the heat and simmer uncovered for 6 to 8 minutes, or until the apples are tender. Remove them from the pan and drain on a cake rack.

Preheat the oven to 350°. With a pastry brush or paper towel, grease a shallow baking dish (just large enough to hold the apples in one layer) with the 2 teaspoons of soft butter. Place the apple halves in it side by side, cut side down. Cream the ¼ pound of butter by using an electric beater set at medium speed, or by beating it against the sides of a bowl with a wooden spoon until it is smooth. Now beat in the ⅔ cup of sugar, a little at a time, then the egg yolks one by one, and last the almonds and lemon juice. With a balloon whisk or electric beater, beat the egg whites with a pinch of salt in a large mixing bowl (preferably of unlined copper) until they form stiff, unwavering peaks. Mix 2 tablespoons of the stiff egg whites into the creamed sugar-butter-egg mixture, then gently fold the remaining mixture into the egg whites with a rubber spatula, using an under-over rather than a stirring motion. Spread the almond topping lightly over the poached apples and bake in the center of the oven for about 20 minutes, or until the surface is golden. Serve at room temperature.

Banana Fritters
Buñuelos de Plátano

To serve 4 to 6

1 cup flour
¼ teaspoon salt
1 egg, lightly beaten
1 tablespoon butter, melted
½ cup milk
1 egg white

2 tablespoons sugar
¼ cup dark rum or brandy
6 firm ripe bananas, peeled and cut
   lengthwise in half, then crosswise
   into quarters
Vegetable oil or shortening for deep-
   fat frying
Confectioners' sugar

To prepare the batter, sift ½ cup of the flour and the salt into a deep mixing bowl. Stir in the beaten egg and butter and then the milk and continue to stir until the batter is smooth. Then beat the egg white until stiff and fold into the batter just before using it.

Meanwhile, in a large bowl, combine the sugar and rum or brandy, and stir until the sugar dissolves. Drop in the bananas and turn them about with a spoon until they are thoroughly moistened. Set aside at room temperature for 30 minutes, turning the bananas occasionally.

Heat 3 to 4 inches of oil or shortening in a deep-fat fryer or large heavy skillet until it reaches 375° on a deep-frying thermometer. Pat the pieces of banana dry with paper towels, dip them in the remaining ½ cup of flour and shake vigorously to remove the excess. With tongs, dip them into the batter and then deep-fry them, 5 or 6 at a time, for 2 or 3 minutes, or until golden brown on all sides. Transfer the fried fritters to paper towels and let them drain. Serve warm, liberally sprinkled with confectioners' sugar.

Cherries Jubilee
Cerises Jubilé

To serve 6 to 8

2 pounds Bing cherries
1½ cups water

1 cup sugar
2 teaspoons cornstarch dissolved
   in water
½ cup kirsch

Wash, stem and pit the cherries. Cook the water and sugar until syrupy. Add the cherries; simmer until they are tender but still firm. Drain the cherries and place equal amounts in individual heat-proof serving dishes. Cook the syrup over high heat for 5 minutes. Add the cornstarch to the syrup, cooking and stirring until thickened. Spoon over the cherries, pour a little kirsch over each portion and set it aflame at the moment of serving.

NOTE: Two large cans of pitted Bing cherries may be used when cherries are out of season. Heat the cherries in their juice, then proceed as above.

Peaches with Raspberry Sauce
Pêches Cardinal

To serve 8

6 cups water
2 cups sugar

8 large ripe but firm peaches, peeled, halved and stoned
1 four-inch piece of vanilla bean or 3 tablespoons vanilla extract

In a heavy 3- to 4-quart saucepan, bring the water and sugar to a boil over high heat, stirring until the sugar dissolves. Boil this syrup briskly for 3 minutes, then reduce the heat as low as possible. Add the peeled peach halves and vanilla and poach them uncovered at a very low simmer for 10 to 20 minutes, or until they are barely tender when pierced with the tip of a sharp knife. Refrigerate the peaches in the syrup until they are cold.

SAUCE CARDINAL

2 ten-ounce packages frozen raspberries, defrosted and thoroughly drained
2 tablespoons superfine sugar
1 tablespoon kirsch

SAUCE CARDINAL: With the back of a large spoon, purée the raspberries through a fine sieve into a small mixing bowl. Stir 2 tablespoons of superfine sugar and the kirsch into the raspberry purée. Refrigerate, tightly covered.

CRÈME CHANTILLY

¾ cup heavy cream, thoroughly chilled
2 tablespoons superfine sugar
1 tablespoon vanilla extract

GARNISH

Whole fresh raspberries or defrosted frozen raspberries

CRÈME CHANTILLY: With a wire whisk, rotary or electric beater, whip the cream in a chilled mixing bowl until it begins to thicken. Sprinkle in 2 tablespoons of superfine sugar and the vanilla; continue beating until the cream is firm enough to hold soft peaks on the beater when it is raised out of the bowl.

To serve, transfer the chilled peach halves with a slotted spoon to individual dessert dishes or arrange them attractively on a large platter. If you wish, you can place the halves on top of one another to resemble whole peaches. (Discard the syrup or save it to use for poaching fruit again.) Mask each of the peaches thoroughly with the *sauce cardinal*. Decorate the peaches with the *crème chantilly*. Then garnish them with whole raspberries.

Pears Stuffed with Cheese
Pere Ripiene

To serve 4

4 small firm ripe pears
1 tablespoon lemon juice
2 ounces imported Gorgonzola

cheese (about ¼ cup), at room temperature
2 tablespoons soft unsalted butter
2 tablespoons crushed walnuts, pistachio or pine nuts

With a small sharp knife, peel the pears and cut them in half lengthwise, leaving a stem attached to one of the halves of each pear. Remove the cores and scoop a scant tablespoon of pulp out of each of the pear halves. To prevent the fruit from turning brown, paint each section of pear inside and out with a pastry brush dipped in lemon juice.

Cream the Gorgonzola cheese and softened butter together by beating them against the side of a small bowl with a wooden spoon until they are soft and fluffy. Fill the hollows of the pears with 1 tablespoon of the cheese-and-butter mixture and carefully press the two halves of the pear back together again. Roll the pears around in the crushed nuts, then arrange them on a serving plate. Chill for about 2 hours, or until the cheese is firm.

Pears Poached in Wine
Poires Pochées au Vin Rouge

To serve 6

2 cups dry red wine
2 tablespoons lemon juice
1 cup sugar

1 two-inch stick of cinnamon or ½ teaspoon ground cinnamon
6 small or 3 large ripe but firm pears, peeled, cored and halved

In a 12-inch enameled saucepan, bring the wine, lemon juice, sugar and cinnamon to a boil over moderate heat, stirring until the sugar dissolves. Add the pear halves, partially cover the pan and reduce the heat to low. Cook the pears at a very slow simmer for 15 to 20 minutes, or until they are soft but not mushy when pierced with the tip of a sharp knife. Cool the pears in the syrup until they are lukewarm. If you would like to serve the pear halves warm, discard the cinnamon stick and use a slotted spoon to transfer the pears to dessert dishes, small bowls or champagne glasses. Spoon a bit of the syrup over them. To serve the pears cold, refrigerate them in the syrup in a large bowl or baking dish until they are thoroughly chilled.

Strawberry Snow
Mansikkalumi

To serve 6 to 8

2 cups fresh, hulled strawberries or
   substitute 2 ten-ounce packages
   frozen whole strawberries,
   thoroughly defrosted and drained

½ cup sugar
4 egg whites
Pinch of salt
¾ cup heavy cream, stiffly whipped
12 to 16 whole strawberries, fresh or
   frozen

With the back of a large spoon, rub the fresh or thoroughly defrosted frozen strawberries through a fine sieve into a small mixing bowl. Stir into this purée the ½ cup of sugar, a little at a time.

Using a balloon-type wire whisk, beat the egg whites and salt vigorously in a large bowl (preferably of unlined copper) until the whites are stiff enough to form unwavering peaks when the beater is lifted out of the bowl. With a gentle under-over cutting motion rather than a stirring motion, use a rubber spatula to fold first the strawberry purée and then the whipped cream into the egg whites. Pour the strawberry snow into an attractive serving bowl, or individual dessert bowls, and decorate with the whole strawberries. This dessert can be served at once, or it may be refrigerated for a few hours and served later in the day.

Fruit in Vanilla Syrup
Compote de Fruits

To serve 4

3 cups water
1 cup sugar
1 two-inch piece of vanilla bean or

1½ tablespoons vanilla extract
4 ripe but firm pears or peaches, or 12
   apricots, peeled, halved and cored
   or stoned

In a 12-inch enameled saucepan, bring the water, sugar and vanilla to a boil over moderate heat, stirring until the sugar dissolves. Add the fruit, reduce the heat, and cook uncovered at a very slow simmer for 15 to 20 minutes, or until the fruit is soft but not mushy when pierced with the tip of a sharp knife. Let the fruit cool in the syrup for 30 minutes. With a slotted spoon, transfer the fruit to a serving bowl or baking dish. Boil the syrup briskly over high heat until it thickens slightly, and pour it over the fruit. Refrigerate the fruit, and serve it chilled in dessert dishes, small bowls or champagne glasses with a spoonful of syrup to moisten each of the portions.

Party Beverages

Toll House Fruit Punch

To serve 50 to 60

3½ cups sugar
2 cups lemon juice
2 cups orange juice
2 cups grape juice
2 cups strong tea

7 quarts ice water
A block of ice
1 pineapple, cut into small pieces
1 cup sweet cherries, pitted and
　halved
Ginger ale or club soda (optional)

In a large container dissolve the sugar thoroughly with the lemon, orange and grape juices. Add the tea and cold water and stir briskly to combine all the ingredients. Place the ice in a large punch bowl and pour the fruit liquid over the ice. Sprinkle in the pineapple and cherry bits. If you like you may add ginger ale or club soda.

Cardinal Punch

To serve about 30

4 cups fresh cranberries
3 quarts water
2 cups sugar

1 cup orange juice
½ cup lemon juice
1 pint ginger ale
Green-colored cherries

Cook the cranberries in 1 quart of water until the berries are soft. Then strain them through a moistened cloth, pressing to extract all the liquid. Place the juice in a large saucepan and add the sugar. Cook the mixture for about 6 minutes. Chill the cranberry juice thoroughly. Place it in a large bowl or pitcher and add the orange and lemon juices, ginger ale and 2 quarts of cold water. Stir to blend the ingredients well. Pour the punch over crushed ice and serve it with a green cherry in each glass or punch cup.

Lemon-flavored Brew
Sima

To make 5 quarts

2 large lemons
½ cup granulated sugar
½ cup brown sugar

5 quarts boiling water
⅛ teaspoon yeast
5 teaspoons sugar
15 raisins

With a small, sharp knife or rotary peeler, carefully peel off the yellow skins of the lemons and set them aside. Then cut away the white membranes of the lemons and discard them. Slice the lemons very thinly. In a 6- to 8-quart enameled or stainless-steel bowl, combine the lemon slices, lemon skins and the two sugars. Pour the boiling water over the fruit and sugar, stir, and let the mixture cool to tepid. Then stir in the yeast. Allow the *sima* to ferment, uncovered, at room temperature for about 12 hours. To bottle, use 5 one-quart bottles with very tight covers or corks. Place 1 teaspoon of sugar and 3 raisins in the bottom of each bottle. Strain the *sima* through a sieve and, using a funnel, pour the liquid into the bottles. Close the bottles tightly and let them stand at room temperature for 1 or 2 days until the raisins have risen to the surface. Chill the sealed bottles until ready to serve.

Champagne Punch

To serve 50 to 60

1 quart strawberries or raspberries
4 cups sugar
The juice of 12 lemons
1 pineapple, cut in small cubes

3 quarts ice water
1 quart champagne
1 quart white wine
Ice

Wash, hull and crush the berries slightly. In a small bowl dissolve 3 cups of the sugar with the lemon juice. In another bowl mix the pineapple cubes with the remaining sugar and let them stand for several hours. Then pour the ice water into a large punch bowl and add the sweetened lemon juice, the berries and the pineapple bits. Stir thoroughly. Add the champagne and wine and stir again. Add ice and serve.

Claret Cup

To serve 4

Approximately 1 cup of fruits of the season: peeled orange and/or grapefruit sections, lemon slices, hulled strawberries, peach slices, cucumber peel
4 ounces blackberry brandy

4 ounces maraschino liqueur
4 ounces curaçao
12 to 16 ice cubes or a block of ice
1 bottle claret (Bordeaux)
6 ounces cold Perrier water or club soda

Place the fruits of your choice in a chilled pitcher or bowl, then add the blackberry brandy, maraschino liqueur and curaçao. Place the vessel in the refrigerator (or freezer) for at least 1 hour (½ hour if you use the freezer). Remove and fill with ice cubes. A solid block of ice cut to fit the pitcher or bowl is even better, since it will not melt as quickly and dilute the drink. Pour in the claret and sparkling water, stir briefly, and serve in chilled wine glasses or punch cups.

Sauternes Cup

To serve 4

Approximately 1 cup of fruits of the season: peeled orange and/or grapefruit sections, lemon slices, hulled strawberries, peach slices, cucumber peel

4 ounces brandy
4 ounces Cointreau
4 ounces Grand Marnier
12 to 16 ice cubes or a block of ice
1 bottle imported Sauternes
6 ounces cold Perrier water or club soda

Place the fruits of your choice in a pitcher or bowl first, then add the brandy, Cointreau and Grand Marnier. Place the pitcher or bowl in the refrigerator (or freezer) for at least 1 hour (½ hour if you use the freezer). Remove and fill with ice cubes. A solid block of ice that fits the pitcher or bowl is even better, since it will not melt as quickly and dilute the drink. Pour in the Sauternes and sparkling water, stir briefly, and serve in chilled wine glasses or punch cups.

Fruit Shrub

To serve 3 or 4

1 cup cranberry juice
¼ cup lemon juice
½ cup orange juice
½ cup syrup from spiced peaches,

or substitute other sweet spiced-
fruit syrup
1 tablespoon rum
Sugar

Combine the cranberry, lemon and orange juices. Add the syrup, rum and the sugar to taste. Stir thoroughly to mix the ingredients. Place in the refrigerator and chill.

Basque Wine Lemonade
Limonada

To serve 8

6 lemons
1 cup superfine sugar
1 bottle dry red wine, preferably

imported Spanish wine
1 bottle dry white wine, preferably
imported Spanish wine

With a small, sharp knife or a vegetable peeler with rotating blade, remove the yellow peel from three of the lemons, being careful not to cut into the bitter white pith underneath it. Cut the peel into strips about 2 inches long and ½ inch wide. Set them aside. Squeeze the juice from one of the peeled lemons and then slice the remaining 3 unpeeled lemons crosswise into ¼-inch-thick rounds.

Combine the strips of lemon peel, the lemon juice, lemon slices and sugar in a 3- to 4-quart serving pitcher. Pour in the red and white wine and stir with a bar spoon or other long-handled spoon until well mixed. Refrigerate for at least 8 hours, stirring two or three times.

To serve, stir again, taste and add more sugar if you prefer the drink sweeter. Serve in chilled wine glasses or tumblers. If you like, the glasses may be filled with ice cubes before adding the *limonada*.

Wine and Fruit Punch

Sangría

To serve 4 to 6

½ lemon, cut into ¼-inch slices
½ orange, cut into ¼-inch slices
½ large apple, cut in half lengthwise, cored, and cut into thin wedges
¼ to ½ cup superfine sugar

1 bottle dry red wine, preferably imported Spanish wine
2 ounces (¼ cup) brandy
Club soda, chilled
Ice cubes (optional)

Combine the lemon, orange, apple and ¼ cup sugar in a large pitcher. Pour in the wine and brandy and stir with a long-handled spoon until well mixed. Taste. If you prefer the *sangría* sweeter, add up to ¼ cup more sugar.

Refrigerate for at least 1 hour or until thoroughly chilled. Just before serving, pour in chilled club soda to taste, adding up to 24 ounces of the soda. Stir again, and serve at once in chilled wine glasses. Or the glasses may be filled with ice cubes before adding the *sangría*.

Trinidad Rum Punch

To serve 6

¾ cup water
½ cup sugar

½ cup lime or lemon juice
1½ cups light rum
2 teaspoons Angostura bitters

NOTE: This punch is usually prepared a few days before serving.

Bring the water and sugar to a boil, stirring constantly until the sugar dissolves, then cook 5 minutes without stirring. Chill. Mix the chilled syrup with the lemon or lime juice, rum and bitters. Chill and serve very cold.

Fish House Punch

To make 1½ gallons

1½ cups superfine sugar
1 quart fresh lemon juice
2 quarts 100-proof Jamaica rum, or
    substitute 80-proof light or dark
    rum

2 quarts cold water
4 ounces peach brandy
1 quart cognac
A block of ice
1 cup sliced, peeled peaches, fresh,
    frozen or canned (optional)

The original Fish House punch was made in the mid-18th Century at a fishing and social club called "State in Schuylkill" in Pennsylvania. The recipe called for 100-proof Jamaica rum, but as this results in a very heavy, somewhat smoky taste, contemporary American palates might prefer a lighter, 80-proof rum. Despite popular misconceptions, a true punch is made with plain water—fresh spring water if feasible—instead of any carbonated beverage.

Place the sugar and lemon juice in a punch bowl and stir with a muddler or bar spoon to dissolve the sugar thoroughly. Add the rum, water, peach brandy and cognac, stir to combine the ingredients, and allow the punch to "ripen" at room temperature for at least 2 hours, stirring occasionally. Put the solid block of ice in the bowl and garnish, if you like, with sliced peaches. Serve in punch cups.

Holiday Eggnog

To serve 12

10 egg whites
⅓ cup superfine sugar
10 egg yolks
1 quart (2 pints) cold heavy cream
2 tablespoons superfine sugar

1 fifth blended whiskey
12 ounces Jamaica rum
1 pint (2 cups) cold milk
Rind of 1 lemon, thinly slivered
Rind of 1 orange, thinly slivered
Ground nutmeg

Place the egg whites in a large mixing bowl and add the ⅓ cup of sugar. Beat the egg whites and sugar with a wire whisk or an electric or rotary beater until they thicken somewhat and foam. In another large bowl, beat the egg yolks until they thicken enough to drop back in the form of a ribbon when the beater is lifted out of the bowl. Pour the foamy egg whites and sugar into the beaten egg yolks and beat them together until they are thoroughly combined.

Place the cold heavy cream and 2 tablespoons of sugar in a punch bowl and beat until the cream doubles in volume and is thick enough to hold its shape softly. Now, beating constantly, slowly pour the egg mixture into the punch bowl with the whipped cream. When thoroughly combined, slowly add the whiskey and rum and then the cold milk, beating all the while. By this time, the eggnog will have thickened somewhat; it will thicken even more as it chills. Sprinkle the top of the eggnog with the slivers of lemon and orange peel and the ground nutmeg and chill for at least 2 hours, or even overnight.

Hot Buttered Rum

To make 1 drink

1½ teaspoons superfine sugar
A 1-inch piece cinnamon stick
3 ounces rum

1 cup hot milk
1 tablespoon unsalted butter
Ground nutmeg

Heat a mug with very hot water and shake it dry. Place the sugar, cinnamon stick and rum in the mug, and stir to dissolve the sugar. Pour in the hot milk, top with the butter, and sprinkle with ground nutmeg.

Hot Toddy

To make 1 drink

Pinch of superfine sugar
1 strip lemon peel stuck with 1
   whole clove
Pinch of cinnamon, or substitute a 1-

inch piece cinnamon stick
3 ounces bourbon, blended whiskey
   or brandy
Boiling water

Warm a glass or mug by washing it with very hot water and shaking it dry. Place the pinch of sugar, lemon peel stuck with a clove, cinnamon and spirits in the glass or mug, fill with boiling water, and stir.

Hot Spiced Wine
Vin Chaud

To serve 2

2 slices lemon
4 whole cloves

2 tablespoons superfine sugar
1½ sticks cinnamon
2 cups (1 pint) claret or Burgundy

Stud each lemon slice with 2 cloves and combine them with the sugar and cinnamon sticks in a 1-quart enameled, copper or stainless-steel skillet, casserole or chafing dish. Place over moderate heat, stir occasionally with a wooden spoon until the sugar has melted, then pour in the red wine. Continue to stir until the wine has almost reached the boiling point. Remove from the heat immediately, scoop out the lemon slices and cinnamon with a spoon or spatula, and pour the hot wine into mugs.

Mulled Wine
Professorns Glögg

To serve 20 to 25

2 quarts dry red wine
2 quarts muscatel
1 pint sweet vermouth
2 tablespoons Angostura bitters
2 cups raisins
Peelings of 1 orange
12 whole cardamoms, bruised in a
    mortar with a pestle or by covering

with a towel and crushing with a
    rolling pin
10 whole cloves
1 piece (about 2 inches) fresh ginger
1 stick cinnamon
1½ cups (12 ounces) aquavit
1½ cups sugar
2 cups whole almonds, blanched and
    peeled

In a 6- to 8-quart enameled or stainless-steel pot, mix together the dry red wine, muscatel, sweet vermouth, bitters, raisins, orange peel and the slightly crushed cardamoms, whole cloves, ginger and cinnamon. Cover and let the mixture stand at least 12 hours so that the flavors will develop and mingle. Shortly before serving, add the aquavit and the sugar. Stir well and bring it to a full boil over high heat. Remove at once from the heat, stir in the almonds and serve the hot *glögg* in mugs. In Sweden, a small spoon is placed in each mug to scoop up the almonds and raisins.

ALTERNATE: To make a simpler *glögg*, divide the quantities of spices in half and mix them with 2 bottles of dry red wine. Leave it overnight, then stir in ¾ cup of sugar and bring almost to a boil. Remove from the heat, stir in 1 cup of whole, blanched and peeled almonds, and serve hot.

Burnt Brandy Coffee
Café Brûlot

To serve 10 to 12

1 stick cinnamon
12 whole cloves
Peelings of 2 oranges, cut into thin
slivers
Peelings of 2 lemons, cut into thin
slivers
6 sugar lumps
8 ounces brandy
2 ounces curaçao
1 quart strong black coffee

In a *brûlot* bowl or chafing dish, mash the cinnamon, cloves, orange peel, lemon peel and sugar lumps with a ladle. Add the brandy and curaçao and stir together. Carefully ignite the brandy, stepping back, since the flame might flare up, and mix until the sugar is dissolved. Gradually add the black coffee and continue mixing until the flame flickers out.

Irish Coffee

To serve 2

4 strips orange peel
4 strips lemon peel
16 whole cloves
1 stick cinnamon
2 teaspoons superfine sugar
5 ounces Irish whiskey
1½ cups strong hot coffee
Confectioners' sugar
¼ cup whipped heavy cream

Stud the strips of orange and lemon peel with 2 cloves each and place them in a skillet or chafing dish with the stick of cinnamon and the 2 teaspoons of sugar. Set over moderate heat, stirring occasionally with a wooden spoon, until the sugar has melted; pour the Irish whiskey into the pan and light a match to the liquid. Be sure to step back since the flame will flare up instantly. Shake the pan back and forth slowly until the flame dies out; pour in the hot coffee all at once and let it come to a simmer. Remove from the heat.

Rub the cut edge of a strip of lemon' peel around the inside of each glass or mug and dip the rim into the confectioners' sugar so that the sugar adheres to the inside rim. Pour in the coffee, trying not to disturb the sugar. Top each serving with a dollop of whipped cream.

Index

PICTURE CREDITS The sources for the illustrations that appear in this book are: 6—Fred Lyon from Rapho Guillumette. 12—Richard Jeffery. 16—Mark Kauffman. 49—Henry Groskinsky. 61–65—Clayton Price. 79–80—Anthony Blake. 83—Richard Meek. 91, 103, 106—Fred Lyon from Rapho Guillumette. 109–110—Anthony Blake. 121, 126—Richard Jeffery. 137–138—Richard Meek. 139—Fred Eng. 142—Michael Rougier. 186—Charles Phillips. 187–188—Mark Kauffman. 257—Eliot Eliosofon. 265—Arie deZanger. 270–272—Fred Lyon from Rapho Guillumette except 270, bottom row 2 at left, Charles Phillips. 306–307, 308–310—Charles Phillips. 312–313—Mark Kauffman. 385—Henry Groskinsky. 389—Mark Kauffman. 391—Fred Lyon from Rapho Guillumette. 394–395, 397—Anthony Blake. 398—Richard Jeffery.

RECIPE CREDITS   The following books were used as sources for the listed pages: *The Cordon Bleu Cook Book,* © 1947 by Dione Lucas—21, 170, 213, 319, 350 (top), 430 (top). *The Dione Lucas Meat and Poultry Cook Book* by Dione Lucas and Ann Roe Robbins, © 1955 by Little, Brown—127 (bottom), 128 (top), 102 (top), 162 (bottom), 204, 208, 211 (top), 218, 298. *The Embassy Cookbook* by Allison Williams, © 1966 by Little, Brown—13 (top), 14, 15, 16 (top), 23 (bottom), 28 (top), 29 (bottom), 33 (bottom), 117 (top), 169 (bottom), 179, 190 (top), 194 (bottom), 199 (top), 202 (bottom), 217 (top), 219, 232, 245, 291 (top), 320 (bottom), 323 (top), 333 (center), 337 (center), 344, 345, 346 (bottom), 357, 377, 427, 433, 439 (top), 441 (bottom), 451 (bottom). *James Beard's Fish Cookery,* © 1954 by James A. Beard—10 (top), 16 (bottom), 20 (bottom), 22 (bottom), 23 (top, center), 43 (top), 233, 243, 250 (top), 253 (top), 302. *Toll House Cook Book,* © 1953 by Ruth Wakefield—152, 339 (bottom), 340 (bottom), 344, 376 (top), 377, 380 (top), 381 (top), 400, 445, 446 (bottom), 449 (bottom).